D1083363

THE WITNESS

OF THE

BROTHERS

Yaacov Oved

THE WITNESS

OF THE

BROTHERS

A History of the Bruderhof

TRANSACTION PUBLISHERS
New Brunswick (U.S.A.) and London (U.K.)

Library of Congress Catalog Number: 96-574
ISBN: 1-56000-203-4
Printed in the United States of America

Library of Congress Cataloging-in-Publication Data

Oved, Iaácov.
   The witness of the brothers : a history of the Bruderhof / Yaacov Oved ; translated by Anthony Berris
      p. cm.
   Includes bibliographical references and index.
   ISBN 1-56000-203-4 (alk. paper)
   1. Hutterian Brethren—History. I. Title.
   BX8129.B63094 1996
   289.7'3—dc20   96-574
                                                                   CIP

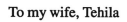
To my wife, Tehila

Contents

Acknowledgments

The writing of this book has its background in my personal relationships with the members of the Bruderhof that have become cemented over a period of many years. These ties were nurtured and deepened by a long series of visits to all the Bruderhof communities and through numerous conversations with their members. The decision to write the book materialized with my realization that there existed an objective need for a work that would review the movement's history. It should be mentioned that this decision did not fall into line with the personal friendships I had made, so it compelled me to maintain an objective distance during my work in order to avoid tendentiousness, which might have cast its shadow on the scholarly character of the book and, thus, prejudiced its credibility.

I made this clear to my Bruderhof friends and they, to their credit, made it clear that they fully understood my position and continued to assist me in every respect. Their assistance was manifested by their unqualified readiness to grant me frank and open interviews on every subject I raised. These interviews appear throughout the book and I am indebted to all the Bruderhof members who spoke to me for their patience, openness, and time.

Special thanks go to all the people who hosted me on my visits, prepared material from their personal collections and from their communes' archives, and in particular to all those who corresponded with me and answered my many questions. Among those who deserve special mention are Andreas and Klaus Meier, Martin and Burgel Johnson, Stan and Hella Ehrlich, and Joseph Ben-Eliezer. I much regret that Hans Meier, to whom I owe a debt of gratitude for our long hours of talks, which gave me my deepest insight into Bruderhof life, is no longer with us.

This study was undertaken with the loyal support of Yad Tabenkin at the United Kibbutz Movement Institute for Research and Documentation, which provided financial assistance for publicity and research facilities through the purchase of books and the provision of office services

vii

for my correspondence. Valuable assistance was also provided by the International Fund for Scientific Relations at Tel Aviv University, which allowed me to travel to the Bruderhof communities as frequently as necessary. During my research I spent half a sabbatical year at Cornell University, which allowed me frequent visits to the Bruderhof, and for this I am grateful to my colleagues from the Department of History there.

Special thanks go to my friends Ze'ev Otitz and Yisrael Sheffer, who read some chapters of the manuscript and made many valuable comments, and to Anthony Berris, who translated the book from Hebrew.

I gratefully acknowledge my colleagues from Yad Tabenkin and the Department of History at Tel Aviv University with whom I discussed questions of methodology during my research.

Many people helped me at various stages of my years of research, but the most loyal and constant assistance was provided by my wife, Tehila (Titi), and my family, who were all part of my work, which necessitated frequent absences from home, and who gave unstintingly of their support and understanding.

Needless to say, although the contributions of so many people are invested in this book, the responsibility for everything it contains is mine alone.

Kibbutz Palmachim
1995

Introduction

In the northeastern United States, off the main highways and in the heart of some beautiful scenery, there are six settlements, the exterior view of which is particularly attractive. At the main gate of each hangs an elliptical wooden sign that bears the legend, "The Hutterian Society of the Brothers," and the name of the community carved below.

A person visiting these settlements has an extraordinary experience in store. Spread before the visitor are rolling lawns, carefully tended gardens, and wide, beautifully clean paths that lead to large houses. At the center of the typical Israeli kibbutz stand the public buildings, and indeed, Israeli visitors in general and kibbutz members in particular have been amazed by this similarity, especially when they discover that the main building houses the dining room, which resembles the large, wooden kibbutz dining rooms of years gone by.

The first encounter with the commune members engenders a somewhat strange impression as the visitor first meets the members of the community, who are dressed in their distinctive attire; the women with their heads covered with kerchiefs and wearing long dresses made of a dark, flowered material, and the men, bearded and wearing suspenders with dark trousers. However, this feeling of strangeness dissipates rapidly once conversation is struck up with one's hosts, who are open and captivating. From that point, a spell begins to be woven on the visitor, winning him over completely.

Conversation with the members of the settlement quickly reveals that they belong to a Christian pacifist commune whose members live according to the precepts of Anabaptism and who practice communal living in the spirit of ancient Christianity. The settlements had their beginnings in 1920 in Germany, and have since undergone numerous changes, which have internationalized their population.

Despite the relative isolation of the settlements, they attract visitors from near and far who have come to hear of their existence. I first visited one of the settlements in Connecticut in 1978, and my visit left an

1

indelible impression upon me. Moreover, that visit played a decisive role in the direction of my academic research and impelled me to write a book on the 200 years of communes in the United States.[1] The book does not discuss these particular communes because they did not fall within the historical parameters set out in the scope of my work, and also because I knew very little about them at the time. The main thrust of my work in the 1980s was devoted to a study of the historical American communes up to World War II, while the writing of *Two Hundred Years of American Communes* was accompanied by comparative historical research, the conclusions of which I continued to study in the light of the accumulated experience of the modern communes.

Among the plethora of modern communes, I found a special interest in the Bruderhof and as a result I have maintained unbroken contact with the movement's members and do not miss an opportunity to visit them. I have to admit that all this was born of the deep kinship I feel for the Bruderhof members, which came about from my first encounter with them and the warm welcome I was accorded. This feeling of kinship became stronger as I became further acquainted with their communal way of life, a way of life that aroused a yearning inside of me for the world which, up until recently, was the world of the kibbutz, one that is slowly disappearing from the reality of the kibbutz movement of today.

Over the years I have managed to visit all the communes in the United States and Europe and have come to know them well. I have met and talked with many of their members who, I discovered, were fascinating personalities. The personal accounts I heard from them revealed enthralling episodes in their history, which prompted me to follow the routes of their wanderings. As I became better acquainted with the Bruderhof, I discovered the important stages of the movement's history: its beginnings in Germany in the 1920s; life under the Nazi regime in the 1930s; the escape to Liechtenstein; the expulsion from Germany and exile in Britain; from Britain, at the height of World War II, the move to Paraguay, which was destined to be a "temporary haven" for the next twenty years; then the move to the United States, which brought about expansion and growth that doubled their population and the number of their communities in the space of a single generation.

The more I learned about modern communes, and as my knowledge of the Bruderhof widened, I realized that their communes were unique in the world of contemporary communal living. I perceived theirs as the most deeply rooted vision of a communal movement and a shining example of a stable and evolving communal life.

My acquaintanceship with them widened as a result of numerous and extended visits and served to reveal their spacial communal wisdom, a wisdom that is manifested in their way of life in which they have succeeded in the harmonious integration of seemingly contradictory elements, and in doing so have proved their ability to maintain communal life over a long period. This integration of these apparently contradictory elements is expressed in their very coexistence: conservatism in their way of life and a controlled openness to modern culture; integrative communality together with intensive family life; refraining from political activity while maintaining their involvement in protest movements whose banners bear the escutcheons, *inter alia,* of civil rights, pacifism, and antiracism; dogmatic adherence to their religious beliefs coupled with a deep-seated tolerance of the beliefs of others; the voluntary joining of new members who take a vow of personal loyalty, and the total rejection of religious coercion by ecclesiastical authorities; charismatic leadership with the involvement of the entire community in decisionmaking by consensus; deep interpersonal relationships; the prohibition of gossip while employing the immediate "brotherly admonition" for those found gossiping; independent educational institutions for their young children while their youth are sent to outside schools; social and labor relations characterized by complete multigenerational integration while each generation enjoys a respected status and active involvement; a livelihood that is based upon industrial manufacturing but without subjugation to market forces and their dictates, and the avoidance of employing hired labor; isolation insofar as their characteristic attire is concerned, but without isolating themselves from their surrounding environment while maintaining close relationships with their neighbors; personal and public spaces that are fully integrated with members' homes, public and economic institutions; a complete absence of radio, TV, and VCRs, coupled with a full communal and cultural life centered around intensive musical activities.

The list could go on and on, but it would not be complete without mentioning the most significant item it contains: the deep, inner belief that their lives are a "witness" or example, and that a life of brotherhood and communal cooperation can be maintained in our world, here and now. This precept, which is deeply rooted in their religious belief, is the source of the strength that imbues their life with its significance, over and above the day-to-day maintaining of their communities. It was that precept that brought me to devote my efforts to the opening of a new, external channel that would convey their message to the specific audience interested in searching for an alternative way of life, and particularly to my own reference group: Israeli kibbutz members who are currently facing one of the most serious crises in their movement's history. But not to them alone; I reached the conclusion that the example of this way of life was worthy of being brought to the attention of a much wider audience, particularly at this point in time.

Although our generation, which has witnessed so many failed social experiments that tried to forge a new society through coercive regimes, has lost faith in an overall social Utopia, it might possibly find a source of inspiration in the "mini-Utopian" communities that have realized a communal way of life out of personal choice and with no officially sanctioned coercion. Moreover, it has become apparent that the spread of the spirit of individualism and privatization throughout the western world, together with the abandonment of the welfare state and all that it entailed, arouses opposing responses. We have recently heard of an organized group of American scholars and politicians who have founded the "Communitarian Movement," the objectives of which, according to the statement issued by its founders, is to arrest the exaggeration prevalent in the struggle for individual rights and endow it with equilibrium by fostering awareness of public obligations to one's fellow man and the community. The group denies the accepted ethos that states that the fostering of individual interests is the true basis for the existence of society. In their statement they assert that, although morals are built on personal conscientious commitment, only community life can nurture and reinforce that commitment. In their activities they extol loyalty to the family, the neighborhood, the school, and the church. It is worth noting that, despite their declared community objective, no real bridges have been built between this movement and the world of modern communes, even to the extent of learning from the rich community experience of the people who live in them. In this context I have no doubt at all that the experience of the Bruderhof and the community wisdom the movement embodies could be a most significant source of inspiration.

It was under these circumstances that I felt that I must undertake this task because it was incumbent on me to place my knowledge of the

Bruderhof in the public domain. Once I had made the decision to present the Bruderhof's message to the public, I devoted my time to reading all the literature that had been published about the movement and to a methodical study of its history. I quickly realized that the external authors of most of the literature on the Bruderhof movement had adopted accepted social science research methods, and despite the fact that these studies employed all the accepted research tools and were based upon professional criteria, they had not succeeded in revealing the essence of the movement. In some ways they reached a dead end, and in fact the Bruderhof movement has some serious reservations about them, even to the point of viewing them as distorting the movement's image and basic qualities. The Bruderhof claims that these authors could be faulted for serious inaccuracy and overgeneralizations that were based upon research tools which, while they might have been suitable for another subject, were totally unsuitable for application to the Bruderhof. There can be no doubt that as far as research is concerned, this is an unhealthy situation, for the truth can never be reached in a study in which the subject does not cooperate.

Without denigrating the importance of sociological research, it seems to me that it would have been desirable to precede such a study with a historical overview that would present the development, wanderings, and changes undergone by the Bruderhof, and which would allow the presentation of sociological generalizations in a fitting historical context, without which current issues would remain misunderstood. To my surprise I discovered that an overview of this kind had not yet been written, and it is this omission that I have endeavored to rectify.

At this point I should mention that the deeper I delved into their history, the memory of my idyllic first encounter with them gradually dwindled only to be replaced by a perspective picture that added the dimension of depth to a multifaceted historical pageant. This picture was inundated with past episodes of internal and external strife, personal dramas and tragedies, social crises, members leaving and being expelled, and even the abandoning of settlements. There were times when it seemed that the movement was in danger of extinction, but each crisis was followed by the re-emergence of a phoenixlike rejuvenation. It would seem that this history of wandering and changes in the composition of the population should, in its turn, have caused far-reaching changes in both the character of the movement and its modes of thought and action, but that is not what happened. One of the most striking phenomena I encountered in the history of this movement was its ability to withstand all the tests of change and still remain true to the values and beliefs that were laid down at its inception and shaped its way of life.

My deep knowledge of Bruderhof history has not changed the high esteem in which I hold the movement. Moreover, it was only through studying the history of the movement that I came to fully comprehend something that one of the elders had told me at our first meeting: "Do not be misled by the pastoral serenity that you see here. Our life is not idyllic, but rather the continuous struggle of each of us with his own weaknesses and of all of us against the deviations which prevent us from fulfilling the task we have set ourselves, that of being a 'witness' to humanity that a life of cooperation and brotherhood is possible in our world."

The description that follows neither presents a history of achievements and victories nor is it a compendium of suggestions for the survival of communes. It does, however, present in the main dilemmas and problems. It presents the "witness" of the Bruderhof through all of its historical changes and its ups and downs. This historical narrative has no heroes; the only real hero in this work is the communal community, a group of people who knew how to stand firm and struggle for their beliefs, to pay a high personal price, but also to feel a sense of satisfaction in a life of bearing a message that has been passed from generation to generation.

I decided to entitle the book *The Witness of the Brothers* in order to fully express the objective of the movement, that of being a "witness," but it could also have been called *The Community of the Brothers*, which might better describe the overview of all the communities that constitute the entire movement in all its present dispersions and past forms. Both of these aspects appear in the book.

Kibbutz Palmachim, Israel
December, 1994

Note

1. Oved, Yaacov, *Two Hundred Years of American Communes* (New Brunswick, N.J.: Transaction Publishers, 1988).

1

The Bruderhof Commune at Sannerz and the German Youth Movements

The Bruderhof movement originated in Germany in 1920, in a country still suffering the impact of military defeat, political disintegration of the Wilhelmian regime, and the economic chaos caused by galloping inflation. Although the middle classes had lost their self-confidence, they persisted in their lifestyle under the illusion that the crisis would blow over.

German society was in a state of ferment and turmoil and was riven by internal strife and civil wars. After witnessing the horrors of war, the collapse of the regime, and seeing its myths shattered and its values debased, the younger generation was bewildered. This generation, trapped by somber reality, was at a loss and sought a way out of the ruins and toward fresh ideals that would enable it to start a new life. Everything was being questioned and the general feeling was, This cannot go on! Some turned to nihilism, others to left- or right-wing political radicalism, and large sectors sought a way out of the maze of feuding.

From 1918 to 1920, a group of German youth held weekly meetings at the home of the Arnolds in Steglitz, a wealthy Berlin suburb.[1] From eighty to one hundred people from various sectors participated in these meetings, among them members of youth movements, youngsters from bourgeois families who despised their parents' way of life, and also some from the families of destitute workers, young people from bohemian circles, atheist anarchists, and members of the Christian Student Union. This motley crew had one thing in common—their dilemma: how to break out of the existing situation and find a new direction that would enable them to choose their own way of life, one that would be true to their aspirations.

7

Who, then, were Eberhard and Emmy Arnold and what impelled them to convene and host that young group?

Eberhard and Emmy Arnold

Eberhard Arnold was born on 26 July 1883 in Koenigsberg in East Prussia into a Lutheran family that was originally Anglo-American and that moved in academic circles. Eberhard's ancestors had emigrated to America from England in 1630, settled in Hartford, Connecticut, and lived in New England for several generations. At the beginning of the nineteenth century, his great grandfather had studied theology at Oberlin College, became a Presbyterian missionary, and was sent to Sierra Leone where he married Maria Ramsauer, a German. Their sons were sent to Oldenburg in Germany to marry and later became German citizens. Although Eberhard's father, Karl Franklin Arnold, was born in Ohio, he married in Germany and became professor of theology at Breslau University. His son Eberhard was born in East Prussia and was brought up in Breslau.[2]

By the age of sixteen, Arnold had become interested in the fate of the destitute in society. Influenced by his uncle, Ernst Ferdinand Klein, a Christian socialist, and inspired by the Salvation Army with which he had contacts, he began to work for social reform for the benefit of the disadvantaged in his town. Under the influence of his parents, he went to study theology at the University of Halle and there he came into contact with the youth of the Lutheran churches and became national secretary of the German Christian Students Union.

In the course of this activity he met young Emmy von Hollander, who came from a similar social and religious background and was training to be a nurse. Emmy von Hollander was born in Riga into a distinguished German Baltic family that held important positions in this northern Hanseatic city and was involved in commerce, administration, and academic activity. In 1880, when education became subject to a policy of Russification, the family emigrated to Halle in Germany and Emmy's father was appointed Professor of Law at the local university.[3]

At the beginning of the twentieth century, the city of Halle was undergoing a religious revival that mainly affected the younger generation. Eberhard Arnold and the sisters Emmy and Else von Hollander all participated in religious revival meetings and this was how they met.

Their faith and shared activities brought the young people closer to one another and they were joined in their radical religious activity by Emmy's sister, Else von Hollander, who from 1907 became their loyal and total ally and who later became a co-founder of the Bruderhof.[4]

In his theological studies, Eberhard was drawn mainly to Christian sources of the early church and to Anabaptist circles, and came to view baptism as an entry into the church that was born of conviction. As a result, Eberhard Arnold decided not to join the Lutheran church because he objected to infant baptism. This appalled his parents, who were conservative Lutherans, and it also interfered with his studies, as he was not permitted to sit his final examinations in theology. In order to be able to continue and complete his studies, he turned to the study of philosophy and education and in 1909 was awarded his doctorate at the University of Erlangen.[5]

He and Emmy were married soon after. The couple did not have any reliable sources of income; Eberhard made a living by writing and lecturing in religious circles and on university campuses. This did not worry the young couple, who accepted it as a way of life: "We have placed our personal life into the hands of God, believing he will guide us along the right path." During the next three years they lived off the fees from the lectures he gave to various evangelical groups and also received some assistance from their families. By 1913, Eberhard had developed tuberculosis and subsequently moved with his wife, their two children, and his sister to the mountains of southern Tyrol. During that period he studied the history of the Anabaptists, who had been active in that region in the sixteenth century.[6]

At the beginning of World War I, Eberhard Arnold, who belonged to an army reserve unit, was called up but was released three weeks later on medical grounds. From then on he was constantly preoccupied with the military question, although it took him some time to reach a pacifist approach. In 1915, Arnold and his family moved to Berlin, where he became the editor of the German Christian Student Union's monthly, *Die Furche,* and literary director of the newly founded Furche Publishing House.

In the articles he wrote for the students' journal and in booklets published by *Die Furche* in Berlin, Arnold preached a return to early Christianity and the revival of the sixteenth-century Anabaptist tradition. As a result of his work, he frequently visited military hospitals and soldiers' families, and it was during these visits that he found out about the discrimination in the treatment of soldiers from different social strata. This intensified his criticism of the corrupt German regime. At the time of the armistice, Eberhard identified fully with the radical pacifist circles. In 1919 he spoke at gatherings of the Union of Christian Students, passionately preaching that the bearing of arms was incompatible with the Christian faith.

Youth Rallies in the Heart of Nature

At the end of the war, the German youth movements, which had been established earlier, attracted all those in search of new directions. At the time, scores of youngsters were joining them, and scores of new factions and impermanent groupings emerged—young people who were coming together for mutual support with fellow searchers. Representative of all these groups was their appreciation of nature, their love of hiking and camping, their longing for a simple life, for equality devoid of class barriers, and their rejection of greed and materialism.

These were also the years of religious revival among the youth and certain groups within the youth movements who had become estranged from religion, the churches, and their institutions, since these belonged to the institutionalized and hypocritical world which youth culture, influenced by Gustav Wyneken and the *Wandervogel*, had rejected. Thus, after the war, contacts were established between graduates of the youth movements and the youth groups from the Lutheran and Catholic churches. Theologians like Paul Tillich tried to bridge the gap between the postwar religious turmoil and the world of the devotees of youth culture. He pointed to the religious element within the search for definitive moral values that were typical of the youth movements.

The church youth organizations, the activities of which began to resemble those of the youth movements, adopted the tradition of meeting in the heart of nature—but the gap between their goals and dogmas remained. Although Eberhard and his wife had not participated in youth movement activities during the war, after it had ended they perceived themselves as belonging to the radical wing of the "Free German Youth" and subscribed to the values that were typical of the youth movements: spontaneity, candor, simplicity, and frugality. In spite of their ages (Eberhard was thirty-six and his wife thirty-five) and their bourgeois status, their contact with the youth groups brought about a change in their lifestyle. Their son Heini writes:

> When Papa came into active contact with the youth movement, I noticed a change in our house.... He was middle class but left wing. At that time most people on our street wore the colors of the German flag but my father wore a red ribbon; and we were called communists or anarchists.[7]

Ten years later, Eberhard Arnold himself described the atmosphere of those days:

> Postwar youth abhorred the big cities as places of impurity for body and soul. They felt that the cities were seats of mammon; they felt the coldness and the poisonous air.... They felt that people did not live as God wanted them to live.... So the young people left the cities.... Their spirit drew them back to nature, to ally themselves with the spirit at work there. To them, the spirit at work in nature and the spirit of God were one and the same.[8]

Referring to the youth circles to which he belonged, he wrote:

> We longed to distance ourselves from the untruthful conditions in churches and schools.... The whole rigid system of tradition and class distinction seemed to us an enslavement of true humanity. We wanted to get away from our social surroundings to the highways, fields, woods and mountains. We fled the cities as often as possible. What were we looking for in nature? Freedom, friendship, community.

During the first years after the war, rallies took place in the heart of nature and on mountain peaks, in accordance with the tradition of the German youth movements. One of the first of these meetings took place in Jena at Easter 1919, and among the 150 participants were several of the former youth movement leaders. The slogan adopted was: "No more talk—the time has come for action!" All political statements were avoided, but the idea of establishing collective settlements arose. This notion was in the air at the time and was supported by people like Martin Buber, who had a great spiritual influence on the young people. Although no specific decisions were made on the subject of collective settlements at that meeting, it created support for that trend.[9]

The Lutheran church tried to exploit this revival to reinforce the church-based organizations. Eberhard Arnold and his group opposed this trend and strove to turn the spiritual revival into a lever in the search for new ways of life and greater involvement in society. This activity led to his resignation from the post of travelling secretary of the Union of German Christian Students and brought him closer to the Christian Socialist Movement—*Neuwerk.*

Among the youth groups that emerged from the former youth movements and from among the church youth after the war, *Neuwerk* was something of a phenomenon, since it combined a religious quest for a new direction with a tendency toward social involvement and a desire for personal commitment. It was the only group that strove to put its ideals into practice by establishing settlements. It emerged during those years as a movement in which a sense of Christian mission was combined with social criticism, and it sought to attain its goals through communities that devoted themselves to social and educational tasks.[10]

The first steps taken by this movement were in the form of a religious group that had emerged from a political movement during the revolution of 1918. At the time, a group that called itself The Christian Democrat (*Der Christliche Demokrat*) emerged within the democratic party and published a weekly of that name. This group soon shed its political coloring and became a purely religious group unconcerned with party politics. It was directly influenced by the theology of Karl Barth, Paul Tillich, and the Christian socialists and inspired by them, it adopted Christian socialism, which did not fit in with any existing party framework. Its main goal was to practice social justice in its own way of life. Although this movement was anchored in the values of the youth movement, it no longer felt the need to stress its independence, self-worth, and superiority over the adult world, which was an attitude typical of the majority of the youth movements.[11]

Like other youth movements, the *Neuwerk* meetings also took place outdoors, and the first was convened at Whitsun (21 June 1919) on the Frauenberg near Marburg. It was attended by young people from various groups: students from the German Christian Students' Movement as well as young Christians from all shades of the radical political spectrum.[12]

For the first time, a religious meeting opened with the folk dancing (*reigen*) that was characteristic of youth movement rallies. The main issue on the agenda was, Can a young Christian change the situation in the world through his actions? Eberhard Arnold delivered a lecture on the message of "The Sermon on the Mount," which caused many aftereffects. Additional issues raised at this meeting were the attitude toward nature and political questions, such as the revolution in Germany and in Russia, and the establishment of collective settlements that was taking place in Germany at that time. This rally generated interest in further meetings and provided an impetus for the fusion of the German Christian socialist youth movement, *Neuwerk*, the publication of its journal, and the founding of its own publishing house.

The second conference, which became a significant landmark in the consolidation of *Neuwerk*, took place in 1919 in Tambach. There its founders and young leaders met representatives of the Swiss religious social movement who were disciples of Leonard Ragaz, and the nonparty line was thus forged, which subsequently led to a split in the movement; those who favored closer ties with political parties left it. The apolitical group was led by Students' Union activists like Eberhard Arnold, the teacher Georg Flemming, and the pastor Heinrich Schultheiss, who nevertheless strove to instil in the movement a willingness to become socially involved through personal commitment.

It was an unusual combination of radical social theories and Christian socialism. The atmosphere at the meeting was also influenced by anarchocommunist philosophers like Peter Kropotkin and Gustav Landauer.

At that time, the proletarian factions of the Free Youth Movement (*Freideutsche Jugendbewegung*) were also stirring. They organized a conference in Inselsberg in Thuringia at Easter, 1920, which was attended by about one hundred young people, most of them radical communists and anarchists, as well as youngsters from religious groups, all of whom shared a spiritual restlessness and expectations of "the beginning of a new era" of radical changes on the economic, spiritual, and religious fronts. They sought new ways of personal commitment beyond asserting their independence by singing and nature walks; they wanted to make a real contribution to society.[13]

It was during these meetings that they began to discuss practical ways of implementing their beliefs. Various proposals were raised, such as establishing primary schools in depressed areas, co-operatives in working-class neighborhoods, and agricultural settlements for the unemployed. This had also been the trend at the meetings held at the Arnolds' home in 1920 and they finally came to the conclusion that the tenets of the Sermon on the Mount and of radical Christianity could not remain merely theological propositions, but had to lead to changes in their own way of life. Thus the Arnolds came to the realization that they had to give up their bourgeois lifestyle in the affluent Steglitz suburb and settle in the countryside.

They thought of various ways of being of service to society, like buying a gypsy caravan and travelling through the villages and small towns, staying a short while to talk to the people and spreading comfort and joy by singing and preaching. But they soon gave up this idea and, influenced by their study of the Acts of the Apostles and the debate on communal life by the disciples of Jesus, decided to establish a communal society (according to Emmy Arnold, Landauer's vision of rural community and communal settlement was an equally decisive factor). It was as though they had experienced a revelation in answer to their search.

From that time onward, Arnold's activity and preaching had a clear direction and this was expressed in his article written at the time, in which he proposed the establishment of settlements where people would work on the land and at various trades, as well as in education, caring for war orphans, and publishing writings in the light of their beliefs. This article caused widespread repercussions and his ideas were discussed at summer rallies. Initially, these were purely theoretical debates, but after some time voices were heard demanding that the idea of establishing a settlement be implemented.[14]

The area selected was near the small town of Schluchtern and had certain advantages: a beautiful landscape as well as historical sites, which were connected to the communal settlements that had been established there by the Moravian Brethren (*Herrenberg*). Besides, the theologian Georg Flemming, one of the *Neuwerk* leaders, lived there. A rally was organized there on Whitsun (21 June) to enable the young members to become acquainted with the place.

The invitations sent out to members of the movement in Germany called upon the young people to arrive well before the start of the meeting in order to do some hiking and visit the historical sites of the *Herrenberg*. Among other suggestions made in the circular was a visit to the collective settlement of Habertshof, the first to be established by the Free German Youth Movement, which was their ideological ally. The program was to combine nature hikes with debates and religious experiences.[15] The rally was attended by some two hundred young men and women from various places in Germany: Berlin, Marburg, Thuringia, and Hessen. From the standpoint of political and youth movement background, it was a heterogeneous group—*Neuwerk* members were joined by people who had belonged to the *Wandervogel*, members of the Free

German Youth Movement, and members of proletarian organizations with communist and anarchist leanings.

The atmosphere was free and informal and participants came with guitars and violins, dressed in shorts and peasant shirts and the girls in bright dresses. Enthusiasm and the joy of youth and spontaneity were in the air.[16] The mood at this rally was described by Emmy Arnold, who came with a group of Berliners:

> We left Berlin on a "*bummelzug*" (slow train).... We traveled fourth class because it was cheapest. With us in the train were a number of people from the youth movement.... Our other traveling companions enjoyed listening to our beautiful songs of nature and of hiking.... When we arrived at our destination, we climbed to the top of the hill where we lit our Whitsun bonfire which shed its light far and wide over the whole countryside. The flames were a symbol of the burning of the old and of hope for the coming of the new.... We sat under the lofty beech trees and listened. There were talks which led into to discussions. After these, with our heads humming, we danced together. We danced folk-dances, real community dancing. We also sang folk songs, songs of love and nature. We sat around on the ground forming a large circle, the girls with garlands of daisies in their hair.... Outward formality and convention were cast off.... There was a spirit of joy, a spirit of comradeship.... The only thing that concerned us throughout those Whitsun days was our urge to carry something new into the world, to blaze a trail for the Kingdom of God and the message of peace and love.[17]

Although the pivotal point of this meeting was the religious quest, radical social issues were also raised since most of the participants were politically aligned with the left. Many were pacifists, although there were also believers in revolutionary violence who vehemently contended that in the wake of the World War, European civilization was about to collapse as capitalism and mammonism had been defeated and would soon be eradicated, and a new society was about to emerge.[18] Above all, the rally was marked by calls for personal commitment. According to the reminiscences of Emmy Arnold:

> About two hundred people, most of them young, came from all parts of Germany with the desire to find an answer to the burning question—"What shall we do?"...We regarded private property and possessions as one of the most evil roots of war and all the wrongness of human life.

> But where were we to begin? In the city or in the country? What was the best way to relieve the misery of the masses? The answer our working class friends gave us was—"Go into the country." It was clear to us from the outset that community life would have to be a life of unity in faith and of community of property and work in voluntary poverty. The writings of Gustav Landauer in particular guided us in that direction.[19]

When the rally was over and the participants had gone their separate ways, Eberhard and Emmy Arnold and a few young people stayed behind, eager to begin living according to the ideals they had propounded. They all went to the nearby small town of Sannerz to look for a home or a piece of land upon which they could establish a collective community. A suitable place was located, but they had no way of paying the rent. Misgivings and uncertainty followed, but Eberhard and Emmy were resolute in their intention of making a start. They went to Berlin to fetch their five small children and returned at once; they were joined later by some friends who had participated in the rally. This was the founding group of what came to be called The First Bruderhof.

On a personal level, the Arnolds had fulfilled their desire to shape their lives according to the ideals in which they believed, while on the public level, they were implementing their decision to create a community that was dedicated to work and their religious faith, which would attract members of youth movements, who were wandering about and enjoying nature without any definite goal. They left a spacious and comfortable apartment in a wealthy Berlin suburb, a good salary, and interesting work, and chose a spartan way of life in order to pursue a nebulous new vision.[20]

Their children were enthusiastic about the move and were delighted by the freedom of the open spaces and beautiful natural surroundings. For the two little ones it was a beneficial change, for the family doctor had recommended a move into the country and a healthier diet. It was summer and the beautiful landscape and friendly villagers created a pleasant atmosphere. In spite of the overcrowding and poverty at Sannerz, their first steps along the new road were filled with joy and optimism.

Sannerz

The land they had leased had a large building with fifteen rooms and attics and adjoining it was a piece of land with an orchard and vegetable garden. The founding group consisted of seven adults and the five Arnold children. Although they had no financial basis, they were soon able to obtain donations from friends, which covered the rent (the largest contribution came from Kurt Woerman of the Hamburg-America Navigation Company) to which Eberhard added the proceeds of his own life insurance.

The members of the commune immediately set to work on the land and began their publishing activities. It was at that time that the *Neuwerk* movement decided to transfer its main activities to Schluchtern, and Arnold's community there provided them with a logistic base. In August, 1920, the *Neuwerk Verlag* publishing house was founded with its office at Sannerz. Despite their poverty and financial difficulties, they contacted a printing press in a nearby town and immediately began to print religious and socioeconomic publications. For Eberhard Arnold, the need to continue publishing was both ideological and personal, and it was an activity that could also become a source of income for the group. The real problem was to obtain start-up capital and once again, friends of the family and wealthy supporters who trusted Eberhard Arnold came to the rescue and expressed their willingness to invest in the establishment of a publishing house in a remote area.

That year the Sannerz commune became the center for the journalistic activity of the *Neuwerk* movement, which was growing and spreading. The bond that united the movement was a sense of mission toward the youth movements and groups in Germany and it found expression in the book *Junge Saat* (*Young Seed,* subtitled *Life-book of a Youth Movement*), which was published in 1921 and was one of the first Sannerz publications. The book was in the form of a discussion between young people, and the authors, aged seventeen to thirty-five, phrased their religious mysticism in expressionist language. The book contained many apocalyptic proclamations on the decline and fall of the depraved world and a millenarian anticipation of a new world, the harbingers of which would emerge from the various religious youth movements. The book dealt extensively with religious and social topics in a socialist vein and contained a call to youth to open their eyes and see that the eleventh hour had come and they must make ready for it.[21]

Another book published during the first year was entitled *Rasse und Politik* (*Race and Politics*), by the Jewish author Professor J. Goldstein, which forcefully attacked the antisemitic tendencies prevalent in Germany and was well received by the Christian press, although it was written from a secular-liberal point of view.[22]

Besides the publication of books, it was decided that the movement's journal would also be published at Sannerz under the editorship of Eberhard Arnold. Beginning in the summer of 1920, the issues of this journal dealt with four main topics: (a) the establishment of settlements in which the way of life would be communal in the tradition of early Christianity; (b) social problems, the relations between capitalism and socialism and the revolution in Germany and Russia; (c) the attitude toward the international peace movement; and (d) the traditions of the German youth movements.

It should be pointed out that the journal was open to debates and to opinions other than those of the Sannerz community. It contained articles that questioned the wisdom of withdrawing to remote settlements, which was seen as a kind of escape from social conflicts. Critics maintained that such settlements could not serve as a model for the masses and did not grapple with the central problems that Germany faced at the time.

The Sannerz community countered this criticism by saying that this settlement was neither intended as an escape from society nor as a model for a new society in Germany. Their main goal was to establish a working and learning community, the members of which could come to terms with their need to shape their lives according to their faith, and where they would be able to find concrete ways of living a life of brotherhood that was devoid of class distinctions. Moreover, a community whose members lived a fully communal life and shared their property contrary to capitalist norms could influence its immediate environment through cultural and educational activity by performing plays with an educational message, organizing study groups, giving talks about topical problems, and organizing community singing and folk dancing. The journal also dealt extensively with the activities of the international peace movement, which was connected with the Quakers and which at that time was active mainly in England, Germany, and Holland.[23]

The books and the journal enjoyed a wide circulation throughout Germany, particularly among the youth who were fervently seeking solutions to their dilemmas, and their sales were a good source of income for the community in its first year. It is worth noting that the *Neuwerk* movement did not advocate the establishment of communal settlements, even though its writings emanated from the Sannerz community. Its main message called for commitment to its ideals in all walks of life, and although the call to establish communes modelled on apostolic Christianity was in the forefront in 1921, it was not intended to be the exclusive goal of the movement. Many of its speakers and leaders explained they did not wish to suggest that this way of life be adopted by all its members; it would suit only those who felt an inner call. Although several attempts were made during that year at organizing the establishment of communes, most of them petered out. Only two communes achieved stability: Habertshof, founded in 1919 in the Schluchtern region, which made its livelihood from agriculture, and Sannerz, which earned its living from publishing and child care.[24]

From the start, the people of Sannerz worked on the land, and although the novice farmers lacked know-how, their romantic belief in the joys of rural life made up for it. Eberhard Arnold tried to learn about agricultural work and bought a book on the preparation of a compost heap. He made a compost heap in the yard and spent time tending it every day after his work in publishing, and in this way he fulfilled one of his ideals—the combination intellectual and physical work. He explained his position on this subject in a lecture he gave at the time:

> We should be ready to spend several hours each day doing physical work. Intellectuals in particular would discover the wholesome effect this has. Daily practical work allows each person's special little light, his or her special gift, to be kindled.[25]

That first summer they had a stream of visitors. Arnold was considered to be one of the leaders of the social and religious ferment among the youth and the news of his family's move to a village spread quickly. Many people were curious to see this group of intellectuals that had chosen to live on a small farm in a remote little town and once the story had spread, the area became a favorite destination for youth movement hikers. The visitors were a very mixed crowd—long-haired radicals in shorts from the youth movements rubbed elbows with intellectuals from the academic and ecclesiastical milieux. People even came from abroad, from England, Holland, and France. The frequent visitors were something of a burden on the people at Sannerz, yet they helped to dispel their feeling of isolation during that first year and strengthen their belief that they were laying the foundations of a movement and heralding a great awakening.

This is how the people of Sannerz summed up their experiences a year later:

> At the *"Neuwerk Sannerz"* a work community has been formed, the entire life and work of which are pledged to the newly awakening movement. There are twelve of us altogether, the majority from the youth movement, who have come together for the common task. In addition to these twelve there is a wider circle of temporary helpers who share our common table. Many hundreds of young people have already (June, 1921) passed through our home.... In our efforts to reach the young

people, we draw our guests into the common work. In our communal discussions, inner gatherings and personal friendships, we seek to witness the way to Christ and to stimulate fruitful work. Then we embark on exhaustive discussions with the young people about the problems of our time.[26]

In spite of the hardships, the experience of the first months inspired Eberhard Arnold to express his elation in an article, written in 1920, bearing the symbolic title, "They Had All Things Common,"[27] words taken from the Acts of the Apostles (2:44), which describe the commune of the disciples of Jesus in Jerusalem. The entire article dealt with the significance of the Christian commune of the apostles, stressing the underlying faith and love inspired by the spirit of Jesus, and which enabled them to live a communal life and to share their property. Arnold emphasized that it was impossible to imitate the external manifestations of sharing property without such faith and love. Any attempt to enforce such an imitation would create a distortion of communal life, which would not last. It was the spirit of love, endowed by Jesus upon his followers, that caused "the concealed kingdom of the Lord to be revealed," as it was in the Jerusalem commune of the Bible. This is how Emmy Arnold described the atmosphere in those days:

Our life in the community was very joyful and filled with the expectation of a new future. Each day that we were able to live together in community was a day of celebration. Everything that happened was used as an occasion to celebrate...and for experiencing fellowship together.

Everybody joined in...everybody wanted to share in the common work.... When I think back to those times...during the period following the First World War, I felt it was a foretaste of what we can expect in a much greater measure in the future in the Kingdom of God. This was so in our life in Sannerz and perhaps in the Rhön Bruderhof.... Something that came from eternity was living among us, something that made us oblivious to the limits of time and space. Thus miracles, as one might call them, were experienced amongst us in quite a natural way.[28]

In the summer of 1921, young visitors again came in droves and helped them cope with building and work on the land, and older visitors from among the radicals who had lost faith in the old regime and who were searching for new directions also came. Emmy Arnold mentions that among the visitors who came that summer was Martin Buber.[29] Eberhard Arnold was away that day and he was very sorry that an opportunity for a meeting between them had been lost as he had a deep respect for Buber, with whose teachings he had become familiar during the war years.

In 1917, when he was still editor of *Die Furche,* he had written an article about Martin Buber's religious outlook, entitled *Der Prophet der neuen Judischen Bewegung* ("The Prophet of the New Jewish Movement," *Die Furche,* November, 1917). In this article he expressed his appreciation of and identified with Buber's perception of the essence of religion, which he defined as "a man's longing, through communion with the absolute, to give shape to the absolute and bring it to bear on man's world; religiousness then becomes action and renewal. Thus religiousness is represented as the opposite of tradition." The article also hinted at views that were to become a part of Eberhard Arnold's teachings, like "the notion that religion is something which impacts on all aspects of life and the emphasis on finding the divine, not in the world beyond, but in all things in daily reality."[30]

Clear evidence of Arnold's profound admiration for Buber can be found in his letter to him about the *Die Furche* Publishing House, written on 10 December 1918:

> It is particularly important to me to form a close relationship with you. I have long followed your career with great interest and the warmest sympathy, for having gained so much inspiration and such great benefit from your work, I need to thank you from the bottom of my heart for everything that you have given me. (The letter is in the Martin Buber archive, file no. 70.1, and in the Bruderhof archives.)

Eberhard Arnold, as well as other intellectually aware Bruderhof members, occasionally corresponded with Buber, especially during the first years, raising theological and philosophical questions.[31]

In the autumn of 1921, the population of Sannerz increased all at once. As the people of Sannerz kept in touch with the large number of visitors who had come during the summer months, some forty people from among the summer visitors decided to come and stay for a trial period during the winter. A circular was sent out to all visitors and friends telling of the activities and thoughts of the members of the commune. The first circular was sent in the autumn of 1921 and it opened with a kind of declaration of aims that stressed they had no indoctrinational or proselytistic intentions, yet they believed that the way of life they had chosen would enable them to live according to their ideals. "We have chosen to live simply in the countryside, in the hope that it will enable us to lead a better life and also enable us to help people living in the cities." They did not consider their home as exclusively theirs. "Even though our home is small, we shall open it to anyone in need of a roof over his head."

The sharing of property was presented as a natural step since it was in line with their goals. They believed that by sharing the work and their property, people would get to know each other better and, thus, come to share their faith. The ideal of service to the community and to society was central to their teaching and was expressed through their educational activities and thus, from the first year, they began to look after children of various ages with the aim of becoming a village educational community, *Landschulegemeinde,* and also an adult education center, *Volkshochschule.* Through this activity they hoped to influence their environment in the hope that they would become "a little city upon the hill," which through its very existence would serve society.[32]

In this circular, the members of Sannerz also raised practical problems, like the shortage of accommodation for summer visitors. They reported that during that year they had hosted 2,500 people and their expenses for housing and food had become a financial burden, but they could neither refuse those who wished to come nor ask for payment for lodging and food. They believed that their visitors came " because they wish to seek the way to God together with us," and in order to allow this search to continue, they asked for contributions from friends and movement members.[33]

In the second year of the commune's existence, after new members with experience in educational work had joined them, educational activity at Sannerz was given a considerable boost. Trudi Dalgas Huessi, a young teacher from Frankfurt who joined them in October, 1921, was to remain in the Bruderhof all her life. Trudi had heard about them through the publications and activities of *Neuwerk* and through Arnold's lectures at the summer conference held at Sannerz on 21 June. She became enthusiastic and left her work at a Frankfurt school in order to join the Sannerz community.

The "Sannerz Letter" to supporters, written in February, 1922, stated that the community numbered nineteen adult members and seven children and that they were already busy preparing for the crowds of summer visitors. It also hinted that they were looking for ways and means of sharing the financial burden, for "we cannot be regarded simply as a youth hostel or a village rest home."[34] But despite this mild admonition, they viewed the waves of visitors with pride and as evidence of their success in the task they had undertaken, and they wrote explicitly that

> a commune of working people can find real meaning in life only if its activity is directed beyond its own limited interests and if it also serves goals beyond the life of the community. Partnership between people doing intellectual work (in the publishing house) and those working on the land and in service jobs is a blessing for all. The people of Sannerz are planning to turn the visits into a learning experience with courses, thus combining work and study. The first course will open at Easter and the subject of study will be Tolstoy, Dostoyevsky, Kropotkin and Gustav Landauer.[35]

In this letter they also welcomed a new member, well-known in young Christian circles: Heinrich Schultheiss, who had been a pastor in the small town of Gelnhaar and who had given up his post in order to live in the commune. Schultheiss joined the publishing house and edited the journal together with Eberhard Arnold. Soon after his arrival, this is how he described the atmosphere at Sannerz:

> What is happening at Sannerz is simply that a few people are taking the risk of living their lives, harming no one, recognizing no law but that of obedience to the living Christ. It must be admitted however, that there is something in Sannerz that easily becomes unbearable for anyone who has already formed a firm opinion, who has a fixed viewpoint.... It is very embarrassing for someone like that to be drawn into the whirlpool of life and movement, and to see nothing regarded as of great importance...except for one single movement: the movement that comes from God, the living Christ. What matters is not that Sannerz grows. The only thing that matters is that a small, keenly active advance force is really there, animated by One Spirit on a single spiritual basis.[36]

During the first two years, the social structure of the Sannerz commune became consolidated, with the group of the seven original members at its center, and committed to the life of the new community. They were usually joined by some thirty temporary residents, friends, and visitors and during the frequent conferences held on the farm, their number would swell to one hundred. The seven original members worked in publishing, in service jobs, and on the small farm, and looked after the children whose number increased rapidly as they took in children from outside. In the winter of 1921 to 1922, there was a total of some sixty souls at Sannerz, and this obliged them to look for additional sources of income.

During the first years, the ideological trends at Sannerz contained many anarchistic elements derived from the teachings of Gustav Landauer.[37] The young radicals of the time believed in spontaneity, which would not fit into any party framework. This was particularly true of the communes, which were springing up all over Germany like mushrooms after the rain. These groups were influenced by Landauer's book, "Call to Socialism," and the majority flourished for only a short time as they had no solid foundations or mandatory framework. Arguments and quarrels soon ensued, which led to their disintegration and subsequent disappearance.[38] Eberhard Arnold also became interested in the teachings of Landauer through his book "Call to Socialism." The social vision it propounded impressed him so much that he adopted and integrated it into his personal social and religious point of view. He particularly approved of Landauer's call to German youth to set up agricultural communes that would foster true friendship while creative work would obviate alienation. The idea of setting up small voluntary units as bases and a springboard for change in society appealed to him, and two years later it led him to establish the Bruderhof community.

An article he wrote at the beginning of 1920, "Extended Households and Communal Life," bears the imprint of the views of Gustav Landauer on communal agricultural settlements that combined intellectual pursuits with physical labor and that were based on full partnership and the sharing of property, work, and spiritual experiences. This article also expressed his appreciation of the anarcho-communist followers of Landauer, and his satisfaction with the growing influence of his teachings, which added spiritual depth to the thinking of young socialists trapped in Marxist dogma. The article also emphasized Landauer's tribute to Jesus and viewed it as a beneficial combination of spiritual open mindedness and a trend toward social criticism.[39] It is worthy of mention that the covenant of the Sannerz community, signed by its first seven members, was formulated in the spirit of Landauer's views.

In her memoirs of Eberhard Arnold, which were written in the 1960s, Emmy Arnold stresses the importance of Landauer's influence on the founders of Sannerz. In the introduction she writes:

From the start it was clear to us that community life would have to be a life of unity in faith, community of property and work in voluntary poverty. The writings of Gustav Landauer in particular guided us in that direction.[40]

During the first year, when the *Neuwerk* publishing house was being set up, one of the first books they intended to publish was a collection of letters by Gustav Landauer and excerpts from his work. Eberhard Arnold raised this topic in his letters to friends whom he wished to interest in the publishing house. He also wrote about it to the writer Karl Joseph Friedrich in his letter of 26 August, 1920:

> One of our important plans is to publish a book by Gustav Landauer. I know you have been very interested in him lately. I am also very fond of him for his beneficial and profound influence on the revolution which has taken place. I am therefore eager to prepare a one-volume collection of excerpts from his letters and writings.... This book is intended to deepen our insight into his mystical teachings and clarify his attitude to God, to Jesus and to communal life.

He added that he did not intend to publish all Landauer's works and letters, since he had heard from Martin Buber that other publishers were already doing so.

Eberhard Arnold worked on this project throughout the publishing house's first year. We learn about the next step from a letter to Z. F. Schwalbe, dated 8 October 1920, in which he said that he wished to contact Landauer's friends in order to obtain letters from them. From another letter to Friedrich, written in November, 1920, we learn that the latter had agreed to undertake the preparation of the book and Arnold even begged him to complete it quickly, "because Landauer's memory must not wane." But despite all his intentions and preparations, the book was never published.

However, Landauer's teachings and personality continued to influence the founders of Bruderhof for years.[41] The profound regard in which Landauer was held became further enhanced by his being considered a martyr after his murder by his political enemies on 2 May 1919. For several years afterward, the members of the Bruderhof used to gather in honor of his memory on the anniversary of his death.[42]

Discord and Schism in 1922

In the spring of 1922, the postwar spiritual ferment in German youth circles was on the wane and the urge to leave the cities to fulfill social missions was beginning to subside. Between 1921 and 1922, debate was rife within the Christian youth movements on the way of life to be sought by their activists. The question was, Is it better to leave society to seek alternative ways or to be the active "leaven in the dough" within society? "Be good men and women," they said. "Do your work responsibly wherever you are—as teachers, craftsmen, doctors, businessmen—and love your neighbor! The discipleship of Jesus does not mean a new order." The little group at Sannerz was pushed out of the movement.[43] These disputes dampened the enthusiasm for creating a new way of life in communal settlements and many young radicals returned to the existing churches to become "the leaven in the dough."

In the summer of 1922, an air of dissension pervaded the Sannerz commune. At first, the charismatic personality of Eberhard Arnold sustained the group, which by then numbered fifty souls, but the situation became progressively more difficult and in the summer of 1922, rampant inflation in Germany exacerbated the tensions within the group. The roots of this dissension could be traced back to the first rallies of the *Neuwerk* movement, when two differing trends concerning the direction of the movement's activity became evident. One was that of the older group, which included supporters of the theological approach of social Christianity propounded by Karl Barth, while the second was that of the group around Eberhard Arnold, which aspired to live according to the principles of apostolic Christianity, in opposition to the churches and their dogmas.

The supporters of the theological approach were dubious about the venture of Arnold and his group in Sannerz. Arnold accused the theologians of skepticism and for causing a decline in the radicalism of German youth. He claimed that their conservative approach was weakening the protest against the injustices perpetrated by the current regime and fostered an atmosphere of acquiescence to capitalism.

In his opinion, the Christian spirit of the Sermon on the Mount was waning, and under the current circumstances a split should be considered, thus enabling each faction to go its own way.[44] These disputes created an unpleasant atmosphere at the 1922 Whitsun *Neuwerk* conference, which took place at Wallroth near Schluchtern where Eberhard Arnold's "mystical Utopianism" was subjected to widespread criticism. In those days, members of political organizations frequently criticized the Sannerz commune, accusing the community of sectarianism, isolationism, and shirking their responsibilities to society.[45]

This view was expressed in an article that appeared in a politically oriented youth journal in February, 1992, and which criticized Arnold's group in the *Neuwerk* movement for focusing their efforts on their settlement and thus distancing themselves from the main struggle taking place in the big cities. The desire of the members of Sannerz to create a new way of life for themselves might be justified from their own point of view, "but if we ask ourselves whether withdrawal, while disregarding the struggle for existence taking place in the towns, is the way to overcome the suffering of the masses, the answer is a definite 'No!'...We cannot wait for the new spirit to sprout from the seedlings in these small communities."[46]

At the same time, the crisis at Sannerz deepened and came into the open in the wake of an affair connected with the Arnold family. In June, 1922, the couple and their children received an invitation to spend a month at the home of their friends Kees and Betty Boeke at their pacifist community in Bilthoven, Holland. During their stay there, galloping inflation in Germany caused many of the investors in the *Neuwerk* publishing house to withdraw their money. The Arnolds were called back, but Eberhard Arnold felt "an inner certainty" that he did not need to cut his vacation short and that "God's hand" would save the situation. He decided to stay in spite of the repeated calls from Sannerz, because he hoped that in Holland he would be able to obtain the necessary funds for keeping the publishing house open. Fortunately, his hope was realized, and at the end of his stay he received a contribution in Dutch currency which, when exchanged for German marks, was sufficient to cover the deficit. But despite their achievement, the Arnolds were too late; in the meantime the publishing house had gone bankrupt and most of the investors and shareholders had withdrawn their capital.[47]

On their return, the family was given a cool welcome by the members of the community and that same evening a general meeting was convened. At this meeting of all the members, the Arnolds were accused of irresponsible conduct and lack of financial skill. It became clear that serious opposition to Arnold's leadership of the community had hardened. The opposition adopted a fundamental position regarding the present regime, favoring integration with it and the dissemination of its new ideology. Contrary to Arnold's belief that faith should permeate and guide their way of life, including its economic and financial aspects, his opponents claimed that matters of faith should be kept apart from economic affairs. The opposition claimed that the "open door" principle, which was held to be the community's guiding light, was hypocritical, since there was an inner circle that held closed secret meetings at night when the rest of the members were asleep, and that the affairs of visitors and new members were discussed at these sessions. The atmosphere at the meeting was morbid and hostile and deteriorated into open crisis after Arnold's speech, in which he said that he would continue to live a communal and frugal life. He was willing to give up his leading position if there was someone willing to replace him. In response, many people announced they were leaving and at that meeting, forty people declared they were abandoning communal life, among them Heinrich Schultheiss and his family.

At the conclusion of the meeting, when the chairman asked who would be staying, only seven members, which was the minimal number legally required to maintain "the association," raised their hands. Had there been one less, the liquidation of the association and the division of all the property between those leaving and those remaining could have been demanded. Several members of the committee that headed the community announced that they were leaving, but as the Arnolds were also on the committee and had the right of signature, this enabled the group to function despite the hindrance of this exodus.[48]

After the meeting they began to divide up the property. They sold the cows, divided up the fruit and vegetables in the store, and the money from the sale of the sawmill. This led to acrimonious arguments and the Arnolds' refusing to accept their share. Harsh accusations flew back and forth and life under the same roof became unbearable. Some of those leaving tried unsuccessfully to find another place in which to continue living together as a community, but apart from their opposition to Arnold's way of life, they had nothing in common. The tensions were somewhat eased with the arrival of Friedrich Klein, Arnold's uncle, who maintained an impartial position and tried to find a compromise, but to no avail. The deep hostility toward the Arnolds stemmed from their uncompromising adherence to the principles of the communal way of life, rather than seeing it as a passing experiment, as did the others.[49]

In October, 1922, the agonizing process of the split came to an end. Emmy wrote of the meeting of those who remained, saying that they felt they must invest a great deal of energy in renewing their communal life: "We could not understand it; we had shared experiences with many of them." Yet, despite of the bitterness of those difficult days, she did not perceive those who had left as "the villains" and those who stayed as "the good ones." She admits they were aware of their mistakes and weaknesses and that they knew they were not yet ready for the great challenge that faced them.

Eberhard Arnold viewed the crisis as a catalyst in a new beginning and summed it up thusly:

> When the call first came to us, we felt that the Spirit of Jesus Christ had urged us to live in full community, in communal solidarity, with an open door and a loving heart for all people.... When we had traveled only a short way along this road, times came upon us that put this power to the test, hostile times of trial, when friends we knew well and whom we had come to love deeply, suddenly reversed their position and became enemies of the way...because they wanted to return to ordinary middle class life...the movement was led once more into bondage through the middle-class influences of capitalism.[50]

In the course of time, this was how the Arnolds summed up this period: "From an objective point of view, the main factor which caused the break-up was the clash between faith and purely economic considerations."

After the crisis, between 1922 and 1924, the little group suffered from isolation and at the same time had to fight to keep out eccentrics who brought "the breath of evil" into their midst and whom the group saw as demonic spirits, the origins of which were in the war and revolution. These people were on the borderline of sanity and hoped to be healed at Sannerz. Some succeeded and some became a burden. Eberhard Arnold describes this period in a letter to a group of young Christians written in April, 1926:

> In the winter of 1922 we faced two difficult challenges: economically, our existence hung by a thread and this struggle exhausted us and left its mark on all aspects of our work. The second and more difficult challenge was the spiritual struggle. We were fighting the dark demonic forces of mammon which had penetrated into our midst and afflicted our life that winter.

Emmy Margaret, the Arnold's eldest daughter, wrote about the visitors who came during those years:

> Those years brought very few new members, but they did bring many struggles for inner clarity—with guests, helpers and with burdened people who were in great need of help just to keep going inwardly. At that time many people came to us who were burdened with sin and an evil life. We all lived in the same house, and Papa had planted in our hearts a deep respect for these poorest of the poor, and he had told us that there was a hidden jewel in each one.[51]

In spite of the isolation, the difficulties and "the breath of evil," Eberhard Arnold felt that the community was inspired by the Holy Spirit during this period, that many of the visitors were influenced by the members' faith and that they served as a bridge to the Kingdom of God on earth.

The Sannerz years, the first seven years of community life, were the novitiate of the community. The one big step, the one great step from private life into the Sannerz community...was a step into *terra incognita*. We actually began without a clear picture of how, in practical terms, such a life would turn out and what it would look like. We are a community of Jesus. And we are a community of the Lord's Supper.[52]

Bruderhof member Gertrude Dalgas Huessi wrote an article describing the situation in 1924 in which she mentions that the community consisted of thirteen adults and twelve children at that time. The little community continued to function in the following four areas along the same lines as before: (a) publishing, (b) education, (c) agriculture, and (d) a youth hostel.

After the liquidation of the *Neuwerk Verlag* publishing house, a new one was established in 1923 under the name *Gemeinschaftsverlag Eberhard Arnold,* because those who had left wanted to keep the company's original name. The new publishing house continued the policy of publishing books on religious and social subjects and this activity was regarded both as a source of income and a way of spreading the word. Gertrud Dalgas wrote of "the urge to create contact with people and bear witness." Among the books published in 1924 was an anthology of youth movement songs, *Sonnenlieder,* a theological volume by Eberhard Arnold, *Innenland,* and a collection of letters by Tolstoy dealing with religious questions.

In her article, Dalgas emphasized that the community was now moving in a new direction by devoting itself to the education of children from the depressed strata of society, who were homeless or came from broken homes. They intended to bring together a group of children of different ages who would be adopted by the adults and become part of the community, studying and working. The older ones would be sent to schools outside the community after a period of training at home, during which "the Berlin atmosphere would disappear." The article presents agricultural work not only as a source of income, but also as an ideal, since it created a bond with nature and provided them with their food. A youth hostel was also set up to institutionalize the open-door policy and enable visitors to come and go in the summer months and join them in their work and social life, and so get to know the way of life Sannerz wished to show the world.[53]

Although the enthusiasm of 1921 and 1922 had waned, many visitors from the youth movements continued to come to Sannerz. "Letters from Sannerz" was published again in 1925 after an interval of three years. The first circular sent to visitors and friends tells of the widespread activity of the publishing house, which had even opened a branch in Leipzig and now sold its books through friends who acted as travelling salesmen. The group of children increased in size and new members joined the community, among them people with families and former youth movement activists.

One of those mentioned was Alfred Gneiting, who was to remain in the Bruderhof all his life.[54] In later years, when summing up his memories of the Bruderhof as one of its veteran members, he gave his impressions of Sannerz in those early days:

> In Sannerz I found again and again what thousands of people longed for in their hearts—a totally new society, the rise of a truly new man. Those people were finding the new way, the way back to God, and they were ready to give up everything to pass this message on. This was the only meaning of their poverty and simplicity, of their move from a comfortable middle-class life to a life of brotherliness.[55]

In this letter he also mentioned a development that was to assume great significance in the history of Bruderhof—the precise formulation of the principles on which their way of life was based. The principle that would later be considered as the most fundamental was called "The First Law of Sannerz," which has remained the cornerstone of their way of life to this day.

The First Law of Sannerz

> There is no law but that of love. Love means having joy in others. Then what does being annoyed with them mean? Words of love convey the joy we have in the presence of brothers and sisters. By the same token it is out of the question to speak about a Bruderhof member in a spirit of irritation or vexation. There must never be talk, either in open remarks or by insinuation, against a brother or sister, against their individual characteristics—under no circumstances behind the person's back. Talking in one's own family is no exception.

> Direct address is the only way possible, it is the spontaneous brotherly service we owe anyone whose weaknesses cause a negative reaction in us. An open word spoken directly to the other person deepens friendship and is not resented. Only when two people do not come to an agreement quickly in this direct manner is it necessary to talk it over with a third person who can be trusted to help solve the difficulty and bring about a uniting on the highest and deepest level.[56]

In 1925, after five years of communal life at Sannerz, the members felt a sense of relief in being able to sum up their experience and define their values, as Eberhard Arnold did in a small booklet, entitled "*Warum wir in Gemeinschaft leben*" (Why We Live in Community). It also included the principles and values embedded and crystallized in their faith, and which were also to guide them in future. The extracts quoted here reflect the religious fervor that prevailed in the community and which permeated the members' everyday life:

Our work is a venture dared again and again. We human beings are not the driving force in this; we have been driven and are being urged on.

The ever-present danger of becoming exhausted and useless is overcome by the faith that underlies mutual help.

Efficiency is aimed at in all areas, but above all other questions, each one...must be faced with the decision again and again, whether or not he is growing into the coming, Christ-determined community and which particular service in the Church community he is called to.... The whole of life, with all the various forms it takes in nature, becomes an image of what is vital in the community of the Kingdom of God. Thus we must make daily meals—the most commonplace of human necessities—into consecrated festivals of community, to be approached with reverence. Likewise each day of working together in community is a symbol of the sowing of life.... The only power that can build community is faith in the ultimate mystery of the Good, faith in God.... For the sake of the call to this way, it is necessary to break with everything else and sacrifice our lives.

Only when we throw our whole life into it, is there any meaning to the public witness to voluntary community of goods and work and in the witness of peace and love.... When a community of deeply moved people believes in the spirit, the freedom of the individual lives in the free decision of the united will brought about by the Spirit.... This will was created to exercise intense powers. It is a fighting will against all destructive powers.... Life in community means discipline in community, education in community, preparing people in the discipleship of Christ.... Educational community of goods and work...is a bond made in free will in surrender, a bond of sacrifice...when working men voluntarily make a joint commitment to renounce everything that is self-willed, isolated or private...

Work alone makes it possible to work in community—work that is joy in working for the whole and joy in all those we work with.... We love physical work, and we love the activity of spirit and mind. We love art and we love to study the spiritual influences at work in the whole of mankind, in its history...we love handicrafts in which man's spirit guides his hand. From God as the source, our common life is built up and led time and again through tragic struggles for life to final victory.

Such a common life is no place to look for the idyllic existence of human comforts and pleasures. It in no way provides satisfaction for romantic desires or selfish cravings for personal happiness. Community life...means sacrificing daily all our strength and all our rights, all the demands commonly made on life and assumed to be justified.... The only way private property, personal assets, or privileges of any kind can be overcome is through the power of the uniting Spirit.[57]

After 1925, there was another period of growth and consolidation, but the movement had changed. From that time onward, the focal point of their lives became the Sannerz commune and although their links with the youth movement grew weaker, they were not totally severed. In the history of the Bruderhof there would again be periods of renewed activity and of links with the youth movements, especially when many of their members came to join the community, but henceforth Sannerz, and later the Bruderhof at Rhön, became the sole ideological center. They had no organized or spiritual leadership outside the commune.

We may say that the foundations had been laid for the Bruderhof as an independent commune movement, which succeeded in preserving the commune as a way of life of its members. From among the many German communes of the twenties, only the Bruderhof became a communal movement that has survived to this day. Although the movement has undergone many changes and has spread far afield, the underlying principles of its way of life, which were formulated at the end of the Sannerz period, continue to serve as a guiding light for the nine Bruderhof communes in the United States, England, Germany, and lately in Nigeria.

Notes

1. *Memories of Our Early Years*, vol. 1 (Collection of pamphlets published by the Plough Publishing House, Rifton, N.Y.: 1973–79), chap. K, 8.
2. Mow, Merrill, *Torches Rekindled* (Ulster Park, N.Y.: Plough Publishing House, 1989), 46. See also the Arnold family tree at the Bruderhof archives in Spring Valley.
3. See the Hollander and Arnold family trees in the Bruderhof archives and in Mow, op. cit., vol. 2, chap. 1, 1–3.
4. *The Plough*, vol. 1 (Quarterly of Bruderhof communities. Bromdon: The Plough Publishing House, 1953): 2; Arnold, Eberhard, and Emmy Arnold, *Seeking For The Kingdom of God* (Rifton, N.Y.: Plough Publishing House, 1974), 14.
5. His thesis was "Early Christian and Anti Christian Elements in the Development of Friedrich Nietzsche."
6. Arnold, Emmy, *Torches Together* (Rifton, N.Y.: Plough Publishing House, 1976), 6–14; *The Plough*, op. cit., no. 3.
7. Memories, op. cit., vol.2, chap. E, 16.
8. In a lecture in April, 1937 at the University of South Dakota. In *God's Revolution* (New York: Paulist Press, 1984), 167; Arnold, Eberhard, *God's Revolution*, 167–68.
9. Laqueur, Walter, *Young Germany* (New Brunswick, N.J.: Transaction Publishers, 1984), 113–15.
10. Vollmer, Antie, *The Neuwerk Movement 1919–1935*. Unpublished doctoral thesis (Berlin, 1973): 78. Members of these groups would found the Habertshof settlement in the Hessen region, which existed until Hitler's rise to power and broke up in 1934. Laqueur, op. cit., 119.

11. Vollmer, op. cit.: 58.
12. Ibid.: 112.
13. Ibid.: 20-26, 69-76; *Sonnherzbuch* (Collection of articles, Sannerz, 1920-26): 34-42, 149-54.
14. Arnold, Emmy, op. cit., 33.
15. *Sonnherzbuch,* op. cit.: 10-14.
16. Ibid.: 56; Vollmer, op. cit.: 76-77.
17. Arnold, Emmy, op. cit., 33-37.
18. Vollmer, op. cit.: 78.
19. *The Plough,* op. cit., no. 3: 4-5.
20. *Memories,* vol. 3, chap. I: 14-15; Ibid., vol. 2, chap. I: 10-11.
21. Vollmer, op. cit.: 98-107.
22. *Sonnherzbuch,* op. cit.: 147.
23. Vollmer, op. cit.: 83-90.
24. *Sonnherzbuch,* op. cit.: 36-39.
25. Arnold, Eberhard, op. cit., 137.
26. Arnold, Eberhard, *Foundations and Orders of Sannerz and the Rhön Bruderhof* (Rifton, N.Y.: Plough Publishing House, 1976), 13-14.
27. Ibid., 5-9.
28. Arnold, Emmy, op. cit., 50-52.
29. Ibid., 60.
30. Between 1915 and 1919, Eberhard Arnold made a living by writing articles on theological and philosophical subjects. He published a series of articles on contemporary philosophers like Kierkegaard, Tolstoy, and Martin Buber. It is evident that he identifies with Buber, calling him "a prophet" of the new religious approach, which has at its center the concept of "the realization of God." This realization is achieved by the wholeness of the person and by overcoming inner duality—*Die Furche* (1917). See also Thomas Stieglitz, interview in Kingston in December, 1991, and his doctoral thesis, published by Paderborn 1991: 129.
31. There are documents in the Bruderhof archives showing that Bruderhof members participated in meetings at which Buber delivered theoretical lectures, and a letter from Schultheiss to Arnold, October, 1921. In the Buber archives in Jerusalem, there are three letters written by Eberhard Arnold to Martin Buber between 1918 and 1927, one of which deals with the plan to publish the letters of Gustav Landauer (see file 70e). In the Bruderhof archives there is a postcard, sent by Buber to Arnold on 11 March 1927, containing his agreement with the Bruderhof attitude regarding integration between faith and life (see *The Plough,* no. 16: 1986). Hans Meier, born in Switzerland (1902), who joined the Bruderhof in 1933, tells of his profound interest in Martin Buber since 1924, when he met him in Zurich at a meeting of Christian Socialists. His regard for Buber also reflected his affinity with Judaism and Israel and later with the Kibbutz Movement, to which he felt a closeness throughout his long life. Hans Meier, and other Swiss members who joined the Bruderhof in the 1930s, belonged in their youth to the Christian Socialist Movement of Leonard Ragaz, who fostered a profound regard for the Jews, Judaism, and the Bible (see Leonard Ragaz, *Signs of the Kingdom,* 105-07). The relations between Martin Buber and members of the Bruderhof were also mentioned by M. Tyldesley in an interview with Walter Huessy in Darvell in 1993.
32. *Sonnherzbuch,* op. cit.: 86.
33. Ibid.: 80-90.
34. Ibid.: 115.

35. Ibid.: 107–18.
36. *The Plough*, no. 26 (September/October 1990).
37. See Arnold, Emmy, *Seeking*, 19. Trudi Huessi mentions the influence of Landauer (see *Memories*, op. cit., vol. 1, chap. M: 20.
38. Regarding this ferment, it is possible during this period to find a similarity in their spiritual sources between the Bruderhof and the pioneer movements in Germany, for Martin Buber and Gustav Landauer were a significant source of spiritual inspiration, influencing their attitude to communal life.
39. The article was published in the *Neuwerk* journal in April 1920.
40. Arnold, Eberhard, *A Testimony of Church Community* (Rifton, N.Y.: Plough Publishing House, 1964): 5.
41. The importance of the influence of Landauer's book on the founders of the Bruderhof in their choice of a way of life is also clearly reflected in their reminiscences. For the influence of Buber and Landauer on the founders, see the interviews with Hans Meier and Georg Barth at Spring Valley in July, 1990, and also, Meier, Hans, *Hans Meier Tells His Story to a Friend* (Rifton, N.Y.: Plough Publishing House, 1979), 5; see Trudi Huessy, *Memories*, 20. Georg Barth, who joined the Bruderhof in 1925, says that when he came to visit for the first time in 1924, he had a long talk with Eberhard Arnold about the views of Gustav Landauer, which were presented to him as the epitome of the Bruderhof's social vision. Interview with Georg Barth, July, 1990. Also interview with Thomas von Stieglitz, December, 1991.
42. Eberhard Arnold's eldest daughter told the author that she remembers that her father stood in memory of Gustav Landauer on the anniversary of his death. Kathleen Hassenberg, one of the Bruderhof veterans, remembers how, in 1934, Eberhard stood on his broken leg on the fifteenth anniversary of Landauer's murder (see also Gneiting, Alfred, *When the Wind Begins to Blow*). The researcher Tyldesley interviewed the Bruderhof veterans and became aware of Landauer's influence.
43. *Memories*, op. cit., vol.2, 12, I: 12.
44. Vollmer, op. cit.: 111–15.
45. Zablocki, Benjamin, *The Joyful Community* (Baltimore, Md.: Penguin, 1971), 72; Whitworth, John McKelvey, *God's Blueprints* (London and Boston, Mass.: Routledge & Kegan Paul, 1975), 170.
46. *Sonnherzbuch*, op. cit.: 149.
47. Arnold, Emmy, op. cit., 69–81.
48. Ibid., 74–76.
49. Ibid., 78.
50. Ibid., 80–81; *The Plough*, vol. 1, no.3, 1953: 6–7.
51. *Memories*, vol. 2, chap. E: 34, 46.
52. Ibid.: 28.
53. *Sonnherzbuch*, op. cit.: 180–86.
54. Ibid.: 191–97.
55. *Memories*, vol. 2, chap. H: 59.
56. Arnold, Eberhard, *Foundations*, 48–49; *God's Revolution*, 130.
57. Arnold, Eberhard, *Foundations*, 20–33.

2

The Rhönbruderhof:
Recovery and Consolidation

By 1926, after new members had joined and fifteen children had been adopted, there were forty-five people living in the community. The group was open and willing to grow and its members were of extremely diverse origins. Some had been anarchists and socialists, others came from proletarian youth movements, and some had belonged to small Christian sects. The motto on the dining room wall read: "Ten have been invited and twenty will come. Add water to the soup and welcome them all."[1]

However, the awakening that had been in evidence in German youth after the war was on the wane and so opportunities for absorbing new members had decreased. As early as 1923, Arnold spoke at a rally about "the funeral of the youth movement" that was imminent. We must bear in mind that in 1923, many were unemployed and runaway inflation had consumed the savings of the middle and lower strata of society and this was a source of incessant social and spiritual unrest. The distress and dissatisfaction of the young people were no longer a central issue.

In 1925, Eberhard Arnold published an article entitled "Our Association at the Crossroads," which dealt with the crisis in the youth movements and in which he described the youth movements as a very significant historical phenomenon that had become weakened and spent itself when the time had come to act. However, the climate that had sustained them had not dissipated and was likely to reappear under different circumstances. In this article he called upon the youngsters in and around the youth movements to abandon their seclusion and soul-searching and dedicate themselves to a transcendental goal as the only way of arresting the decline and overcoming the crisis. Arnold objected to allying the spirit of brotherhood engendered by the movement to the policy of any political party, believing that without a spiritual goal, political struggle was worthless. At the same time, he called for involvement in the struggle to change society and support and assist the downtrodden. All the forces working for change must act together; yet he stressed that his movement would employ only peaceful means. A task force would be set up and sent to distressed areas to assist those in need of food, clothing, and shelter and in this way they would presage the coming of the new social order.[2]

Although the Sannerz commune had left the *Neuwerk* movement, it did not sever its ties completely with the youth movements. The connection was maintained mainly through the activities of Eberhard Arnold, who was often invited to lecture to various groups of students and church gatherings. His lectures attracted large audiences of youngsters in search of guidance, and through them the Sannerz community acquired new friends, including some members of the upper class. Among those who attended his lectures and who later became friends of the Bruderhof was Prince Waldenburg Schoenburg.[3]

Eberhard Arnold often addressed the Free German Youth Movement in Dresden. Hans Zumpe, who heard him speak there, joined the Bruderhof and within a few years had become Eberhard Arnold's assistant in the administration of the commune.[4] In a similar way, young Georg Barth became interested in the commune, first visiting in 1922 and joining in 1925, and subsequently becoming a lifelong member. In his memoirs, Georg Barth says that he had belonged to a group of young Christians called the *Koengener Bund,* which had been formed within the youth movement in his home town. He met Eberhard Arnold in 1922 when he came to address a YMCA group in Breslau and he was so impressed by his personality that he went to visit Sannerz and asked to stay, but Arnold persuaded him to first complete his studies. After becoming a qualified crafts teacher, Barth joined the Bruderhof, taught crafts, and later became one of the commune's leading members. He recalls that at their very first meeting in Breslau, Eberhard showed him Gustav Landauer's book *The Call for Socialism,* and on the way to the railway station in the nearby town they again discussed Landauer's theories on communal settlements.[5]

During the lean years suffered by the youth movements, Eberhard's lectures brought a continuous flow of visitors to the Sannerz commune. People from various groups with varied viewpoints visited the commune; youngsters from the Christian youth associations who raised theological questions on the need to live a communal life and Marxists and communists, too. Some were very impressed by the communal life and described the members as "noble communists," but most were scornful and critical.

In her memoirs, Emmy Arnold writes that they used to tell them:

> What are you doing? Why do you live in a community with forty or fifty people? It's nonsense. It's not worthwhile. You have to wait until everybody does it, then you have to join in! In the meantime you should join our party and fight with us.

Visitors belonging to nationalistic circles also came and their arguments focused on "whether the national interest should take precedence over the personal one," and the question of individual freedom was usually central to the discussions held with the visitors.

At that time, small communal settlements were breaking up because of personal disillusionment and because of extreme radicalism, which could not be fulfilled in practice. Some broke up due to excessive individualism: each person wanted to work independently and "no one was willing to accept instructions or dictates from anyone else." They complained, "We didn't join the community to be told by others what to do...we are not ready to submit to new bosses...we'll only follow our inner needs."[6]

A few years later Eberhard Arnold would refer to the question of the disintegration of the communes in a lecture at the University of Dakota. He maintained that their main weakness was lack of faith in a God-given absolute truth by which they should have lived their daily lives. All the communities that failed lacked a faith that was sufficiently strong to overcome the weakness of human nature. Indeed, communes could only survive by virtue of a compelling faith, which was lacking in all the short-lived communes that had been established in the twenties.[7]

Impelled by this belief, the Sannerz community decided to become a Church community in August, 1925. In a declaration of faith published at the time, they wrote:

> The community feels that its true calling is to establish itself as a Church, to live together as a commune fully united in daily life on the basis of sharing all property, having surrendered all private property.

Some months later, in January, 1926, when members of the *Arbeitsgemeinschaft Neu Sonnefeld* commune proposed amalgamation of the two communes, the members of Sannerz presented them with their declaration of faith, emphasizing the vow demanding lifelong faithfulness to their independent Church, which says:

> There is no true brotherhood without absolute allegiance to the unifying faith and without a struggle against the satanic forces, exposing us to temptations along the way. There is need for obedience stemming from the Holy Spirit, as an anchor for our relationships.

They were also presented with "The First Law of Sannerz" as a mandatory principle that underpinned their way of life, and it was these demands that prevented the amalgamation.[8]

In spite of changes in the general atmosphere and the waning of the ferment within the youth groups, Sannerz continued to pursue the "open door" policy toward those seeking shelter because of personal problems. Trudi Huessi writes:

> The Sannerz house was always full of guests; they came especially in summer, from May on. Whitsun was the most beautiful season, and we used to have conferences and invite people. And suddenly there would be a hundred people all in that house! The boys and the young men had to sleep on hay in a barn we rented from a farmer in a neighboring village and the girls slept in another barn. Everything happened outside around the house.[9]

After several years of accepting people under overcrowded conditions, they came to the conclusion that the house at Sannerz was too small to accept all those who knocked on its door and that their living space would have to be extended. Since the possibilities of enlarging the house at Sannerz were limited, they began to look for a new place. After scouring the surrounding area, they found the Sparhof farm near Fulda in the Rhön Mountains. The farm was known locally as *Hanshof* ("Hans's Yard"), but they called it *Bruderhof* ("Brother's Yard"), which had been the name of the earlier Hutterite settlements.

It was a neglected farm standing on infertile soil, in a region inhabited by poor peasants. Their dilemma was great: the acreage (seventy-five acres) was too large for their group to cultivate, ten thousand marks ($6,500) had to be paid immediately, and they did not possess such a sum. Nevertheless, they decided to buy it, believing that the money would eventually be found and indeed it was: In the fall of 1926, a few days before the first payment was due, they received a donation from Prince Waldenburg Schoenburg, who had befriended them after hearing Eberhard's lectures.

At the beginning of 1927, the group moved to the new farm, which was renamed *Rhönbruderhof*. The transfer was executed in stages; first they moved the children and the youngsters, who helped harvest the potatoes in the new vegetable garden. It was a cold winter, so they had to seal their living quarters as well as prepare the land. The slow and gradual transfer created tensions between those who remained at Sannerz and those who moved to the new farm. The publishing house continued to function for some time in Sannerz, and although the number of people working there was limited, it was their main source of income. Eberhard Arnold remained in Sannerz because of his work, and the maintaining of harmony between the two groups called for a great effort and many visits to Rhön in order to alleviate the social tensions. The final move took place at the end of 1927.

The move to Rhön did not entail a radical change in the structure of the commune, but in the wake of the new situation, changes in the way of life took place. Life in the Bruderhof became quieter, more stable, and institutionalized, and meetings that had previously been open to all now became limited to those who had taken the vow of faithfulness. The community's population became stable and the differences between members and visitors were more clearly defined. The spontaneity and emotionalism that had characterized Sannerz diminished and work became the focal point of life in the commune. Emmy Arnold writes:

> There was plenty of work to do and the times when the whole household worked together were an important part of the communal experience.... The day was spent in work and the evening in discussions, in which either the whole household or only the brotherhood took part. We went on hikes and tried to make contact with the neighboring peasants.... Occasionally we performed plays in the neighboring villages and tried to present a simple message. On summer evenings we often gathered under the big beech tree on the hill overlooking the community. Here, with our guests and those who had worked with us, we sought the true inner liberation of the individual from himself, for true peace and a just society.[10]

The first years of the Bruderhof at Rhön were years of poverty and financial problems. They were short of both food and money and on a few occasions they almost went bankrupt. Checks bounced and two members were constantly engaged in trying to make ends meet. A police officer would often come to confiscate some of their possessions in lieu of their debts. Eberhard joked about this, saying that judging by his numerous visits, he could easily be considered a member of the Bruderhof. The farm was in a bad location; the soil was poor and the area exposed to winds that damaged the crops. The wheat crop hardly covered their own needs. They were constantly short of bread and the situation deteriorated to the point that visitors were asked to bring loaves of bread with them. In some instances, instead of a birthday cake, bread was baked instead. In the winter of 1928, the vegetable and potato crops were poor and the community was short of food throughout the year. This left its mark on the health of both adults and children.

Despite the economic situation they did not change their open-door policy and continued to absorb people and adopt homeless children because they wished to assist the needy. From the moment that they had arrived at Sannerz they had begun taking in homeless children, mostly war orphans and children from broken homes and this, too, had a financial aspect. One of the of the veteran women recalls:

> The community was too poor to take children in, to see to their education, clothe and feed them. Sannerz and the Rhön Bruderhof were just too poor. So they arranged a kind of sponsor or guardian for each child, people outside the community whom they found by writing letters or by appealing to friends. Each guardian would take on a child...and pay a monthly sum of money or send a package of food or clothing to contribute in a concrete way so that these children could be educated in the community. Especially in the Rhön Bruderhof, the children's community was a source of income through those friends who helped support a child.[11]

Payment, however, was not conditional to accepting the children and concern for their welfare was uppermost:

> When we heard about children in need somewhere, we just took them in. We never asked beforehand whether we would be paid, but once the child was there, we tried to obtain some means.[12]

It is remarkable that they persevered in their educational work within such a small framework.

Children in the Rhönbruderhof were organized as an independent community and life in the community made a powerful impression on them, as can be seen from their reminiscences years later:

> The Rhön Bruderhof was for years a "land of children".... Through the years a wonderful children's home came into being.... The idea of the "study and work" school was incorporated into our children's community. We worked on the farm and in the garden, cared for the goats and rabbits and were a real help with the harvest.[13]

During those years a religious spiritual group called the *Sonnentruppe* became active in the children's community, with eleven-year-old Heini

Arnold organizing it. Eberhard Arnold encouraged it as an expression of the independence of the children's society. The group gathered to participate in religious experiences. Emmy Margaret, Heini's elder sister, recalls that they used to go out in a group into the nearby woods and return elated by spiritual experiences after long hours of wandering around in solitary contemplation and prayer.[14]

Their inner world was suffused with a religious spirit and replete with symbols and ceremonies that stemmed from the old youth movement. They used to gather in the heart of nature around a bonfire, sing together, and read from the Scriptures. They sometimes invited adults to their meetings and also composed songs and ditties that reflected their affinity with the community's faith. This activity was central to the children's lives. Sophie Lober writes:

> We gathered every day, during playtime or whenever we wanted to. We would stop playing or even working. We had to work very hard from morning till evening in the summertime, weeding the fields, hoeing or haymaking.... When we felt the need to be together, we just left off work and sat down to sing or to share our feelings.[15]

From the outset, the ideal of a school combining study and work was realized. The children worked on the farm and also looked after their goats and rabbits. With their meager means, the community maintained a school for the fifteen children living there, the eldest of whom were aged twelve and thirteen, and they were taught by teacher-members of the community and friends who volunteered to help. After much debate, they decided to send the older children to a school outside the community, where they could also receive vocational training. The most gifted child was Hardy, Arnold's son, whose father intended him to become a teacher in the commune. Since no suitable school could be found for him in that district, in 1927 he was sent further afield to study and on graduating from high school he went to Tubingen University. Hardy kept in close touch with the community, spending the various vacations there and devoting himself to activity on behalf of the community among his fellow students. Some veteran members of the Bruderhof who joined in the 1930s claim that his lectures in student circles coupled with his personality played a crucial role in their decision to join.

With the growing number of children, a school building had to be built and they obtained a loan on easy terms from the district council for this purpose. Trudi Huessi writes:

We built the children's house as soon as we could, but we had no money, we had to get a mortgage. That may have been in July 1927. In November 1928, the children's house was completed. There was a wonderful inauguration celebration when it opened. The President of the province of Hesse, Dr. Friedensburg, came. He was a broad-minded person and very interested in new movements.[16]

In addition to their educational activity, they also owned a small publishing house, which they had kept after the split at Sannerz, called *Gemeinschaftsverlag Eberhard Arnold*. Funding was provided by their Dutch friend, Kees Boeke, who contributed a sum that enabled them to start work. In 1925, they contacted the Berlin *Hochweg Verlag* publishing house and proposed a partnership in the publishing of source books of theology and the history of Christianity. Their collaboration began with a pretentious plan for one hundred basic books, comprising all the important works in the history of Christian theology, but circumstances prevented the plan from reaching fruition. Collaboration with the Berlin firm continued until 1932, but between 1925 and 1932, only twenty-one books were published. The books were selected with the intention of promoting their mission in German society. Eberhard Arnold writes:

We have always believed that our mission can be carried out by way of the printed word as effectively as by the spoken word.

The branches of their publishing activity were diverse and on various levels: preparation, editing, and also the employment of travelling salesmen. Moreover, they had links with writers who came to visit the Bruderhof, and in this way they gained new friends.[17]

Work in publishing was combined with agriculture and services. Emmy Arnold describes the enthusiasm with which they did the proofreading and the discussions that went on while they worked in the house and on the farm. While they were preparing Eberhard Arnold's book, *The Early Christians*, for publication, for example, they all became involved in the choice of extracts from the sources and at the same time they became familiar with writings on the sources of Christianity and different creeds and sects like the Moravian Brethren, the Quakers, and the Anabaptists.

In May, 1930, the Mennonite scholar Harold Bender visited the Bruderhof and described it in an article published in the *Christian Monitor* in January, 1931. The article gives some idea of the way of life at the Bruderhof ten years after its founding and reflects the impression it left on visitors to the commune. Bender describes the beautiful surrounding landscape and stresses the simplicity, cleanliness, and orderliness of the small community, as well as its poverty. He writes:

> It was from this fact of the Brotherhood's poverty that I received one of my strongest impressions, namely the devotion of these people to their faith and principles. Many of the members had formerly held good positions in society, as school teachers, social workers, laborers and others, but they had given up everything and were willing to suffer and sacrifice and bear hardship for the sake of their cause.... Theirs is an honorable poverty, and they are least of all concerned with "worldly goods," since they have given up the principle of private property...and a community of goods has been set up in its place.

After describing their humble ways, he writes about their origins and faith:

> The members' background was quite varied. All had been shaken loose from their previous life through the upheaval of the World War and the years following it. Many had gone through the youth movement, seeking something better, tired of the sham and artificiality of the world, and dissatisfied with the deadness of much of the evangelical church life. At present there are about seventy persons, adults and children...of this number about thirty are members.... It should be said that the Brotherhood has a strong missionary spirit and a definite program of evangelization...which is to be accomplished through the testimony of the many guests who come to the Bruderhof. In the course of a year, the number of guests reaches a thousand or more.[18]

Despite all the troubles and material hardships, it was indeed their belief that the commune was destined to spread the word and serve as a model of communal life for their generation that sustained the group during the hard days of isolation and kept their hopes alive. Emmy Arnold writes:

> In the fall of 1928, Eberhard said in a talk to the Brotherhood...that one day our movement would grow considerably...all manner of people coming—men from industry, professional people, workers, teachers and the poorest of all kinds. All of them would like to live in community...it was our task to make room for them and to build for them.[19]

Yet, in spite of their exalted hopes for the future, their isolation was disheartening and impelled them seek contact with similar groups. Ever since the establishment of their settlement, seeing no point in an isolated existence without being part of a wider social movement, they had sought out other communes. But in the Germany of that time there was little chance of setting up additional movements and this was a problem that was the cause of great concern to Eberhard Arnold.

The Vision and Teachings of Eberhard Arnold

Life at the Bruderhof revolved round Eberhard Arnold. His primary task during those years was to stimulate, deepen, and clarify the life of this socioeducational community of work, as it was called, and in addition, he continued lecturing to youth movement groups. Emmy Arnold recalls:

> During the years at Sannerz...Eberhard gave lectures in various cities in Germany, Austria and Switzerland, and took an active part in Youth Movement and pacifist group conferences. His book, *Die Ersten Christen nach dem Tode der Apostel* (The Early Christians after the Death of the Apostles) appeared in 1926.[20]

Arnold was a charismatic figure, possessing not only knowledge of theology, imagination, and vision, but also a talent for creating personal relationships and inspiring others with his enthusiasm. Interesting evidence of the impression made by his personality can be found in the memoirs of Gladys Mason, a young Englishwoman who joined the Bruderhof in Germany in the early 1930s:

> This is what always impressed me very much about Eberhard: his humility. He was a man who, before living in Sannerz in a small group, had done evangelizing work and thousands of people had come to listen to him. He was asked to speak everywhere, but he chose the way of building up the little group of the Church Community.... He gave his whole life for that. And it was such a little circle at the Alm, also at the Rhön, all together a hundred people with children. I used to look at Eberhard when he was talking to us and think—such a poor little circle, nobody special, and yet he was giving us all that.[21]

Eberhard Arnold developed an original theology, combining various religious and spiritual sources. His teaching can be seen as a special manifestation of the dialectical theology that emerged in Germany after World War I and in the atmosphere of confusion prevalent at that time, it was an intellectual reaction to the liberal theology and values of Wilhelmian Germany. This theology rejected the anthropomorphic conception of the deity, insisted that Christianity remain unassailable in the face of the efforts of science to negate its value, and revitalized the belief in the coming of the Kingdom of God. Like the dialectical theologians, Arnold emphasized the "objectivity" of the Christian message and claimed that the path revealed by Jesus called for obedience to the Will of God and entailed suffering by the believers who strove for its sake. His own particular contribution lay in his insistence that communal life, work, and the sharing of property were interconnected and must be realized in everyday life.[22]

The sources that inspired his thought were Apostolic Christianity, Anabaptism, and the teachings of Johan Christoph Blumhardt, Sr. and his son Christoph, both of whom were Protestant preachers who lived in the nineteenth century in the small spa of Bad Roll in the State of Wurttenberg. They were believed to employ supernatural powers in their struggle against demonic forces, in faith healing and in the laying on of hands. They had gathered around them a small community of believers who lived as a commune. The son became interested in the theories and goals of the social democrats and although he dissociated himself from their atheism, he even represented the SPD (*Sozialdemokratische Partei Deutschlands*) in Parliament. The Blumhardts diluted their ties with the Lutheran Church and maintained their independent views, which were anchored in the Christian faith and anticipation of the Kingdom of God, as well as in the ideas of socialism. Eberhard Arnold valued their teachings highly and from them derived his criticism of the Churches and also his call to Christians to fight against the prevailing regime and the demonic forces it aroused. As we can see from recent articles published in *The Plough,* the spirit of the Blumhardts' legacy has been preserved in the Bruderhof.[23]

Arnold regarded himself as an instrument of God's will on earth whose mission was to establish and disseminate a way of life based on the ethic teachings of Jesus. He believed that he was one of a long line of reformers and fighters against Church institutions who had been entrusted with the mission of the Holy Spirit: some members of the Early Church, the Montanists, the disciples of St.Francis of Assisi, the Bohemian and Moravian Brothers, and especially the Anabaptists. His interest in the Anabaptists preceded the establishment of the Sannerz commune and it became heightened when he realized that the Hutterites still existed in America.

Arnold writes that on discovering the Hutterites, he had felt great respect toward them for their unremitting faith and communal way of life, which had been preserved for over 400 years. From the theological point of view, his deepest respect was reserved for the Apostles of the Early Church who were known for their purity, pacifism, and harmonious communal life. He claimed that they were men of charity who were willing to help the wretched and oppressed whom they welcomed. They regarded work as their calling; living as equals, they were poor and humble. Living according to the apostolic way meant working together

zealously and in a spirit of generosity. This way of life was also reflected in the simplicity of their clothing, housing, and utensils. This is
how Eberhard Arnold expressed his affinity to apostolic Christianity:

> We represent a different social order, that of the Communal Church as it existed in
> Jerusalem, when its members gave up all private property and shared everything of
> their own free will.[24]

Arnold perceived the world to be controlled by evil forces, particularly
at that time:

> There has hardly ever been a time when it was as evident as it is today that God and
> His righteousness do not yet rule.... We see it in the unjust distribution of goods,
> although the earth offers unstintingly of its fertility and all its potential. The world
> is going to pieces everywhere. It is crumbling and rotting away. It is going through
> a process of disintegration. It is dying.... The only help for the world is to have a
> place of gathering, to have people whose will, undivided and free of doubt, is bent
> on gathering with others in unity.

His views on the existing regime were critical and pessimistic:

> This regime is falling apart, disintegrating, rotting and expiring.... The root of all
> evil is private property, fostering covetousness and greed. Private property is a
> curse, preventing decent relations between people and impairing man's relation-
> ship to God. Private property stems from egocentricity, selfishness and greed....
> Money is a personification of Satan; it is the Devil personified. It is a means to
> power over people's lives. This is what is devilish about it.

Arnold denounces capitalist society for its worship of private property
and individualism. His position is similar to that of the socialists and the
communists, and he confirms that "the attack by socialism and communism on the status quo is a call to our consciences—those of us who
consider ourselves Christians."

Shortly before his death, Eberhard Arnold spoke to a group of visitors
to the commune about the sources of his spiritual world and stressed his
concern with social problems as a component of his Christian faith:

> In searching for the foundations of my faith, I turned not only to ancient writings
> and to Jesus's Sermon on the Mount...I also sought to get to know the state of the
> working class...both through books and by observing the situation closely, en-
> abling me to share their life. I did so in order to follow in the footsteps of Jesus,
> Francis of Assisi and the prophets.

This attitude is confirmed in the reminiscences of the veterans of the
German Bruderhof, as told by Alfred Gneitling, for example:

Eberhard's strong feeling for justice came out very clearly in a speech he once made at a First of May celebration in neighboring Schluchtern, at a time when we still took part in it. He said: "We must not forget that every piece of clothing we wear represents the blood of workers." His identification with the struggle of the workers and their martyrs was manifested when at suppertime he once asked the whole community to stand in silent respect for quite a time. It was the anniversary of the death of Gustav Landauer.[25]

During the Bruderhof's first formative decade, Gustav Landauer's book, *Call to Socialism,* exerted a great deal of influence on him. Landauer's influence on Eberhard Arnold was notably evident, especially his call to set up communal agricultural settlements, in which spirituality would be revived through the combination of life and work in a natural environment with an intensive spiritual life. It was Arnold's belief that such communities would sow the seeds of society's renewal.[26]

The affinity between Eberhard Arnold and Gustav Landauer stems from the deepest strata of their respective *weltanschauungs.* Arnold was intellectually aligned with Landauer with regard to the importance he ascribed to spiritual forces as an active agent in society and to spiritual regeneration as the mainspring of social revolution. Both men believed that real change could only be achieved in the wake of a voluntary change of heart and not by a policy of compulsion.[27]

Eberhard Arnold consistently opposed the use of political forces to further the social struggle:

We refused to attempt the reform of social conditions by political means. It may seem as though we were withdrawing and isolating ourselves, as though we were turning our backs on society. In fact we are building up a life.... Such a life means that a quite new reality has to determine everything in social, economic and religious affairs.

Arnold's attitude toward the state was as ambivalent as Landauer's. Both perceived it as indispensable under the circumstances preceding the revolution when it would gradually become obsolete as the people became spiritually transformed. Before such a change in social relations occurred, the political framework had to be preserved to safeguard life itself. Nevertheless, he consistently expressed his aversion to the state and all it represented, and viewed it as a coercive framework that was unable to advance spiritual change.

As he was aware of the importance of the state as a temporary institution that would fulfil vital functions during the period preceding the Kingdom of Heaven on earth, he acknowledged:

> We give our full consent to the government and its legitimate fight against sin and crime: lying, impurity, murder and avarice. We are glad to cooperate with the authorities insofar as they do something constructive to counteract these horrible things.

Yet at the same time he sought to make clear to the members of his community that they could not become part of the state apparatus:

> We take no active part in politics or in the use of violence. We refuse to get involved, but we are not indifferent. If the government needs our help in a purely peaceful action, we are of course ready to cooperate. Only we must obey God more than men.

Eberhard Arnold advocated pacifism and nonviolence as the duty of every faithful Christian:

> We are friends of peace and we want to help bring about peace. Jesus said: "Blessed are the peacemakers!" And if we really want peace, we must represent it in all areas of life. So we must do nothing that conflicts with love. That means we cannot harm anyone in business; we cannot lend our approval to a way of life that provides a lower standard of living for manual workers than for people in academic positions.

He rejected the claim that he and his friends were Utopians who sought to build a future that could never be realized, and explained that he believed that the uprooting of evil would be carried out by people who became enlightened through their own efforts and their way of life: "This is the only way to change the world, to make it pleasant to live in"; and he called on his disciples: "See to it that you lead a blameless life. That means you must look to the future and shape your life in accordance with the forthcoming Kingdom of God."

It must be stressed that Arnold's theology was rooted in reality. He saw the role of the Bruderhof as a community existing in this world while serving as a model of the Kingdom of God to come:

> To be ready for God's Kingdom does not mean to stop eating and drinking or to reject marriage; it means recognizing the signs of the times and living now as we shall live in the future Kingdom of God. God's economy, His plan for the Kingdom of God, must be given well-defined practical expression in the household of the Church. Then even the blindest will have to realize that here is a place where they can find something of love and joy that God's Kingdom will bring to all humankind at the end of time.

Eberhard Arnold prized the joy of family life and described the monogamous family as an all-important basis for the growth of fellowship and alliance among people:

Being united in faith is the only foundation on which life, and that means marriage too, can be built up. From this it is plain that in marriage too, the issue is not marriage as such but unity in God's Kingdom, unity in Christ and His Holy Spirit. Families are founded within the framework of the community. We keep strict discipline in our family life.... Family does not suffer from the communal life, on the contrary; the joy of a married couple in each other and in their children is especially strong and deep.

He did not view marriage as a communion of equals. Through his study of the early Christians he came to the conclusion that a wife's duty was to be loving, faithful, and retiring. She could influence her husband but would not dominate the relations between them:

Woman's role is to be loving and motherly and to dedicate herself to protecting, preserving and keeping pure her family circle and all those in her care; to train, foster and care for them. A woman may be active in different spheres—intellectual, cultural, practical, or any others; that will vary a great deal. But if she remains a true woman, her caring love for those entrusted to her will always be present, whatever she does. Man's work, the struggle and pioneering and conflict with the world outside is under no circumstances to be more highly prized than this inward and creative giving of life and depth to the church community. It is not a matter of different values; it is the calling that is different.

Arnold was fully aware of the individual personalities of the members of the church community:

The more original an individual is, the better we like it. We have found that the greater the differences between people, the closer they may come to each other inwardly. We affirm the individual personality: each person is unique.

But this does not lead to the antagonistic individualism that he views as the tragedy of life in the modern world:

Individualism and materialism lead to the disintegration of the web of life, the result being that most people live differently from the way they yearn for.... Spiritual rebirth will take place when they give up covetousness and personal ambition. The alternative to such individualism is communal life which is in essence the surrender of the individual's will to the Will of God. Such a life has always been the goal of enlightened people in society.

Eberhard Arnold summarizes the role of their commune in these words:

We have to make this possibility known: people can live in community! We bear witness to this reality: people are living in community! We bear witness to the wellspring of this reality: the future Kingdom of God. We want to live this way to the end of our lives because we believe that this is our calling for the sake of all humankind.

He stresses the rules that underpin the Bruderhof way of life:

> On joining the community each one brings into the unity everything he has. He keeps nothing...what he has in his possession is given him to use only as long as he needs it to do his work.

Educational work within the community was considered to be of great importance and was intended to constantly improve mutual relations and strengthen the fundamental belief that upheld the commune. Eberhard Arnold often spoke of it:

> The Bruderhof is an educational community, both humanly seen and in the sense that every one of us has to be taught by God. That process is never finished.[28]

Education begins in childhood and he believed that "the only true service to our children is to help them become what they already are in God's thoughts."

He did not believe in a liberal upbringing devoid of discipline:

> The question of authority is crucial in bringing up children. The Bruderhof rejects these two extremes: authority based on physical force and a blind lack of authority. Freedom for individual children...does not mean that a child can follow every mood and every whim without restraint. No, guidance is necessary. It is the greatest love we can show children. Children want to be guided, helped and given direction, but they do not want to be coerced or crushed. It is important not to get into the habit of being too lenient with children's moods...children must learn to take themselves in hand.

Eberhard Arnold called upon the Bruderhof not only to bear witness to the possibility of leading a Christian life of fellowship, but also "to conquer the world," not only to attain perfection, but to evangelize. According to this teaching, the Bruderhof members must not only serve as "a bridgehead to the Kingdom of Heaven on earth," but also fight "the rule of mammon."

> We know of course that this Kingdom has not yet come on this earth. Not only God has great power; the mighty national governments have great power; lying and impurity have great power. Forces that are entirely opposed to God assert themselves. The Kingdom of God is not yet realized in our day.

The church community must take part in the struggle against the forces of evil:

> It is a great thing if we can go out and tell people about God's Kingdom. But it is a much greater thing if a historical reality is presented to the world, a witness to the

truth of the Gospel...by representing with our lives the way of love and peace
and justice in the midst of a hostile world that is bristling with weapons.

He calls upon them to accept a missionary role:

> The colossal need facing humankind in this hour of history makes it urgent to show
> a new way. The time is here for a communal Church to be a light in the lampstand,
> a city on the hill.... The time is here when the message of God's unity, justice and
> brotherhood in his Kingdom must spread abroad. If we are no longer here for all
> people, if we can no longer concern ourselves with the need and suffering of the
> whole world, community life has lost its right to exist.

> No commune can survive if it lives only for its own sake and for its members'
> benefit. Such a commune will become a sect divorced from reality. It will lose its
> way, even if it retains the communal way of life. The spirit of the commune leads
> us to care about all people...this is expressed in our "open door" policy. Our
> door is open for those entering and leaving...here is no monastery. We are a part
> of this world and our doors are open. We wish to maintain a mutual relationship
> with all that is happening outside. We wish to feel the needs of the outside world as
> an incentive for our activity there.[29]

In a letter to his friends, written a few days before his death in November, 1935, he again called upon them to fulfill the mission of the
Bruderhof, to become involved in every social movement, even if they
identified only partly with its aims.

> We had searched for travelling companions, for proved and tested groups of pil-
> grims on the same way.... We never cared the least to assert our so-called inde-
> pendence or to win the reputation of having a lifework of our own! All that mattered
> to us was that our call was clear, our freedom pure and our unity real. So we looked
> out for men and women, for individuals and groups, who might be following this
> call to freedom, purity and unity.... And we did in fact encounter several commu-
> nity attempts, some large and some smaller groups, some old and some of recent
> origin. Many little communal groups in our own neighboring countries were young
> and frail in their origins; but we also found several movements that had been living
> in full vigor for two, three, or even four centuries in complete community and still
> are living today!

Eberhard Arnold was the Bruderhof's spiritual teacher and leader and
was admired by its members during the movement's formative years.
He was aware of his leader's status, yet sought to clarify his opinion on
the role of leadership in the Bruderhof and the responsibility and dangers it involved:

> In our community life, "servant" is the best word to describe any bearer of social
> responsibility.... The place of the Servant of the Word is a burdened one. He does
> his service in a brotherly spirit, the spirit in which all brothers and sisters are of

equal worth.... We have no fixed offices here, only services that grow out of the stream of love, the moving current of the Spirit. As soon as those who do these services want to do something independent of this stream of love and of this Spirit, their life is a lie, an impossibility. Not even the most gifted person has anything to say if he believes in himself. (God's Revolution, 119)

Pointing to the dangers lurking in distorted perceptions of leadership, he said:

First is bureaucracy and bossiness, the presumption of brothers who look upon their service as a means to elevate their own persons. This threatens to enslave the rest of the community. Second comes the tendency to arrogant moralism, the audacity of a person who places himself and his moral convictions above others. The third danger is a spirit of business efficiency: the constant concern about earning money, about the productivity of daily life. And finally there is sheer pride, some people think they are the most capable and others less competent.

The teachings of Eberhard Arnold remained the Bruderhof's authoritative writings after his death and the subsequent leadership did not make any changes in the Bruderhof's theological foundations. Most of them followed in his footsteps, but the individual interpretations differed and gave rise to tensions and conflicts, which will be discussed later.[30]

The Journey to the Hutterites

Bruderhof interest in the Hutterites and their way of life dates from the first days at Sannerz. This is evident from an article by Eberhard Arnold published in their journal Das Neue Werk in December, 1921, entitled, "The Bruderhof Communes of the Hutterites."[31] Although they respected and identified with the Hutterites, this did not lead them to make contact with their communities in America, for at that time their activities centered on Germany.

At the end of 1927, they became interested in direct contact with the Hutterites. Concrete steps in this direction were taken at the beginning of 1928, at the time that the Bruderhof members were studying the sources of the Anabaptist movement in the sixteenth century. Eberhard brought in a great deal of literature on the subject, having obtained it from public libraries and archives.

They were surprised to find a similarity in their spirit, faith, and communalist teaching, and much of what they read bore a great similarity to the way of life that had developed at Sannerz and Rhön. They were particularly interested in the beginnings of Hutterite communal life in the sixteenth century, their way of bringing up children, and their collective social organization and economy, and they were greatly impressed by descriptions of the Hutterites' suffering and their martyrology. Their wonder and excitement grew when they heard that the Hutterites still existed and even had dozens of settlements in the United States and Canada, with a total population of some 5,000 people. Some members suggested that contact with them be established and that a merger might be considered.[32]

When this subject was raised in the Bruderhof, the general reaction was positive and as a result, Eberhard Arnold began to seek contact with the Hutterites through correspondence. First he turned to scholars who specialized in the subject: Robert Friedman, a Viennese Jew, well-known for his research on the Anabaptists; and John Horsch, who had studied the Mennonites, and with their help he was able to contact Elias Walter, "The Elder" (one of the elders of the Hutterites), from the Canadian "Stand Off" settlement in Alberta. Arnold sent him a letter on 23 June 1928, in which he described the Bruderhof in Germany and pointed out the many similarities he saw between them in both their faith and way of life. This was the first of a series of letters in the same vein that he wrote in 1928 to other elders, David Hofer at Rockport and Johannes Entz of Elmspring, South Dakota, in which he not only stressed the similarities but also described the Bruderhof's set of rules that were inspired by Hutterite principles.[33]

In his letter of 6 November 1928, Eberhard described the small Bruderhof community in Germany (which numbered twenty-eight members at the time) and put forward his request for amalgamation with the Hutterites. With regard to the Bruderhof's decision, he explained that this would involve "a resolute will, which shall never be withdrawn, to be really united with you and your communities. We want to be completely incorporated for our spiritual and material welfare."[34]

The Bruderhof members waited impatiently for a reply, but it was slow in coming. After a long delay, a letter arrived from the Hutterites, which was written in positive yet noncommittal terms, and which led to an extensive correspondence throughout 1929.

In May, 1929, Eberhard Arnold wrote a letter to all the Hutterite settlements (*"kleiner Sendbrief"*), in which he stated unequivocally that they wished to belong to the Hutterites in their faith, as loyal and obedient

members, and appealed to them: "Accept us! Charge us with missions!"
And in another letter he wrote: "We ask you to take our Bruderhof as a
most humble daughter colony like an adopted child and set us up and
equip us."[35]

Arnold's emotional appeals convinced the Hutterites of his serious
intentions and as a first step they sent him their books of rules and in
August, 1929, he thanked them for *The Orders of the Hutterian Brothers*, and wrote that they were starting to adapt the Bruderhof rules accordingly. In the same letter, he wrote about the financial aspects of the
possible merger, stating that the Bruderhof had undertaken the repayment all their debts without incurring new ones, but since they were
involved in extensive absorption of new members, they were in urgent
need of financial resources to enable them to fulfill their mission.

In his letter to Jacob Hofer in Canada, dated 14 September 1929, he
elaborated on the difficulties of the Bruderhof:

> Our need is great and since we are hardpressed by about $7,000 of our worst debts,
> with the danger of being driven from our house this fall...I am forced to make a
> repeated plea.... For the sake of our sixty young and old people, I take it upon
> myself joyfully to stand again and again at your doors as a beggar.[36]

In the fall of 1930, after correspondence lasting almost a year, Eberhard
Arnold was invited to visit the Hutterites in America. This visit had numerous objectives: becoming acquainted, establishing a relationship with
the Hutterite spiritual leadership, obtaining consent for the amalgamation of the Bruderhof with the Hutterite Church, and the appointment
of Eberhard Arnold as "the elder" of the German Church. Clearly, at a
time when all the communes in Germany had disappeared, the Bruderhof
had no desire to remain a small group, unique but isolated. Emmy
Eberhard writes:

> Eberhard and I never wanted to be "founders" of our own enterprise. We had always believed that we belonged to the camp of those who had fought since the 16th
> century for a collective way of life.[37]

At the beginning of 1930, a short time before Eberhard left for his
tour of the Hutterite settlements, he contracted a serious eye inflammation from a splinter while he was chopping wood. The doctor treating
him recommended that he postpone his journey, but he did not heed this
advice as he regarded the journey as extremely important and urgent,
and decided to leave immediately. Apart from the religious motivation,

his journey was also of vital financial importance as the Bruderhof was in dire financial straits and in urgent need of assistance. This is evident from their being forced to sell twenty acres of their land and also their piano, in order to finance Arnold's journey.[38]

At this stage, the journey was of mutual interest: From the Hutterites' point of view, relations with the Bruderhof could invigorate a 400 year-old movement that was saddled with outmoded traditions in their way of life and dress. The Hutterites were particularly impressed by the Bruderhof members' knowledge of the old texts and even their own publication of some of them, as well as by the spiritual leadership of Eberhard Arnold.

Eberhard travelled among the Hutterite settlements in the United States and Canada for a year, during which contact with him was very limited since his letters were sent by sea and took a long time to reach his friends, who were anxiously awaiting them. His first letters, written after his visit to the Hutterite settlements in South Dakota, were full of admiration:

> The spirit and truth of today's Hutterism, also here and now, surpass by far our expectations.... The faithfulness to one another, to Michael Wetter, the Word leader, to the servants and the stewards, seems to me perfect, as they keep a firm discipline in conversation, speaking openly to one another and not about one another. Joy and happiness are expressed in the humor of deep contentment, and in still deeper sayings from the Scriptures and from experiences. The simplicity of the life is still kept fairly well. For instance, cars are not bought for any Hof.... The Hutterian religious faith is real and genuine. It is deeply rooted in the hearts of all. They do not wish to live, nor can they, in any other way than in community.[39]

Most of Arnold's letters were written to his wife and they show that he was warmly received during his visits to the Hutterite settlements, especially at those of the *Schmiedleut*. He writes enthusiastically about their great interest in his lectures on the way of life at the Bruderhof, which lasted until midnight. Besides the many letters he wrote about the problems caused by the painful eye inflammation, which hurt him a great deal throughout the journey, he also made sure that he wrote in his journal every day. It included his reflections, which were not expressed in public during his journey, and in it he expressed his appreciation and his criticism of the Hutterites, when compared to the Bruderhof:

> The difference between our Bruderhof and American Hutterism consists largely of this: We seek to find our spiritual nourishment and foundation in the first and the second Hutterian periods of 1525 to 1578, with their joyfully going on the attack,

whereas in the American communities it is the late period that serves that purpose. What Michael Waldner (the Hutterite Bon Homme) has expressed is probably correct: These teachings from the time of Andreas Ehrenprise to the approaching decline fit the present situation in our communities best.

There are differences between the origins of our modern culture and classical education...and the quite unique Hutterian culture, which is very deep but difficult for strangers to understand (not for me).... It can be sensed that we come from the world and religion of the twentieth and, worse still, of the nineteenth century, so different from the fighting church of the sixteenth century with its readiness for martyrdom, and also from the conservative-minded church of the eighteenth to twentieth centuries, so careful to preserve true communal piety.

The journal also criticizes the split between the three streams of Hutterism, and especially the considerable differences between the rich and poor settlements, which, in his opinion, is not compatible with the Hutterite Christian values known to him from ancient letters:

There is no true community between Manitoba (*Schmiedleut*) and the *Lehrerleut*, even though the two groups profess the same basis of faith. Here lies the deepest harm to present day Hutterism: the all too great independence and the self-sufficiency of the three individual groups, the individual Bruderhofs.[41]

Eberhard also writes about the differences of opinion between him and his hosts from the *Lehrerleut* group, that surfaced during his tour:

From all the *Lehrerleut* I get the impression of a very earnest, deeply founded and firmly rooted stand for community and Hutterism; they live harmoniously and in their clothing and style are purer and less subject to outside influences than the *Schmiedleut* and *Dariusleut*. But that basically wrong feeling for the economic and financial independence of the individual hofs, with every hof claiming the right to do with its money as it pleases...is perhaps stronger among them than among the *Dariusleut* and the *Schmiedleut*. I put up a most passionate fight against this cursed collective egoism.

Moreover, during his tour, Eberhard did not hesitate to tell his hosts that "today the devil is using a much more cunning way to take you in. Instead of tempting you with individual property, he is getting you through collective property."[42]

Emmy Arnold writes that she understood from Eberhard's letters that while the Hutterites were very up-to-date regarding the needs of the economy and were using modern agricultural machinery, they were very conservative and traditional in their appearance. They still wore the kind of clothes worn by seventeenth-century Tyrolean peasants, together with elements that had been added during their stay in Russia: the women wore long skirts and head scarfs, the men were bearded and wore black. They objected to music, pictures, paintings, and smoking. Emmy admits that the Bruderhof members in Germany were concerned about the traditionalism of the Hutterites; they were embarrassed by their rigidity because, according to the Youth Movement tradition (which was somewhat anarchist), they were not inclined to subject their lives to a system of rigid rules that was not based upon their own experience.

We must also remember that the social and ideological sources of the Bruderhof were different—the German Youth Movement with its own values, Quaker pacifism, the Labor Movement, and general Protestant influences—and so it is hardly surprising that some Bruderhof members thought that the disadvantages of amalgamation would outweigh the advantages. Emmy Arnold writes that while the women were not opposed to the scarfs and long dresses that were similar to the peasant dresses in the Youth Movement tradition, which they liked to wear, the men had reservations about their dark clothing. The greatest difficulty lay in the need to give up their beloved musical instruments, the recorders and guitars that accompanied all their meetings. Eberhard himself mentioned that the intransigent stand of the Hutterites on the matter of musical instruments and pictures could interfere with the merger. They rejected not only the piano and the organ, but also recorders and guitars. He often spoke about it with the Hutterites, but the elders were unrelenting in their opposition:

> The obstacles that present-day Hutterism puts in the way of our cultural work and task should not be overlooked. Up to now, it seems to me that instrumental music, for example, is absolutely rejected and fought against.[43]

Eberhard knew that the Bruderhof members would find it very hard to give up their tuneful choral singing and their playing. It would be a great sacrifice and it was discussed exhaustively, even to the point where many of them wondered whether the merger justified such sacrifices. The Hutterites raised the subject of smoking, which was then accepted at the Bruderhof, although in the past, under the influence of the youth movement, they had objected to both tobacco and alcohol. In the course of time, smoking had gradually penetrated into the community, but the Hutterites were adamant on the subject. Yet some of the Hutterite customs were not difficult to accept, like their distinctive simple clothing, since this was in line with Bruderhof Youth Movement preferences, albeit they did not like the men's clothing, the black cape and suspenders. However, in his letters, Eberhard urged them to overcome their reservations for the sake of the desired amalgamation.

We understand from his letters to Emmy that Eberhard's tour initiated an awakening among the Hutterites. In one of his letters he wrote: "My visit and our 'invigorating zeal' are significant for them and cause a great stir." And he adds:

> A number of serious-minded brothers are expecting that God will one day give me the task of revolutionizing the life of the communities and leading it back to genuine, truly communal Hutterism. But I believe and hope I am only called to testify to the need for such a change; I am not in a position to become the right man for a task involving so hard a struggle.[44]

Eberhard mentions that he often found himself in embarrassing situations, like when the elders proposed that he should be the "Head of the Bruderhof" and lead them as Jacob Hutter had done in the early days. He reacted with sincere modesty, "I know only too well that someone different from me would be needed for this."[45] We can find evidence of the profound impression Eberhard made on the Hutterites in a letter from Joseph Stahl, from the village of Huron, to Elias Walter:

> It seems to me that Arnold is a second Jacob Hutter in all his efforts, especially against greed and personal money in the church.[46]

A central problem raised at all their meetings was the differences in their attitude to the "mission." David Hofer of Rockport said:

> The Hutterian mission differs from evangelization by lecture in that it seeks out the "zealous"—and them only—in every place, challenges and gathers them and calls them to their true home. If the Church is on the right path, then there will be a mission; if not, there will be none.

In his view:

> The Church in America today is not on the right path and is all too imperfect and endangered, so that one can have questions about mission.... All brothers are unanimous in that we should stay (over there in Germany) so long as the "zeal" is maintained and the authorities are not against us.[47]

Eberhard's journal tells us about his theological dispute with the Hutterites on the place of the vision of the millennium in guiding them on their way:

Joseph Kleinsasser, the elder, goes too far in declaring: "The millennium is of no importance to us. The one thing that matters is that we lead a devout life and attain eternal blessedness." I suppose though, what he means is the way the idea of the millennium is presented...by other evangelistic groups who set their hopes on the millennium.... They put off all justice on earth to some future millennium and in the meantime plod along in the same unchanged injustice as the whole wide world. However, we religious-socialist Europeans will reply to that...we on our Bruderhofs live "here and now" in the strength, the spirit of the world to come.[48]

In his letters to the Bruderhof written in December, 1930, Eberhard Arnold mentioned that he was accompanied on his travels in Western Canada by Elias Walter. He complained that his eye was very painful and interfered with his writing at a time when he was particularly eager to share his experiences with them—at the climax of his tour: a gathering of Hutterite elders convened to discuss the admission of the Bruderhof into the Hutterite Church and his appointment as an elder.

After a series of discussions between the local elders and Eberhard Arnold to clarify the conditions of admission that had been laid down by the Hutterites and also the German Bruderhof's requests, the Hutterite leadership came to the conclusion that conditions for the merger were now ripe, and a general meeting of elders was called. It took place on 9 December 1930, in the colony of Stand Off in Alberta and in the presence of all the spiritual leaders ("Servants of the Word"), and it was there that Eberhard Arnold was baptized as a Hutterite. A few days later, on 19 December, he was ordained as a spiritual leader ("Servant of God") of the Bruderhof, and this was authenticated in his letter of appointment: "With this Eberhard Arnold is given by the Church the task for Germany, to proclaim the Word of God there, to gather the zealous, and to establish the Bruderhof near Fulda in the best order."[49]

In a letter to his wife that was written immediately after this event, he expressed his pride in writing to her as "a real Hutterian Brother," and explained the significance of his appointment:

My confirmation gives me unlimited authority to establish a genuine Hutterian community life, both temporally and spiritually, to the best of my perception. It means that the brothers in America will fully and forever support our Bruderhof both in its inner life of faith and in its outward economic life, also when the two of us and all our fellow fighters are no longer alive.

He states with great satisfaction that his appointment has led to rare cooperation between the three factions:

> It should be seen as a divine confirmation of the task I am given with this journey that we are now the first Bruderhof to belong at the same time to the *Dariusleut, Schmiedeleut* and *Lehrerleut*.[50]

In December, 1930, the Bruderhof community was admitted to the Hutterite Church and Eberhard Arnold was installed as a Hutterite elder. This was confirmed in a letter signed by Elias Walter that was sent to the Bruderhof communities from Canada on 20 March 1931.[51]

A short time later, Eberhard set off on another tour of the Hutterite villages to continue in his fund-raising efforts, since he had achieved very little in this respect in the previous months. In his letter of 8 October, he complains that he had been able to speak very little about the financial needs of the Bruderhof because his Hutterite hosts had insisted that spiritual matters must come first. When he raised his request for a grant of $25,000 that he would like to send to the Bruderhof on Christmas Eve, he received the ingenuous reply, "So much all at once?"

In a letter written in January, 1931, after his appointment as a Hutterite elder, he writes that raising money is still a slow process with only meager results, and complains of the embarrassment of such soliciting:

> My fund-raising journey is not without results, and yet so far distant from the goal Hans and I have, that one can have doubts about reaching it. I hope that you will not be too dissatisfied with me if I only bring back part of the $25,000, the sum truly needed and set as our goal. At any rate, I am trying my utmost, and force myself to a most unpleasant begging journey to all the Bruderhofs which are not deeply in debt. This work is unpleasant to me only because I do not like this pressing for money. However, it must be, otherwise only part of my journey will be accomplished, even though it is the most important part.[52]

Emmy Arnold tells of the disappointment felt at the Bruderhof when they heard about the limited financial success of Eberhard's journey, for they were in dire straits at the time. Although small sums that Eberhard had managed to send did arrive from time to time and were vital for the repayment of loans and debts, they were a long way from filling their needs. It should be added that one of the secondary achievements of his visits to the Hutterite villages was the discovery of old Hutterite manuscripts, which he found lying around untouched. The Hutterites themselves were unable to read them because they were written in old German and they willingly agreed to Eberhard's request to take them with him to the German Bruderhof. These manuscripts were of great historical and literary value, especially to researchers of religions and the Bruderhof members, most of whom were scholars, were most appreciative of this particular achievement of Arnold's journey.

Notes

1. Arnold, Emmy, *Torches Together* (Rifton, N.Y.: Plough Publishing House, 1976), 62.
2. Central Bruderhof Archives, document (YM 11) EA 25/20, 1925.
3. *Memories of Our Early Years*, vol. 1 (Collection of pamphlets published by the Plough Publishing House, Rifton, N.Y.: 1973-79), chap. A, 18. In vol. 4 of *The Plough* (Quarterly of Bruderhof communities. Bromdon: The Plough Publishing House, 1957), interesting evidence is provided by Hans Joachim Schpass, who describes the profound impression made on him by his meeting Eberhard Arnold.
4. Elizabeth Bolken Zumpe in *KIT Annual 1991* (The Collected Newsletter of the KIT Information Service. San Francisco, Calif.), 60. Another young man who, influenced by those meetings, adopted the Bruderhof faith and way of life was Arno Martin, who became a loyal member of the Bruderhof until his death n 1978. Arno joined the Sannerz commune in 1926 and was one of the mainstays of the agricultural team that established the farm at Rhön, and later the one in Liechtenstein. *Memories*, chap. J.
5. See Barth's memoirs (July, 1973) in the Bruderhof archives, and also an interview with the author.
6. Arnold, Emmy, op. cit., 116-17.
7. The Bruderhof archives, document (YM/15) EAE 31/17.
8. Arnold, Eberhard, *Foundations and Orders of Sannerz and the Rhön Bruderhof* (Rifton, N.Y.: Plough Publishing House, 1976), 35-37, 51-53.
9. Huessi, Trudi, in *Memories*, vol. 3: 16.
10. *The Plough*, vol. 1, no. 3 (1953): 7-9.
11. Annemarie Wachter, in *Memories*, vol. 2 D: 2.
12. Huessi, op. cit., vol. 3 C: 49.
13. Keiser, Manfred, in *Memories*, vol. 3 C: 23.
14. Emmy Margaret in an interview with the author, October, 1992.
15. Lober, Sophie, in *Memories*, vol. 3 A: 54.
16. Huessi, op. cit.: 54.
17. Zimmerman, Chris, *Mission Through the Printed Word* (unpublished thesis, Plough publication): 5-7.
18. *Brothers Unite* [An account of the uniting of Eberhard Arnold with the Hutterian church (Rifton, N.Y.: Plough Publishing House, 1988), 227-34].
19. Arnold, Emmy, op. cit., 123.
20. *The Plough*, vol. 1, no. 3: 7-8.
21. *Memories*, vol. 1, chap. G: 28.
22. Whitworth, John McKelvey, *God's Blueprints* (London and Boston, Mass.: Routledge & Kegan Paul, 1975), 171-73.
23. For his attitude to the Blumhardts, see *Torches Together,* 171-79. This is also mentioned by Tyldesley.
24. Unless a different source is mentioned, this quotation, and the following quotations, are taken from Arnold Eberhard, *God's Revolution* (New York: Paulist Press, 1984).

25. *Memories,* vol. 3, chap. C: 64.
26. See article from 1928 in the Bruderhof archives, document YM/12 EAE 28/13, and also his speech in 1929, document YM/13 EAE 29/19. M. Tyldesley also mentions Gustav Landauer's influence on Eberhard Arnold, quoting the article by Pfeiffer (see note 48) in an article to be published.
27. Tyldesley, ibid. (unpublished).
28. Buber's influence and that of his book, *I and Thou,* is mentioned in Tyldesley's article and in *God's Revolution,* 156.
29. See the text of the speech in the Bruderhof archives, document YM/13 EAE 29/19.
30. Whitworth, op. cit., 171-77.
31. *Foundations,* 60.
32. Arnold, Emmy, op. cit., 115, 125.
33. *Foundations,* 60.
34. *Brothers Unite,* 6.
35. Ibid., 15; *Foundations,* 64.
36. *Brothers Unite,* 39. In an interview with the author, Thomas Stieglitz claimed that Eberhard Arnold had turned to the Hutterites for financial assistance because he believed that the Bruderhof deserved it as a result of their mission among German youth, proclaiming the Hutterite way of life.
37. Arnold, Emmy, op. cit., 115.
38. *Memories,* vol. 1, chap. F: 9; *Brothers Unite,* 56-57.
39. Ibid., 68, 73.
40. Ibid., 129.
41. Ibid., 141.
42. Ibid., 174-76.
43. Ibid., 128.
44. Ibid., 177.
45. Arnold, Emmy, op. cit., 139-40.
46. *Brothers Unite,* 212.
47. Arnold, Emmy, op. cit., 141; *Brothers Unite,* 121.
48. Ibid., 124.
49. Ibid., 149.
50. Ibid., 186-87.
51. See the complete text of the letter in Ibid., 184-85.
52. Ibid., 192.

3

The 1930s in Germany

Eberhard Arnold returned to Germany on 10 May 1931, having been clearly unsuccessful in obtaining funds, and this was very disappointing. His journey to forty Hutterite settlements had provided very little financial support for the Bruderhof, who had incurred heavy debts while trying to build their settlement during a period of high inflation, and they now realized they would have to shoulder the burden alone. Eberhard's long absence provided the Rhön community with the opportunity of discovering how they could manage without him and according to Emmy Arnold, things had gone well:

> On the whole it went really well. It had been given over to Hans (Zumpe), then 23 years old, to represent Eberhard...the whole Brotherhood supported him. Life was not without a struggle. Ambition, arrogance, the perpetual enemies of community life, came to the fore soon after Eberhard's departure. Again and again we had to occupy ourselves with our own and others' weaknesses.... It was given to Hans at that time to see the way and the direction and to hold on to it in a very loving and clear way.[1]

Elizabeth Bohlken Zumpe, Hans Zumpe's daughter, supplements Emmy's account by stressing the difficulties in adapting to the Hutterite ways:

> My father, twenty-three years old, was left with Oma (Emmy Arnold) to run the place and lead the little group through very difficult times.... Letters arrived from Opa (Eberhard Arnold) asking them to accept the Hutterite ways of dress, to grow their beards, to do away with music, to eat their meals with men on one side of the room and women on the other. The women had to accept the *kopftuch* (the head covering). My father was not very happy because it was his job to try and explain to the Brotherhood again and again all these new forms and rules. The group wanted Opa to feel they were fully supporting him. On the other hand many things seemed absolutely incredible to them and the distance separating them was so large.[2]

When Eberhard returned, he was pleased to find that many of the Hutterite customs had already been adopted by the German community.

The men had started to grow beards and the women were wearing traditional Hutterite dress. Particularly striking was the way in which the equal status of the sexes, which had its origins in the youth movement, had changed and been replaced by different roles for men and women, which was typical of the Hutterite tradition.[3]

The transition to the Hutterite way of life was not easy. Numerous discussions had taken place at the Bruderhof while Eberhard was away in America and they continued after his return. This is made evident from the contents of a letter written by Bruderhof member Irmgard Keiderling to Emmy Arnold's sister, Else von Hollander, who was in Switzerland for medical treatment, and which describe their dilemmas thusly:

> At the end of the past year we often concerned ourselves with the questions of pictures and musical instruments. In this connection the question of law and freedom came up.... We want to strive courageously for a simple and pure style, but continue seeking our direction in regard to pictures. With music it is more complicated. It is not forbidden. It amounts to this: no music is tolerated which produces religious ecstacy. The Hutterites cannot say that instrumental music is evil in itself; the main point is that living the truth should be free from any musical suggestion...so it is not music, also not pictures which the Hutterites reject, but idolatry in every form; the intrusion of music into worship; art should not lead us into an illusion which displaces our clear recognition and decisiveness.

She goes on to describe the debate at the general meeting at which Eberhard summed up his mission to the Hutterites during which the merger and his appointment as "elder" were confirmed. At the meeting, Hans Zumpe was relieved of his responsibility as leader of the community and appointed Eberhard's deputy. Irmgard Keiderling quotes Eberhard Arnold's view of his mission:

> The overall impression of my journey is as follows: The community life of three thousand five hundred souls in America is something overpowering, great. That means that the spirit of community in these thirty-three Bruderhofs is genuine, pure, clear, true and deep...there is nothing in the whole world, neither in the available books and writings that have been handed down nor in present-day communities, which can be compared to the essence, character and spirit of the Brotherhood men known as Hutterites. So, in full recognition of our origins inspired by the Youth Movement, of our experience of communal living, and of the Sermon on the Mount, I want to work for our growing fully into Hutterism. I am given the authority by the Hutterites to commence a great missionary task for this kind of life throughout the whole of Europe, so that even the money we accept from the Hutterites is untainted. Our entry into Hutterism is quite independent of our need for money.... The question of financial support is of a secondary nature, but fol-

lows the first step of becoming incorporated.... That in short is the outcome of my journey.[4]

Eberhard Arnold used all of his influence in an effort to convince his friends that it was vital to replace the spontaneity of the youth movement with the strict rules of the Hutterite Communal Church, which were based on the experience of many generations. In a speech he made in July, 1931, he reviewed the disintegration of the hundreds of short-lived communes that had their origins in the German Youth Movement and had failed to create a stable way of life and preserve their values. He said that they had lacked transcendental goals and values and the ability to overcome skepticism and transform the revolutionary ardor of the postwar years into a constructive force, while the Bruderhof drew their strength from the Hutterite Church by living according to the values of the Early Christian Church. He ended his speech by saying: "We are duty-bound to adopt mandatory rules and precepts. Yes, like those of religious orders. That is the only way to survive.[5]

The strictness of the Hutterite way of life served to counteract youth movement spontaneity and proved extremely valuable in preserving the community's framework after Eberhard Arnold's death. After all, the merger with the Hutterites was Eberhard Arnold's greatest achievement and reflected his charismatic leadership of the commune and proof of the wisdom of this step was his success in ensuring the continued existence of the commune after his death, which was something that few charismatic leaders had been able to accomplish.

Eberhard's prolonged stay in the Hutterite colonies had enhanced his ability to observe the unique features of the two movements and assess the prospects and the dangers that they faced. He did not express these views publicly, but hints can be found in a letter to his Elder friend, Elias Walter. In summing up his visit he writes:

> After a whole year's absence and some deep study of the dignified, serene and peaceful atmosphere among you, our Bruderhof strikes me as rather passionate, youthful and impetuous, and in need of your maturity and long experience.

In his letter he spells out ten specific points and elaborates on the danger of the existence of private property:

> Every trace of personal property and private money ought to be completely done away with.... The most serious danger to your present-day communities

will be overcome in the following way: In the future, an individual Hutterite community will no longer consider itself the legal owner of its property, goods, fields, income and harvest. Instead, the community will see itself as a steward of its goods and possessions, its livestock and fixtures, in the name of the whole Church of God. I do not believe that the habit of communal living can prevent the collapse of the community. Only the fact of daily asking for the Holy Spirit in the proclamation of the Word and in the communal work can keep us in truly full community.[6]

The Years of Expansion

During 1931 and 1932, the Bruderhof expanded more than at any other time and the members considered them to be the community's best years, despite the fact that they were quite poor financially. Many people came, either to visit for a short time or as potential candidates, and among them were visitors from Switzerland, England, Sweden, and Holland. In the summer of 1932, 2,500 people visited for short periods and thirty became candidates.[7]

Among the visitors were many young people from the youth movements who were searching for a meaning in life and found their way to the Bruderhof. Annemarie Wachter, who later married Heini Arnold, was a typical member of this group, joining the Bruderhof in January, 1932 at the age of twenty-two after years of youth movement activity. She described her experiences during her first days at the Bruderhof in a series of letters to her family and devoted an entire chapter to them in a book of letters written in her youth.[8]

Of particular interest are her first impressions and her explanation of why she joined the Bruderhof. A month after her arrival, she wrote to her family:

> The people who live here are filled with one purpose common to all. They come from groups with the most widely different outlooks: the Religious Socialists, the Socialist Movement and the youth movements.... The most important thing is the strong faith these people are given through an encounter with God...this faith makes it possible for them to discard everything from their previous lives that clashes with it.
>
> The kind of communal life that the Bruderhof is trying to live cannot accept class distinctions.... Capitalism is absolutely rejected, and the aim is to live in the total sharing of goods, as in the Early Apostolic Church. Personal property and all personal earnings must be given up.

She goes on to tell of her decision to join, whatever the cost:

I have decided for the life at the Bruderhof, which means that my life and my work belong from now on to the cause of the Bruderhof.[9]

In the letters that followed she explains what brought about her decision:

My decision has not been influenced by any human being or group of human beings.... No one has made it or brought it about. Rather I was gripped by it. My only active part in it was to allow myself to be fully gripped. And even this was something greater than my own doing. You must not think that I was urged to take this step by people here or that I was influenced by some power of suggestion. They certainly would let me go and not try to hold me back if my decision had been otherwise. What urged me to this attitude and decision is something I felt quite personally—an encounter with another world.[10]

In 1932, some students from Tubingen University came to the commune, having been swayed by Hardy Arnold who was studying there and lecturing on the Bruderhof to student groups. That summer they had numerous visitors from various circles: Catholics and Protestants, both left- and right-wing supporters. In their memoirs, several Bruderhof veterans mention that while seeking a youth movement able to satisfy their longing for true friendship, a lofty ideal, and the creation of a new society, they fell in with right-wing circles that later joined the Hitler Youth. 1932 was the year in which the aggressive nature of that movement became apparent, and the sensibilities and conscience of some of those who had heard about the Bruderhof brought them there on the eve of Hitler's rise to power.[11]

Vagrants also found temporary shelter at the Bruderhof. Although these visitors helped with the work on the farm, they spent most of the time talking with the members about ideological questions and Bruderhof principles. Among the topics discussed were their relations with the Hutterites, their attitude to the family within the commune, and even vegetarianism and the naturalistic diet. The discussions took place under the beech tree in their yard and often continued for many hours, during the midday meal or after supper. This sometimes interfered with the work, since it was customary not to cut short an interesting discussion or leave it unfinished—even for such essential work as dish washing. A discussion was considered to be an exhilarating collective experience, something similar to teamwork. Annemarie describes the wave of summer visitors:

It is very difficult to feed an ever-increasing household. When we came there were not quite eighty of us and now there we are 110. We also have twenty-four to thirty guests almost all the time. It is becoming more and more difficult to accommodate them. For the summer, a kind of youth hostel has been arranged in one of the new attics. Most of these new people are working on the farm and in the garden, and some are in the print shop. The women guests usually work in the kitchen. Some strange people meet here. Some from the youth movement, but not all.... We have some interesting talks.[12]

The beginning of 1930 saw the establishment of some contact between the Bruderhof and members of the Jewish religious Hechalutz Movement, who were training on a farm at Gheringhof, near the Rhönbruderhof. According to Georg Barth, these relations had been initiated in the late 1920s:

We had long been aware of the group which lived nearby, a commune preparing itself for life in a kibbutz in Palestine.... When they visited us we were impressed by their profound idealism.... They adhere to the Jewish religion, but this does not impair our relations. Respecting their wish to eat kosher food, we offered them something suitable.... They were very curious about our way of life and wanted to understand how we manage the commune and our work. They were former town people and quite unused to agricultural work. We had some lively talks and discovered we had mutual interests. We regarded the fast-growing kibbutz movement as a partner in achieving an ideal of brotherhood and social justice. Communal life is perceived by both our movements not merely as a value *per se,* but as the first step towards a new society.[13]

The Bruderhof archives have a copy of a transcript of a conversation that took place at the Rhön Bruderhof on 17 August 1932, between a group of visitors from Gheringhof and members of the Bruderhof community. This document is devoted mainly to the visitors' account of themselves, their *weltanschauung,* and their motivation for living in a kibbutz in what was then Palestine. They presented themselves as a religious-socialist group that aspired to settle at Kibbutz Rodges (a training farm near Petah Tikva, Israel) and maintain a community in which the social vision would be integrated with a religious, Jewish way of life. Members of the Bruderhof wanted to know in what way the Bible had inspired them and sought to understand their Zionist conviction; whether it was merely political or whether it had been inspired by the prophets. According to the transcript, the visitors replied that they were strongly motivated by their belief in socialist principles, which correlated with the prophets' vision. The hosts asked whether they were a closed community or whether their doors were open to all religious Jews, to which they replied that every religious Jew was welcome as long as there was work and accommodation.

The conversation ended with a discussion of internal problems and the hosts enquired about the ways and means in which personal rivalries were resolved, saying that after twelve years experience of communal life, they were well aware of the fact that personal rivalries were unavoidable and in order to diminish their impact, everyone should struggle against his own selfishness. The visitors replied optimistically that they hoped to overcome their egotistical mentality during the training period for their future life in a collective community.[14]

In an interview with the author, Rudi Hertz, a member of Kvutzat Yavneh, Israel and a veteran of the religious kibbutz movement, recalled the meeting and added that it took place on a Sunday, which was a zealously observed holiday in the region, and that it had taken place as a result of their curiosity about their neighbors. He recalled that they were impressed by the cleanliness and order, but that they were rather disappointed by the standard of their agriculture and remarked, "In that respect we were far more advanced; they managed their farm like the poor farmers in the area." He recalled how hospitable their hosts had been and that they had spent several hours in lively conversation. The Bruderhof members had been interested in the kibbutz, while members of the training farm were fascinated by "those Christians who live the same kind of life as we do" and by the fact that "their (communal) life ensued from their religious convictions." Rudi also noticed that they were influenced by Gustav Landauer and remarked that "Landauer was deeply admired by myself and by many of my generation. His book, *A Call to Socialism*, served as the basis for our socialism, a non-Marxist kind of socialism."[15]

In 1931, the Bruderhof established contact for the first time with individuals and groups outside Germany. First came a Swedish couple, Nils and Dora Wingard[16] and soon after, close contact was established with groups in Switzerland and families from that country began to arrive at the commune with a view to joining the Bruderhof. The Swiss families were an important and valuable addition and the first of these was the wealthy Boller family, which handed over all its property on joining.

Other families did so too, and their contribution was vital at the time, considering the thin financial harvest reaped by Eberhard Arnold on his North American tour. Emmy Arnold writes that "these families brought in the money we needed—almost the whole sum we had expected to get

from the Hutterites in America." The Boller family came from Christian
Socialist circles that were influenced by the teachings of Leonard Ragaz,
who tried to establish a commune in Zurich. The father, Hans Boller,
was a pastor who had been greatly respected by his congregation, but
the gap between his sermons and reality caused him and his wife to
distance themselves from the Church and seek to join a commune. They
first tried to do so in Zurich, but when they heard about the existence of
the Bruderhof in Germany, they decided to join in 1931, preferring it to
the *Werkhof* commune in Zurich.

Eberhard Arnold considered their joining very significant:

> Our encounter with them reminded us of our own new beginning when we left
> Berlin and went to Sannerz.... Their way to full community had been long pre-
> pared for them through their innermost calling, rooted in the very depth of their
> being.

They visited the Bruderhof for the first time shortly after Eberhard's
return from his tour of the Hutterite villages, on the day of the wedding
of Eberhard's daughter to Hans Zumpe:

> They came in the middle of a wedding. That certainly is quite significant. Just this
> question of marriage and its relationship to religion and society...has been a
> burning one for them.... For a long while they had wrestled with the question:
> how is it possible to live a true life in a marriage and the family in a community
> that demands absolutely everything? Else especially had strong reservations. And
> now they were plunged into the experience of our wedding. And the strongest and
> greatest impression they received was that the marriage was a symbol of full
> unity.... Actually, they were won over on that wedding day.

> In all our meetings we hardly touched on money matters except on the last evening
> when Hans and Else Boller began talking about it, but we only referred to it very
> briefly. It was my innermost endeavor that we should meet Hans and Else Boller
> with the same love and care...as we would any poor person whom we have rec-
> ognized as a brother through our common humanity.... No one should be favored
> and no one discriminated against. We have always accepted the poorest with joyful
> hearts and loving readiness. Therefore, we have endeavored, in the authority of the
> Church, to tell Hans and Else the truth and to keep nothing back. In this connec-
> tion, the question of surrendering all our property became clear, and thus it also
> came to the point that we could explain the difference between giving goods and
> valuables into safekeeping when entering the novitiate and handing them in when
> accepted into the Brotherhood. Whereupon they answered in all firmness—"in the
> sense of the Brotherhood."

> We could foresee that when they returned to Switzerland they would certainly hear:
> "How can you give up your wide sphere of influence and all the good a pastor can
> do, to withdraw to the solitude and the narrow limits of the remote Rhön?" We

spoke about this point with the Bollers, showing them that our communal life has meaning in history, in the experience of the Kingdom of God, only because our actual living in community is of decisive consequence for the mission.

When Hans and Ilse Boller returned to Zurich they declared their withdrawal from the established Church in Zurich, resigned their pastorate and broke off all their connections.

At the same time they were given a letter for the people of the *Werkhof,* challenging them to start on their way and come to us.[17]

The *Werkhof* commune near Zurich was one of the short-lived communes that had been established in Europe in the late 1920s. It was founded by young people with a socialist religious background and reached a membership of twenty, but failed to become an integrated group or attain internal unity.

After some time, people began leaving and the majority turned to the Bruderhof with which they had contact and where they thought they could find greater inner harmony. At one stage, negotiations for a merger between the two groups took place but failed because of differences in their principles. Differences of opinion within the Zurich commune led to its disintegration and twelve of its members who believed in the religious communal idea, decided to join the Bruderhof.

Among the members of the *Werkhof* commune were Hans Meier and his wife, who were both from Zurich. Hans came from a socialist family, but with the traumatic experience of World War I he became deeply disillusioned with socialism because of its inability to prevent the bloodshed, and became a pacifist. In his youth he had been a member of the *Freischar* youth movement where he had met Margaret, his future wife. His pacifist principles prevented him from serving in the army and he was imprisoned for three months. While he was in prison, the Bruderhof members sent him a telegram in which they identified with him and invited him to visit them and so, after his release in 1929, he married Margaret, his youth movement friend, and they followed up the invitation and spent three weeks at the Bruderhof. Later, they left for a tour of European communes and what they found was far from encouraging: All the communes were about to break up. But the couple were undeterred and Hans writes in his memoirs:

In spite of these failures, we felt the urge to begin living communally...because we felt that such a life of brotherhood, of justice and peace, must be possible, otherwise we would be forced to abandon all hope.[18]

The Werkhof commune in Zurich did not last because of differences of opinion on questions of faith and the education of children. Of the three families that made up the commune, it was Hans's that knew something of the Bruderhof and they asked their friends to give the German commune a try before giving up on communal living. And that is how the Swiss commune found its way to the Bruderhof in Germany.

After a long period of hesitation that resulted from their religious doubts, as they considered themselves socialists who believed in Jesus, the Meiers were the last to join. They had belonged to a socialist religious movement headed by Leonard Ragaz and were nonpolitical socialists and pacifists. Like many of their generation, they had been influenced by Gustav Landauer and his book *The Call to Socialism*. When the Zurich commune began to break up, Hans's wife decided to join the Bruderhof and later he followed suit, joining in January, 1933, on the day of Hitler's rise to power.[19]

The Bruderhof under the Nazi Regime

When the Nazis came to power in 1933, the Bruderhof community numbered 140 members to whom Hitler's appointment as Chancellor came as a great shock as they knew that from now on things would be difficult. News of the persecution of the Jews and seizure of their property appalled them. Reports of schools being closed down, people being taken to concentration camps, the persecution of Catholics and other religious sects, and especially the discrimination against Jews, were the cause of deep concern in the Bruderhof commune. Yet many visitors still came and went that year, some of whom were opponents of the Nazi regime who wished to become members, but not all shared the same opinions and although many discussions ensued, they had to be wary of informers. Outside the Bruderhof, the people joining were regarded with displeasure and some of the members were forced to sever their ties with their families.[20]

During the first months following Hitler's rise to power, they tried to maintain their daily routine. Their community was growing and eighteen new members were baptized that summer, among them Hans Meier and his wife. The increase in membership raised their morale and also assisted them politically as under the new regime, the fact that some of them were foreign nationals curbed harassment by the authorities. "Having foreigners among us enabled us to continue with the most indispensable work," wrote Georg Barth.[21]

We can also learn something of the atmosphere at the Bruderhof in the summer of 1933 from Emmy Arnold's letter to the Hutterite elder, Joseph Hoffer:

> In spite of the present situation, new, zealous, seeking people keep coming to us to live in community, leaving good jobs behind. Poor people also come to us, who have grown weary of the hardships of the times and no jobs, and seek help and salvation with God and his church.... It is a great strengthening to all of us when new ones come, but you can imagine what a great burden it is.... We have only 175 acres of land.... Above all, think of us in your prayers and don't forget to send us help so that we don't have to send anybody away in winter, and can equip rooms for the eager new ones. If we want to do all this, it has to be done soon or else it will be too late.[22]

In those days, the possibilities of contact with the outside world were greatly reduced. The local Nazi authorities forbade them to let people stay overnight and any visitors risked their lives by doing so. In spite of these restrictions, they maintained their contacts with their Jewish friends. We know this from Georg Barth, who recalled that "they were among the only people willing to visit us." For their part, the Bruderhof members were not deterred from keeping in touch with Jewish circles. Hans Meier said that in 1936 he visited Martin Buber at his home together with another Bruderhof member, where Buber warned them of the danger they faced by visiting him and Hans replied, "We face the same danger. We too have been forbidden to receive visitors." During that visit Buber gave them a copy of the Old Testament, which he and Franz Rosenzweig had translated into German.[23]

Eberhard Arnold immediately grasped the nature of the Nazi regime and warned of its dangers. Speaking to the community, he made it clear that "it means a real decision if we want to follow the way of Jesus; it may mean martyrdom and death—being put into a concentration camp and put to death," although at that time very little was known about those things.[24]

The question of whether to openly demonstrate their opposition to the Nazi regime was debated at numerous meetings. They ignored the Nazi orders to use the "Heil Hitler" salute. As usual in their relations with the authorities, Eberhard Arnold approached the district official and explained that their adherence to the teachings of Jesus did not permit them to fulfill the demands of the Nazi government. The question was, What were they to do? They decided to try to continue "to bear witness" and speak out openly.

In the spring of 1933, the authorities began to hector the Bruderhof. The police and the SS conducted repeated searches on the pretext that the Bruderhof community was spreading communist propaganda and although no evidence of "guilt" was found, they continued with their inspections and questionings. On 11 October 1933, Bishop Ludwig Miller, head of the German Evangelical Church, called upon Eberhard Arnold to explain the principles of their faith and their relationship to the state. Eberhard replied in a detailed letter, setting out the main points of the Bruderhof dogma. The bishop did not reply.[25]

On 12 November 1933, the Nazis held a plebiscite. The members of the Bruderhof came to the conclusion that a simple "no" was not sufficient. Eberhard formulated a sentence that summed up their fundamental position based upon their Christian faith. All the members wrote it down and inserted the pieces of paper into the ballot box in the district town of Veitsteinbach and they were very surprised to read in the newspapers next day that all the people of the town had voted "yes"! But the authorities were now fully aware of those who had voted against.

Four days later, on 16 November, the settlement was surrounded by 140 men of the Gestapo SS and SA units and every room was searched. They scrutinized the books and personal letters, especially those from abroad. The Arnolds' rooms were searched very thoroughly and also the archives and library, where they looked for books "hostile to the state."[26] Eberhard had recently broken his leg and had undergone surgery and so he was bedridden, which saved him from being sent to a concentration camp as the leader of the community.

Several days after this raid, Eberhard Arnold made another attempt to come to an understanding with the district authorities and sent them a long letter in which he explained their principles and included some of the theological books they had published. He wrote, *inter alia*:

> The wave of National Socialism has caught us quite unprepared, and even now we know far too little about its philosophy.... We brethren are called to the love of Christ, to love alone. This explains our misgivings on the one hand, and our declarations of respect for the present national government on the other; we can perceive no contradiction in our attitude. We love our German land and people and want to belong to them all our life. As you will gather from my writing, especially from my book "Inner Land," my German background and outlook were formed by the old folk songs and by German mysticism. For that reason alone I had hoped we

would be increasingly able to respect the present government, and vice versa, and that we would be granted the privilege of living in the midst of the new Germany unmolested, following our consciences as Germans and Christians.

Since there was no reaction to the letter and the harassment increased, Eberhard Arnold made another attempt, which caused him great mental stress: He wrote to the Gestapo headquarters in Berlin, explaining his views and requests:

> The present government demands the primacy of the state more strongly that ever before, claiming absolute authority and dominating the nation with its Weltanschauung. For a Church bound to Christ, obedience to God and dedication to His Kingdom takes precedence over everything without exception and must remain paramount.
>
> Of particular concern is the freedom of speech and education... without which we cannot live.... We would appreciate a clear statement about the extent to which this freedom will remain in Germany.... The seemingly absolute belief in Aryan and especially Nordic blood arouses fear in a Christian that the divine measure of justice and equity toward other kinds of blood will suffer.
>
> We know ourselves to be completely free of all hostility to the government, to the state and to the nation, and innocent of giving support to any movement or group hostile to the present state, even though we are not and can never be National Socialists.
>
> We would have to resort to emigration as a last and most undesirable measure, if the German Reich and the Prussian state were to deny our urgent request to continue the work we are doing for the benefit of society at the cost of self-sacrifice: namely rural settlement work, mission work among the people and communal education. It would be unspeakably hard to leave our home and fatherland, to give up working for our beloved nation... but if we are not allowed to live in community as our conscience dictates, we must and will do that.[27]

The situation of the Bruderhof commune was extremely difficult. Apart from the raids, the searches, the confiscation of printed material, and restrictions on outside visitors, the conditions of the mortgage repayment were replaced by a short-term loan to be repaid within two weeks. As they had no income from the farm at the time, their only income was from the sale of books, which they continued to print and distribute. This activity was not only a means of livelihood, but primarily a way of "bearing witness," but this, too, soon came to an end when they were forbidden to sell their books. The reason given was that they were spreading "propaganda dangerous to the state" and that their worldview disregarded the primacy of the interests of the nation and state, "in refusing to accept the basic national socialist laws concerning the purity of blood and race."[28]

We find some interesting information on the worries and difficulties of the Bruderhof in a letter by Hardy Arnold that was smuggled to the Hutterite Elders at the end of 1933. The letter describes the harassment by the authorities because of their religious beliefs and pacifism, the authorities' intention of closing their school, and their being forced to follow the Nazi curriculum, which brought about their decision to send their children to Switzerland. This is how he describes the community:

> In spite of some increases we are only 110 people, because some unbaptized novices have broken their word and lost their faith in the face of our tribulations, and children whom we have loved and cared for over a long period have been taken away.

> We plead for your counsel and help.... When you write to the Foreign Minister and the Minister of the Interior of the German government, make it clear that our Bruderhof does not belong to us but to the Hutterian Church in America and to all its communities, as expressed in our statutes. Could you try to get permission for our immigration into Canada? Could you send us some money?[29]

At the beginning of 1934, the Nazis closed down their school and they were no longer allowed to care for children from outside the commune. Nazi supervision of their local school was very irritating. An inspector was sent to check out the national socialist education being given to the children and was, of course, very disappointed. As a punishment for their not providing such education, they were forced to employ Nazi teachers and it was this step that made them decide to send their children to Switzerland. They had to obtain passports immediately, but as the district official was also a Nazi, he made it extremely difficult for them. Once normal procedures were not available to them, they tried their luck in unconventional ways and the children were smuggled into Switzerland in the dead of night. Annemarie Arnold writes:

> I remember that night very clearly. It was late one November night. It was very foggy and we all walked together—all the Bruderhof members walked with the children to a certain crossroads.... From there, different ones went in different directions, either on bikes or by wagon or maybe even walking.... It was a very frightening and serious moment.... All the children reached the places to which we sent them safely.[30]

The children's home to which they had been sent agreed to keep them there for only a short time, and so it was imperative that shelter be found for them immediately. Emmy and Eberhard Arnold had to find a solution and came to the conclusion that they should go to Liechtenstein and after they had been taken there, they searched secretly for a suitable place and found it close to the small town of Silum. It was a summer resort hotel situated at an elevation of 1500m, which had not been used recently, and the owner agreed to rent it out to the Bruderhof. It was winter, the roads were in a bad state, and the neighbors advised them to postpone the transfer till the spring, but time was running out. A friendly farmer agreed to take them on his sledge, but they could not get all the way up to the hotel and had to walk the last part of the way. This was very difficult for Eberhard, whose broken leg had not healed properly since his surgery. When they reached the hotel they found that it lacked proper heating and that there was only lodging for 100 people in nearby huts. Moreover, the hotel owner demanded a deposit of SF1,500, and as they had had to pay for the journey of the twelve children from Switzerland to Liechtenstein, such a sum was not at their disposal.

Under these circumstances, the first thing they had to do was raise the money. On their way down the mountain, they visited a friend in a hospital in a nearby town and when she heard what had happened, she gave them SF8,000 on the spot! They saw this as an act of God as it enabled them to pay for the transfer of the children from Switzerland and acquire the hotel, which would provide shelter for them. The place became a new settlement, which they called Alm Bruderhof.[31]

Gradually, members and their children gathered in the new settlement in Liechtenstein. First came the children and then some youngsters from England, who were the first English people to join the Bruderhof, and among them were Arnold and Gladys Mason, who were to remain in the Bruderhof all their lives and play an active role in it. These young people had heard about the Bruderhof from Hardy Arnold, who had been a student at Birmingham University and had addressed the students on the Bruderhof. The Masons had been very impressed by him and his lecture and they invited him to their home, and thus social as well as ideological ties developed between them. This relationship eventually led them and a group of their friends to join the Bruderhof in Liechtenstein.[32]

The new English members were very enthusiastic and particularly remarkable was their willingness to hand over all their property to the commune, including personal effects such as diamond rings. Someone else who joined at that time was an Edinburgh-born woman, Kathleen Hamilton (Hassenberg), who had been a member of the Presbyterian Church in her youth. She had subsequently become a Quaker and worked as a teacher, and became active in pacifist circles. She, too, had become acquainted with the Bruderhof through Hardy's lectures, and like the Masons, had been very impressed by his description of the communal way of life and of the stressful situation of the group in Germany as a result of Nazi persecution. She was particularly moved by the suffering of the children, who had been prevented from receiving proper schooling, and she resolved to join the Bruderhof commune in Europe and so Kathleen and her friend, Winifred Bridgewater, contacted the Bruderhof and expressed their desire to join. Like the Masons, they were first asked to go to Liechtenstein, but later, when the Bruderhof members who were liable for military service were being smuggled out of the country, they were transferred to Germany. Kathleen admits that "under the circumstances, I would have been reluctant to join the commune in Nazi Germany, but owing to developments at the time, I could not refuse.[33]

On 7 April 1934, Eberhard Arnold made the following report to the Hutterites on the latest events:

> We now have a second Bruderhof, a Hutterite community up in the mountains—the Alm Bruderhof near Silum.... The new community will begin with forty-five souls, while seventy-five remain in the old community, our Rhön Bruderhof in Germany.
>
> Since January 1934, our children and young people have been fleeing from that violation of their consciences which is threatening all schoolchildren and young people of military age in Germany today with an evil, compelling force to make them hate and take part in civil war and war between nations. First, some of our children and young people were kept hidden at different places in Germany with friends or relatives, so that after a few weeks they could be taken across the border without risk. We have now gathered nearly all of them at the new little community. Many people, zealous for the truth, will certainly come to us there after a time, for it will become ever clearer to people "outside" that all who want to be serious Christians in Germany will be subject to oppression.[34]

The founding of the Liechtenstein settlement created a new situation at the Bruderhof, and for the first time there were two settlements in two different countries. Eberhard Arnold, as their spiritual leader, now faced new difficulties and challenges. He and Emmy chose to spend that year in the new settlement and faced numerous difficulties during that transitional period. In the summer of 1934, the new community underwent a spiritual crisis, as we can see from a letter sent from Alm to Rhön in July. The community became depressed and many people became addicted to soul-searching and self-criticism that bordered on real suffering. This atmosphere paralyzed the community and impaired their ability to function within the community and on external missions. Members filling educational functions asked to be relieved of their duties, maintaining that they were unable to relate to the children. In his letter, Eberhard Arnold called upon them to cast off their despondency and break out of the vicious circle of brooding and self-pity in which many of them enmeshed. He denounced their tendency to blame themselves for failing, saying that he considered it a sin that was disastrous for the commune. He wrote that "in recent months the life of the commune has been a swamp in which people are sinking so deep they might drown." Depression, soul-searching, and self-pity had struck these youngsters, who had lost their natural joy of life. Eberhard believed that the way to arrest this decline was to devote themselves to their tasks and to concentrate on the problems of their generation and those of the surrounding society. "Instead of each one asking himself—what is happening to me?—he should ask—what is happening to the world? What is going on in Germany under Hitler's leadership? And in Soviet Russia? How will the Kingdom of Heaven come upon this earth?[35]

In the winter of 1934 to 1935, Eberhard and Emmy Arnold returned to the commune in Germany where they were needed even more because of Nazi harassment. On their return they realized that their isolation from society and the church had increased. The radical Protestant churches were swept along on the tide of German patriotism and their leaders rejected any pacifist tendencies. They stated that if they were called upon, their response would be positive.[36]

At the end of 1934, Germany was about to pass a law introducing compulsory military service and once this fact became known abroad, Hans Meier, who was in Switzerland at the time, informed the Bruderhof that there were rumors that the first age groups would be conscripted immediately. The Brothers held a long meeting at night to consider what was to be done. Were they to remain in Germany and continue the struggle or get out of the country? Seventeen young men were liable for conscription under the new law. Emmy Arnold describes that meeting: "After a time of silence to ask God for the right guidance at this hour, we decided to send the young men to the Alm Bruderhof."[37]

They fled on foot, on bicycles, and in various other ways, but because of the lack of money, not by train and finally, all of them crossed the border safely and were joined by their families a short time later. So by the time the law was passed in March, 1935, all the young men of the

Bruderhof were safely housed in their Liechtenstein refuge. In a letter to the Hutterites, Emmy described the situation of the Bruderhof:

> On March 16, Germany introduced compulsory military service.... In spite of our great problems, new people are finding their way all the time into the life on both hofs. Altogether on both Bruderhofs, the Alm here in Liechtenstein and the Rhön in Germany, we were able to accept twelve novices into full membership of the Church.
>
> On both hofs we have many guests who want to experience life in community.... The need in both our places is very great.... On the Alm Bruderhof we are now ninety altogether...our living conditions are particularly poor.... We are hit by severe poverty. The Principality of Liechtenstein is friendly toward us, but of course we do not know how long we can stay here, especially if war breaks out.

On 28 October 1935, she wrote to the Hutterites:

> As long as our task is still here, we think that we must stay in Europe and especially serve the people of our homeland.... If things continue like this we do not know if it will be possible for us to stay here.[38]

The situation at the Liechtenstein commune was not easy, and gradually hostility toward them increased:

> The community lived mainly on what the publishing house earned and by selling books and turnery products, and there were constantly brothers on the road selling books.... In Liechtenstein there were also National Socialists. They used propaganda against us and against the Jews who had fled to Liechtenstein. They tried to get sufficient signatures to force the government to push us out.[39]

In 1935, they heard that the German government was calling on all its citizens of military age to return to Germany. The young Bruderhof members found themselves in a position of some danger in little Liechtenstein as the number of places available was limited and the Alm could house only the young men and their families. It thus became imperative that they find additional places of refuge in other countries and to this end emissaries were sent to Holland, Switzerland, and England. In May, 1935, Eberhard Arnold came to the realization that his community had become international and now consisted of people from England, Switzerland, Sweden, and Holland, with only a small number of the Germans who had originally come from Sannerz. It became clear that an alternative site must be found, as the conditions in the German homeland had become unbearable.[40]

While searching for a new location Eberhard Arnold went to England with his son Hardy, who had maintained his contacts there from his student days. The journey was very hard for Eberhard, as from lack of funds they often had to walk and this was very painful for him. From England, he went straight back to Alm. He had succeeded in obtaining a contribution from the Society of Quakers and these funds were to be used for developing hot-house cultivation, as this was the only way that vegetables could be grown on the Alm mountaintop. They also acquired a piece of land that was leased to them in the valley below the hotel and the members had to go up and down the hill every day to work there.

Once the situation at Alm had returned to normal, Eberhard went back to Germany. At that time, the tension regarding the acceptance of the Hutterite ways resurfaced. The strictness of the Hutterite customs displeased those members who wanted to preserve the tradition of spontaneity in "a free spirit," while others who were steeped in Hutterite writings were ready to adopt their ways in all their severity. Others, among them Emmy Arnold, were in favor of a middle-of-the-road position; while greatly appreciating the Hutterite way of life, they were loath to sever their ties with the tradition that had guided them so far. In a discussion on this subject that took place at Rhön, Eberhard Arnold said:

> If we devote ourselves solely to the study of the ancient writings of the Hutterites and force others to accept them, I shall not remain with you.[41]

After some time, the atmosphere at Alm once more became one of despondency and Eberhard was forced to go back there for a few days. And so in the autumn of 1935, for a period of many weeks, Eberhard and Emmy Arnold travelled back and forth between the two communities. These journeys were not only very dangerous but also very painful for Eberhard because of his broken leg. At the beginning of October he decided to stay at Rhön, because the atmosphere there was very bad and he felt that his presence there was vital and once again he tried to combat their depression. Emmy Arnold describes the low ebb at the Bruderhof at the time:

> People did not have a listening ear; they were unreceptive to what this time had to say to us...sometimes they coddled one another instead of correcting one another...there was talk about others behind their backs. And this at a time when we were seriously threatened because of our spiritual message.

> In the end it became clear to all of us that if we went on like this, we were not truly a brotherhood. The brotherhood was dissolved by the agreement of all. There were to be meetings, but they would be held in silence. Each one was to go into himself

and seek the spirit of awakening, the uniting Spirit. It was an hour of bitter gravity when we came to this decision.[42]

This was a difficult period for the Bruderhof in Germany, perhaps the most difficult of all, and it was then that disaster struck: Eberhard Arnold was taken from them. On the very day when the Rhönbruderhof called to the Liechtenstein Bruderhof for help, a telegram came from the doctor at the Darmstadt hospital, telling Eberhard to come for a checkup on his leg. He travelled to the hospital, never to return. At the hospital they decided that he had to undergo complex surgery, which was unsuccessful; his leg had to be amputated. In the operating room, Eberhard's condition deteriorated, and he died on 22 November 1935.[43]

The Death of Eberhard Arnold and the Expulsion of the Bruderhof from Germany

Upon Eberhard's death in December, 1935, Hans Zumpe was installed as Servant of the Word and from this position of leadership, he began to make drastic changes in the founder's policy, especially with regard to the Bruderhof's relationship with the Hutterites. The Arnolds were not in Germany at the time; Eberhard's sons Heini, Hardy, and Hans Herman were studying in Zurich and could not come to Germany for fear of being conscripted into the army. The Arnolds, including Eberhard's wife Emmy, were displeased by the change of policy and protested against it. A meeting was held in Zurich between the Arnolds and Hans Zumpe to clarify and discuss the changes and this meeting became known as the *Zurich Handel.*

Hans Zumpe had the upper hand and sanctions were imposed on Eberhard's sons. Zumpe's followers accused them of being overemotional and rigid in their insistence on following in their father's footsteps. Hans Zumpe led the community during the difficult period from 1936 to 1937 when it was torn from within and was also under pressure from the Nazi regime.

At the time, the Liechtenstein authorities made it clear they could not guarantee that the Germans would not conscript the young men of the Bruderhof, but fortunately, Arnold and Gladys Mason, Freda Dyroff, and Hans Zumpe, who had been sent to England to find a suitable place for a new community, managed to do so.[44] The place they found was a farm near the small town of Ashton Keynes in the Cotswolds and they described the circumstances of the purchase thusly:

> Freda borrowed her father's car and we drove around England, looking for a place and fortunately we found one which seemed suitable—in the Cotswolds, west of Oxford, but we didn't have enough money to buy it. We stayed in one of the abandoned buildings and gave the owners eleven pounds, all the cash we had, as an advance payment.[45]

With the help of friends from English Quaker circles, the group succeeded in raising funds to buy the farm and by September they owned the 200 acres that belonged to the farm. The first group of seventeen members arrived and they were followed by those of army age who had clandestinely left the settlements on the continent.

As the threat to the safety of the young members in Liechtenstein increased, they sought ways of escape to the new refuge in England. They decided to organize a band of wandering pipe and guitar players, led by Hans Meier. They planned several routes: by sea from Genoa after crossing Italy or through Switzerland and France, and finally chose the latter route. At the border crossing the guard looked at Hans Meier's Swiss passport and was satisfied; he did not check the others. They were also lucky that their passports were not checked during the train journey through France, which was most unusual at the time. Other young members took different routes and slipped into England via Italy and Holland and although these journeys involved a high degree of risk, they all ended safely when they were allowed to enter England on invalid passports. Gradually, all the young Bruderhof members gathered in England, just before the liquidation of the German community by the Gestapo.[46]

During those difficult years when the community was being moved to England, the source of the strength of the Bruderhof lay in the loyalty of its young members. Only a few left during the years that followed the death of their spiritual leader, Eberhard Arnold, and the Bruderhof's growing international character, coupled with the refuge they had found outside continental Europe, helped to preserve this strength. In the summer of 1936, the situation of the German Bruderhof deteriorated. Their requests to the authorities to be allowed to sell their books, which was their main means of livelihood, were rejected. A few years ago, a copy of the official report refusing their request was found in the district archives and it is interesting to read the arguments used in the report, which elucidate the Nazis' attitude toward the Bruderhof:

My refusal to issue a vending license to the Bruderhof is based on the fact that the propaganda emanating from them is hostile to the National Socialist state.... They do not recognize the basic National Socialist laws pertaining to blood and race...they refuse all military service. When the new conscription law came into force, the Bruderhof promptly sent all its qualifying members to their branch in Liechtenstein, thus avoiding military service.[47]

At approximately the same time, a meeting of the Council of Hutterite Settlements in Canada and the U.S. was convened at which it was decided to send emissaries to investigate the state of the German branch of their church in the wake of Eberhard Arnold's death. The delegation was to also reaffirm their ties, since the man they had known and trusted was Eberhard Arnold. They began their visit in England at the beginning of 1937 and then went on to the German community. The Hutterites' visit to Germany was valuable in several ways: first, their presence as Canadian tourists in itself had a restraining influence on the Gestapo at a time when the community was under threat and second, it also influenced relations within the community. At the time, Hans Zumpe was the only Servant of the Word serving all three settlements and the Hutterites declared that such centralization was not standard procedure and that each settlement should have its own Servant. Their opinion was accepted and two days before they left England, Hardy Arnold and Georg Barth were installed as Servants of the Word and Hans Zumpe was deposed. Hans Zumpe's daughter wrote in her memoirs that in 1938 her father was excluded from the Cotswolds Bruderhof for a year. According to her account, this was due to his attitude toward the Hutterites in that the Bruderhof members felt that he ignored the Hutterite leadership and was too independent in his decisions as leader of the community. Heini Arnold expressed this by saying that "Hans Zumpe wanted to learn from the Hutterites but not merge with them."[48]

Hardy Arnold and Georg Barth continued to correspond with the Hutterites on this issue after their return to America and their correspondence exposes the problems created by Hans Zumpe's leadership. In one of their important letters, the Hutterites recommended his dismissal. This letter, sent to Hardy and Georg by the Elders Joseph Kleinsasser and David Hofer of the Milltown, Manitoba colony, never reached its destination, having disappeared under strange circumstances and it only came to light in 1960. The letter accuses Hans Zumpe of employing a policy that ran contrary to the values of Christianity and their Church, and demands his exclusion from the community:

Hans has shown himself to be an unwise and undiscerning leader. He did not understand the deepest meaning of the Lord's Supper according to the teaching of Paul.
And if he understood it, he acted very irresponsibly and proved himself to be an
unworthy servant of the Church. He should not be reaccepted without serious
repentance...and he cannot carry the Service of the Word any more.[49]

In the meantime, a very serious danger to the community loomed on
the horizon. On 14 April 1937, the Bruderhof members received a telephone call from Gestapo headquarters ordering them to leave the farm
within twenty-hours and informing them that they would not be allowed
to take any of their shared possessions with them. The order was based
on the law against "communist activity" that had been passed in 1933,
and according to the terms of which the Bruderhof members were defined as "undesirable" and were to be expelled or sent to a concentration
camp. The language of the official indictment was "violent resistance to
the people and government of Germany," and considering the very nature of the Bruderhof, it was totally unfounded.[50]

The order came as a great shock to the Bruderhof members, despite
the fact that they had been preparing for such an eventuality for some
time. Their greatest fear was of being sent to a concentration camp.
Fortunately, the two Hutterite visitors, David Hofer of Bonne Homme,
South Dakota, and Michael Waldner of James Valley, Manitoba, were
there at the time and their presence prevented this and deterred the Gestapo from any acts of brutality.

The Bruderhof members recall that the Hutterites told the Gestapo:

Look here! You can't do this! This place belongs to us, it is a Hutterite Brotherhood. We've come from Canada and this is our property.[51]

Their presence did not prevent the expulsion of the Bruderhof members, but forced the Gestapo to change the charge, which had been rejected by the two Hutterites. And so, a few days after the liquidation, the
Gestapo changed the charge to one of "criminal bankruptcy and grave
suspicion of fraud and embezzlement," and for this purpose a creditor
was persuaded to sign a document stating that he had been deceived by
the Bruderhof through nonpayment of a debt. At first the man had refused, but later he submitted to Gestapo pressure.[52]

The Hutterites, who had witnessed this entire sequence of events,
beginning with the raid on the settlement, the siege, the searches and
confiscations, and ending with the expulsion, documented them in a

detailed letter, written by David Hofer.[53] The letter reveals the central role played by Hans Meier, who was a Steward at the time and considered by the Gestapo to be their leader, so he was arrested together with two other brothers, Hans Boller and Karl Keiderling. Recalling these events fifty years later, Hans Meier maintained that it was an act of God that the two Hutterite visitors happened to be there during that particular period, for when the Gestapo realized that the two American Hutterites were present and claimed that the Bruderhof was a branch of their Church, they were afraid that their actions might be publicized in America as persecution of Christians. The active intervention of the Hutterites, who argued and negotiated with the officers in charge of the raid, prevented the dispersion of the members to their previous homes, and they were allowed to leave as a group, albeit without their books and possessions. Meier recalls that the Mennonite leader, Michael Horsch, arrived but was afraid to remonstrate with the authorities and later justified the Gestapo's allegations.[54]

It should be pointed out that the leadership and press of the German Mennonites played a despicable role in this affair: not only did they refrain from protesting against the expulsion of the Bruderhof, but also justified it in their journal by confirming the Gestapo's claims that it was due to the community's inability to pay its debts. The submissiveness of the German Mennonites was immediately denounced by the Dutch Mennonites, who rallied to take the Bruderhof refugees in after they had crossed the Dutch border.[55]

In mid-May, 1937, after the entry visas had been obtained and the conditions for their absorption into the Cotswolds commune had been prepared, approximately 100 adults and children travelled to Britain and joined the first group, which had been there since 1936. The German refugees' arrival at the farm near Ashton Keynes was favorably received by the local press. Comprehensive articles appeared describing the history of the group, its international character, and pacifist, anti-Nazi position. Their suffering under the Nazi regime and their expulsion from Germany aroused sympathy and were widely reported.

Initially, the group aroused suspicions because of the strangeness of their attire, but the mystery was soon dispelled and the friendly and hospitable group became integrated within the region. They were particularly appreciated for their diligence, which brought about a rapid and impressive development of the neglected farm. The Home Office and the Ministry of Agriculture spoke favorably of them and soon after their arrival in England, the *Manchester Guardian* published an article by E. C.Arnold (Hardy, Eberhard's eldest son) in its prestigious weekly supplement, in which he introduced the group to the English public and described their beliefs and mission.[56]

In a gesture of hospitality they were invited to the local Rotary Club where Arnold Mason explained their religious pacifist beliefs and communal way of life. In answer to questions, he said that in Britain, their group had found an atmosphere of freedom and an understanding of their motives.[57]

While the Bruderhof refugees were being absorbed in England, three of their most active members (Hans Meier and two others) were being held in the district prison at Fulda and were in danger of being sent to a concentration camp. Fortunately, they did not have to stand trial and were released after being held for three months, thanks to a friendly district judge who had examined their file and had realized that they were innocent. He knew about the Gestapo's intention to send them to a concentration camp and he planned the trial for a day when the Gestapo officers were absent at a Nazi mass rally in Frankfurt. In his verdict, the judge maintained that there was no evidence of guilt and ordered their immediate release and expulsion from the country before the Gestapo could discover what he had done. In order to get them out in time, the judge contacted their lawyer who took them to the border in his car. At great risk, the three reached the Dutch border near Neimegen having crossed a German forest with the help of a map and a compass, but they miscalculated and returned to the German border where they were arrested by German frontier guards, who miraculously did not maltreat them but showed them the way into Holland. Thus the last Bruderhof members left Germany on their way to refuge in England. The release of the three prisoners now reunited with their families was widely and sympathetically covered by the British press.[58]

Notes

1. Arnold, Emmy, *Torches Together* (Rifton, N.Y.: Plough Publishing House, 1976), 152.
2. *The KIT Annual 1991* (The Collected Newsletters of the KIT Information Service. San Francisco, Calif.): 62.
3. Zablocki, Benjamin, *The Joyful Community* (Baltimore, Md.: Penguin, 1971), 79.

4. *Brothers Unite* [An account of the uniting of Eberhard Arnold with the Hutterian church (Rifton, N.Y.: Plough Publishing House, 1988), 244–52.
5. Bruderhof archives, document EA 31/4B (YM/14).
6. *Brothers*, op. cit., 259–63.
7. See Durnbaugh, D; "Relocation of the German Bruderhof to England, South America, and North America," *Communal Societies*, vol. 11 (Communal Studies Association, 1991): 66.
8. Arnold, Annemarie, *Youth Movement To Bruderhof* (Rifton, N.Y.: Plough Publishing House, 1986).
9. Ibid., 166–67.
10. Ibid., 181–83.
11. See memoirs of Gerhard Weigard in *Memories of Our Early Years*, vol.1, chap.1 (Collection of pamphlets published by the Plough Publishing House, Rifton, N.Y.: 1973–79). One of them was Herman Arnold, Eberhard's nephew, who participated for some time in Hitlerite circles and left them in 1934 after being swayed by his uncle in the Bruderhof. See G 2.
12. *Youth Movement*, 206.
13. Interview with Georg Barth, Deer Spring, Conn., July 1990.
14. See file S407B/EAE17 in the Bruderhof archives at Spring Valley.
15. Interview with Rudi Hertz, February, 1992.
16. See *Memories*, vol. 2, chap. F.
17. *Brothers*, op. cit., 271–72.
18. Meier, Hans, *Hans Meier Tells His Story to a Friend* (Rifton, N.Y.: Plough Publishing House, 1979), 4.
19. Ibid., 4–5.
20. Arnold, Emmy, op. cit., 181–84.
21. Barth, Georg, in *Memories*, vol. 2H, 20.
22. *Brothers Unite*, 317–18.
23. Interview with Hans Meier, July 1990.
24. Arnold, Annemarie, in *Memories*, vol. 2 D, 15.
25. Hindley, Marjorie, *One of the Lesser Known Confrontations with the National Socialist State, 1933–1937*, German History, vol. 11, no. 2 (The German History Society, 1993), 210–11.
26. According to Hans Meier in an interview with the author, the Gestapo removed from the library, which contained some 20,000 volumes, all the books that had red covers and that were suspected of being communist literature.
27. Hindley, op. cit., 214–15.
28. From the letter sent by the district Chief of Police, dated 10 June 1936.
29. *Brothers Unite*, 319–20.
30. Arnold, Annemarie in *Memories*, vol. 2, chap.D, 38.
31. Arnold, Emmy, op. cit., 192–93.
32. Interview with Arnold Mason, Woodcrest, N.Y., November 1991.
33. Interview with Kathleen Hassenberg, October 1992.
34. *Brothers Unite*, 322–23.
35. *kleiner Sendbrief, The Plough* (1974), 30.
36. Hindley, op. cit., 216–17.
37. Arnold, Emmy, op. cit., 196.
38. *Brothers Unite*, 330–32.
39. *Memories*, vol. 1, chap. K, 18.
40. Arnold, Eberhard, The Bruderhof archives, file no. EA 360 (YM/6) (1935).

41. Arnold, Emmy, op. cit., 196–200.
42. Ibid., 202–03.
43. In an article that appeared in the periodical published by people who had left the commune, Eberhard Arnold's grandson, John G.Arnold, Hardy's son, claims that his grandfather died as the result of intentional neglect by the Darmstadt hospital doctors, who had been instructed to get rid of him because he was an anti-Nazi leader [see *KIT,* vol. 2, no. 5, (1990)]. This claim is repeated by another Arnold grandchild, Elizabeth Bohlken Zumpe, Hans Zumpe's daughter, in her autobiography *Torches Extinguished.* She writes that she heard this when she herself was a patient at the *Elizabethen Stift* hospital in Darmstadt, where her grandfather had undergone surgery and died. The episode was revealed to her by a senior nurse who had worked in the hospital in the 1930s.

> I was told that the order came from "higher up" never to let Opa awaken from the anaesthetic. I suppose that we will never know for sure. [*Torches Extinguished,* (Carrier Pigeon Press), 167–68 and *KIT Annual 1991,* 63]

44. Interview with Freda Dyroff, Pleasant View, 1991.
45. Interview with Kathleen Hassenberg, 1992; *Memories,* vol. 1, chap. G, 34.
46. Arnold, Emmy, op. cit., 215–16.
47. *The Plough* no. 9 (Quarterly of Bruderhof communities, March/April 1985).
48. Zumpe, Elizabeth Bohlke, *Torches Extinguished,* 37, 173; also *KIT Annual 1991:* 65.
49. Mow, Merrill, Torches Rekindled (Ulster Park, N.Y.: Plough Publishing House, 1989), 114–15; *Brothers United,* 335.
50. For the official allegation for the liquidation of the Bruderhof and the expulsion of its members, see *The Plough,* vol. 1, no. 1 (1953), 22 and vol. 5, no. 2 (1957), 62–63.
51. *Memories,* vol. 3, chap. I, 25.
52. *Memories,* vol. 1, chap. I, 10.
53. The letter was published in *The Plough* in September 1939, and also appears in its entirety in Emmy Arnold's autobiography, *Torches Together,* 219–28.
54. Interview with Hans Meier, 1992. Emmy Arnold spoke of the penetration of Nazi influence into the German Mennonites when she participated in their international conference that was held in Amsterdam in the summer of 1936 (see Arnold, Emmy, op. cit., 218).
55. Hindley, op. cit., 218; Durnbaugh, op. cit., 68–70. In a paper he presented at the "Remembering for The Future" conference, which took place in Berlin on 13–17 March 1994—"The suppression of the Rhönbruderhof by the National Socialist authorities on April 14, 1937"—Durnbaugh extensively reviewed the position of the German Mennonites, who had deep reservations about the Bruderhof and who justified the Nazi's reasons for their expulsion.
56. *North Wilts Herald* (25 May 1937); *Bristol Evening Post* (25 June 1937); *News Chronicle* (24 June 1937); *Evening Advertiser* (28 May 1937); *Manchester Guardian Weekly Supplement* (June 1937).
57. *Evening Advertiser* (2 September 1937).
58. *Torches Together,* 228; *Evening Advertiser* (3 July 1947). In addition to the author's interview with Hans Meier in July 1990, see also Meier's own memoirs in *Memories,* vol. 1, chap. L, 14–19.

4

The Bruderhof in England

In March, 1938 in the wake of the Anschluss in Austria, the Liechtenstein Bruderhof was closed down, all its members moved to the commune in England, and thus the curtain was rung down on the Bruderhof movement in continental Europe and the period of enforced divisions was ended. From then on it became possible to live in a multigenerational community and invest efforts in social and economic organization according to the traditions and lifestyle that had been recently adopted from the Hutterites.

In their first year in England they were joined by some thirty new members from Switzerland, Holland, and Great Britain, which swelled their number to 200 souls. Among the new members from Britain was a group of seven people from Birmingham who, prior to joining the Bruderhof, had lived for some six months in an urban commune and had maintained social and ideological contacts with the Cotswold commune. As part of these contacts, the members of the Birmingham group were invited to spend Easter and Whitsuntide at the Bruderhof commune.

The Community Group, after having spent Easter and Whitsuntide at the Cotswold Bruderhof, soon became convinced that as a separate urban community they were unable to offer a full life to those who came to them in need. Each day they grew more certain that although the gift of friendship expressed both in material and spiritual assistance was part of any Christian witness, these in themselves were not enough. Nothing less was needed than a complete life revolution. Furthermore, as a group they longed to be fully united with all those living this life of complete surrender to God. It was clear to them that the Bruderhof was actually going in this direction, so quite spontaneously and out of deep conviction, the two communities became united, spiritually and economically.

The joining of this group was the most significant social experience the Bruderhof had undergone since their arrival in England. Much later, Herman Arnold, Emmy and Eberhard's youngest son, would mention it in his memoirs:

> In 1938, we experienced a period of awakening and revival in the Cotswold commune. The most tangible expression of this was the arrival of the Birmingham group.[1]

With their settlement in England, a new chapter in the history of the Bruderhof was begun. For the first time, a new commune had been established beyond the borders of the movement's birthplace in Germany and the neighboring countries. With the arrival of the English members who joined those from Switzerland and Holland who had come to the commune earlier, the way was open for the transformation of the Bruderhof from a German movement to an international one, albeit the German hegemony was maintained and the majority of the English began to learn German.[2]

The five years that followed the death of Eberhard Arnold were the years of collective leadership, and the positions adopted by the leadership during this period were left in the hands of the Arnold family: Eberhard's widow, children, sons-in-law, and their close aides. None of them yet knew how to lead a growing community like the Bruderhof and the leadership was guided by the administrative traditions and methods of the Hutterites and with their direct counsel. It was at that time that the offices of "Servant of the Word" (a spiritual and social leader in Hutterite and Bruderhof communes; a kind of local secretary and rabbi) and "Witness Brothers" (active, central members of the commune who assisted the Servant with advice when necessary), which were both Hutterite in origin, came into being in the Bruderhof commune. These officeholders were accorded the status of a collective leadership, which was extremely vital. It may be said that the Hutterite methods they employed helped them to preserve their framework and internal unity during the transitional period that followed Eberhard Arnold's death.[3]

At the Cotswold Bruderhof, Hardy was installed in the office of Service of the Word by David Hofer and Michael Waldner, and he served the Cotswold Bruderhof and its many guests during the very critical and stirring time that preceded World War II.

Hardy Arnold was very active in the establishment of the Bruderhof's English-language publishing house. Initially, and once it had become clear that they had a wide readership, they began by publishing newsletters in English (*Bruderhof Letters*) and later had the idea of founding a publishing house for books in English to replace the one that had gone under in Germany. The Cotswold Bruderhof Press was founded in 1938 and commenced its operations with the publication of the movement's periodical, *The Plough,* which was generally a quarterly. Its first editor was Hardy Arnold, whose command of English had become fluent in his student days at Birmingham University. This periodical was popular in England and it made a great contribution to the dissemination of articles on the pacifist Christian communes and a variety of information on life in the Bruderhof.

A German-language periodical was published at the same time, and in their first year these publications had a readership of 500 English subscribers and some 200 in Germany and Switzerland. Apart from the periodicals, they began to publish religious books written by Eberhard Arnold, the first of which was *The Individual and the World Need,* followed by a translation of *Confession of Faith* by the Hutterite theologian, Peter Ridman. A more general volume on the British communes, *Communities in Britain* (not published by the Bruderhof), was very favorably received and included the first comprehensive review of attempts at establishing cooperatives in Britain in the 1930s, and also a comprehensive review of the Bruderhof by Hardy Arnold. This particular article contained a detailed report on the social and economic situation in the summer of 1938, according to which:

> At the Cotswold Bruderhof there are 230 men, women and children of several nationalities, mainly German, Swiss, British and Dutch. As there are nearly ninety children, educational work is one of the most important activities.... English, German and Swiss teachers, kindergarten teachers and nurses look after the children, and about fifteen people are engaged in this work.
>
> Apart from the housework, which includes cooking, washing, baking, cleaning, sewing, etc., the members of the Bruderhof are engaged in the following branches of work:
>
> Firstly, farming and gardening. Nearly 200 acres are under pasture and there are also 100 acres of arable land, including ten acres of market garden. A tuberculin-tested herd of Shorthorn dairy cattle is kept and part of the milk is sold and some is consumed by the large household. Further livestock includes 120 Shropshire sheep, 4 horses, 2 working oxen and a pony. The community has a veterinary surgeon who looks after the cattle. A large poultry section of more than 1,000 birds is one of the most successful branches of the community's activities. In addition to this, thirty beehives are kept.

The arable land produces the grain for the community's bread and potatoes for the household, and also fodder for the cattle. Most important for the running of the household is the market garden of ten acres which produces all the vegetables required. Some fruit trees have already been planted. The entire farm and market garden are worked by modern scientific methods, although it is essential that the natural conditions of rural life should not be destroyed.

The other large branch of work is the publishing, printing and bookbinding department. The Cotswold Bruderhof publishes a quarterly journal, The Plough, and also books for the promotion of its ideals together with publications for the Hutterites in America.

Smaller branches of work include wood-turning, carpentry, smithing and similar occupations. For the furtherance of intellectual work there is a large collection of about ten thousand books, mainly in German and English. Lectures are held periodically throughout the year and every individual also has, as far as time permits at the present pioneering stage, ample opportunities for education through music, both vocal and instrumental, folk dancing, and other arts and crafts.

From time to time, people are sent out to give talks in various parts of England and the continent, and a great number of visitors are received every year, including many unemployed, refugees and other destitute people, who the community endeavors to help to the best of its ability.

Recently, the community has started work in Birmingham.... It has a building which is used as a center and meeting-place for all those interested in a Christian life in the Birmingham area.[4]

Just as they had at Sannerz and Rhön, the Cotswold Bruderhof invested great efforts in turning the publishing house into a central branch that would employ both male and female members in editing, proofreading, printing, and binding. Although they had only few books to publish, they did succeed in bringing out the quarterly *The Plough* over a period of three years.

It is worthy of note that one can find some Bruderhof interest in the kibbutz movement in what was then Palestine, in the first issues of *The Plough*. In the April, 1939 issue, there appeared a book review of *The Handbook of the Jewish Communal Villages in Palestine, 1938,* published by the Head Office of *Keren Kayemeth LeYisrael and Keren Hayesod,* Jerusalem. The reviewer, Gertrud Huessi, one of the veteran members of the commune, wrote:

Reading this Handbook, a member of a Christian community at once asks...what are the roots of such a life and what are the causes of its success?...How is it possible that so many people—twelve thousand in number—decided upon this way of life?...The book tries to show the reason for this enormous success. There are some practical advantages in living in a *kvutza*; life is more rationalized than on a private farm; farming is mechanized and the cost of production lower.... Manual and intellectual life are combined in a splendid way. The *kvutza* is a mutual insurance against unemployment and ill-health.

But the deeper reasons seem to lie in this: the movement of Zionism was combined from the beginning with a deep longing of many Jews to get back to manual labor, back to the land! A. D. Gordon, who was deeply influenced by Leo Tolstoy, impressed the young people with an almost mystical fervor drawn from Jewish Hasidic sources. Socialism plays a great part in these settlements.... The deeper reason for their development seems to be an idealistic socialism, a kind of religious strength not called by name, but sensed by an urging power.

And in the spirit of her religious beliefs, the reviewer claimed that

these are the urging powers which enable people to love such a life. The higher the enthusiasm for this new way of living, the smaller was the number of those who left.[5]

The clouds of war gathering over Europe in 1938 were reflected in pacifist articles and reports that appeared in the Bruderhof periodical. The community's contacts with British pacifist groups and the Quakers were strengthened at this time and the publications of these groups carried articles in support of the Bruderhof communes, their German background, and the contribution of the Bruderhof in Britain as an example of communal living between people of different nationalities, particularly between Britons and Germans.[6]

The Bruderhof members were active in pacifist circles and lectured throughout Britain. In 1938, they held some fifty meetings in cities like London, Bristol, Nottingham, and Birmingham, and in the nearby smaller towns of Swindon and Cheltenham.

At the beginning of 1939, a leaflet was circulated locally in which the "Brothers" announced a series of lectures that was to take place in a central hall in the nearby town of Ashton Keynes, beginning on 15 February. The announcement included the following note:

Considerable interest and attention has been shown by the residents of Wiltshire and Gloucestershire in the activities of the Cotswold Bruderhof.... The members of the Bruderhof wish to meet their neighbors in order to provide them with a full explanation of the objectives and purpose of their life.... It is their wish to enjoy the friendliest relationship with their neighbors and to cooperate for mutual help.

The Cotswold Bruderhof is a Christian community, the objective of which is to demonstrate a life of practical Christian brotherhood in all things. It includes German and Swiss as well as British members, and is witness to a life of love and Christian brotherhood irrespective of nationality or social standing.[7]

Despite a lack of capital, 1938 was a year of economic success on the Bruderhof farm. The turning point came at the end of the year with the receipt of donations from friends and the establishment of "Friends of the Bruderhof, Ltd.," a public company in which friends of the Bruderhof in Britain were able to buy shares and thus help in the expansion of the Bruderhof's activities. This enabled the Bruderhof to invest in both agriculture and building, and one of the first projects to be undertaken with the assistance of the investment company was the purchase of land for the establishment of a new community. This was Oaksey Park, a big farm of 300 acres not far from the existing commune, which had a dairy herd of sixty head and farm buildings in good condition.[8]

There were some 230 souls living at the Cotswold Bruderhof in the autumn of 1938 and this was the moving force behind the decision to establish a new commune. The Hutterites divided their communes when their population reached 150. The new commune was close by and thus allowed the joint use of services such as a bakery and a school. The buildings were in good condition and enabled the immediate housing of some seventy people, and there was a spacious room that was used for meals and meetings. The purchase of the farm met some opposition from the area's wealthy landowners, but the Brothers were undeterred and the day after the farm was purchased, some thirty people, half of whom were adults, moved in. The farm's branches were a dairy herd, pigs, approximately 800 chickens, and forty acres of arable land. After the Oaksey commune was established, the members felt the need to give their movement a name and "The Brothers" was chosen, and from then on they were known as "The Society of Brothers."[9]

At the end of 1938 it seemed that the Bruderhof had become firmly established in Britain and this feeling was expressed in the December, 1938 issue of the magazine, *The Cotswold Bruderhof.* The introduction to this issue contained an invitation to the British public to visit and become better acquainted with the Bruderhof: "We expect our visitors to respect our way of life and its meaning." The invitation was directed at the general public, to anyone who felt a need to make contact with a communal lifestyle, regardless of whether his or her motives were religious, social, or secular; the magazine did, however, emphasize that their life was based on belief in God, that Jesus Christ was their source, and that they were inextricably linked to the American Hutterites. The magazine included a concise review of the tenets of their faith and the

history of the Bruderhof from the time of the Free German Youth movement in Germany in the 1920s. The last section of the magazine contained a review of what was to be found in the Bruderhof communes at
the beginning of winter, 1938, including the fact that in December of
that year there were 250 men, women, and children. The issue also reported on the dissemination of information about the Bruderhof that
their people conducted in the cities of Britain, particularly in Birmingham, where they used the house that had belonged to the group that had
joined them during the past year for this purpose.

As in the Bruderhof communes in continental Europe, in England,
too, independent educational activities held pride of place. Once the
new farm had been purchased, room was set aside for the various educational institutions: a nursery for the babies, a nursery school, kinder-
garten, and primary school. In 1938 there were some 100 children at the
Bruderhof, ranging in age from infants to teenagers, and true to their
tradition from the Sannerz days their educational facilities were open to
children from outside, especially those from deprived backgrounds and
the poorer neighborhoods. 1939 saw a special issue of their magazine
that was devoted to a review of their educational principles and a description of what went on in their educational institutions. One article
dealt with the particular difficulty of teaching English to children who
were native German speakers. The author lauded the openness of the
Bruderhof toward foreign languages while they were still in Germany
as part of the concept of their internationality and the need to communicate with people from other cultures. Another facet of their educational
concept was their proclivity to make the family part of the child's education and socialization. The importance of this increased in England,
where the commune had forty-five families who had children.[10]

On the eve of the war in 1939, a large number of British pacifists
and foreigners who had sought refuge in Britain arrived at the two
communes.[11] Many of the pacifists who had become close to the
Bruderhof perceived their communal lifestyle as a way of life that
demanded a far greater commitment from them than demonstrations
of passive protest and they felt that life in the commune enabled the
realization of a positive alternative to the existing regime. British pacifists were particularly impressed by the life of cooperation that existed between Britons and Germans, and many of them sought a way
of joining such a community.[12]

As had happened previously, the Cotswold commune, too, became an attraction for visitors and the first half of 1939 saw some 1,000, among whom were socialists and communists from universities and workers clubs, vegetarians, pacifists, and also people from various oppositionary religious groups. The number of visitors was so great and the task of hosting them so intense that the Bruderhof was forced to limit visitors to certain days, and those who intended to stay and work were asked to inform the commune in advance.

Up to the winter of 1939 to 1940, The Brothers maintained good relations with the British government. In April, 1939, the members of the Bruderhof wrote to the Home Secretary, Sir Samuel Hoare, thanking him for his courageous stand in the Parliament in December, 1938. As mentioned earlier, the purchase of Oaksey Park had aroused the ire of some of the local residents and petitions were sent to the Home Office and to Parliament complaining of the sale of land in England to German settlers. Attacks were directed at the Home Secretary, who was asked why he had not exercised his authority in preventing this. In his reply, the Home Secretary stated that the Bruderhof had been given permission to settle in the area on condition that they would not seek employment outside their settlement, and that they had fulfilled that condition. Moreover, the purchase of Oaksey Park had been effected in order to absorb the British citizens who had joined the Bruderhof and to enable them to work within the confines of the community.[13]

In 1939 the Bruderhof membership rose to 300 souls and despite the fact that war was looming, the flow of new members continued unabated. Ten new members and the same number of refugee children joined at the beginning of the year. It is worthy of note that out of a feeling of anxiety and concern for the fate of the Jews being persecuted in Germany, the Bruderhof members expressed their readiness to absorb "non-Aryan" refugees from Vienna, and thus twenty adult refugees arrived at the commune and apart from them, the members cared for refugee children whose parents had been killed or sent to concentration camps. Some of these refugees left after a while and found their place outside the commune. The Brothers viewed the provision of shelter for refugees from Germany, Austria, and Czechoslovakia as a vocation, and a few dozen more refugees from these countries found their way to them, among them babies and young children who had been smuggled out with their parents' consent, and had been either fostered or adopted by Bruderhof families. Especially praiseworthy was their readiness to absorb "thirty young Zionists," all of whom were refugees from Germany, and who, it was agreed, could live with them for a year and be given their agricultural training in the two Cotswold communes.[14]

The *Hashomer Hatsa'ir* Trainees at the Cotswold Bruderhof

The absorption of the *Hashomer Hatsa'ir* trainees, who had managed to escape from Germany during the last days before the outbreak of war, gave the Bruderhof members the opportunity get to know something about the kibbutz movement. The group was sent to them by the *Hechalutz* office in London. At that time, a large number of refugees had reached Britain and among them were members of the Jewish pioneering movements who did not possess the necessary documentation, thus making the finding of a suitable place for their agricultural training necessary, until they could leave for Palestine. During the search for suitable farms, Arthur Ben-Yisrael, the *Hechalutz* emissary in London, and two training instructors, Ze'ev Weiss and Edith Freundlich (who are today members of Kibbutz Hazorea), found the Bruderhof farm with which they fell in love at first sight. The farm looked good, clean, well-organized, and spacious, the location was beautiful, and above all, it was a communal settlement that was reminiscent of everything they had ever heard about the kibbutz.

The trainees began to arrive at the Bruderhof in July, 1939. The group of thirty young men and women were accommodated in a separate building, ran their lives autonomously, and ate their meals, which came from the communal kitchen, separately. Eight of them are living in Kibbutz Hazorea today and I met with four of them to hear their recollections of the Bruderhof and without exception they spoke of that time with warmth and praise. They recalled that their first encounter had been quite embarrassing because of the Bruderhofer's attire: the women wore long dresses and had kerchiefs over their hair, while the men wore suspenders with their trousers. However, they soon got to know and trust one another.

Yael Gilad recalls:

Despite their odd clothing, we soon got used to them and even learned to admire their modest way of life. Moreover, we soon realized that theirs was an idealization of the collective, the just and egalitarian way of life.... Personally, I was charmed.... Without identifying with their ideals or religion, I admired the way in which they realized them.

Members of the Bruderhof called them "the Zionists" and went out of their way to treat them fairly. Larry El'or recalls:

> The Bruderhof were experienced in absorbing refugees, most of whom had arrived from various places, and some were very odd characters indeed. The Jewish trainees, on the other hand, formed a homogeneous group of people who joyfully fulfilled the tasks of communal life. Members of the Bruderhof tried to make it easier for us to adjust. They allowed us to live as a group and abstained from anything that might be considered as missionary activity. We were allowed to eat separately but were invited to join them on festive occasions. They were eager to hear about the kibbutz which they perceived as the ideal of a successful communal life. In certain cases they would even admonish us and say that our behavior was unfitting for a future life in the kibbutz.... All together, we lived side by side. We were mainly involved with one another during work hours, which we shared equally. They tried their best to train us in farm work and did this with typical German thoroughness.

Werner Weiss still has the "diploma" he received at the end of his time with the Bruderhof. It is an interesting document, which reads:

> The Society of Brothers known as Hutterites   Date: 18.10.1940
>
> Werner Weiss who led the group of Zionist refugees...has shown the keenest possible interest in all the branches of farm work.... He has also concerned himself with the theory and practice of farm work.... We have no hesitation in testifying to the character and integrity of the owner of this diploma.

There were also some misunderstandings that ensued from differing concepts of work and property. Larry El'or recalls:

> One of our members was working in the orchard when suddenly his ladder collapsed. Members of the Bruderhof said that he should be punished for sabotaging a work-tool by doing extra work. We objected, claiming that it had been an accident and that the entire group would make good the damage. We insisted because their demand conflicted with our principles, and eventually we intended to call a strike. Faced with our resolute refusal, the Bruderhof held consultations and finally accepted our proposal. They even said that "We have realized that 'the Zionists' have some fine principles."[15]

The encounter between the two groups impressed both sides and left mainly pleasant memories. Georg Barth, who held a senior position in the community's leadership wrote:

> The Zionist group lived with us for many months.... They worked in all the farming branches.... From time to time they were visited by representatives of the

London office who wanted to find out how they were doing.... Despite our differences, we developed a mutual understanding.... They were Jews and we Christians, but this did not interfere at all.... We were very interested in the kibbutz movement and wanted to find out how they maintain communal life without religious beliefs.[16]

I heard some recollections in the same vein from Arnold Mason, who was born in Birmingham and was among the first Englishmen to join the Bruderhof in Germany. He held a senior position in the Cotswold community and had negotiated the acceptance of the Jewish trainees with the *Hechalutz* representatives. "We agreed gladly," he recalled, "because we urgently needed hands. Furthermore, it was very much in the spirit of the times to absorb young refugees from Germany."[17]

In general terms one may say that the members of the Cotswold Bruderhof remember "the Zionists" fondly. I had the chance of talking with some of the Bruderhof old-timers and heard recollections that bore a striking similarity to those of the Hazorea people. It was amazing to find that they, too, recalled "the ladder affair" exactly as it had been related by Larry El'or. Both sides remarked that the trainees were of great help during the dark days that befell England at the time, and especially as their neighbors' hostility increased. Larry recalled a significant episode, which he recounted as follows:

> There was a refugee living and working on the Bruderhof temporarily. He used to go to the village pub and on one occasion overheard the local farmers planning a pogrom against the Bruderhof because they suspected them of being German spies. He immediately returned to warn the community, whose members were confused by the dilemma of how they should react in the event of an attack because their pacifist principles forbade them to defend themselves or even to call the police. After some lengthy deliberation, someone came up with the idea of approaching Ze'ev Weiss, who was in charge of the trainees. He was told, "Since we don't want to rely on the police, we can't call them, but we cannot forbid you to report what is about to happen." Having taken the hint, we acted straight away and told the police. On the following day, as the farmers advanced on the Bruderhof, they found the police blocking their way and the pogrom was averted (this story has been verified by Bruderhof sources).[18]

Arnold Mason recalled another instance. In 1940, after the evacuation of Dunkirk, relations between the Bruderhof and their neighbors deteriorated even further. Rumors were circulated to the effect that disguised Gestapo agents were running the farm, that all the members were members of the Nazi movement, and that they maltreated the Jews on the farm. Accusations were published in the local press and readers letters began to appear. The Wilts and Gloucestershire Standard went so far as to publish a letter from a local resident who wrote that members of the Zionist training group were fleeing the farm as a result of harsh treatment by "the Germans."[19]

On reading this, Ze'ev Weiss immediately wrote a letter to the paper, in which he stated categorically:

> I wish, on behalf of the Jewish group, to refute these false allegations...Hitler has driven us out of Germany and we are happy that we have found at the Bruderhof a settlement prepared to give us good training.... Our work here is exactly the same as that of the Brothers.... We feel, therefore, no injustice of any kind. Contrary to the allegations made by Mr. Pressland, we have no complaints of any kind to make against the Bruderhof's attitude towards us.
>
> On behalf of the Zionist group,
> Werner Weiss[20]

According to Arnold Mason, Weiss's letter was of the utmost importance in putting a stop to the defamation campaign against the Bruderhof, albeit it could not prevent their ultimate emigration from England.

World War II and Emigration from England

During the early days of the war, the good relations that had previously existed between the Bruderhof and their neighbors were still maintained. In October, 1939, the Bruderhof communes were visited by the tribunal that dealt with the status of "enemy aliens" and it determined that all the Bruderhof members were eligible to remain where they were and carry on with their lives as before. At the time, Germans resident in Britain were not yet under the threat of internment in detention camps, and the only constraint imposed upon them was that their movements were limited to within the county borders.[21]

In April, 1940, a prominent London newspaper published an article in support of the Bruderhof and their way of life, without bothering to conceal their pacifist beliefs which were, as far as many of their neighbors were concerned, like a red rag to a bull.[22] It was at this time that The Plough published a report on a series of lectures and meetings with various groups that had continued undisturbed:

> During the past six months, since the outbreak of war, hardly a week has gone by without two or more of our members visiting friends and addressing meetings up and down the country. For this we feel thankful—for what is the use of a community

without a "sending out?" What is the use of a message if is not delivered? About thirty-five meetings were held, and a great number of friends visited privately.

There are now one hundred and thirty active members at Oaksey and Ashton Keynes. The novitiate, strengthened by fourteen newcomers since September, now numbers nineteen...making a total of one hundred and fifty-three fully surrendered members. With 130 children and thirty-five guests and helpers, 318 men, women and children were living at both communities at the beginning of March, 1940—eighty-four at the Oaksey Bruderhof Community and 234 at the Cotswold Bruderhof Community.

Since our last full report in the summer of 1939, there has been a great deal of forward movement in the economic sphere. The considerable increase of land in 1938-39 from 300 acres to 820 acres has been consolidated and new activities have arisen from this increase; for instance, a vegetable, poultry and bread round in Swindon that was inaugurated last autumn, and a milk round in Wroughton.

Later in this review, the writer expresses gratitude to the British government for the correct relations it maintained with them:

We are most grateful to the government for their kind and considerate treatment which enables us to devote all our resources to the prosecution, not of war, but of peace and brotherhood among men, which we feel is the best expression of gratitude we can give to this country.[23]

As the war progressed, the situation of the Bruderhof was further exacerbated, for an international group of pacifists whose roots were in Germany and the majority of whose membership was in fact German, was a potential source of problems and tension during wartime. In a newsletter published in October, 1939, the Bruderhof declared that despite the fact that they were unable to participate in the war for reasons of conscience, they were prepared to do their bit and ease the privations of the civilian population of the county by supplying agricultural produce and especially milk for the children. They were aware of the sensitivity of their presence in the area, and reported on the closure that had been imposed upon them, according to the conditions of which the Germans among them were prohibited from leaving a radius of five miles from the border of their farm, which made the marketing of their produce very difficult.[24]

The summer of 1940 saw a serious deterioration in the situation of the Bruderhof in Britain. After the fall of Holland and the evacuation of the British Expeditionary Force (BEF) from Dunkirk in May, 1940, the ring of hostility around them tightened. The local papers published letters calling for the detention of Bruderhof members in internment camps, and a question on this matter was asked in Parliament. Voices in their defence were heard in the debate that followed, saying that they were an anti-Nazi group that had found refuge in Britain.[25]

But the situation deteriorated and anti-German feeling in Britain reached new heights. Hostility, boycotts, and physical attacks on Bruderhof members by their neighbors and local residents increased. Hysteria replaced suspicion, with the Bruderhof now viewed as a fifth column. There were rumors that signals had been seen from the farm at night, and that their fields were covered with concrete blocks "to prevent German aircraft from landing." There were numerous cases of harassment by members of the Home Guard, who conducted spot searches to uncover arms caches.[26] Horrifying rumors told of a "dictatorial regime" within the commune and of "Gestapo methods" through which the community's elite held sway over the rank and file members. Despite the fact that these rumors were vigorously denied, the feelings of suspicion between the Bruderhof and their neighbors remained.[27]

It was during this period that the hostile elements lay economic siege to the Bruderhof. They tried to limit their rights to sell their milk in Swindon on the grounds that as they were not liable for conscription, they enjoyed an unfair manpower advantage and, thus, their competitors exploited the atmosphere of patriotism that prevailed in Britain at the time to create hostility toward the Bruderhof.

One of the most prominent inciters was the local vicar, the Reverend R. H. Wells, who claimed that he had received letters from members of his flock daily with complaints about the great freedom still enjoyed by the Bruderhof, whom the writers perceived as a fifth column. He concluded his letter with the warning that if the authorities took no action, there was a distinct danger that the Bruderhof's neighbors would take the law into their own hands.[28]

The campaign against the Bruderhof shifted to the political arena when the matter was brought before Mr. W. W. Wakefield, Member of Parliament for the Swindon Division. The members of the Bruderhof met him, but had no success in convincing him of their right to refuse to serve in the armed forces on religious grounds; they also did not succeed in convincing him of the sincerity of their opposition to Nazism and of their readiness to contribute to the war effort through agriculture. In the course of their meeting, the MP had some harsh words to say to them:

> I must say quite frankly that I have no sympathy with you.... We are engaged in a life-and-death struggle, and you do nothing but hide behind our soldiers, sailors

and airmen...you are not going to get my support for anything that is going to shelter people like you from taking their proper place in the defence of the country which has given you and your members protection. As for taking another man's business while he or his assistants are in the fighting line, that is something which I shall fight with all my power.[29]

The Home Office, despite its earlier sympathetic attitude toward the Bruderhof and in the light of the prevailing state of belligerency, now found it necessary to discuss the possibility of detaining the German members "for their own safety." The entire issue was discussed at high level in both Parliament and the House of Lords. In the course of the debate, the Duke of Devonshire referred to the plea that a closure be imposed on the Bruderhof, and said that the matter was being dealt with by the Home Secretary. At the same time, he derided those who suspected them of being a fifth column, saying that as an ex-intelligence officer, "the last person I should dream of employing as a German spy would be one who spoke little, if any, English and wore a long beard and a long dressing gown. These unhappy brothers have become the victims of so much suspicion and antagonism that they themselves are begging to be interned, and in fact they are in some danger unless they are interned."[30]

His Grace's remarks were not, however, completely accurate because the Brothers had not requested protection in an internment camp. A short while after this debate, the Bruderhof members were given to understand from the Home Office spokesman's remarks that all their foreign members would have to be detained in an internment camp. This of course meant that the community was liable to be split up and in order to prevent an internal schism, they decided that there was no choice but to emigrate from Britain.

In the summer of 1940, the Brothers petitioned the Home Office with a request to allow them to leave Britain. This emigration of some 350 people in wartime, with the Atlantic swarming with German U-boats, was both very difficult and extremely dangerous, but this did not deter them. A frantic search for a new country of refuge got under way. The Swiss Hans Meier and the Briton Guy Johnson (a pacifist with a legal background who had joined the community in 1938) were chosen as the community's vanguard to lands across the ocean.[31]

Travel in wartime was no easy thing for pacifists and commune members. Their first problem was to obtain visas to one of the American countries to which they intended to emigrate, and this was solved in a most unusual manner. The Bruderhof had maintained contact with the Jewish committee that dealt with the absorption of refugees from Europe, and as a result had absorbed about a dozen refugee children. The parents of one such child had managed to save themselves and had reached Venezuela, and they had requested the committee to send their son to them there, but because of the high risk involved in such a journey, no volunteers could be found to accompany the boy. When the Bruderhof heard of this, they immediately expressed their readiness to accompany the child and the task was given to Hans Meier, who had already been chosen to further their emigration from Britain. Hans and the child reached New York in August, 1940, but the American immigration authorities and the Jewish committee in New York were not happy with the fact that a Christian was accompanying a Jewish child, and so Hans's assignment was cancelled. Luckily, he was given a ninety-day visa for the United States and Canada, and this short period allowed him to begin looking for a refuge for the Bruderhof.[32]

There were numerous friends in North America who were ready and willing to provide assistance: The American and Canadian Hutterite leaders, members of Congress, and public figures who had good relations with the commune movements (Henry Lasserre, for example). The initial attempts at finding a new location took place in Canada, where the Bruderhof could be close to the Hutterite communities. The Hutterite leaders put out the first feelers for a refuge for the Bruderhof as early as August, 1940, but the Canadian immigration authorities rejected them on the grounds that they were not interested in accepting German pacifists with the war at its height—they had problems enough with the Hutterites. The requests made by other friends were also rejected.[33]

Once the attempts in Canada had failed, the Bruderhof turned south. They had many American Quaker friends and also one of Eberhard Arnold's relatives who held a senior position in the American administration, and through their good offices they succeeded in reaching Eleanor Roosevelt, the President's wife, who invited them to breakfast at the White House. She showed them a great deal of sympathy during their talk but explained that at present, on the eve of the upcoming Presidential election, her influence on the President was limited. She suggested that they wait until after the election, but time was running out as the British government had told the Bruderhof that they must leave the country without delay, otherwise they would be forced to intern all the communes' foreigners.

There were also some attempts to purchase land at the Shaker settlement near New Lebanon, which was very suitable for communal life, but once the Shakers heard that the Bruderhof maintained family life, which was something diametrically opposed to their principles, the projected purchase fell through. And so it became clear that under the prevailing circumstances, the Bruderhof had no chance of finding refuge in the United States.[34]

Once these efforts had failed, help eventually came from the Mennonite Orie Miller, an old friend of the Bruderhof from Germany in the twenties. When he heard of the dead end they were facing, he approached the Paraguayan ambassador to the United States with whom he had maintained contact from the time the Mennonites emigrated to Paraguay in 1929. The ambassador contacted the President of Paraguay, who immediately gave his permission to absorb the Bruderhof under the same conditions that had applied to the Mennonite immigrants; in other words, they would be given the right to organize their settlements according to their principles, to speak their own language in their schools, and be exempt from military service. Meier promptly sent the news to the Bruderhof in England and received an affirmative response together with instructions to obtain Paraguayan entry visas and transit visas through Argentina. And so Hans Meier, who had set out to accompany a Jewish child to Venezuela, found himself enmeshed in making immigration arrangements to a South American country, the language and location of which were unknown to him. Much later, he admitted in his memoirs that "when we set out to find refuge, we had never even thought of Paraguay, and now we had to find out where it was on the map!"[35]

The Bruderhof members in England received the news with surprise and confusion. On the one hand, they were very happy that they had finally found a country of refuge, while on the other, they realized that not a single one of their number knew anything at all about it. What were the people like? What kind of climate did the country have? Was there room for settlement? Was it all jungle? They immediately opened their atlases and encyclopedias and began to collect information about Paraguay.

Meier remained in South America. His job was to do everything necessary to facilitate the journey to Paraguay, including the obtaining of transit visas through Argentina. The Argentine government demanded a

$7,000 bond as surety that the immigrants would not remain in Argentina and once again, the American Quakers came to the rescue and put up the bond. Entry into Paraguay also had to be arranged, and to this end Meier had to travel alone to the port of Buenos Aires before the group arrived. On a horrendous journey by leaky ships, trains, and river boats, Meier travelled south via Brazil and Paraguay, finally reaching Buenos Aires where he was to meet the Bruderhof groups that were to begin sailing from Liverpool in December, 1940.[36]

At the same time the Bruderhof in England began to ready themselves for their journey. They first had to sell their farms, and Oaksey was sold immediately, its inhabitants moving to the Cotswold farm. It should be noted that the Home Office gave them every assistance, helping in the sale of the Cotswold farm and also in reserving berths on the Blue Star Line's transatlantic vessels, which carried meat and wheat from Argentina. The problem was not only that these ships had a very small number of first-class berths but because they had to split up into groups, the fares were very high. It was also not easy to organize the emigration in groups from a social point of view.

In their last year in England their numbers were swelled by many British pacifists. These new members were faced with having to make a speedy decision to emigrate to an unknown tropical country and at the same time adopt a new faith and way of life by baptism and making a vow that would bind them for life. Those who chose to do so underwent a rapid process of acceptance.[37] It is worth noting that British pacifists continued to join the Bruderhof even after emigration had got under way and the first group was on its way from England to Paraguay.

One of the pacifists who joined at this time was John Winter, who is today one of the Bruderhof's older members. He says:

I joined in 1940 when I was twenty. The war was at its height and I felt that my Christian beliefs forbade me from taking part in it. I sought a way of realizing my opposition to war which would benefit society. I first heard of the Bruderhof when I was a farm worker on farms around London and so I went to visit them. My visit coincided with the first group leaving for Paraguay. Something that defies definition happened to me on this first encounter but it was something that made me want to visit them again and get to know them better. A great many people of pacifist persuasion visited the Bruderhof at that time. At the beginning of 1941 I decided to link my destiny with theirs. I knew that this would oblige me to emigrate to Paraguay with them because the last group was due to leave in a few months time. I would not say that I really wanted to travel to an unknown country called Paraguay...on the contrary, I had every reason to be frightened by the prospect of sailing off across the Atlantic and leaving England behind for a distant tropical country. But I was driven to seek a way to a life of brotherhood with people of like faith. I therefore had no hesitation in asking to become a candidate and to be baptized before leaving England. I did not feel that I was fleeing, avoiding the vagaries of life or abandoning a country at war. On the contrary, I felt that I was going to a life of sacrifice which was, to a certain extent, equivalent to the sacrifices being made by my friends and peers out of their loyalty to their country and the rules of war imposed upon it, and in the belief that this was the right thing to do...under those circumstances I felt an inner wholeness in that I, too, was giving my life to something I believed was right.... It was with this feeling that I was baptized, joined the commune, and left for Paraguay with the last group.[38]

In the autumn of 1940, 350 men, women, and children of the Bruderhof readied themselves for the journey to distant South America. Sailing the Atlantic at the height of the submarine war was fraught with danger. The first group of eighty people sailed from Liverpool in December, 1940, and landed at Buenos Aires just before Christmas. The voyage in first class was an expensive and unavoidable pleasure that took its toll of the community's meager funds at a time when the hardships and privations of the Paraguayan jungle awaited them. Two of the community's children, Elizabeth Zumpe and Nina Wright, recall:

The Cotswold Bruderhof was bought by the British government—the Home Office—so there was a considerable amount of money available for the expensive trip to South America.... The Blue Star Line vessels were large freighters with only a first class for passengers. To us children, our ship seemed like something out of a fairy tale—beautiful and luxurious.[39]

It was a very dangerous voyage because it was wartime, and there was a big submarine war going on so it was very difficult to cross the seas. We had to zigzag north to Iceland, then across the Atlantic and down the coast of America to avoid the German submarines. I do not remember any fear in the group. We felt we were under God's protection.[40]

Elizabeth Zumpe recalls the sad farewell from the ship's crew in Buenos Aires:

We had all made drawings for our favorite stewards, and many of us cried as they stood in a long line to say goodbye to us. We all knew that their voyage back would be a dangerous one, and in fact all the Blue Star Line ships were sunk by German submarines during the war.[41]

Arnold Mason, too, summed up the community's Atlantic crossing with amazement at their great good fortune:

> Our people crossed the Atlantic eleven times during those years and nothing happened to them. A large number of the vessels on which we sailed were torpedoed on the return voyage. We had the feeling that God was protecting us.[42]

It was hardly surprising that when they reached South American shores, all the passengers experienced a sense of release from what had been a long nightmare.

The English Bruderhof—The Establishment of Wheathill

The last group of the Bruderhof left England in April, 1941. Three British members, Stanley Fletcher and Charles and Hella Headland, were left behind to complete the sale of the farm property to the Home Office, which had purchased the farm for the establishment of an approved school. During an air-raid on London, the office of the solicitors who were handling the transfer of the property was hit, thus compelling the three to continue living at the farm for two months longer than originally planned, and while they were there they continued to be the contact address for old pacifist friends and supporters. It should be mentioned here that prior to the departure of the last group, Heini Arnold, who was Servant of the Word, authorized the three who stayed behind to become the nucleus of a new community, and he did so because of the uncertainty that clouded the fate of those sailing for Paraguay.

Indeed, by the summer of that year the three had been joined by ten pacifists and they became a small community that wished to live according to the tenets of the Bruderhof.[43] Stanley Fletcher recalls the forming of this small group:

> The last group left for South America and on that very day the first person with the serious intention of joining us arrived; three days later, Dick Whitty, a Scotsman, arrived. One after another, people came, including some we had never heard of before. We did not have permission to take them to Paraguay with us, so we knew we were running into a problem.[44]

By the winter of 1941 through 1942 this group numbered nineteen, including two married couples. At Christmas of 1941 they decided to continue living as a commune and it was at this time that the "Brothers" decided to write to Paraguay and seek advice on the continuation of the Bruderhof in England. However, before they were able to receive a reply from Paraguay they had to find somewhere to live because the ownership of the Cotswold farm had already been transferred. They searched throughout Wales and the Midlands and finally found a farm on the North Wales border in the county of Shropshire. The story goes that they found the farm after Charles Headland, a member of the Bruderhof, told the man who was driving him that he was a pacifist. On hearing this bald statement, the irate driver told Headland to get out of the car and left him at the roadside. Headland, who was left to find a roof for the night, reached a lonely farm which, it transpired, was not only up for sale, but also at very good terms. And thus Wheathill Farm was purchased.[45]

The farm of one hundred and eighty acres was situated on a ridge of hills at an elevation of 1,000 feet overlooking the mountains of North Wales. "It was a poor farm with an amazing view," said John Bazeley, who joined the group in its early years. There were twenty people in the founding group in March, 1942. The land had been neglected and so Wheathill had been graded as a Class-C farm, and the problem that faced them was how to make a living out of the farm with people who had no farming experience at all. There was no agricultural machinery to help them clear up the disorder because during the war, industrial production was directed to the war effort and it was difficult to purchase agricultural equipment. Dick Whitty had this to say about the difficulties they faced: "To build up a farming Bruderhof in the middle of a war, with no farmers among us, was a task that could frighten us or one we could only tackle in faith."[46]

Fortunately, they enjoyed good relationships with their neighbors and the local farmers gave them the benefit of their experience and sometimes their labor, particularly in renovating the farm buildings and converting them into suitable accommodation in the face of the harsh winter they experienced in their first year there.

Poverty and hardship were their lot and although they were without even basic furnishings during their first days on the farm, their spirits were high. They felt that they were laying the foundations for the realization of their ideals. "They were poor but they had a wealth of spirit and this was why we were attracted to them. We were particularly captivated by the vision of communal life, towards the realization of which they strove," writes John Bazeley on why he joined. "There was a special magic, because apart from the communal lifestyle, they lived together with Germans who were thought to be 'the enemy.'"[47]

It is noteworthy that the great majority of those who joined at that time were pacifists who sought a way of positive expression of their opposition to war. The commune's way of life of brotherhood and harmony appealed to a large group of pacifists as a worthy alternative to a regime of hostility and wars. As their consciences directed them to disregard the call to participate in the war effort, they experienced a strong desire to find something positive, of which they would be able to say, "This I can do." Derek Wardle, one of the pacifists who joined them says, "We wanted to find an alternative way of life...we needed to find a place in which people could live together on a joint basis." Regarding the attraction that Wheathill held for him and others like him, he said:

> I think that it must have been the atmosphere of the place, because the exterior was depressing: a dilapidated farmhouse, ramshackle farm buildings, fields covered with weeds, mud everywhere and wretched buildings...but there was an atmosphere of faith and hope that was replete with an inner enthusiasm and joy. I know that this was what attracted me, nothing external. I am sure that this was how it was with the others who joined at that time.[48]

In the meantime, the Bruderhof in Paraguay had sent their approval for the establishment of a new community in England. Encouraged by this news and an influx of new pacifist members, the members of the group decided to establish a new community in England, to be called "The Wheathill Bruderhof."

Notes

1. *The Plough,* vols. 1 and 2 (Quarterly of Bruderhof communities. Bromdon: The Plough Publishing House, 1938); ibid., no. 1 (1939): 16; *Communities in Britain* (Cotswold Bruderhof Press, 1938), 79–80; *Memories of Our Early Years,* vol. 2 (Collection of pamphlets published by the Plough Publishing House, Rifton, N.Y.: 1973–79), chap. H ; ibid., vol. 2, chap. H, 35.
2. Allain, Roger, *The Community That Failed* (San Francisco, Calif.: Carrier Pigeon Press, 1992), 25–26.
3. Zablocki, Benjamin, *The Joyful Community* (Baltimore, Md.: Penguin, 1971), 82.
4. *Communities in Britain,* 28–30.
5. *The Plough,* vol. 2, no. 2 (1939): 63–64.
6. *The Friend* (21 July 1939).
7. The leaflet is in the Bruderhof archive at Spring Valley.
8. *The Plough,* vol. 2, no. 1(1939): 17–22; vol. 2, no. 3.
9. Ibid., vol. 2, no. 2: 49–52.
10. Ibid, vol. 2, no. 3 (Autumn, 1939).

11. Allain, op. cit., 40.
12. *The Plough* (1938, 1939); Interview with Arnold Mason, November, 1991.
13. Correspondence between the Bruderhof and the Home Secretary, Sir Samuel Hoare, in *The Plough*, vol. 2, no. 2 (1939): 60-61.
14. *The Plough* (2 February 1939). See also unpublished survey of the Bruderhof members, Steph and Gill Barth, on the rescue of Jewish refugees (Pleasant View, 1992).
15. Author's interview with members of Kibbutz Hazorea, July, 1991.
16. Interview with Georg Barth, July, 1990.
17. Interview with Arnold Mason, November, 1991.
18. This incident was described by Hans Meier in an interview in July, 1990, and his description tallies with that of Larry.
19. See 8 May 1940 issue of the *Wilts and Gloucestershire Standard*.
20. See 11 May 1940 issue of the *Wilts and Gloucestershire Standard*.
21. *The Plough*, vol. 2, no. 3 (1939).
22. "German Exiles Share All Possessions," *Evening Standard* (4 April 1940).
23. *The Plough*, vol. 3, no. 1 (Spring, 1940).
24. Letter in the Spring Valley archive (October, 1939).
25. *Swindon Advertiser* (24 May 1940); *Daily Herald* (27 May 1940).
26. Allain, op. cit., 64.
27. *Wilts and Gloucestershire Standard* (11 and 18 May 1940).
28. *Evening Advertiser* (23 and 24 April 1940); *News Chronicle* (24 April 1940).
29. *Evening Advertiser* (25 May 1940). Also published in the London *Daily Express, Daily Mail,* and *Daily Herald,* from 27 May 1940.
30. *Parliamentary Debates—House of Lords,* vol. 116, no. 58 (12 June 1940).
31. See Hans Meier's memoirs in *Memories,* op. cit., vol. 1, no. 12: 27.
32. Meier, *Memories,* 22—24.
33. Durnbaugh, Donald, "Relocation of the German Bruderhof to England, South America, North America," *Communal Societies,* vol. 11 (Evansville, In.: Journal of Communal Studies Assoc., 1991): 72.
34. Meier, op. cit., 84; Zablocki; op. cit., 73; Durnbaugh, op. cit., 24-28.
35. Meier, *Memories,* vol. 1, chap. L: 37.
36. Arnold, Emmy, *Torches Together* (Rifton, N.Y.: Plough Publishing House, 1974), 218-19.
37. Allain, op. cit., 74-75; Cocksedge, Edmund, *Vagabond for Peace* (House of Freedom Christian Community Publication, 1991), 55.
38. Interview with John Winter, October, 1992.
39. Zumpe, Elizabeth Bohlken, in *The KIT Annual, 1991* (The Collected Newsletters of the KIT Information Service, San Francisco, Calif.), 110
40. Wright, Nina, in *Memories,* vol. 3A, 58.
41. *KIT Annual, 1991*: 112.
42. Interview with Arnold Mason, November, 1991.
43. *50th Anniversary of the Wheathill Bruderhof* (Rifton, N.Y.: Plough Publishing House, 1992), 1-6.
44. *The Plough*, no. 31 (May/June, 1992).
45. *50th Anniversary,* 29.
46. *The Plough*, no. 31 (1992).
47. Bazeley, John (Woodcrest, 1991); Zumpe, Elizabeth, in *KIT Annual* (1991): 289.
48. Wardle, Derek, in *50th Anniversary,* 27.

5

Isolated Communities in Paraguay

The first group of Bruderhof emigrants landed at the port of Buenos Aires on 12 December 1940 and immediately continued on their journey north. They arrived at the port of Asunción after a long journey up the Paraná River on an Argentinean vessel, and after the luxury of the first-class accommodation on the transatlantic voyage, the conditions on this vessel quickly brought them face-to-face with the kind of reality that awaited them in South America. They spent a further three days in the Paraguayan capital until they found a river boat that would take them on to Puerto Casado and from there they travelled by train to the station at Kilometer 145, where their Mennonite hosts awaited them. From there, their hosts took them to their settlement, Fernheim, which was located in the jungle region of the Paraguayan Gran Chaco. The members of the Bruderhof immediately saw that this region was unsuitable for the establishment of a settlement because of its isolation, transport conditions, and tropical climate. They remained at the Mennonite settlement for some two months and at the same time began looking for a more agreeable location to the east of the Paraná River, which was thought to be more suitable for settlement. It was then that the Mennonites from the Friesland settlement came to their aid and recommended a 20,000 acre farm which was located not far from them and which was owned by a German settler named Rutenberg. A delegation that visited the farm decided that it was indeed suitable for settlement, and so it was duly purchased and the first group moved in before the second group arrived from England.[1]

The farm, Primavera, was located in the eastern part of the country, some 160 kilometers northeast of Asunción, in a subtropical region of woods, forest, and grassy plains. Access to the region from the capital was by river boat along the upper reaches of the Paraguay River to the small port of Rosario, and from there by ox cart along dirt roads for approximately eighty kilometers. As none of the Bruderhof members had any experience in farm work in a subtropical region, the early days on the farm were very hard. Although the Mennonites from the nearby Friesland settlement, who had been in Paraguay for many years, made the Bruderhof very welcome and gave them every assistance as they took their first steps, relations between the two communities did not become close. It quickly became clear to the Bruderhof people that these German settlers who, in the distant past, had been close to the Hutterites in their Anabaptist faith and had fled Russia in the wake of the forced collectivism there, hated communism and therefore had certain suspicions and reservations about the Bruderhof communes. What aggravated their relations even more was the National-Socialist propaganda that permeated the Mennonite group and the fact that they maintained spiritual and cultural ties with Nazi Germany. They were sent German school books and equipment, and during the war a number of their young people decided to go to Germany and join the army. Years later, Hans Meier would say of them that "they were a strange mixture of Anabaptist Mennonites and German colonialists who had been infected by Nazism," and added that "although they were only six miles away from Primavera, neighborly relations did not develop and we had no cultural contact with them."[2]

The remaining groups of Bruderhof emigrants arrived from England during the first months of 1941, including the new members who had joined on the eve of the departure for Paraguay. The last group crossed the Atlantic and reached Primavera in June, 1941, thus completing the arrival of the entire community at their new settlement. They numbered 350 men, women, and children.

On their arrival at the old farm they found only one building and a number of lean-tos, which could not be used for accommodation as they were already occupied by some of the farm workers, so their first task was to build temporary housing for the population of the new settlement. Despite their principles regarding hired labor, they had no choice but to seek the help of local workers whose skills they needed for putting up the first buildings and cutting down the trees needed for this purpose.

During the first few months they lived in lean-tos, which were a kind of wide hall, or *hallen,* covered with a straw roof. Each family was allotted a roof and a small piece of land, the borders of which were marked by hanging screens. A lean-to dining room was built in this fashion, with an adjoining kitchen and a "hall" in which they sat on benches at tables made of the local wood. Using this method of construction they also built the rest of the farm buildings with the help of the Paraguayan workers, who were the only ones who possessed the necessary skills for building lean-tos and thatching roofs.

Initially, they cut down the trees using the primitive native methods, but they quickly realized that these were both difficult and inefficient. As a result, they immediately set to work building a sawmill, and with the first wooden beams they produced they built the first buildings of the first commune, Isla Margarita. Fortunately, they had been able to bring with them a large number of tools and machines from the Cotswold farm, and with these they commenced their agricultural operations, but not before they had prepared the land suitable for cultivation and by burning parts of the forest that encroached upon the borders of the settlement. They later began to prepare a market garden and land for other field crops.

While these initial preparations at the farm got under way, the women and children remained at the nearby Mennonite settlement. The adult brothers employed in the preparatory work at Primavera were divided into work teams: the building team which, together with the local farm workers, built the first buildings, and a wood-cutting team, which worked together with the Paraguayans, learning their skills at the same time. There was also a team that dug a well. During the initial period, water was brought from the nearby stream in barrels on ox carts, and this was done by yet another team who were taught how to work with horses and oxen by the Paraguayans. In the old farmyard they kept several cows that supplied them, and the children in particular, with fresh milk.

May of that year saw the arrival from England of an old steam engine (made in 1910!), which made an important contribution to the operation of the sawmill, and later to the running of a generator, which provided the settlements with electricity. Some agricultural machinery and a printing press, which had been despatched separately, also arrived from England together with the last group. This was essential equipment that improved the living conditions and enabled them to organize their work more efficiently.

After the first temporary buildings had been put up at Isla Margarita and each family had been allotted living quarters, the time had come to bring in the families that had been living at the neighboring Mennonite settlement. As work on the dining room and kitchen had not yet been completed, the first meals were taken outdoors. The most acute problems, particularly during the first few months, were the bad housing conditions and the poor diet. Hygiene conditions were particularly bad and the harsh climate, to which they were still unused, added to their hardships even further. During this period the majority suffered from malaria, infections, and tropical sores, and the suffering of the children was particularly great. Many of them suffered from contagious diseases and various epidemics, and in that first year nine children died of malnutrition and as a result of the poor hygienic conditions.[3]

It quickly became clear that the new settlement, Isla Margarita, was too small for 195 adults and fifty-five children, and so they immediately set about establishing a second one at Loma Jhoby, on the site of an old farm about two miles away from Isla Margarita. The first pioneering group moved there in January, 1942, and they were joined by an additional seventy people a few months later.

A third settlement on the lands of Primavera, called Ibate, was established under special circumstances four years after Loma Jhoby. The purpose of its establishment was the Bruderhof's wish to absorb European orphans immediately after the end of the World War II. The original plan called for the establishment of a children's community at this settlement, who would be adopted by members of the new commune. Upon realizing that the plan called for financial assistance, which they hoped to obtain from friends, they published its details in the local press. The Montevideo newspaper, *La Idea*, published an article about it together with an open letter from the Bruderhof:

> The Hutterian Society of Brothers seeks to absorb thirty orphans from war-torn Europe and is making arrangements to bring them here. The responsibility and obligation of helping innocent children devolves upon all those who were not forced to suffer the horrors of the war.... This assistance involves a financial investment for the absorption of each child; for the building of suitable housing and the purchase of equipment, before the necessary outlay for living expenses. As we ourselves are too poor to bear this burden alone, we hereby turn to our friends with a plea for help.[4]

In 1946, even before any donations and other assistance had been received, people were sent to Europe to take charge of the children. The plan was to have been put into action with the cooperation of the

Bruderhof community in England. The emissaries from Paraguay toured the refugee camps and interviewed hundreds of children from whom they were to select the group. The international bodies that were dealing with the refugees gave them every assistance, but it was the German authorities that set bureaucratic obstacles in their way at every turn and prevented the plan's fruition. It became clear that the German authorities were not interested in sending the children off to this religious group in far-off Paraguay and so, after months of hard work, the emissaries returned to Paraguay empty handed and deeply disappointed. Once the plan for a children's community fell through, Ibate became a conventional commune.[5]

As an alternative to the plan for bringing orphaned children to Paraguay, it was proposed to the Bruderhof representatives in Europe that the communities absorb displaced persons from the refugee camps. The Bruderhof accepted this proposal with alacrity and expressed their readiness to accept a group of 120, including forty children. It was obvious that a group of this size and composition could not undergo the usual procedure of acceptance as candidates to the Bruderhof, so it was agreed that the refugees would be accepted as guests in the English and Paraguayan Bruderhof communes for a two-year period, at the end of which they would be free to decide whether to join the commune or leave. This arrangement was accepted by all the bodies concerned and the Bruderhof representatives immediately set to work on the selection of candidates. At the same time, work was begun on the preparation of living quarters in both the English and Paraguayan communes and once all the preparations were completed, approximately 100 refugees set out for Paraguay in October, 1948. The group was a diverse one, with the majority of East European origin—Poles, Lithuanians, Latvians, Czechs, and Ukrainians—and although their unwillingness to return to their communist homelands was a common factor, they agreed to go to the Bruderhof communities despite the communal aspects of the absorbing communities. There were some grounds for suspicion regarding the sincerity of this agreement when from the moment they arrived at the first South American port of call, they began to disappear. It quickly became apparent that all they had wanted was to get away from the camps in Europe by exploiting the Bruderhof's offer in order to find a country of refuge. Even those who finally did arrive at the Paraguayan communities showed no real desire to be absorbed and by the end of 1948 there were only a dozen or so of them left, and they, too left a short while later.[6]

Social Order and Economics at the Primavera Communities

The three Bruderhof communes at Primavera were established at a distance of two to three miles from one another and although the production and service branches of all three were separate, all their economic activities and income were managed jointly. Isla Margarita had its sawmill, wood workshops, a fruit juice factory, and a bookbinding shop, while Loma Jhoby kept a beef herd and a slaughterhouse, and it was there that the central hospital was later built. The third community, Ibate, had a bakery, shoemaker's shop, sewing workshop, dairy herd, chickens, and the biggest central library in the Paraguayan settlement, which housed some 20,000 volumes, mainly in German and English.

The three communities made their livelihoods from the various branches of agriculture that they had established. On the cultivable land, which covered approximately 40 percent of the total acreage, they grew maize, wheat, sugarcane, manioc (or cassava, a tuberous potatolike root), and rice. Adjacent to the settlements they cultivated market gardens for the supply of vegetables to the local population, and there was an abundance of fruit that grew wild all around. There were tall citrus trees, overloaded with fruit which, so the story went, had been planted in the distant past by Jesuit settlers. Initially they employed European farming techniques, but soon began to combine these with local methods, which increased both their productivity and yields.

One of the most important production branches was the sawmill they had set up in the early days, which provided wood for building and later supplied raw material to their decorative wood products factory. Much later, this factory was to become an important source of income and gain a fine reputation in the capital, Asunción. Another central agricultural branch established in the early days was the beef herd, which consisted of 2,500 head of Cebu stock, some of which were crossed with Holsteins. Sixty of the best cows were selected to become the nucleus of the dairy herd and although it attained relatively high yields, it was not profitable and could not even supply the quantity of milk required for home consumption.

The Paraguayan communities had to aim toward self-sufficiency and here they enjoyed the advantages provided by the size, constituents, and variety of their population. At the beginning they had their steam engine, which provided them with energy, and in 1950 they installed electricity in all the communes for lighting, agricultural and industrial use, services, the dining room, laundry, and especially the hospital. A number of agricultural implements were brought from the United States, including two tractors, and two trucks were imported from Britain. Due to the underdeveloped Paraguayan technological know-how, it was impossible to operate this machinery under normal service conditions and the mechanics were forced to improvise repairs on site, which in Europe would have been done in garages and service workshops.[7]

Despite the variety of agricultural branches, it was difficult to make a living from farming and so the Bruderhof members were forced to seek additional sources of income, which led to a number of members working outside the commune. Among these were members who had been employed as agricultural advisors in government agricultural and engineering companies, at United Nations experimental stations, and in the various agencies of the Pan-American Union.[8]

In 1942 they rented a house in Asunción, which was used as an office that represented the Bruderhof in all their dealings with the government, and which also filled the role of their agency for the buying and selling of produce to and from local merchants. The treasurer was responsible for the sale of their produce sent to the Asunción market. Next door to the house there was a shop that sold the Primavera decorative wood products, which gained a fine reputation and were bought mainly by tourists. As life in the communities became more firmly established and Primavera's economic activity increased, the number of products that had to be purchased in the shops of Asunción also grew. As a result of this, Bruderhof economic and financial representatives took up permanent residence in the house. Initially there were twenty of them, but as time went by this number increased to fifty.

The majority of those who lived in the house were young people who had been sent to Asunción for higher education. The girls were sent to the nursing school, teachers training college and to learn sewing, while the boys were sent to vocational schools. This period of education in the capital was designed, *inter alia*, to give the youngsters a chance of having a good look at the outside world before deciding whether to join the community as full members.

Apart from its economic functions, the house in Asunción was also the contact address for friends of the Bruderhof. Many local youngsters, particularly students, showed great interest in the Bruderhof beliefs and way of life, and these encounters served to reveal the hardships of life in Paraguay under a fascist-dominated dictatorship to the young people of the Bruderhof. The meetings were of great value in broadening the Bruderhof youngsters' political horizons.[9]

Jean-Pierre Allain tells us something of the special atmosphere that pervaded the Bruderhof youngsters at the house in Asunción:

> At Bruderhof House there was a much freer atmosphere both among boys and girls and among the youth and the adults. The atmosphere was different from [that at] Primavera and also from [that at] El Arado. Nearly all the young people participated much more in community life. There was more of a happy friendship between us boys and [the] girls. There were wonderful outings…interesting talks and meetings with visitors, friends from outside.[10]

During those years relations were formed between the Zionist pioneering youth movements and their emissaries in Paraguay and Uruguay and the young people living in Bruderhof House in Asunción. This came about as a result of the house's proximity to the Jewish centers in the capital and the age of the people who lived in it, and it was these that attracted them to the Jewish youngsters.[11] Fida Meier, a member of Woodcrest, recalls:

> The young people who lived in the Bruderhof house in Asunción formed very good relations with members of the Zionist youth movement in Paraguay. We would meet once a month at either their club or our house. We were taught Israeli songs and dances and had many conversations about their way and ideals. In time, closer friendships developed and we were even invited to visit their homes.[12]

Transport conditions in Paraguay compelled the communities to use air transport between the settlements and the capital. A small airstrip for the use of light aircraft was built near Primavera and these were used mainly for medical purposes, if and when it was necessary to send people to the capital for medical treatment. The proliferation of contacts in the city also compelled the Bruderhof to establish a radio link between the settlements and the house in Asunción. The Primavera settlements also had a number of radios that enabled them to maintain some contact with the outside world.[13]

Life at the Primavera settlements was managed according to a fixed and routine order of the day that began at 5:00 A.M. and continued until

10:00 P.M.[14] Meals were taken at noon and seven o'clock in the evening in the dining rooms, which were the centers of community life. Breakfast and afternoon tea were taken in the family circle or in groups.

> At three every day, following the midday rest and tea-time, the men gathered to peel mandioca (manioc, the Paraguayan equivalent of the potato) and discuss problems pertaining to work. This was called the *Bruderrat* or brothers' work council, the body that managed work and directed community work. The main income-producing work departments—the dairy, farm, sawmills, turnery and building crew—were directly responsible to the *Bruderrat*.[15]

There was a division of labor between the men and women in which the men worked in the stables, with the dairy herd, on the farm, and in the sawmill and carpentry shop, while the women worked in the sewing workshop and in the childrens' houses. In the kitchen, the women worked under the guidance of a professional cook and there, in the laundry, the hospital, and the school, men and women worked together. Each branch had a head or coordinator and in discussions on work matters there was participatory democracy. Certain work assignments, such as guard duty, were done according to a rota system. There were two work coordinators; one for the men and another for the women.

The communities' members lived in extremely crowded conditions. The rooms were small and without glazed windows, and each family was allotted living quarters according to its size. Acclimatization to the primitive living conditions in the Paraguayan outback was one of the hardest things in their lives, and getting used to the subtropical conditions was particularly difficult for the Germans and English, who were used to a totally different climate. John Bazeley, who came to Paraguay from England in 1949 and lived there for thirteen years, admits that "getting used to the climate was hard. We expended a great deal of energy on acclimatization. It was only after we reached the United States that we realized how hard life had been in Paraguay."[16]

Despite the harsh conditions of life in Paraguay, the communities enjoyed a very active cultural life. They organized lectures, slide shows, movies, and plays. A small string orchestra was founded and true to Bruderhof tradition, choral singing was nurtured while the books and newspapers, which were sent from Europe, kept them abreast of world events.[17]

The communities maintained intensive educational activities from the earliest days in Paraguay, and these were embarked upon the moment that the physical conditions permitted. Suitable land was prepared, the trees upon it were burned, and lean-tos with walls and room dividers were built. The windows were unglazed, so the frames had to be closed with shutters during stormy weather.

Due to a lack of textbooks and notebooks, teaching in the early days was concentrated on oral instruction and later, after the war, they received donations of German and English textbooks. German was the language used for teaching in the early years, but teaching in English gradually gained a foothold and as time went by it became the second teaching language. It was only in the late fifties that Spanish became the third teaching language and the children became fluent in all three.[18]

By the end of the first year at Primavera there were 170 children, seventy of whom were of primary school age, and by 1952 the children numbered approximately 300. Thus, from the early fifties each community had its own school up to the ninth grade. The children attended school during the morning and either worked or played under the guidance of an adult during the afternoon. These activities, which were a kind of supplementary education, were called *Hort*. From the fifties onward efforts were made to expand the educational framework by adding a tenth year to the curriculum, which would prepare the pupils for the government matriculation examinations, and to this end they increased the number of hours devoted to Spanish. The subjects studied at school were the same as those at the state schools, with the exception of religious instruction, which took pride of place in the educational syllabus.[19]

A central high school serving the three communities was built after a number of years at Isla Margarita, and each day the children walked the three kilometers that separated the communities from the school. In order to reach the school the children had to pass through a forest that was reputed to be a home for wild animals, and so they were always accompanied to and from school by a number of adults. The teaching staff consisted of some twenty brothers and sisters, and apart from teaching *per se,* they engaged in social activities with the children, taking them for walks and picnics in the nearby woods and swimming and fishing in the rivers. Although hunting was forbidden, it was an open secret that the older boys would use these opportunities to sneak away and hunt small animals in the forest.[20]

Both the primitive conditions in which they lived and the harsh natural environment had their effect on the children. It was difficult to foster a cultured lifestyle in an environment such as this and as a result, discipline among the youngsters became lax over the years and observation of the Hutterian way of life, which had characterized the youngsters' life in the past, waned. John Arnold, Hardy's son, tells us something of the atmosphere that prevailed at the end of the forties:

> I noticed one major change. Religion became meaningless and was mocked. Hans Zumpe allowed hunting and the shooting of birds, while Hans Herman was fighting against all the killings in the Isla Margarita School.... In the most difficult years, Hans Herman managed to make us aware of moral values.[21]

In general, the children liked school and its special atmosphere, and Christoph Boller tells us:

> Our parents found it hard to adapt to the climate but for us, the children, there were no such difficulties. We loved the place, its atmosphere of freedom and even its distinctive climate. We were happy children and the hardships did nothing to diminish our happiness. The surrounding orange groves provided us with a great deal of fun, particularly at picking time.

And his wife adds:

> Despite all the handicaps, the teachers in Paraguay did a good job and this became evident when we went to external institutions for further education and training. It was then that we able to see that we had been given solid educational foundations. Life at Primavera provided us with a great deal of stimulus for study and our teachers gave us the best possible guidance for exploiting what we had learned and for making further progress.[22]

Once their school studies had been concluded, the youngsters worked in the various branches of the farm for about a year and during this period they had time to consider their future: work within the community, further education outside, or to leave for a break, during which they could decide whether or not to become members of the Bruderhof. It was accepted practice at Primavera to allow the young people to live outside the Bruderhof for a certain period before they made their decision to join. No pressure of any kind was exerted on them and they were allowed to reach their decision freely and individually. Andreas Meier tells us something of the adolescents' soul-searching:

> We, the children of Primavera, grew up harboring the ambition of leaving one day and seeing the big and fascinating world of cars, airplanes, and the stores in the big cities about which we only heard from the stories of the adults. Apart from that, there was no possibility of acquiring a comprehensive higher education in Para-

guay, so we sought ways of enabling the young people to leave the country and experience life in the big world outside. We sent them on various missions to Argentina, Uruguay, Chile and Brazil where the Bruderhof had circles of friends. These people were the bridgehead from which the Bruderhof's young people made their first contact with the outside world.[23]

It must be borne in mind that the people of the Primavera Bruderhof lived in isolation. A wide barrier separated them from the native Paraguayans with whom they came into contact. The natives harbored deep suspicions about the *gringos,* and although many of the brothers had learned Spanish, the local native population spoke Guarani, the language of the Guarani Indians, which the brothers never succeeded in mastering. Eric Phillips, one of the Primavera teachers who addressed the members of the Wheathill commune on the hardships of life in Paraguay, admitted that

the barriers were not all from the Paraguayan side. We on our own part were afraid—especially in the first years when conditions were very primitive—of contracting contagious diseases. This kept us somewhat isolated, but it was not an unfounded fear because leprosy—often concealed—and other tropical diseases were and still are present in the neighborhood.[24]

During the early years, relations with government authorities were normal and in 1945 the President of Paraguay, General Morinigo, visited the Bruderhof communities and was very impressed by their economic achievements. The products of the wood workshop caught the President's eye and later, when he sought an original Paraguayan gift for presentation to the President of Brazil, he ordered a decorative wooden bowl from the Bruderhof! It is said than in order to avoid singing the Paraguayan national anthem at the reception, the Bruderhof composed a special song in honor of the occasion, which was extremely well-received by the presidential retinue.[25]

1947 saw the outbreak of a civil war between the supporters of the two political parties, the Liberales and the Colorados. Hostilities broke out in March of that year and continued through August, with armed bands from both sides raiding and looting the Bruderhof communities. The army conducted searches and confiscated their horses, but those soldiers who knew the Bruderhof also knew that they would not find arms there and as a result their searches were cursory. Fortunately, the local population managed to persuade the looters not to damage the Bruderhof settlements and local families with children asked for refuge there in the knowledge that the Bruderhof were opposed to violence and not involved in the conflict. The bitter experiences of the civil war proved to the Bruderhof that their situation in Paraguay was vulnerable and reinforced their inclination to seek refuge in another country.[26]

Despite all the obstacles and limitations, the brothers tried unceasingly to maintain good relations with their neighbors and did not miss any opportunity to visit them in their homes and learn something of their customs, culture, and songs. They also tried, albeit with only limited success, to master Guanari and often invited their neighbors to festivals at the Bruderhof. When they needed help in thatching roofs, they called in the locals who were experts in this rural art. Although these encounters did contribute to the cementing of friendships, they were only short-term ones and the cultural gaps remained.[27]

Very few of their neighbors actually joined them. One family native to the region that did was that of Venceslao Jaime,[28] but they did not succeed in striking roots and finally left.[29] The only permanent relations that the Bruderhof had with their neighbors were established through the hired workers. The Bruderhof, who employed local hired labor for building in the early days, did not sever the connection later. The workers continued to work in construction, brick making, preparation of building materials, wood cutting in the sawmill, haulage, and weeding in the market garden. Thirty to forty Paraguayan workers would come to work every week and although the Bruderhof members tried to convert them to their beliefs through lectures in Spanish, the fact that they knew little Guanari blocked any attempt at developing real relations with them. An obstacle far more serious than the language barrier was the fact that the hired workers were employed to perform the most menial tasks, and this constituted an invisible barrier, which was felt mainly by the children, who both sensed and expressed the alienation between the Paraguayan workers and themselves.

Their standard of living also set them apart from the natives. Although in the early days, the brothers had lived in primitive conditions with living quarters that were no more than lean-tos, it did not take them long to improve these conditions with the construction of brick buildings and wooden huts. All the buildings were supplied with electricity, furnished, and equipped with household appliances, which the natives perceived as luxuries. This rapid improvement changed their image in the eyes of their neighbors and they were perceived as an affluent society, acceptance to which was conditional to being a property owner. All of the brothers' explanations were to no avail, for they were not prepared to allow every new member a partnership in the commune's assets. The natives simply did not believe them, and moreover, they held the opinion that even if they were accepted as members they would continue to perform all the menial tasks, and this despite the great efforts made by the brothers to share every job with them as equals.[30]

The Hospital at Loma Jhoby

The hospital established in the early days of the settlement was the principal contribution made by the Primavera settlers to the local population. It was initially designed to provide medical services for the Bruderhof members in the light of the poor hygienic conditions and the tropical climate to which they were unused. A short while after their arrival, epidemics broke out, which mainly affected the children, but fortunately three of their number were doctors (one man and two women) and one a pharmacist, all of whom had joined the Bruderhof on the eve of their departure from England. In the early days, the hospital worked under the most primitive conditions, occupying two rooms in the general living quarters. With the establishment of the second community at Loma Jhoby the medical service was transferred to there and work was begun on the construction of permanent buildings for a small hospital. It was decided to build the hospital at Loma Jhoby because there were still some of the old farm buildings on the site and also because it was some distance from the crowded Bruderhof settlement.

The hospital rapidly began to provide medical services to the local population too, and needless to say, these were people who had never known what medical service was. The rumor about the group of *gringos* who had come with three doctors who provided medical service for all comers spread like wildfire throughout the region. Scores of natives began to make their way to the hospital on foot and by primitive means of transport and once they reached the site, they encamped close to the Bruderhof settlement and waited their turn for treatment. The patients generally suffered from a variety of tropical and contagious diseases: worms, stomach gastritis, dysentery, trachoma, malaria, venereal diseases, pneumonia, and a variety of injuries and snake bites.[31]

The hospital's reputation reached distant ears and a multitude of patients travelled long distances to the Primavera hospital. Some died en route and to this day one can see the simple markers that were put on the roadside graves of those who died on the way to Primavera. The medical contribution of the hospital was immense and gained the admiration of both the local authorities and the Paraguayan government. Some even compared it with Albert Schweitzer's hospital in Africa, for at Primavera, too, patients and their families travelled great distances to get there and camped in the lean-tos outside the hospital until they had been treated. In cases that called for extended hospitalization, the families camped near the hospital and helped care for the patient.[32]

The medical services, which in the early days had been provided under primitive conditions, became more efficient. For a long period, the hospital was the only medical facility in the region. In 1949, it consisted of two wooden buildings that housed twelve beds, and more rooms were added for an out-patient clinic, a pharmacy, and operating room. A surgeon, another pharmacist, a laboratory technician, and three nurses joined the medical team in 1948. Maureen Burn, an Edinburgh-born medical student who decided to join the Bruderhof in 1944, was asked to study to become a laboratory technician in order to join the hospital's medical team. In the course of her work she specialized in snake-bite sera, which she prepared herself with the help of the commune's children, who became experts in hunting and catching snakes. Maureen tells us that she used to meet patients' families and hear stories of medicinal herbs and traditional medical techniques, some of which she used with great success. Apart from her work in the laboratory she also taught biology in the local school, and it was in the role of teacher that she would take the children into the forest to look for snakes and thus obtain the rare venom that she needed for the preparation of sera.[33] She says that the most awesome experience of her medical work was a visit to a leper colony of which she had heard from a patient who had been cured and who visited the hospital and later stayed in the commune for a while. Maureen recorded her story and later published it in her book.[34]

In 1949, there were 3,600 patients listed in the hospital's files; by the early fifties the number had increased to 7,500, and in 1954 there were 10,000 patients on file. It was in 1954 that the hospital's activities underwent a sharp increase with the addition of new buildings, which brought the number of beds to thirty. As time went by, the area covered by the hospital's medical services was extended to 1,000 square miles and the target population increased to 30,000 souls. It is worthy of note that the medical services provided were not only limited to those patients who actually came to the hospital, but the Primavera doctors also made "house calls" to distant native huts, which necessitated journeys of many hours on horseback. The medical team consisted of some twenty people—male and female nurses, laboratory technicians, and doctors.

Although the natives were extremely grateful for the treatment they received, they were only able to pay their hospitalization expenses in kind, usually agricultural produce, and through health insurance payments, but this covered only a small part of the cost of the treatment. The natives were able to obtain some small assistance from the government, which in 1945 enacted a national insurance law (*Institutio de Prevision Social*) that was designed to benefit the working class and their families, but which did nothing for the medical needs of the unemployed. The necessary financing for the extension of the hospital came from donations from sister churches like the Mennonites and the Quakers, but in the final accounting the brunt of the burden fell on the Bruderhof. It was a burden that grew continuously and so it was hardly surprising that at the end of 1954, the hospital's operating balance sheet showed a $30,000 deficit. The Bruderhof hoped to cover this with the help of donations from and appeals to friends in Europe and America.[35]

Leadership Struggles

In the course of the first decade of settlement in Paraguay, internal tensions were created within the commune as a result of power struggles and shifts in the Bruderhof leadership. The isolation that was their lot in Paraguay, together with the great changes that had taken place in the human makeup of the commune following the massive absorption of new members, brought with them the consolidation of an authoritarian leadership to which the members became inured as a result of the day-to-day hardships, the isolation, and the hard physical labor. These internal struggles have had numerous interpretations and some, which have been published recently by members of the Bruderhof and also by members who left because of them, are worthy of mention.

Heini Arnold, who had been elected Servant of the Word in 1938, after their gathering in England, led the group during the transitional year of emigration to Paraguay. In August, 1941, a short time after the group had become established in Paraguay, he fell seriously ill and vacated his place in the leadership, and this event left an opening for crises and tension, the echoes of which reverberated throughout the community for many years. Years later, in his book, *Torches Rekindled,* Merrill Mow recalled this episode and this is how he described the turn of events in the version accepted by the Bruderhof:

> In 1941 in Paraguay, Heini had a flare-up of an old illness—he had been treated for it in England—an ailment that became extremely serious down there. It continued to affect him for the rest of his life but it became deadly serious in August of that year. He was put under sedation for relief from pain. We were fortunate to have doctors in the community...but they did not have the right medicine to treat this illness.... Over a period of two months it got worse and worse; Heini became very seriously ill, showing signs of a dying man.... At that time, Heini was the only active Servant of the Word; for one reason or another the others had been temporarily removed.... Now because Heini had been told that he was on his deathbed, and because his father had wished it in his last letter, he believed that if the services of Hans Zumpe and Georg [Barth] and Hardy could be restored, then God's blessing would be on this church.... And so on October 3, 1941, in a meeting from his deathbed, Heini confirmed these servants.

> Heini survived the illness, but because of the medication he was given, the side-effects became increasingly serious.... It got so serious that he was taken from Primavera to a hospital in Asunción.... Heini was in Asunción for a couple of months in the hospital, where they had the right kind of medicine and treatment and he was able to return home. Now, the Asunción doctor had made no stipulations to Heini about his work, but Hans Zumpe, only recently reinstalled to the service by Heini, said to him and the community, "Heini should have a rest from all spiritual work because he has not recovered." And with that Heini was effectively removed from the Service of the Word...and this continued into 1942.[36]

The leadership crisis has also been described in Roger Allain's book, *The Community That Failed.* In his description, Allain focuses on the oppressive atmosphere that prevailed in the commune, describing it as "the first leadership crisis." He describes the assemblies that took place by the veranda upon which the deathly ill Heini's bed had been placed. Heini, who at the time had made a personal and public moral stocktaking, perceived the recent period as the lowest ebb the community had known; in his view, the members of the community had devoted themselves to the material matters of everyday living while neglecting the spiritual, which had typified their life in the past. Instead of devoting themselves to the Kingdom of Heaven, they had engaged in matters of money and food and thus the atmosphere of despondency had permeated their ranks. In order to break free of these shackles he called for personal and public repentance, which would return God's grace to them.

These assemblies outside Heini's room continued for many nights. Both work and the daily routine were disrupted and in the absence of leadership, everyone experienced a feeling of helplessness. Heini's condition improved after a few weeks, and according to Allain's account, he asked to be relieved of the office of Servant of the Word. The man who had cared for him during his long illness and to a great extent had filled his shoes, was Hans Zumpe, and so it was more or less obvious that he was the natural candidate to replace him. According to Allain's description, there was a deterioration in Heini's physical condition, so it was decided that he should be sent to Asunción accompanied by his wife and a number of close members of the community, for medical treatment. As travel conditions from Primavera were extremely difficult, it was decided to fly him to the capital, and so an airstrip that would take light aircraft was built. The arrival of the plane that was to take Heini to the capital caused a sensation in the community as it was the first time that an aircraft had landed in the region, and in fact, the occasion served to open the small airfield that would serve Primavera during the entire period of the community's existence.[37]

Bette Zumpe, Hans's daughter who left the Bruderhof, adds some details from her memories of the episode:

> Heini had a very bad kidney infection with a very high temperature and a great deal of terrible pain. Cyril, our doctor...had just finished his studies in England when he decided to join the community. He had no antibiotics.... He gave him morphine injections but it seemed like nothing would help.... It seemed as though Heini's hours were numbered.... Heini thought he was a dying man and kept calling the brotherhood to repent.... Heini had reinstalled my father as Servant together with Georg Barth. The brotherhood decided that Heini should see a specialist in Asunción.... There he got the best care anyone could ask for.... At some point, my dad was asked to have a confidential talk with the doctor.... He went with Annemarie. The doctors said that he needed a lot of rest, fresh air and good food...and that his mental state was very highly strung.... Papa felt that when a servant needs rest under such circumstances that this is a very confidential matter. Therefore, he did not discuss that talk with the brotherhood.[38]

According to Merrill Mow, Heini's removal from the leadership caused a chain reaction that was to become the cause of crises in the coming years:

> In July, there was a meeting of the responsible brothers, the witness brothers, in the woods near the community, and Fritz Kleiner was one of them. He stood up and

voiced a very strong protest against the direction in which things were going.... After this meeting in the woods there came a human judgement and Fritz, Heini, Hardy, Emmy Arnold and Hans Meier were excluded from the brotherhood and household, placed in a very serious exclusion.[39]

Fifty years after these events, Hans Meier told the author that he was excluded from the community and the church in an act that he defined as a "small exclusion," because he had proposed Hardy Arnold for the office of Elder. As the decision was made by Hans Zumpe and a group of his followers and not by the entire community, the exclusion was both temporary and partial and did not contain an element of church discipline.[40]

Although the ones excluded in 1942 had been reaccepted by 1944, the internal situation was becoming so difficult that Heini and Hardy began to meet, although it had been forbidden. They were both in the transport department, driving wagons, but they lived in different communities. The internal condition of the community was pretty impossible.... A bureaucratic approach to community life had gained control, a humanistic approach centered not on God but on the brotherhood, not on the united church but in "the will of the people" and not on the leadership of Jesus but on that of Hans Zumpe.[41]

Once he had recovered from his illness, Heini Arnold returned to Isla Margarita, but not to his former office. Hans Zumpe took care to keep him apart from his brother Hardy and as the two had been forbidden to meet, they were forced to do so secretly. As a result of the limitations imposed upon them by Zumpe, they used to meet along the road and exchange a few words before going their separate ways.[42]

There was another leadership crisis in 1944 when the members of Loma Jhoby made a stand against Hans Zumpe, who at the time was Servant of the Word at Isla Margarita. The Loma Jhoby brothers wanted to seek the advice of the Hutterites on how to respond to Hans Zumpe's leadership, which was diverting them from the Hutterite ideology they had adopted. In secret meetings held by the Loma Jhoby brothers, complaints were voiced against the newer members from England on the grounds that they had not become imbued with the original Bruderhof spirit and had remained "cold-hearted." Once these secret meetings became public knowledge, there was an outcry. General meetings were called at which the "plotters" were accused of conniving and arrogance and it was decided to mete out the harshest sanction of all, the "great exclusion." This punishment was imposed upon seventeen central members of the community, among them, yet again, Eberhard Arnold's three sons. They were excluded from the community and separated from their families; Heini Arnold for two years and the others for shorter periods, although it must be said that these, too, were relatively longer than the periods of exclusion that had been meted out in the past. This was the longest exclusion imposed up to that time and there were those who claimed that it left a residue of bitterness and anger, especially in Heini Arnold, which was to surface in the future. When those who had been excluded left the community, they had to shave their beards, they were forbidden to wear the traditional Hutterite dress, and each one had to make do with the small sum of money given to him on his departure. Heini found work as the farm manager at the leper colony.

Looking back at the crisis of 1944, Elizabeth Zumpe admits that the punishment was greater than the crime and further points out that some of those excluded bore a deep grudge against those who had punished them, and this burst out into the open in the crisis of 1961.[43] Eberhard Arnold's son-in-law, Balz Trumpi, who at the time was a member of the Bruderhof leadership, comments on the exclusion in his moral stock-taking of much later, and admits that

> In 1944, five brotherhood members were sent away to Asunción. Twelve more were excluded but stayed at Primavera. I agree that how they were treated in 1942 was wrong and what Hans Zumpe, Georg Barth and the brotherhood did to them in 1944 was much too harsh.[44]

In the late forties, Heini Arnold was returned to the community and once again began to fill central leadership offices. The tables were turned a short time later when Hans Zumpe's status went into decline. His daughter Elizabeth writes on the atmosphere that prevailed:

> There was a crisis. We didn't understand any of it. Wagons kept rolling to community meetings. Then there was the great exclusion. The reason was that Heini, Hardy and Hans Herman felt that my father was not "Hutterite" enough.[45]

By the middle fifties it seemed that the problem of leadership crises had been overcome and that the Bruderhof was on the right road. In the Bruderhof settlements in Paraguay, solid foundations had been established for community life both socially and culturally, albeit from an economic standpoint they still found it difficult to function. The Paraguay years were years of poverty and although the Bruderhof tried various ways of making an honorable living, they did not succeed in doing so. Despite the fact that the community was maintained by its own agricultural production, there was not enough food to go around. The modern dairy and herd, the yield of which was among the highest in the country, did not produce enough milk for all and in fact, most of it was reserved for the children and the pregnant women. The market for the decorative wood products was limited and these were sold mainly to tourists—and they were not too numerous in Paraguay at the time. The Primavera settlements were always dependent on the community in Britain and donations from American Quaker friends.

But despite the economic difficulties, there was an optimistic atmosphere at the Bruderhof, and this gained expression in articles that were published abroad and in those that appeared in their own publications from which one may learn that during the decade in Paraguay, the population of the Bruderhof was doubled and reached 700, half of them children and teenagers. The international character of the community was highlighted in everything that appeared in print and one can gather that despite the isolation and remoteness, the fervor of their desire to take their "witness" to groups in distant Europe and North America had been preserved. Some of the articles reported on delegations to Argentina, Brazil, and Chile and the forming of relations with similar communities in the United States.[46]

In 1952, a booklet was published at Wheathill in England that contained a chapter on ten years of Bruderhof settlement in Paraguay and in which the author expressed great faith in the future of the Paraguayan settlements:

> Primavera is in a particular way suited for communal life on a large scale, since the government of Paraguay has much sympathy for such colonies and concedes far-reaching liberties. We are also less hindered in our work of building our community life, as many restrictions which exist in more highly developed states are absent.... So far, Primavera, where there are almost 700 gathered together, has only once experienced severe obstacles, namely through the civil war of 1947.[47]

A short time later in 1955, a pacifist doctor, Milton Zimmerman, and his wife Sandy, arrived at Primavera from the United States for a period of alternative service, a period that began as one year and has continued to this day. Zimmerman, who was a supportive "participating observer," received a different impression of the situation of the Bruderhof in Paraguay in those days. He said:

> The Bruderhofs here are an island of foreigners in their surrounding environment
> and the extent of their contribution to their neighbors makes no difference at all.
> Only half of the members speak Spanish and very few speak Guarani. How can a
> community such as this make any kind of spiritual contribution when the language
> barrier still remains intact after fifteen years of neighborly relations?[48]

In retrospect and despite the fact that they were the result of circumstances, the Bruderhof view the years in Paraguay as an interim period, but one that played an important role in the community's development. The Bruderhof became consolidated as a movement in Paraguay and the years spent there were something akin to the Biblical "forty years in the wilderness" for them. From the small flock of Eberhard Arnold's disciples, the majority of whom were German, it became a truly international community.

From the time of the move to England, the Bruderhof adopted an open-door policy, but in Paraguay in the forties this was of no real consequence because of the isolation and distance. The population's increase stemmed from natural reproduction and the joining of the younger generation. It should be mentioned that the Bruderhof have never exerted pressure on their children to join and they have done so solely out of belief. But the environmental conditions in Paraguay reduced the scale of people leaving and a large group of young people remained. After the end of the World War II, when the routes to Europe were reopened, links with the outside world became stronger. There was a constant stream of visitors from Europe and new members joined each year, initially people from Europe and later from America, especially North America.[49]

The El Arado Settlement in Uruguay

With the increasing tendency to extend their relations with other countries, the Bruderhof leadership sought an opportunity to do so. The leadership viewed the sending of their young people abroad as one way of breaking away from the isolation and cultural backwardness imposed upon them by the community's location. In 1951, an opportunity to do so was given them by Robert Slovak, a wealthy Bruderhof friend in Uruguay who owned a large dairy herd of 300 head that was run on modern lines not far from Montevideo. He suggested that the Bruderhof manage his dairy herd on a contract basis and replace his hired workers.[50]

Some time before this, Bruderhof emissaries had been sent to Argentina and Uruguay to make contact with friends in those countries and raise funds for the hospital. They made contact with various groups, particularly with Swiss and German Jews who were anti-Nazi refugees. The emissaries also visited Argentina but received the impression that suitable conditions for the establishment of a Bruderhof settlement under the Perón dictatorship could not be created.[51]

Uruguay was then thought to be a liberal country with an untroubled political climate in which there was political and religious tolerance and no military conscription, and so the Bruderhof accepted Robert Slovak's proposal. They viewed it as an opportunity of establishing a bridgehead near Montevideo for the establishment of a settlement in Uruguay and decided to send a group of young people who were skilled dairymen. The five who went to Uruguay worked and managed the dairy herd as contractors, but three months after their arrival it became evident that the work took up most of the hours of the day, it was too hard, and their relations with the owner were both strained and not suited to commune members. Therefore, they decided to quit, leave the farm, and look for land on which to establish an independent agricultural settlement.[52]

In an article published some years later in the *El Arado* magazine, there was a concise description of the move to Uruguay and of what had happened to the group in that first year, prior to the purchase of their own farm:

> The Hutterian Society of Brothers in South America tried to reach more densely populated areas than in Paraguay. For some years we had maintained personal contacts in Chile, Brazil, and especially Argentina. In 1951, some twelve people settled a three hectare tract of land at Carrasco, twenty-four kilometers from Montevideo. The group gradually increased in size and it quickly became clear that the farm's area was too small. At the end of 1952 they moved to the El Arado farm on the Osvaldo Rodriguez road, which had eight hectares, was closer to the center of Montevideo and allowed closer contact with the population.[53]

Although conditions on the farm in the early days were primitive, it had economic potential. They slowly began to improve the living conditions, built a special building for the dining room, and added a second story to the living quarters with the objective of absorbing up to 100 people. The soil was good and they planted fruit trees, cultivated a market garden, grew strawberries, planted a vineyard, and kept a small dairy herd and chickens. Their main source of income was the sale of their agricultural produce in Montevideo; the market was close by and the members sold the produce from stalls in the markets and also to regular customers who were, in the main, foreign residents and members of the staffs of the various embassies. There were also some members who worked outside the commune in order to swell the community's income and one of them was Charles Headland, who worked as an accountant at the American Hospital in Montevideo.

The work was hard and long but the atmosphere was good and the way of life at El Arado was the same as that in all the Bruderhof communities. The thing that set this particular settlement apart was the fact that Spanish was the day-to-day language. The community hosted a great many visitors and a lively exchange of views was conducted with them on problems of faith and philosophy. May, 1955 saw the first issue of their Spanish-language magazine, El Arado, which was aimed at building a bridge to the local population and conveying the ideological message of the Bruderhof.[54]

From its early days, the community at El Arado fostered their relations with the local population. They maintained an open-door policy, which found the following expression in all their publications:

> Anyone seeking a life of brotherhood will be warmly greeted at our community regardless of their class, race, nationality or ideology. They can enjoy for a while the opportunity of joining us in our work and way of life. If, during this period, they find a joint basis with Bruderhof beliefs, they will be accepted as candidates.[55]

Roger Allain, who had played a central role in preparing the community for the move to Uruguay, was sent there from Primavera in 1955 to serve in central offices—Servant of the Word and editor of the Spanish-language magazine. Even then he was aware of the need to become more involved in outside society and cement relations with friendly circles in Uruguay and Argentina, and he was helped in this mission by his fluent Spanish. It was on his initiative that relations were formed with pacifist circles, similar religious groups and an anarchist group.[56]

In January, 1956, Allain was heard on Radio Del Pueblo in a rare public interview with a member of the Bruderhof. The Bruderhof was presented to the Montevideo public as a way of life, not a religious sect:

> This is not about new dogmas, a new sect, or socio-political theory, but rather a way of life in which the love of God and one's fellow man is a basic principle of life. As far as we are concerned, this is not a fleeting experiment. We have found

here a personal lifestyle and social structure towards which we believe that many people would strive. So therefore our door is open to all men of goodwill who would like to become acquainted with this way of life.[57]

Further testimony of this desire to become involved in outside society and fulfil their mission in it can be found in an advertisement that appeared in their magazine, *El Arado* (no. 8), in 1958:

We are ready to give lectures at any time and anywhere in the country and to establish contact with groups and individuals who are interested in our communal life, either by correspondence or personal meetings.... We will be happy to receive invitations to speak on various aspects of communal life and are interested in hearing about groups and individuals, both in the capital and in the interior, who would like to establish contact with us.

The open-door policy was also mentioned in the same vein and at length in the Primavera newsletter:

We are unable to influence political events and mass opinion. Our only hope is that we will be able to cause an awakening here and there and arouse conscience... in a world of steel, perhaps our soft whisper will find its way into hearkening ears and hearts which are waiting to hear it...we shall not try to prove anything with arguments. If there is an argument we would like to use, it is this: come and see and live with us for a while. Our life together will speak on our behalf. We do not intend to say that we have achieved our objective...but there is something here which contains a creative power that is likely to bring about a change in people's spirit, to raise them from out of nations and different situations and draw them towards unity which is freedom and freedom which is responsibility.

Our origins are middle-class...we represent eighteen nations. Most of us are sons of the modern world but some have grown up in the commune during all the thirty years of its existence...from the standpoint of our past, we are, as an American in his first week at Primavera put it, "a very strange collection indeed." We mention this in order to emphasize the fact that we have found unity in togetherness...we live in a commune because we are convinced that until a real solution to some of the world's problems is found, it is incumbent upon people to find their way towards the organic unity of life...the way towards the primal sources of human society. The door is open to anyone who wishes to join us in our search and work towards such a life.[58]

Relations with the Jewish Pioneering Movement in South America

The search for contact with similar groups prompted the establishment of relations with Jewish Zionist groups and the Jewish pioneering movement, the latter finding a common language with the Bruderhof against their common background of communal life. Not long after the establishment of the settlement near Montevideo, far-reaching relations began to develop between the Jewish pioneering movement and the Bruderhof. Part of these relations included exchange visits between the members of the *Ihud* and *Hashomer Hatsa'ir* training farms, which were not far from El Arado. I heard of the relations that existed between the members of the training farms and members of the Bruderhof in interviews I held with Bruderhof members who were living in Uruguay at the time. Of special interest were Andreas Meier's reminiscences in which he acknowledged the important role played by his encounter with the members of the training farm in his return to his Bruderhof origins. Andreas was among the first Bruderhof youngsters who was allowed to leave the commune and discover the outside world. At first, he and some friends worked on a modern dairy farm in Uruguay, but later, on reaching the conclusion that this was not the way to "find out about the outside world," he left his friends and went to live alone in Montevideo. He recalls this period:

> I lived alone in Montevideo for about a year. I found work and made a good living...but after a while I realized that my life was empty of meaning and significance. I missed the company of the brothers to which I was so used. I had no interest in making money and having to take care of myself...it was at that stage of my life that I got in touch with the *Hashomer Hatsa'ir* training farm, about which I had heard earlier, and spent two weeks with them.... I remember that time as an uplifting experience...it was a new and invigorating experience and totally different from my life in Montevideo. These young people, who were enthusiastically preparing themselves for communal life, reminded me of the days of my own youth in the commune in Paraguay. In certain respects, their commune was far more extreme than that to which I was used. They had a communal clothing store in which all the garments were divided by size—small, medium and large—and everyone just helped themselves according to size...there were no personal clothes...this encounter with a collective community made me homesick for my past and aroused my desire to return to the communal way of life. It was my experience at the training farm that impelled me to return to the Bruderhof. I had experienced the taste of loneliness in Montevideo while at the training farm I had tasted togetherness.[59]

Andreas was not the only one to share his reminiscences of encounters with members of the Zionist pioneering movements with me. His brother Klaus, who went to El Arado to study medicine at the University of Montevideo, recalls meeting Jewish youngsters and members of the training farms:

> The thing that brought us together was our belief in communal life and what separated us was belief in God. They believed that a commune could be built through

human effort, while we said "No! God alone can do it." That was the main difference between us.[60]

Further testimony on these relations was also provided by Charles Headland, who recalled the visit of a young Jew called Raul Weiss whose visit to the commune was one of the highlights of his experiences as a young Uruguayan radical.

Raoul, today a member of Kibbutz Ga'ash in Israel, visited El Arado in 1958. At the time he was a young student who was close to *Comunidad del Sur*. When I met him, he admitted that the three days he had spent with the Bruderhof at El Arado were etched on his memory as an unforgettable experience from which sprang the desire to maintain contact with the Bruderhof for a period of many years. Like Andreas Meier, Raoul felt that his encounter with them strengthened his ties with communal life and indirectly influenced his decision to live in a kibbutz in Israel.[61]

An interesting visit to the Bruderhof by a member of the Religious Kibbutz Movement took place in November, 1957. Mordechai Nissan from Kibbutz Ein Zurim was a kibbutz movement emissary to Uruguay at the time, and his impressions of his visit may be found in his movement's magazine. Nissan was impressed by the commune's exterior similarity to that of the kibbutz, although the small Uruguayan settlement reminded him of "a kibbutz training farm prior to permanent settlement...everything bears a marked similarity to the kibbutz, but on a much smaller scale." He held long conversations with his hosts about their religious convictions and was impressed by the way they had combined their Christian beliefs with Martin Buber's book, *I and Thou*. When describing El Arado, Nissan felt that "their collectivity is total and encompasses every aspect of their life," and found many similarities with kibbutz life: "It was surprising to find similarities between the work roster problems there and those in the kibbutz," and that "their collective consumption is governed by bodies similar in structure to our own." He was also very interested in comparing problems of the children sleeping at home, those of the younger generation and their return to the commune after having spent some time away from it.

Mordechai Nissan concluded that "an unmistakable line differentiates between the kibbutz and the Bruderhof. The kibbutz has a definite national character...while the Bruderhof has an international one...

the people here base their way of life on their religious beliefs and it is entirely possible that they have taken as an example...the Essene sects."[62]

Several years after the publication of the above-mentioned article, Moshe Unna, the spiritual leader of the Religious Kibbutz Movement, referred to it as an expression of "our first encounter with this religious collective movement" (the visit to the Rhön Bruderhof had probably slipped Unna's mind. See above.—Y.O.), and emphasized that "it is hardly surprising that from a number of points of view we are interested in their movement." He said further that "I personally have been in touch for some time with their community in Paraguay." Unna states categorically that, "in my opinion, it is important for us to get to know them, their concepts, ideas and deeds. We must learn about our existing similarities and also of the differences that separate us, which may give us food for thought with regard to our own problems. A study of their ideology and objectives might provide such an opportunity." The main thrust of his article, however, is devoted to a review of Emmy Arnold's book, *Torches Together*. Unna concludes his exhaustive review admiringly:

> These people have indeed shown great fortitude, a fortitude that must surely arouse our amazement and admiration. What was the source of this indefatigable strength? In my view, the only answer can be true belief, not in themselves but in Divine power which guides man's way throughout his life, and a sincere and unrelenting desire to fulfill the commandments of their religion, to realize them together, for only thus will their realization become real.[63]

"An Encounter with the Kibbutz" in the *El Arado* Magazine

In 1957, Dick Whitty, who was then living at Primavera, was the driving force behind an extraordinary initiative to devote half of one issue of the Spanish-language magazine, *El Arado,* to the theme of the kibbutz. It is noteworthy that until that time, no communal movement had been given such great coverage in any of the Bruderhof's publications.[64]

And so, in August, 1958, issue number 7 of *El Arado* was published, with half of the magazine's content devoted to a section below the title, "Encuentro con el Kibbutz"—"An Encounter with the Kibbutz." The lead article, which served as an editorial, discussed the unique relationship between the Bruderhof and the kibbutz:

> Even though we are divided on many issues, we attach great importance to the fact that there exist groups of people who are devoted to a communal and integrative

way of life in a world in which everything is breaking down. We have one thing in common, namely our hope for a new mankind, for a new society in which the individual can put his potential at the service of his brothers and at the same time develop his own personality. Nevertheless, we must emphasize that to our mind, the acquiescence of kibbutz members to the necessity of an army for defence is utterly opposed to the spirit of brotherly love. This is one of the issues on which we shall never reach a consensus of opinion with the kibbutz movement.... Yet this should not prevent us from feeling close to them, if only because like us, they aspire to an ideal of togetherness in communities where property and work are shared collectively. Most of the articles in this section originated from an extensive correspondence over many years with kibbutz members in Israel. It should be noted that this publication deals with the common denominator of true communal life rather than with differences of opinion.[65]

In addition to a number of informative articles on various aspects of kibbutz life, several others are concerned with the dialogue between the movements. The most outstanding is entitled, "Humanismo o Fe? El Fundamento de la Vida en Comunidad," written in the form of a dialogue between a *kibbutznik* and a member of the Bruderhof on the tenets of both movements. The kibbutz member opens with an assumption that there are enormous differences of opinion, but then declares:

> We are looking for points at which our movements can meet. To be honest, I believe that there is a vast spiritual difference between the Bruderhof and the kibbutzim in Israel.... In the eyes of the world, the kibbutz represents a secular Utopian movement which has succeeded.... It is a movement that has no religious philosophy (with the exception of the religious kibbutzim). This immediately raises the question of whether humanistic ethics may replace ancient traditions of religion.

According to the kibbutznik, it may. However, he takes it for granted that a commune should be based on spiritual motivations. He remarks that in his Kibbutz Federation, political and revolutionary Marxism served as the driving force and as the basis for a future society. In addition there was a tremendous enthusiasm for building up the country. He asks the Bruderhof member what kind of spiritual power had inspired them.

The Bruderhof member's reply is based on Martin Buber's book, *Paths of Utopia* in which, according to the author, "one may find the key to our doctrine expressed by the non-religious Jewish philosopher, Gustav Landauer, who was one of the personalities who influenced our community." He refers to a number of Landauerian ideas that became the cornerstones for the Bruderhof's patterns of life: for example, the community as a union of people who act as a living organism; people's need for internal renewal in order to change their society; the community's unity is not enforced externally, but is the result of a live, internal spirit that affects each individual.

In the second round of the dialogue, the "kibbutznik" touches on the Bruderhof's belief in the exclusiveness of Christianity. He asks, "If your profound belief in Christianity were to disappear from your life and you no longer believed in Jesus, would you be able to continue living in a commune?" The Bruderhof member's reply is indirect. He answers by emphasizing three of their basic tenets: (a) the commune is intended for anyone; (b) it objects on principle to every kind of bloodshed; and (c) true brotherhood exists through direct and open relations between people. He adds: "We perceive non-violence as the basic element of early Christianity. Therefore, we cannot it as it is the source of our doctrine and our belief in a life of love and brotherhood."[66]

Several articles discuss the Religious Kibbutz Movement. Dick Whitty, the author of one of them, assumes that religious Judaism does not call for communalism to the same extent as did early Christianity, which aspired to the kind of brotherhood that was realized in the Apostles' Jerusalem community.

He deals directly with the Religious Kibbutz Movement in his review of Arieh Fishman's book, *The Religious Kibbutz Movement,* and poses some rhetorical questions to its members, for example: "Could you maintain a communal life without your religion? Does the Jewish concept of 'A Sacred People' require the realization of kibbutz communalism?" He then goes on to point out the lack of a direct relationship between orthodox Judaism and communal life. The author also wonders whether it might be possible to perceive the religious kibbutzim in Israel as an expression of a new kind of Judaism, one that is much more radical than the concept of social justice in antiquity. The author suggests that kibbutz life and its abolition of all private property is actually a realization of *shmitta,* not only every seventh year, but also throughout life. Dick Whitty concludes his review with the hope that the religious kibbutzim may perceive the value of their communal life from a much broader and more significant perspective, namely, as a message for modern man. According to him, that is what the Essenes did when they appealed to all the people through their way of life.[67]

The links forged with the members of El Arado were also the starting point of a flourishing correspondence between members of the

Primavera Bruderhof and members of kibbutzim in Israel. The most assiduous correspondent at that time was Richard (Dick) Whitty.[68] From the early fifties Dick corresponded with a number of kibbutz members, among them Shalom Wurm. Whitty recalls that the first letter in this long-lasting correspondence was the one he received from Avraham Ben-Yosef, a member of Kibbutz Sasa, who sought contact with worldwide communes in 1954. Whitty says that Ben-Yosef referred him to other kibbutz members who might be interested in forming relations with the Bruderhof, which was how he contacted Shalom Wurm and Arieh Fishman, a sociologist who had published several studies of the Religious Kibbutz Movement. Although he corresponded with them, Whitty stresses that their correspondence was the result of personal initiative and did not encompass the Bruderhof as a whole. In a letter to the author he explained that "in the fifties, the membership of the Primavera Bruderhof were not as interested in these contacts as they were in the eighties."[69]

On the part of the kibbutzim, Zvi Shahar of Kibbutz Tel Yosef (which at the time was still called Giv'at Zeid) took up correspondence with the Bruderhof. He was born in Paraguay and as a member of the *Dror* youth movement, had heard of the Bruderhof while living in Asunción. After his emigration to Israel and the kibbutz he wanted to learn more about their way of life and in a letter dated 2 May 1956, he wrote to the Primavera community, proposing an exchange of information that would strengthen their relations.

Shahar received replies from Dick Whitty at Primavera and Charles Headland at El Arado, Uruguay, both of whom welcomed his initiative and said that they were extremely interested in the kibbutz movement. Dick gave a detailed report of their life at Primavera and expressed his hope that some day they might get to know each other through mutual visits. He enclosed a Primavera farm inventory and data on the populations of all nine Bruderhof communities in the world, according to which their movement had 1,200 members, 680 of whom were at Primavera. He also sent booklets on their religion and ideology, noting that

the enclosed literature may raise a multitude of questions.... No doubt it differs from the Israeli way of thought.... However, after getting to know Martin Buber's and Max Brod's writings, I have reached the conclusion that we are closer to the Jewish entity than to the large Christian churches. The connection between us and

Judaism stems from our aspiration towards a new social order, towards a classless society...and towards the establishment of a nation that is based on justice and brotherhood.[70]

We learn of a further initiative from the June, 1958 edition of *The Plough*, which published a letter from a group of young Israelis:

We belong to the Federation of Kvutzot but differ from them in our concepts. We read and heard about you and feel ourselves very near to you, to your beliefs and to your way of life. We want to do here in Israel something very near to what you realize in the life in your communities. Of course there are differences but they are of a secondary nature. We should like to establish relations with your community, from the experience of which we hope to learn very much.

Our group was created three and a half years ago when we left secondary school. We looked for the meaning of life. We found the way back to religion, not the orthodox one, but the living and spiritual one. We left town, wishing to begin a new life in the country where spirit, love, brotherhood, God's commandments in their full significance will dominate life, daily life.... We live in a community on a farm which is not our own, working for the company that owns it and getting a daily wage. We hope to establish a place of our own in a year or two. All of us are very young, between nineteen and twenty.[71]

Actually, their move to a populated area should have ensured widespread relations with members of the kibbutz movement, who had been visiting them since the fifties, but this did not happen. There is no documentation of encounters or even correspondence during those years in either the Bruderhof archives or in those of the kibbutz movement. What happened? Klaus Meier explains that in the sixties, the Bruderhof movement was undergoing a severe crisis that affected all its communities. They were deeply involved in internal problems and were unwilling to foster as many external relations as they had previously. The few that survived were on a personal level. Moreover, financial difficulties prevented travel and as far as external relations were concerned, the Bruderhof's priorities were aimed at contact with former members who had left during the crisis and at an effort to bring them back.[72]

Under these circumstances, relations between the kibbutz movement and the Bruderhof were put on the back burner. Neither movement showed interest in reviving them and there were no external incentives to do so. The issue of *El Arado* that was to have opened up an intellectual and written dialogue between the Bruderhof and the kibbutz movement failed to achieve its purpose and it remains unwanted in the Bruderhof archives.[73]

Relations with Anarchists and Members of Communes

Relations of a special kind were established between members of the El Arado Bruderhof and young anarchists from Montevideo. These youngsters, who were mainly students, showed great interest in ideological meetings with the Bruderhof members in which the doctrines of Kropotkin, Gustav Landauer, and Martin Buber were discussed, together with questions of religious belief and communal life. The effect of these meetings motivated a group of fifteen anarchists to form a commune on a small farm near Montevideo called La Canuta, and its members became known as Los Canuteros. These young anarchists were so affected by their encounters with the Bruderhof that they established a number of collective enterprises in the city, one of which was a printing press.[74]

Pedro Scaron, a member of the group, has the following to say of the influence of the Bruderhof:

> The first communal group to penetrate our world was the Society of Hutterite Brothers.... We held our first talks with them in October, 1952 and thus the first contacts between them and us—a group of anarchist students—were established. There were further meetings in the wake of the first and then both short and extended visits to the Society of Hutterite Brothers' commune. The upshot was the idea of establishing a commune like theirs...but our small commune differed from the others in that we perceived it to be part of general society...we did not want it to be a place of seclusion and solitude but rather one of organization for struggle and creativity.[75]

Contact with the anarchist group was maintained throughout the existence of El Arado in Paraguay, and information about them can be found in the majority of the Bruderhof periodicals that were published in Paraguay and Uruguay.[76]

Charles Headland recalls the strong relations between the Bruderhof and the anarchist group, which were maintained until the Bruderhof's last days in Paraguay:

> We were very involved in their lives. We were happy to meet people who believed that it was possible to live in a commune, albeit there were vast differences in our religious beliefs.

As time went by, the mutual visits increased in frequency until some of the Bruderhof leadership felt that in the light of their religious differences, the relationship had become *too* close. When it was decided to close down the El Arado commune, their anarchist friends were deeply disappointed and felt that they had been abandoned. "I felt that our relations with them had gone too far," said Charles Headland.[77]

In 1957, Lanza Del Vasto, the spiritual leader of the French communal movement, which combined Christianity with the doctrines of Mahatma Gandhi, visited Uruguay. Del Vasto, a well-known literary figure, had been invited to South America by academic circles in Montevideo and Buenos Aires. Some of his lectures were attended by members of the Bruderhof and, thus, relations between them were established. Their invitation to visit them was accepted and the visit opened the door to a dialogue between two differing approaches to communality and religion. In issue number 6 of *El Arado*, Roger Allain reports that he initiated Del Vasto's visit to their commune. Del Vasto told them how he had first gone to live in a commune in France ten years earlier, that in the present commune, El Arco, there were forty members; families with children and young unmarried people of both sexes. There was no private property and the members received no wages.

After writing of the similarities between the two movements, Allain focuses on the differences between them:

> They have taken a vow of non-violence, frugality and loyalty to the commune. This vow is valid for one year at the end of which it is renewed.... For us, on the other hand, joining the brotherhood means total and lifelong dedication.... We use tractors, typewriters, telephones and electricity...they zealously reject modern technology and mechanization.

Allain disputes their concept of an isolationary life while at the same time pointing out the dangers that lurk for communes that shun the modern world. Awareness of this danger was what had led the Bruderhof to build its communes close to populated areas and El Arado was living proof of this. He further writes of the abandoning of traditions and customs that separated them from those strata of the population with which they wanted to establish contact:

> As the commune grew and its desire to spread its message increased, it tried to reach the maximum number of people possible. We saw that it was this that differentiated between them and us.... We abandoned traditions and lifestyles because we wanted more than anything to preserve and extend the possibility of relations with people of our own generation.[78]

The conclusion of the dialogue elucidated the deep disparity between the two communes, and this is explained by Felipe, a member of the commune, in an interview for the *Marcha* newspaper:

> Not only do we at El Arado use tractors, typewriters, the telephone and electricity, while at El Arco they zealously reject modern technology.... It is immaterial to Lanza Del Vasto whether his followers have differing religious convictions; whether they are Catholic, Protestant or Quakers. We of the Bruderhof find it hard to see an intimate union of people, all of whom have their separate faiths and who are loyal to their past traditions as the El Arco people are.

Yet, despite these differences, Lanza Del Vasto expressed a sense of closeness to the Bruderhof:

> I sense a feeling of great closeness to you...because small groups such as yours and ours will form the nucleus of a new world order that will rise after the flood.[79]

The Uruguayan commune had to extend its mission in South America. The members of the Bruderhof still had great but unfulfilled expectations, and we can learn something of their feelings from the December, 1956 edition of *The Plough*:

> It seemed that the Uruguayan commune, El Arado, because of its location and the attention it had drawn in various Uruguayan, Argentine and Brazilian circles, could have had a greater influence on its milieu had it had the manpower necessary for this task. The need to consolidate its economic foundations compelled this small group to become introverted and its members were unable to disengage themselves and devote their efforts to what was happening from Cordoba to Santos in Brazil. In order to face these tasks, it was recently decided to move a number of families and young people from Primavera to El Arado...over the coming year we plan to increase their numbers to eighty and thus hope to provide them with the manpower necessary to accomplish all the tasks of spreading our message and ideals.[80]

The issue was raised again in the movement press in 1957 when it was said that relations with the Spanish-speaking population in South America were far from satisfactory because of the Bruderhof's preference for relations with German-speaking circles. Yet at the same time, the El Arado group's adoption of Spanish for daily use within the community was lauded.

Hardy Arnold, who was one of the Bruderhof's leaders at the time, visited the commune in 1957 and was most impressed by the members' ability to foster relations with their neighbors as a direct result of their fluent Spanish and in his report of that visit, he wrote:

> We were very moved by the spirit and dedication prevailing in the whole brotherhood and by the keen awareness of the problems of our age and by the will to do more in our efforts to reach the people of South America. I feel that the tendency that more of our young people should be trained in South America and become fully acquainted with the Spanish language and also with the particular problems of South America, is a good one.[81]

In his book, *The Community That Failed,* Roger Allain, who played a major role in the establishment of El Arado, devotes an entire chapter to his life in the commune and in it he looks back fondly at the early days there. He describes their intensive activity and points out that despite the heavy work load, the members still found time for intellectual pursuits. Their spiritual interests were broad, and as evidence of this he mentions the rich variety of reading material they discussed, which included works by Aldous Huxley, George Orwell, Simone Weil, Romano Guardini, Martin Buber, and Ortega y Gasset. Then, he says, "we felt as though we were a big family. Our children enjoyed a very free atmosphere...there were no barriers between the office-holders and the other members of the commune. There was an atmosphere of freedom in the commune."[82] Jean-Pierre Allain, Roger's son, describes life as a teenager:

> During the first five years, we were a small group and there was a very good, friendly and understanding atmosphere among all the children and teenagers. I didn't feel, as I did at Primavera, the division between the children and grownups. There was often a real, healthy friendship between children and adults.... It was natural for a boy to play with a girl and for a girl to have a friend who was a boy.
>
> I often participated in the talks some members of El Arado had with Sunday visitors and I was impressed by the ideas of some of our friends (I particularly remember the Comunidad del Sur).[83]

But another, more personal vein creeps into the concluding part of this chapter of Roger Allain's book on El Arado. In retrospect, and after making a trenchant stock taking of his past, he severely criticizes his own strict approach and that of his co-leaders on matters of intimacy and problems of sex that existed within the Bruderhof membership. The community's extreme puritanism created tensions and mental problems that permeated the community. In the summer of 1958, deep tensions surfaced between Roger himself and some of the veteran members of the commune, and as a result, Roger and his wife were asked to return to Primavera and hand over the commune's leadership to others and indeed, he returned to a reality of a great impending crisis, the seeds of which had already sprouted at El Arado.

Despite the efforts of the members of El Arado, they did not succeed in attracting new members from the local population. Although they had many visitors and numerous friends in Montevideo who spent weekends with them, very few decided to stay. All of the community's new members came from the Primavera communes in Paraguay.

Their most significant additions from among their circles of friends in South America were Stan and Hella Ehrlich from Buenos Aires. This young couple left behind an apartment, good financial standing, and good jobs, and out of a deep belief that they were giving meaning to their lives, went to share a life of hardship in Paraguay. Years later, at their home in Woodcrest, they related how they joined the commune and their story is an enthralling human document that bears testimony to the idealism that the Bruderhof emissaries succeeding in awakening among those young people who were then seeking a way. Hella recalls:

> We met the Bruderhof people at the home of friends in Montevideo.... We both had good jobs, lived comfortably and had a circle of friends with whom it was nice to meet and discuss matters of paramount importance...but we still felt that there was something missing in our lives, that there were more important things than a sound financial standing.... When we met the members of the Bruderhof, the idea of community entered our world and we were curious to see what it meant, so we decided to go to Primavera to see for ourselves. We stayed for two weeks and what I experienced was so strong that on our return home it was clear that we would join them. At that time, we were about to buy a house and that was the moment to decide whether we were to continue with our old routine or follow the inner call that we had both heard...it was then that we decided to move to Primavera. We both wanted to begin in that harsh and distant place.... it was only later that we were transferred to El Arado because of our fluent Spanish.[84]

Stan and Hella's joining the community was the fruit of the efforts invested in the establishment of relations with friends outside the Bruderhof. It was at this time that there was a clear tendency in the Bruderhof to send emissaries throughout the continent, particularly to densely populated areas. Some were sent to Buenos Aires and others reached Chile and Brazil, but as mentioned earlier, these efforts proved unsuccessful.

Notes

1. Meier, Hans, in *Memories of Our Early Years,* vol. 2 (Collection of pamphlets published by the Plough Publishing House, Rifton, N.Y.: 1973-79), 40.

2. Interview with Hans Meier, October, 1991. Also Allain, Roger, *The Community That Failed* (San Francisco, Calif.: Carrier Pigeon Press, 1992), 102.

3. Ibid., 104-14; Cocksedge, Edmund, *Vagabond for Peace* (Australia: House of Freedom Christian Community Publication, 1991), 65-68.

4. *La Idea,* no. 343 (Montevideo, November, 1945).

5. Allain, op. cit., 173-74. News of the attempt to absorb the children also appeared in the European press: the Swiss *Weltwache* on 10 January 1947 and *Tsror Michtavim* (Hakibbutz Hameuhad, Israel, 1947) (Hebrew).

6. Allain, op. cit., 180-82; also an interview with John Winter, October, 1992. On the episode of the displaced persons, see also Elizabeth Zumpe's autobiography, *Torches Extinguished* (Carrier Pigeon Press), 97-101; Cocksedge, op. cit., 84-85.

7. *Ten Years of Community Living—The Wheathill Bruderhof* (England: The Plough Publishing House, 1952), 34.

8. *Ten Years of Community Living,* 37, and also Wagoner, Bob and Shirley, *Community in Paraguay* (Rifton, N.Y.: Plough Publishing House, 1991), 75.

9. Allain, op. cit., 153-58; *Ten Years of Community Living,* 36; Cocksedge, op. cit., 79.

10. *The KIT Annual, 1991* (The Collected Newsletters of the KIT Information Service, San Francisco, Calif.), 217.

11. See *The Plough,* vol. 4 (Quarterly of Bruderhof communities. Bromdon: The Plough Publishing House, 1956): 112-16.

12. A talk with Fida Meier, Woodcrest, November, 1991.

13. On activities in Asunción, see *The Plough,* vol. 1, no. 1; vol. 3, no. 4; vol. 4, no. 4.

14. See order of the day, Wagoner, op. cit., 177-78.

15. On the organizational and administrative structure, see Wagoner, op. cit., 164 and 166-68.

16. Interview with John Bazeley, November, 1991.

17. Allain, op. cit., 230.

18. Wagoner, op. cit., 70. Interview with Kathleen Hassenberg, October, 1992; Cocksedge, op. cit., 88.

19. See Wagoner, op. cit., 203-10.

20. Allain, op. cit., 170; Cocksedge, op. cit., 71, 81-82.

21. *KIT Annual, 1991,* 19.

22. Interview with the Bollers, November, 1991.

23. Interview with Andreas Meier, November, 1991.

24. "Barriers Can Fall," *The Plough,* vol. 5, no. 4 (1957).

25. Interview with Dick Whitty, October, 1992. See also reports in *El Paraguayo* (23 October 1945) and in *El Pais* of the same date.

26. Allain, op. cit., 176-78; Cocksedge, op. cit., 75-76.

27. See "Barriers Can Fall," op. cit.

28. On the joining of Venceslao Jaime see *The Plough,* no. 4 (1953), 9-13.

29. *KIT Annual 1991,* 220.

30. On relations with the neighbors see *The Plough,* vol. 2, no. 3; vol. 3, no. 2; vol. 3, no. 4; vol. 4, no. 4; and also Allain, op. cit., 146, 232.

31. Allain, op. cit., 126-28; Cocksedge, op. cit., 86.

32. Allain, op. cit., 201-03; Interview with Maureen Burn, October, 1992.

33. Ibid.; Cocksedge, op. cit., 83.

34. *Outcast But Not Forsaken* (Rifton, N.Y.: Plough Publishing House).

35. See *The Plough,* vol. 1, no. 1; ibid., vol. 1, no. 4 (1954); and also *The Primavera Medical Service, 1949* [Pamphlet put out by Hospital in the Backwoods: Sanatorio Primavera (1954)].

36. Mow, Merrill, *Torches Rekindled* (Ulster Park, N.Y.: Plough Publishing House, 1989), 117-19.
37. Allain, op. cit., 120-23.
38. *KIT Annual, 1991,* 41. See also Bette Zumpe's book, *Torches Extinguished,* 54-56.
39. Mow, op. cit., 119-20.
40. Interview with Hans Meier, October, 1992.
41. Ibid.; Allain, op. cit., 146.
42. Mow, op. cit., 121. Georg Barth, who was then Hans Zumpe's associate and whose ways later parted, admits that after Eberhard Arnold's three sons had been excluded and later came together again, Hans Zumpe would tell him (Barth): Make sure that the three brothers do not live in the same community. Ibid., 163.
43. Ibid., 121-22. See also Elizabeth Zumpe's remarks, op. cit., 65-68.
44. *KIT Annual 1991,* 240.
45. Ibid., 41-42.
46. "Pioneering in Paraguay," *Mennonite Life* (January, 1950).
47. *Ten Years of Community Living* (Bromdon: *The Plough*) 39.
48. Wagoner, op. cit., 271.
49. See *The Plough,* vol. 1, no. 1; vol. 1, no. 2; vol. 4, no. 1.
50. Interview with Charles Headland, January, 1992.
51. Allain, op. cit., 214-15.
52. Interviews with Hans Meier and Charles Headland and also Allain, op. cit., 218-23.
53. *La Sociedad de Hermanos* (Montevideo, 1956), 4-5.
54. Interview with Stan and Hella Ehrlich, November, 1991, and with Charles Headland.
55. *La Sociedad de Hermanos* (Montevideo, 1956): 6.
56. Allain, op. cit., 256-60.
57. *El Arado,* no.3.
58. Wurm, S., *Communes and Their Way of Life* (Hebrew) (Ayanot, 1968), 515-16.
59. Interview with Andreas Meier, November, 1991.
60. Interview with Klaus Meier, January, 1992.
61. Interview with Raoul Weiss, September, 1991.
62. See *Amudim* (138) (December, 1957) (Hebrew).
63. Unna, Moshe, *Bruderhof—A Religious Collective Movement* (Amudim) (October, 1964) (Hebrew).
64. Correspondence on this subject between Dick Whitty and Roger Allain, who was then Servant of the Word at El Arado, began in June, 1957. All the correspondence that preceded the preparation of the special edition of *El Arado* on the kibbutz is preserved in the central archive at Spring Valley, together half-edited articles that were not included in the published issue.
65. *El Arado,* no. 7: 15.
66. Ibid.
67. Ibid.: 23-26.
68. Ibid.: 28-34.
69. Dick Whitty, a Primavera veteran and pacifist who was born in Scotland, joined the Cotswold Bruderhof and was very interested in Jewish culture and the establishment of relations with Israel and with Jews. He himself married a Jewish refugee from Vienna.
70. From Shahar's correspondence (May-September, 1956), to which the author was given access.
71. "Young Community in Israel," *The Plough,* no. 1 (1958).

72. Interview with Klaus Meier, Deer Spring, 3 January 1991.
73. In 1964, John Arnold, grandson of the founder, wrote to Martin Buber requesting his assistance in establishing contact with the kibbutz movement in Israel. Whether such contact was indeed established as a result of this letter is unknown. The letter itself is in the Buber archives.
74. Allain, op. cit., 225. Also *El Arado*, no. 2, and *The Plough*, vol. 3, no. 4.
75. *El Arado*, no. 2 (August, 1955).
76. See *The Plough*, vol. 1, no. 3; vol. 2, no. 1; vol. 3, no. 4. *El Arado*, no. 9.
77. Interview with Charles Headland in December, 1991. Roger Allain also says of this close relationship that he was to blame when the Bruderhof leadership criticized his leadership in Uruguay. Allain, op. cit., 283.
78. Allain, *Encuentro con Lanza Del Vasto*; *El Arado*, no. 6 (December 1957).
79. *Marcha* (4 September 1959), Montevideo.
80. On the missions to the South American countries, see *El Arado*, no. 8, and also *El Arado*, no. 5 (July, 1957); *The Plough*, vol. 1, nos. 1 and 2; vol. 4, no. 1; Cocksedge, op. cit., 89.
81. *The Plough*, vol. 6, no. 8 (1958).
82. Allain, op. cit., 275.
83. *KIT Annual 1991*, 216.
84. Interview with Stan and Hella Ehrlich, October, 1991. See also Allain, op. cit., 235-36.

6

The Bruderhof in England and Germany:
1943–1960

When the three people who had remained in England to arrange the sale of the Cotswold farm were joined by the British pacifists, the enlarged group was able to establish the Bruderhof community at Wheathill. In its early days the community was isolated from the mother movement in Paraguay, but it took only a short time for links to be established with the brothers across the sea, links that, because of the war, were by necessity limited. Two families of British origin who were sent to reinforce the links between the Bruderhof and the Wheathill group arrived at the beginning of 1943, and they proved to be an important addition, both as skilled workers and experienced commune members. One of these was the Mason family, who were originally from Birmingham and who had joined the Bruderhof in Germany in 1935. The two families from Primavera had six children between them and they became the foundations upon which the community's educational institutions were built.[1]

From 1944 to 1945, with the purchase of two adjacent farms, the community's acreage was increased to 545 and the location of the new farms brought the community closer to the main road, thus improving access and egress for agricultural produce. It was at this time that the water supply problem to the community was resolved and new living quarters were built. As a result of the diversion of all available resources to the war effort, it was impossible to obtain building permits for new buildings and for the improvement of the existing ones, so buildings that had been originally intended for chicken houses became the new living quarters! That year the settlement began to take on all the characteristics of a Bruderhof community in its administrative bodies, too:

apart from Stanley Fletcher, who was Servant of the Word, a work organizer, a steward (treasurer), and a house mother were elected.

The objective on the farm was to move to intensive farming, and the members began to extend their agricultural knowledge and learn new methods that had been previously unknown to them. Agricultural implements were purchased and yields rose, and in 1945 they succeeded in improving the farm's land from Grade C to Grade A, and while this improved the farm's yields, the lack of ready cash persisted. Although the new members who joined them from time to time brought some assets with them, part of them were transferred as donations to Primavera, as was the farm's surplus. The transfer of donations from England to Paraguay gave full expression to the Bruderhof principle of mutual assistance, a principle that was gratefully appreciated at Primavera and totally accepted at Wheathill. One of the commune's women recalls:

> The land and the dairy herd produced good yields and they had a good chicken farm. In addition, quite a few of the new members from England brought property and personal effects with them and these were handed over to the commune, but the members who had come from Primavera suggested that any surplus income be sent to Paraguay.[2]

True to the principled approach of the Bruderhof, the Wheathill commune, too, maintained an open-door policy for new members and so, toward the end of the World War II, Wheathill's membership increased continually with almost all the new members coming from pacifist circles. In 1943, the community numbered sixty-nine souls, including twenty-two children, and by 1945 the number of children had increased to thirty-two. According to Derek Wardle's estimate, they were joined in those early years by some thirty people each year. The majority of the people who joined were aged between twenty and twenty-two. "We were young and filled with enthusiasm," recalls Wardle, and adds, "Not only were we undeterred by the difficulties, they also filled us with joy and energy.... We had the feeling that this was the calling needed by the world at that difficult time." Those were the bleakest days of the war and true conscientious objectors felt that they had to shoulder part of the burden "so that out of all this, something new and positive would grow after the war."

The joining of the English youngsters was bound up with a split from their families, who could not accept their pacifist ideology and their choice of a life of poverty on the impoverished farm. Their move to Wheathill was a burning of bridges that justified giving up all their personal possessions. Derek Wardle says that "each of us gave all of his personal possessions to the commune with a sense of inner wholeness.... I personally brought with me a bicycle that was very close to my heart, but after a few days I felt that I had to hand it over to the commune, despite the fact that I was not yet a candidate for membership and that formally, I did not have to do so." The ruling ethos in the group was to give up all private property as a way of life and a symbol of a new beginning.[3]

At the time that new members were joining, an effort was made to reinforce the nucleus of Bruderhof members with a cadre of people from Primavera who guided the group in the organization of everyday life and their agriculture, and particularly in the direction that their ideological and religious education was to take. This stemmed from the fact that the new people were of a wide variety of faiths and beliefs, and some of them even saw themselves as agnostics. The leadership in Paraguay feared that the commune might deviate from the Bruderhof's religious path and, thus, reinforced the English group's leadership.

In those early days, the group's spiritual leader was Stanley Fletcher, one of the three Bruderhof members who had stayed behind in England. Before joining the Bruderhof he had been a wandering preacher who was blessed with great personal charm and he contributed a great deal to the consolidation of the group around Bruderhof beliefs. In 1945, the Bruderhof leadership decided to move Fletcher to Paraguay and replace him as spiritual leader with Llewellyn Harries, whose leadership was both strict and dogmatic as a result of his desire to maintain the characteristics and spirit of Primavera.

> The Wheathill Brotherhood fell more and more into "trying not to do the wrong thing" and taking the advice of the experienced community members from Primavera without as much as questioning any of the rules and regulations imposed upon them. This was a dangerous way to live together.[4]

The difficulties were great, particularly in view of the fact that the veteran Bruderhof members had brought with them the traditions of discipline and the example set by the Hutterites, while the majority of the new members, who had come from British pacifist circles, were "seeking people" who were possessed of a high degree of openness.

The Bazeleys, for example, who had joined the commune in 1943, and prior to their joining had been conscientious objectors with socialist and atheistic views, have this to say about the atmosphere of the place and its influence upon them:

> The place looked impoverished but it was rich in spirit.... We had no Christian belief when we first arrived, but we were gradually won over to the prevailing spirit of the place and came to the understanding that it was impossible to live a communal life without a deep love of one's fellow man.... Hence, we reached the conclusion that we must follow the footsteps of Jesus and become Christians. It was not easy, because we had been agnostics and the transition called for a great deal of convincing. Some of the veteran members had immense powers of persuasion. Life was full of the tension of seeking a way. The ethos of "brotherly admonition" reduced this, obviated an accumulation of fresh tension and encouraged candid clarification. The atmosphere was changed with the arrival of the Brothers from Primavera, where the theocratic and ecclesiastic Hutterite traditions were more firmly rooted.

John Bazeley illustrates the differences metaphorically:

> They (the Hutterites) rode on a train which moved forward on a fixed track, while we travelled on a road upon which we had to be alert every moment and be ready to deal with unexpected situations.[5]

In the summer of 1944, intensive discussions were held at Wheathill on the community's ideology and faith, at the conclusion of which a manifesto was formulated, which became a kind of declaration of their principles:

> Life at the Bruderhof is a way of life utterly opposed to the injustice and competition of the world today.... The door is open to all men and women of all classes and nationalities, so that all who desire a brotherly life may join together and share their lives for always. This longing for a life of peace and justice has led to the breaking-down of every barrier that stands before them, so that they have no property of their own but share their material goods one with the other according to their needs, in the manner of the Early Christians.

In the summer of 1948, the Wheathill community was accepted as a full member in the Bruderhof movement. The community's spiritual doctrine, which was based upon Early Christianity, was formulated in a document bearing the title, "Memorandum and Articles of Association."[6]

At the beginning of the fifties, much effort was invested in improving conditions at Wheathill. Burgel Johnson (Zumpe) moved to Wheathill from Primavera with her family in 1952, and she recalls that even compared to the settlements in Paraguay, the English community appeared impoverished and backward. There was no proper drainage or piped water, and it was only in 1953 that a central drainage system, proper toilets, and piped water were installed. The building of a large, spacious dining room, which would also serve as a hall for social, cultural, and general activities, was begun in the same year. The building was completed in 1954 and the opening was attended by dozens of their farmer neighbors.

In 1955, a generator that supplied electricity to the community was purchased and the building of a new school in the center of the community got under way. The old school building at Cleeton Court was about a mile and a quarter from the housing area and the farm and made the integration of the children in communal activities somewhat difficult. The building work was done in the main by young volunteers who spent the summer months at Wheathill in international work camps, which brought together young people from various European countries. Apart from their great work contribution, these camps provided an opportunity for a refreshing encounter between the community's young people and groups of enthusiastic youngsters and enabled the establishment of many future relationships. The joint efforts of the Bruderhof members and the forty young campers who participated in each camp helped complete the buildings and courtyard, and in 1956 the community's children had their first lessons in the spacious classrooms of their modern school in the center of the community. Cleeton Court Farm was sold a year later.[7]

In general terms, one may say that the Wheathill Bruderhof was formed by a young and dynamic group of people, which sought to form relations with various circles of the outside population and thanks to the numerous summer visitors, there was ample opportunity for this. One such visitor was Ellen Yacht, a young Jewish woman from a middle-class New York family, who was a pacifist. Ellen heard about the commune from some friends and while on a summer vacation in London, she decided to visit the remote Bruderhof community. She says, "From the moment I arrived at Wheathill, I knew in my heart that this was where I wanted to stay."[8]

Another visitor to Wheathill who was won over to the Bruderhof way of life was Martin Johnson from York. The son of a Quaker family, he had been imbued with Quaker values and heritage from childhood and while a student at Cambridge he visited Wheathill and wanted to stay, but the Bruderhof members persuaded him to postpone his arrival until after he had fulfilled his parents' wishes and completed his studies. And so, after receiving his B.A. in biology, he moved to the remote farm. "My parents were very disappointed by my decision. After my education and training at Cambridge, I suddenly decided to leave everything.... Happily, they changed their opinion after a few years and today our relationship is very amicable."[9]

Despite the fact that the community was isolated and off the beaten track, it was not all that far from the cities of Birmingham and Manchester, and in Birmingham the members of the Bruderhof found a platform from which to voice their views and disseminate their message. This was the famous "Bull Ring," which was the Hyde Park of the Midlands, and it was to there that the young people of the Bruderhof would go every Sunday, put up a soapbox, and address the public in the best traditions of British free speech. Audiences of hundreds would gather round to listen and argue, and sometimes the Bruderhof members would break into dance and organize community singing.[10]

The custom of going into Birmingham and speaking in the Bull Ring began in 1950 and continued without a break for seven years, in the course of which they opened a stall for the sale of their fresh farm eggs and this, too, became a permanent feature of their Sunday gatherings. Their perseverance and the quality of their produce gained them a good reputation, which helped them both commercially and in the dissemination of their message.

Their efforts, it turned out, were not in vain, and among their audiences were people who were interested enough to visit the Bruderhof, and some even became members. The best example of the effect the Bull Ring speakers had was the joining of a local journalist, Derrick Faux, and in a letter he wrote to the editor of *The Plough* some time beforehand, he explained the circumstances. This is how he described his first meeting:

> While waiting for a bus on Sunday in Birmingham, I was able to listen to one of your speakers. Although I had only a few minutes, I was deeply impressed.... I also received a leaflet about your community and its work. Until last May I was a newspaper reporter in Chesterfield.... For some years my wife and I have been seeking a way of life in accordance with true Christian principles, but in so many movements there is the constant dependence on financial gain, and the members are bound to separate their religion from their day-to-day lives. Your community does seem to find the answer in putting all work into the category of service [thus] eliminating the profit motive.... Do please let me know more. D.F.[11]

Faux was not satisfied with simply writing a letter to the editor and a short time later took his family to visit the commune, where he was won over to the Bruderhof way and beliefs and subsequently joined. He quickly found his place working in the publishing department and editing the commune's magazine, and sometimes publishing articles in the popular press. As a devotee of Esperanto, he also published articles in publications that appeared in that language (testimony to the distribution and influence of publications in Esperanto may be found in the story of Bruderhof member Joseph Ben-Eliezer, who says that he first read of the Bruderhof in an Esperanto-language publication). It was Faux's articles that first brought reporters to the commune and in 1951 the media drew attention to the Bruderhof in Britain, who then numbered 200 souls.[12]

This publicity brought public interest in its wake and at the same time encouraged the commune's leadership to initiate activities of a general nature, one of which was a conference directed at the general Christian public on the subject of "The Sermon on the Mount in Our Time." The conference was attended by some thirty people, the majority of whom were British friends of the Bruderhof and some who were clergymen and scholars attracted by both the location and the subject. There were also some scholars from abroad, among them representatives of the Italian Waldensians with whom the Bruderhof established relations. Some of the participants remained at the commune for an extended period, taking part in the daily life and work of the host community. If the responses of the participants were anything to go by, it would seem that the high standard of discussion served to enhance the Bruderhof's reputation and extend the circle of interest in it in both Britain and Europe.[13]

Beginning in the early fifties, Bruderhof emissaries from Wheathill visited a number of European countries: Switzerland, Holland, France, Italy, Germany, and a number of Scandinavian countries. These delegations, which were made up of adults and young people alike, made contact with many sectors of the population but in particular with the Reform Churches: Mennonites, Quakers, Waldensians, and others, and also with international pacifist organizations. Relations were also established with French Catholic circles who were interested in becoming acquainted with the Bruderhof's communal way of life and a special effort was directed at visits to post-war Germany. Wheathill's location enabled it to become the bridgehead for activities on the Continent and faced its members with a tremendous challenge, while at the same time weighting them with a burden they found difficult to bear.

Despite the fact that Wheathill's population had grown, it was still not large or strong enough to carry the burden of the growing farm that was their main livelihood. The various Bruderhof missions, together with the assistance they provided for the other Bruderhof communities, caused a manpower shortage with a consequent reduction in the farm's activities, but in spite of this, the community preserved its agricultural characteristics in both its culture and traditions. In October of each year the Harvest Festival was celebrated and all their neighbors were invited to take part. According to the tradition of this agricultural festival, the participants were seated on bales of straw in the field and were treated to a program of music, song, and plays. Toward the end of the fifties they experienced a number of hard years on the farm and there was a drop in yields, but despite these difficulties the community's activities continued in full flow, housing conditions were improved, and the farm's branches were extended.

The new set of circumstances that had been created after the war brought in its wake some changes in the direction of the Bruderhof communities' activities, and with them came the dawn of a period of extroversion, which was aimed at increased involvement in what was happening in the outside world. One significant expression of this trend was the revival of the publishing house and the quarterly *The Plough*, publication of which had been suspended in 1940 with the Bruderhof emigration to Paraguay.[14] Relations with Europe, and with Germany in particular, were reestablished in 1947 and Bruderhof emissaries went to Germany to seek contact with people who wished to atone for the sins of the past and also those who sought a renewed Christian way of life. Their disappointment was great when they found only confusion and nihilism, but this did not deter them from continuing with the establishment of relations and even from trying to reestablish the Bruderhof in that country. At the same time, efforts were made to publicize their existence in both Britain and on the Continent. Numerous letters and circulars were sent out to old friends in order to show them, and the general public, that not only had the Bruderhof survived, but that it was alive and well. Relations with Primavera, too, were strengthened and new members were sent to England. The press began to show an interest and sympathetic articles on the Wheathill community were published.[15]

In December, 1956, representatives from all the Bruderhof communities worldwide met at Primavera to discuss the objectives of their activities in outside society. Also discussed was the question of Wheatill's status in the light of increased activity on the Continent. The view was aired that the community had reached its optimal size and could not absorb more new members. There were suggestions that a new location for the Bruderhof commune in Britain be found, one that had the required absorption capability for new applicants, and these were based on the assessment that there were many people in Europe who were seeking an alternative way of life. Another claim was that they needed to find a location closer to London that would allow greater mobility, and more particularly, greater accessibility for all the potential visitors. The upshot of all this was that in the summer of 1956, the search began for the location for a second Bruderhof community in England.[16]

The Bulstrode Bruderhof

The search for an additional location led the searchers some twenty miles from London to the abandoned Bulstrode Palace at Gerrards Cross in Buckinghamshire. Bulstrode was a seventeenth-century palace surrounded by a 500 acre park that had been the residence of the Duke of Portland and which, like so many other stately homes, had been recently abandoned. Negotiations for the purchase of the property between Bruderhof representatives and the custodians of the property in the County Council began in October, 1957.[17]

In the summer of 1958, the Bruderhof concluded the purchase of the palace and seventy acres of the park and on 18 July the first group of twenty people arrived and began work on repairing the huge building. The 100-room palace had not been lived in for fifteen years and was in a state of total neglect. The purchase imposed a heavy financial burden on the Bruderhof and appeals to their friends for financial assistance in renovating the building and converting it into suitable housing appeared in the British press. By autumn of the same year there were already some 100 people living there, the majority of whom were members who had come from Wheathill, and there were also some English members who had returned to Britain after many years at Primavera. One of the latter was Gwyn Evans, who had joined in England in 1938 when he was a Congregationalist minister. With the help of friends in the towns, the rooms were furnished and converted into living accommodation, but the problem of heating the huge building during the winter months remained unsolved.

Among the first people to move to Bulstrode from Wheathill were Ullu and Ellen Keiderling, whom I met in their apartment at Woodcrest thirty-three years later. They told me about the move to Bulstrode and recalled that the need to alleviate the problem of overcrowding at Wheathill had been accompanied by a desire to break out of their enforced isolation; a need to be closer to London, concentrations of young people, colleges and universities, and the seeking people. Wheathill was in a remote location, "on the north-western edge of the map of England," and was off regular public transport routes. In some respects these were the same objectives that had brought the Bruderhof in Paraguay to establish a community near Montevideo.[18]

It turned out that from the standpoint of contact with the outside population, the choice of location was fully justified and this was a source of great satisfaction for the people at Bulstrode. In a letter to the editor of their quarterly, they wrote:

> Proximity to London has justified our expectations of many visitors and Bulstrode has continued to be the center of much activity. A new departure has been that we have held open meetings on Sunday mornings to which friends and neighbors have been invited.... Also, on five successive Sundays we have sent a small team into London to speak in Hyde Park.[19]

In general terms, life at Bulstrode was easier than at Wheathill. The palace and the park were full of treasures and hidden corners that delighted the community's young people on their wanderings on the property. Burgel Johnson, who had been among the first to move to Bulstrode and was secretary to Arnold Mason who was Steward, recalls:

> We made a great effort to turn that huge palace into a pleasant place in which to live, and it was no easy job. The building was neglected and cold and the roof leaked in many places, but life there was full of surprises. We youngsters would wander through the park, the halls and the cellars and discovered treasure troves of antiques; statuettes and paintings, and especially caches of vintage wine... but in the final accounting, the main problem was to find sources of income that would enable us to make our livelihood. We lived in a magnificent palace under conditions of poverty and hard work. At first we produced wooden toys along the lines of "Community Playthings," but our main source of income was the manufacture of

steel doors for farmhouses. The work was laborious and as we had to market our products by ourselves, the income was not large. We also sold flowers we picked from the garden and cultivated a piece of land for growing vegetables for our own consumption...but that did not provide a livelihood. The shortage of cash prevented us from renovating the building and even from repairing the leaky roof.

Burgel recalls that there was not an overabundance of food and in order to be able to eat one meat meal a week, they contacted a Jewish butcher in London and in return for laundering his staff's overalls they were given half a cow every week.[20]

The steel door factory slowly got on its feet, their financial situation improved, and with the help of friends they also managed to raise money for medical equipment, agricultural machinery, and clothing for the communities in Paraguay.

With the arrival of the big group at the beginning of October, the Bruderhof held an open house for some 300 people from the local population. This was the first opportunity that their neighbors had been given to become acquainted with the Bruderhof members, their communal way of life, religious beliefs, how they made their living and their cultural level.[21] In an effort to win their neighbors over, the Bruderhof repeated the open house event several times over the next few years and the number of their neighbors who took part increased. In the spring of 1959, some 600 visitors attended the event and spent a whole day in the park, which was in full bloom. The openness displayed toward the outside world brought visitors from various church circles, including some French Catholics who were interested in learning from the Bruderhof's communal experience. In 1957, they had some visitors from India and also pacifist groups from Holland and Germany.

There were also reports from Wheathill on a large number of visitors from various groups and countries, among them families from Holland, Scotland, and France, and even a lone student from Ghana. There were also young people from India and South Africa and an Italian professor from the University of Rome who all came to see the communal way of life for themselves. For their part, the young people of the Bruderhof organized social activities in the slums of Liverpool and Manchester during those years.[22]

On the crisis that beset Bulstrode in 1965, Merrill Mow writes:

An atmosphere of complacency and laxity threatened to destroy the life of the community and sapped its inner vitality. During the winter and spring, a number of brothers and sisters travelled from America to Bulstrode and called the members of the community to face challenges which would arouse them from their slumber.

He says that at the time, when almost all the Bruderhof were settled in the United States, and after all the *Hofs* in Paraguay and Europe had been closed down, it appeared that there was no justification for the continued, separate, and isolated existence of the Bulstrode Bruderhof. In a joint decision made on 20 March 1966, by its members and members of the *Hofs* in the United States, it was decided to close Bulstrode down and move its members to the United States. The decision was effected that same year and in December, 1966, the last of its members left Bulstrode Palace.[23] The building and park were bought by a missionary association, which invested large sums in renovation and the proceeds of the sale of the property paid for the member's journey from England to America. Thus ended thirty years of Bruderhof communities in Britain.

The Revival of the Bruderhof in Germany

At the beginning of 1950, after some earlier efforts at establishing relations with religious and pacifist circles, a plan was formulated for the establishment of a bridgehead in Germany with the opening of "Bruderhof House." The house was designed to be a contact address for visitors and guests and also as a base for the dissemination of the Bruderhof message and its literature. The plan was inaugurated in 1955 when the Bruderhof acquired a big house capable of housing some twenty-five people at the historical site of Hohenstein Castle, in the mountains of Franconia in Bavaria, not far from Nürnberg. The first group of six people left Wheathill for the new location at Easter, 1955, driving the length of Germany to the Bavarian mountains and the castle, which was situated on one of the highest peaks. It is worthy of note that the revival of the Bruderhof in Germany coincided with the twentieth anniversary year of the death of Eberhard Arnold, the movement's founder. The first group consisted of German, Dutch, and British members whose task it was to begin preparing the house, which had stood abandoned for a long time, for housing the members and guests.

The house they had at their disposal stood outside the castle itself, in the area that had in the past held the outer fortifications. According to some estimates, the large building dated from the tenth century and had been used in the past as housing for the estate's tenant farmers and later as a guest house. It was solidly built and after some minor repairs could easily be used for housing, but its greatest advantage was its location: atop a peak overlooking a magnificent view of the Bavarian mountains as far as Nürnberg and the forests of Bohemia. Soon after the arrival of the first group, the first visitors began to arrive: lone hikers and organized groups from Nürnberg who had heard rumors of the Bruderhof's arrival. To facilitate contact with their visitors, the Bruderhof members set up a stall that sold fruit and fruit juice and from which their German-language literature was distributed, and it was in this way that they also established relations with the inhabitants of nearby Hohenstein.

The Bruderhof group remained at Hohenstein Castle for six months, during which time they were visited by over 100 people, the majority of whom stayed with them for short periods. The most significant relationship they established was with the members of the Nürnberg pacifist group, "The Brothers of Common Life," and this proved to be one that would endure for many years. They were also visited by Germans who had been close to them in the past and at the end of that summer they held a conference for graduates of the *Freideutsche Bewegung,* a movement with the which the Bruderhof had maintained relations in the distant past. The conference was attended by approximately sixty people and the problems of postwar Germany were discussed. Emmy Arnold, widow of the Bruderhof's founder, who had been given the opportunity of travelling from Paraguay to visit the movement's historical sites in Europe, also attended the conference. But despite the success of the summertime visits, the Bruderhof members reached the conclusion that they would be unable to remain at Hohenstein Castle during the winter months and so, in October, 1955, it was decided to move to another location in Germany.[24] Fortunately for the Bruderhof, they were presented with the opportunity of buying an estate called Sinntalhof, near the spa of Bad Bruckenau.[25]

The estate covered twenty acres and included a number of buildings, and prior to the Nazi rise to power it had been a boarding school, which had later moved to Connecticut in the United States. The buildings that dated from the end of the nineteenth century were fit for accommodation and part of the land was ready for cultivation, so these conditions enabled twenty-five people to settle there and begin living in an independent community, which was thenceforth known as Sinntal Bruderhof, the eighth Bruderhof community (there were three in Paraguay, one in Uruguay, one in the United States, and two in England).[26]

The man who was the most active in bringing the Bruderhof back to Germany was Hans Zumpe. From the early fifties he had devoted most of his efforts to finding ways of reaching groups in Germany with which the Bruderhof could renew its relations. In 1956 he wrote an article in the Bruderhof quarterly in which he set out the reasons why, in his opinion, it was necessary to renew their activities in Germany at the same time as maintaining those in South America and Paraguay. In his view, in the Germany of the fifties, conditions were ripe for a Bruderhof community to fill a role in the spiritual enthusiasm that had gripped the young people of that country. Zumpe felt that the enactment of the compulsory military service law, with its possibility of a choice of nonmilitary service, could well put the Bruderhof on the map of Germany as a place in which young people could perform a service of peace in community life and agricultural work. This view found support among conscientious objectors outside the Bruderhof and they went so far as to emphasize the fact that it would be in the Bruderhof's interests that this service should not be institutionalized, but rather be one of free choice and on a voluntary basis.[27]

The Sinntalbruderhof immediately set about fulfilling the tasks that they had set themselves in Germany, and emissaries were sent out to various circles. In August, 1956, a Bruderhof delegation took part in a German Quaker conference where they were warmly received and given an opportunity to present themselves and their community. Immediately afterward they participated in the annual Conference of Protestant Churches in Germany, which took place in Nürnberg and which was attended by some 7,000 people from all over the country. Despite the conference's size, the Bruderhof delegation succeeded in presenting their position before the participants.[28]

The Sinntalbruderhof allocated three of its members to fulfil these missions throughout Germany on a rota basis and they were also assisted by members from England, especially in tasks of a more general nature, like the antinuclear campaigns. These activities attracted the attention of the press, which resulted in the publication of a number of articles in both the local and national papers.

During the community's first years, the buildings were renovated and converted to the specific uses of a Bruderhof community and a dining room and kitchen were built, which were planned to cater for a large popula-tion. 1959 saw the commencement of construction of an additional build-ing, which was designed to house families with children and accommodation for their numerous guests. The reputation of the Sinntalbruderhof spread and the summer months brought so many visi-tors that in the first year, they did not have enough room to accommodate their visitors and were forced to rent rooms in the nearby town. Although the majority of the visitors were German, they were also visited by paci-fists and conscientious objectors from France, Holland, Switzerland, and England, and also by a delegation from the Aituru commune in Nigeria.[29]

In 1958 they began to set up a factory for the manufacture of decora-tive wooden boxes and wooden toys in cooperation with the central factory, "Community Playthings," which had been set up in the United States at about the same time. Their products penetrated the local mar-ket and were also bought by tourist visitors to the nearby spa.[30]

As in all the other European Bruderhof, the Sinntalbruderhof made efforts to establish relations with the local population. In 1959, Bruderhof members visited a nearby refugee camp where they organized a Christ-mas party that brought some joy into the lives of the camp's inmates. In general, it was obvious that the Sinntalbruderhof members were ex-tremely sensitive to the revival of their community on German soil and could not ignore the burden of the past, which cast its cloud over that country. Evidence of this may be found in a 1960 issue of *The Plough,* the main part of which was devoted to a protest against the reappear-ance of antisemitism in Germany, news of the desecration of graves in Jewish cemeteries, and of the obscenities scrawled on synagogue walls. The same issue mentioned that the Bruderhof members had devoted a whole week to "the Jewish Question," in which they had read books on Jewish history, Hasidic tales from Martin Buber's book, listened to Jew-ish music, and hung paintings with Jewish motifs in the dining room. In their discussions they had sharply criticized modern-day Germany for not doing enough to eradicate the spirit of hatred that had spawned the abomination known as antisemitism.[31]

Notes

1. Interview with Arnold Mason, Woodcrest, 1991; *Ten Years of Community Liv-ing—The Wheathill Bruderhof* (England: The Plough Publishing House, 1952), 15–19.

2. Zumpe, Elizabeth Bohlken, in *The KIT Annual, 1991* (The Collected Newsletters of the KIT Information Service, San Francisco, Calif.), 290; Ibid., 104. Also *50th Anniversary of the Wheathill Bruderhof* (Rifton, N.Y.: Plough Publishing House, 1992), 30-32.

3. Wardle, Derek, in ibid., 35.

4. Zumpe, E. B., in *KIT,* vol. 3, no. 11; Ibid., 107-09.

5. Interview with John Bazeley, November, 1991.

6. *Ten Years of Community Living,* 19.

7. *The Plough,* vol. 3, no. 3 (Quarterly of Bruderhof communities. Bromdon: The Plough Publishing House, 1955), 79; vol. 4, no. 4 (1956), 122-23.

8. Interview with Ellen Keiderling, November, 1991.

9. Interview with Martin Johnson, November, 1991.

10. *The Plough,* vol. 2, no. 1 (1954); vol. 3, no. 3 (1955).

11. Ibid., 22.

12. Faux, Derrick, "All Things In Common," in *British Weekly* (3 May 1956); Brown, Peter, "The Happiest People in Britain," in *Everybody's Weekly* (6 June 1956).

13. *The Plough,* vol. 4, no. 2 (1956).

14. The first issue of the quarterly was published in Spring, 1953. *The Plough* was also published in German and later in Spanish and Dutch, and later still in Esperanto.

15. *Sunday Pictorial* (20 May 1951); *Mennonite Weekly Review* (2 September 1948).

16. *The Plough,* vol. 5, no. 3 (1957).

17. *The Buckinghamshire Advertiser* (25 October 1957).

18. Interview with Ullu and Ellen Keiderling, Woodcrest, November, 1991.

19. *The Plough,* no. 3 (1959).

20. Interview with Martin and Burgel Johnson, Woodcrest, November, 1991.

21. *The Plough,* nos. 2 and 3 (1958).

22. Ibid., no. 3 (1959).

23. Mow, Merrill, *Torches Rekindled* (Ulster Park, N.Y.: Plough Publishing House, 1989), 255-56.

24. *The Plough,* vol. 3, no. 2; vol. 3, no. 4 (1955).

25. According to Elizabeth Zumpe, it was her parents who discovered the estate and brought about its purchase. It happened when they were on their way to visit the site of the old Rhön commune. They stopped for coffee in Sinntal, which they had known before the war. The owner offered them the estate on very good terms on the condition that they allow her to try to join their community in England. The Zumpes liked the place, saw that it had settlement and economic potential, that it was close to public transport services, and it was decided to purchase it. Zumpe, E. B., op. cit., 144.

26. Ibid., 144-45.

27. *The Plough,* vol. 4, no. 1 (1956).

28. Ibid., no. 3.

29. Ibid., no. 1 (1960).

30. Ibid., no. 3 (1958).

31. Ibid., no. 1 (1960).

7

The Move to the United States

With the end of World War II, there was evidence of an increased desire at Primavera for the establishment of contacts with outside society. Kathleen Hassenberg, a native of Scotland who spent the war years at Primavera, says that even then she raised the need to send emissaries to countries outside Paraguay:

> We have a mission and we do not exist solely for ourselves; we must make contact with people like ourselves who are seeking a way of communal life.[1]

Bette Zumpe describes the prevailing atmosphere in her memoirs:

> After the war people became restless. They wanted contact with the civilized world. They wanted to be part of the rebuilding of a destroyed Europe. There was a restlessness which caused brothers and sisters to reach out into the world.... The trouble was, where to start? Europe, where we came from, or the USA? Heini was sent to the USA and my dad (Hans Zumpe) to Europe.... The people of Europe had just been through the war. They were scared of anything that smelled of communism. The Americans, on the other hand, were very enthusiastic about communal life.[2]

The first signs of American interest in the communes appeared in 1948, when the wanderings of three Harvard dropouts brought them to the Primavera Bruderhof. The three, Bob Peck, Jim Bernard, and Art Rosenblum, were looking for a meaningful communal life through which they would be able to cast off their frustration with American society. They were very impressed by the Paraguayan communes and published their impressions in the American press. One of the articles appeared in the pacifist Quaker magazine, *Fellowship of Reconciliation*, and helped to spread word of the Bruderhof in North America even before their emissaries reached the continent.[3]

Among the visitors from America who came to become acquainted with life in the Bruderhof in the fifties were the Wagoner couple. Their impressions of their extended stay appear in their comprehensive book, which contains a somewhat ambivalent appreciation of the Bruderhof in Paraguay:

> Here is certainly no Utopia in any sense of the word. I should like to dispel that idea entirely. The work is hard, there are disagreements and personality clashes.... But there is one tremendous difference between this and any other group of people I have ever seen: they have a common basis among them for meeting people and overcoming them. The common basis is a spirit of love, "and love overcometh all things." The life here can only be described; it cannot be communicated.[4]

In 1947, a discussion was held at Primavera on the question of sending a mission to the United States to raise funds for the hospital at Loma Jhoby. The Bruderhof also sought to use the opportunity to travel the country and sense its mood, for they had received the impression that with the end of the war, the beginnings of a wave of communal awakening had become evident in North America. Following these discussions, emissaries were sent to the United States from Paraguay from 1949 onward, and from that time not a year went by without at least two such emissaries in the eastern and western United States. Two Bruderhof emissaries reached California in 1952 and were extremely impressed by the scope of communal awakening on the west coast, where they met with organizations and groups who lived in communes and cooperatives, and these in turn showed great interest in the Bruderhof.[5]

In those early years, the Bruderhof emissaries were mainly engaged in fund-raising and obtaining equipment and medicine for the hospital at Loma Jhoby, but at the same time they sought contact with groups interested in a communal way of life. These efforts were crowned with success among the wealthy Quaker community from whom they received large donations, and also among the pacifists who had formed cooperative communities while they were interned in the camps for conscientious objectors during the war, and who were also very generous.[6] The Bruderhof emissaries were popular speakers at colleges and theological training colleges and wherever they went, they were asked, "Is communal life possible in an America that is drowning in wealth? What is the basis needed to begin communal life?"[7]

By 1952 the number of Bruderhof emissaries in the United States had reached six and their main objective was to establish contact with those communal groups that had expressed an interest in their ideology. These were the cooperative communities of Koinonia, Macedonia,

Kingwood, and Celo. The largest and most prominent was Macedonia, which had been founded by Morris Mitchell as a cooperative group prior to World War II. Toward the end of the war the community was joined by a group of young pacifists who had come together in North Dakota and who aspired to found a commune, and on their arrival at Macedonia they began to realize their dream by moving the community over to communal lines. In 1947, the members of this group had founded a small industrial enterprise for the manufacture of wooden toys called "Community Playthings," and while still in North Dakota they had first heard of the Bruderhof through a booklet published in England in 1939, called "Children in Community," which dealt with the Bruderhof way of life and the education of their children. When the members of the group heard that Bruderhof emissaries had reached the United States, they made contact with them, the Bruderhof people were immediately taken to the hearts of the Macedonia veterans and from the outset relations between them were excellent.

Among the emissaries sent abroad during those early years were Eberhard Arnold's three sons. The first to go was Hardy, whose fluent English impressed his listeners. He was followed by Heini and Hans and their wives, and they managed to establish good relations with a number of people from the smaller American communes. Heini and his wife, Annemarie, left on their mission in the first half of 1953 and they managed to establish strong ties with potential candidates for the Bruderhof, especially from among Quaker families. The most notable of these was the wealthy Potts family from Philadelphia who enjoyed high status among the Quaker activists in the eastern United States. The head of the family, Tom Potts, was a senior executive in a steel mill and had been active in Quaker peace organizations during World War II. His encounter with the Bruderhof emissaries changed his life. He was won over to their way of life and beliefs, put himself and his home at their disposal for the dissemination of information, and later decided to join them and live, with his family, in the Primavera commune, only returning to the United States in 1955 when the Bruderhof commune was established there. "They sent us back to the States because we were too old to ride horses on the Paraguayan prairie," he would say laughingly.[8]

The mission was a moving and impressive experience for Heini and Annemarie, and twenty-five years later Annemarie would sum it up thusly:

> The time when Heini and I were sent from Primavera by the Brotherhood to travel here in the United States and take up contacts with friends that the brothers had made on an earlier trip, and if possible to raise some money for Primavera—this whole time meant very much to both of us. We came into contact with so many different people who were seeking something different for their lives.... After having been in Paraguay for about twelve years, where we were shut off from everything that was happening in the world, it was like a fresh, new wind for us.[9]

In his memoirs, Merrill Mow, who at the time was one of the youngest Americans to be won over to the Bruderhof way, tells us something of the atmosphere in the United States of the fifties that inspired young idealists to seek communal life:

> In the wave of idealism following World War Two, many people were looking for something new, and some were looking in the direction of community. It was not as in more recent years when young people were living in community because they felt it should follow from being a serious Christian. Rather, in this grouping of communities in America, the motives were social concerns and these "intentional communities" were of all sorts. some were anarchistic, some semi-communal, and cooperatives.[10]

The Bruderhof emissaries reached the United States at the time when intensive activity was under way for the establishment of federative ties between the various communal groups. A prime mover in this respect was the Fellowship of Intentional Communities, an umbrella organization bringing together groups and scholars who dealt with communes and cooperation. This organization held a conference at Macedonia at the beginning of 1954 and the Bruderhof emissaries who attended were received with much interest by the delegates of the community groups. But there were also some who viewed the Bruderhof's participation with something less than enthusiasm and it was one of these who attacked them as a fundamentalist group that endangered the free spirit of the American communes. These attacks, however, were isolated incidents and the majority of the community members took them to their hearts and defended them from their critics. It was these encounters and the visits to the communities that brought about the linkage between the awakening to community and the Bruderhof. Alan Stevenson, one of the first emissaries, summarizes it this way: "There was some serious seeking of a way among young Americans.... and the 'witness' of the Bruderhof carried some weight."

It gradually became clear that there was a great deal of interest in communes and that the chances of their establishment on this continent fully justified the establishment of a Bruderhof community in the United States. In her memoirs from that period, Gertrud Arnold writes: "That mission led to the feeling that we should establish a Bruderhof in the United States."[11]

Heini and Annemarie Arnold were also very impressed by the idealism they found among young Americans. During their mission they met young people who were prepared to take social tasks upon themselves, work in the poorer neighborhoods and fight racialism, and they write:

> When we went back to Paraguay we knew that we had somehow to find a way to begin a communal life in the States to which some of these people might be able to come. We had to share our lives with them.[12]

It was under these circumstances that a meeting of the General Council of Bruderhof delegates was held at Primavera in July and August of 1953. Delegates from Europe and North American friends also attended, among them Francis Hall, the spiritual leader of the Kingwood commune and also the Wagoners from the Church of Brethren. Heini and Annemarie Arnold, fresh from their mission to the United States, were also there.[13] At the conference, some differences of opinion emerged with regard to the continuation of the Bruderhof missions throughout the world. Heini Arnold was in favor of deepening and extending their ties in the United States and he reported on relations that had been established with the Macedonia and Kingwood communities, saying that in both places there was a readiness to hear about communal life. Hans Zumpe, who had come from Germany, told the council of links he had forged with old friends of the Bruderhof, but according to his later comments, the council was unresponsive and he did not succeed in engendering the feeling that Europe was interested in the Bruderhof's message. The general feeling was that Europe had only recently emerged from a war and was still licking its wounds, but America on the other hand aroused euphoric expectations, and so Zumpe was isolated.[14]

The Council of 1953 was an event of special significance that represented a stage in the new beginning and a breaking out of the long isolation of Paraguay. *The Plough*, reporting on this, said:

> Several years ago we felt how cut off from the world Primavera was. Through the activities of the members we have sent out to various countries and through the arrival of new friends, our backwoods solitude is now a thing of the past.... For us at the Bruderhof, the arrival of new friends is always an encouragement.... Their

presence broadens our point of view and gives our children and young people a vivid awareness that there are people in all parts of the world who are seriously struggling for a new meaning of their lives.[15]

The role of the Council was to decide on a policy of missions to Europe and the United States, and after prolonged discussion it was decided to send a seven-man delegation to the United States that would undertake the groundwork for the establishment of a community in North America. The members of the delegation met with members of the various cooperative communities with whom they had contact, and after several weeks of talks and clarification the parties reached the conclusion that they should unite. Moreover, once they had got to know the members of the Bruderhof delegation through their talks, a number of the Macedonia people indicated that they wanted to participate in the establishment of a new community in the United States. They wrote a letter to Primavera in this vein and were told that they should not act too hastily, for their acquaintanceship was but brief and it was still too early to allow their integration. It was, however, agreed that it would be preferable to become further acquainted and only later to decide on the possibility of amalgamation.

The main factor that prevented immediate amalgamation was the nonexistence of an agreed position on matters of belief and religion. The community groups were a real conglomeration of faiths, ranging from Buddhism to agnosticism. A clear instruction was sent from Primavera saying that any amalgamation must be conditional to the acceptance of Bruderhof principles and the agreement of prospective members to become "novices" according to accepted Bruderhof practice. Prior to acceptance as a member, the novice, or candidate, had to participate in seminars and discussions on the principles of faith and on day-to-day norms. The process of formulating the principles obliged all the potential candidates to gather in one place, and so the Macedonia community in Georgia, the community with which the Bruderhof had the strongest ties, invited them all to be their guests.[16]

Art Wiser, a member of the Bruderhof today who then belonged to Macedonia, told me about the amalgamation with the Bruderhof:

> We were very happy about the relations with the brothers because they had come to us at a very difficult time in our existence.... Seasoned families had left us at that time because they could see no future in our group.

In the wake of a number of members leaving the group, the people at Macedonia began to discuss their future and the Bruderhof members who visited Macedonia at the height of these discussions were invited to stay despite the internal crisis that was raging. The discussions on amalgamation with the Bruderhof went on for some three months and at their conclusion, on 28 March 1954, seven families decided in favor of amalgamation and three decided to continue as an independent group. Art Wiser opted to stay because he had remained an agnostic and the Bruderhof's religious objectives were unacceptable to him. So, the community was split with the full agreement of the parties concerned and arrangements for coexistence were made with mutual understanding. It was decided to divide the property (and the debts) proportionately, but one knotty problem that remained was what was to be done with the toy factory. At first it was decided to divide it up, but it was later agreed that it should be transferred to the majority group on the assumption that it would have a greater chance of furthering its progress. Art Wiser, who represented those who were remaining, says that the detailed arrangements for the division of the property were made in an atmosphere of understanding and friendship; "We did not fight for rights and advantages." Thus, the industrial enterprise that was to become the movement's most important economic asset in the coming years was transferred to the first Bruderhof group in the United States. It should be mentioned that relations between the two groups continued to be extremely amicable and the people who remained in the Georgia community expressed their readiness to continue talks with the Bruderhof.[17]

Apart from the people from Macedonia who joined the Bruderhof, there were also some newcomers from other communities: Five members of the Kingwood community from New Jersey who decided to dismantle their community and join the Bruderhof; a number of members of the Koinonia cooperative community, and several members from Celo. This last group had in the past combined cooperation in private housing and independent jobs. Their ideal was life in the bosom of nature according to Thoreau's doctrine and the majority were vegetarians. They had first heard of the brothers in 1953 and had invited their emissaries to visit them. A further meeting took place at a conference of the Federation of Intentional Communities and it was there that they were won over. For four years the members of this group had tried unsuccessfully to find their way to communal life and had been faced with a dead end. Meeting the brothers revealed a previously unknown world and they, like other such groups, had held talks with the Bruderhof, but not all of them had been convinced. The news that the Bruderhof intended to establish a community in the United States convinced several of them to join.

This was how quite a large group was formed in the United States and it was clear that they had to find a place for the new community immediately, one which could absorb the newcomers and the others who would undoubtedly follow. A series of preliminary survey trips was undertaken in the north-eastern part of the country in which seventy-five sites were inspected. The seventy-sixth and last place they saw was the one they chose, close to the town of Rifton in New York State. It had been previously owned by a wealthy carpet manufacturer called J. W. Dimmick[18] and was called Woodcrest Farm.

Woodcrest: The First Bruderhof in the United States

The decision to purchase the ninety-five acre Woodcrest Farm was made at the end of May, 1954. The small delegation that visited the farm was most impressed by what it found: the buildings were large and spacious, the farm itself was close to several main roads, and a magnificent view of the Catskill mountains could be seen from the top of the hill. Fortunately, they were able to raise the money required for the purchase, for at more or less the same time, they had been joined by John Houssman, an elderly man who was suffering from a terminal disease, whose only desire was to live out the rest of his life as a member of a commune and who contributed $30,000 to the community.[19]

The advance group arrived at Woodcrest on 8 June. The property had been abandoned for four years and was in a state of total neglect. On 4 July, the thirteen people there celebrated the establishment of the new community and two months later the entire group of sixty-five souls, including twenty children, had arrived at Woodcrest. It was a varied group, consisting as it did of people from different communes. The group's nucleus was comprised of Bruderhof members from Paraguay and it was they who filled both the social and spiritual offices, with Hans Herman Arnold as Servant of the Word. This core group was joined by the people from Macedonia, who brought their "Community Playthings" toy factory to the new community. With them came the people from Kingwood who in the past had been Quakers, but who in recent years had sought their way in oriental religions and in meditation, and finally the group from the Celo cooperative community in North Carolina.[20]

Dick Domer, one of the Celo members, has the following to say about those early days:

> Those first days were very exciting and filled with enthusiasm. We all had different views on life, education and food.... We were vegetarians and ate at a separate table, but after a short while we felt that our vegetarianism was hindering the group's social consolidation and that it wasn't really that important to us, so we had no hesitation in stopping. As we all came from different groups with an openness to different philosophies and beliefs, those early days were filled with a great many ideological struggles. But at the same time there was a great deal of admiration for the Bruderhof veterans. They did not try to force their way of life, which had been accepted in Paraguay, upon us but together with us they tried to find suitable ways of combining the various traditions.[21]

By December, 1954 they numbered eighty souls. In February, 1955 Heini Arnold and his family arrived and Heini took the leadership of the community upon himself as Servant of the Word. The largest group of newcomers was that from Macedonia and it was they who had the strongest tradition of communality. The Macedonia group had brought with them a great number of assets, and in particular the woodworking machinery that was to lay the foundations of the Woodcrest toy factory, which kept the name "Community Playthings." The machinery and the rest of the factory's inventory were moved to Woodcrest at the end of 1954, and in order to ready the factory for production they worked right through the winter without suitable heating. The products were in the main the fruits of the members' powers of invention and some were improved models of toys that the members of the Bruderhof had made for their own children. In the first years, the factory had been divided between the two parts of the original Macedonia community, but once full amalgamation went into force in 1957, it and its production facilities passed into full Bruderhof control.[22]

Tom Potts, the man who got the factory running at Woodcrest and who managed it for many years, recalls:

> The first few years were very hard. We lacked experience and had no knowledge of the market. We sent some of the brothers out selling but without much success... but it was not long before things changed. The sixties saw the enactment of a federal law in the United States which obliged primary schools to open kindergartens or a kind of pre-school. It was called "Head-Start" and its objective was to give educational motivation to the children of the poorer communities. The federal govern-

ment injected a great deal of money into this project and all at once an almost unlimited market opened up for our products, which apart from toys also included school furniture. The possibility of expanding our production coincided with the beginnings of the Bruderhof movement's expansion in the United States and this provided us with solid economic foundations for our activities.

Tom repeatedly emphasized that "we view our success as a gift from God and believe that He guided, and will continue to guide us along the right road."

Regarding the factory itself, Tom says:

We feel that the work in factory is particularly suitable for our way of life...there is work for all sectors of the population and it can be adjusted to meet a particular need. Work is not seasonal and there is no need to work on festivals and holidays. Our products are not patented but we are not afraid of competition for the products enjoy a fine reputation, thanks to our high work ethic. The factory has gradually grown and developed from almost nothing and as a result of our experience we can enjoy the fruits of our labors.[23]

Woodcrest's population increased and by March, 1955 some 100 souls were living there. The first task that faced them was to convert the buildings into living quarters. The buildings were large and spacious and although they contained numerous living rooms and larger rooms, neglect was everywhere. In 1957 they were joined by the second half of the Macedonia group, which in the past had refused to reject the pluralism of its beliefs. The group's leader, Art Wiser, had entered a deep theological discussion with Heini Arnold and in the end had been persuaded to accept the Christian beliefs of the Bruderhof. Once agreement had been reached on matters of religion, the group transferred its land and property to the Bruderhof. There was some deliberation on whether to remain where they were or to move everyone to another Bruderhof community. Macedonia was situated in a beautiful mountain region but it was isolated and access was difficult, so it was decided to move the population and the property to Woodcrest temporarily. The move was temporary because the population now numbered some 150 people and the community was approaching the limit of its absorption capability, so it was decided to purchase a new property in Connecticut called Evergreen.[24]

One of the most notable events that occurred during the first years at Woodcrest was the big fire that broke out on 4 February 1957. The fire destroyed the community's central building, which housed the dining room, the kitchen, and the food store. It also housed the offices of both the community and the factory. The flames rapidly destroyed a great deal of property and caused extensive damage to the archive, destroying *inter alia,* Eberhard Arnold's manuscripts. All the members who were there at the time recall those hours with pain and sorrow and the only happy memory was the speed at which their neighbors rallied round to help extinguish the fire, and also their help in the days that followed. It was the first and most significant indication of the good relations that had developed between the community and their close neighbors. But of course the brunt of the rehabilitation work fell on the shoulders of the community's members who at the time numbered 200, and on those of the teams that had been sent to help from all the Bruderhof communities.[25]

The special spirit of enthusiasm and openness that characterized all the Bruderhof communities was also evident at Woodcrest. Heini Arnold felt it and years later would say:

> There was one thing that was refreshing for Annemarie and me: a new straightforwardness and honesty...people wanted a straight relationship...this is something that for me belongs to the strong impressions of the early Woodcrest.[26]

Despite the primitive conditions at Woodcrest in those early days, the community attracted many visitors and guests, some of whom were simply curious or just passers-by, while there were others who had serious intentions of joining. Such were Merrill Mow and his wife, of the Church of Brethren in Chicago, who came to stay and six months later were accepted as novices. Rumors of the new community spread far and wide, around the neighboring areas and New York City, and at weekends the community was flooded with visitors. Some members were appointed to meet with the visitors for long talks and discussions on their way of life and beliefs, and these, coupled with Woodcrest's special atmosphere, had a great effect on many young people who were seeking a meaningful way of life. One can hear evidence of this in talks with many of the Woodcrest veterans who came to the community individually and through a variety of motives. Dick Domer recalls:

> We were flooded with visitors every Sunday, many of whom were religious and secular Jews from New York. They came to see us because of our proximity to the popular Jewish resorts in the Catskills and we had talks with many of them. We held special meetings for visitors on Sundays; they asked incisive questions and we had to find answers. These meetings took place at the same time as the brothers' regular Sunday meetings at which we would study together. We did not read only religious books but also philosophical works...this was in 1956 and 1957 and we

were visited a great many beatniks...some of whom meditated every day and who were not overly enthusiastic about work. There were people from a variety of walks of life and a variety of outlooks. All in all, the meetings were very interesting and were accompanied by a spirit of mission.[27]

The Alexanders, who had lived in a commune near Toronto, were also among the visitors to Woodcrest in that first year. In their reminiscences, twenty-five years later, they recall that when they asked to come and visit they were told that because of the great demand and the small number of available beds, they would have to wait. When they finally arrived, they immediately fell under the spell of the atmosphere of enthusiasm that pervaded the young people there and were captivated by the warm welcome they received; "We felt as though we had come home." I heard similar remarks from Woodcrest member Donna Ford, late of the Church of Brethren, who came on her own. Donna had heard of the Bruderhof through *The Plough* and what she had read encouraged her to find a way of joining them. She wrote in the summer of 1956 and received a prompt and positive reply. Donna, too, recalls the warm welcome as something that captivated her from the first moment. Some of the community's young people were waiting for her at the railroad depot and from there to Woodcrest on its hill, they walked singing together, and when they reached the top of the hill she, too, said emotionally, "I feel as though I have come home."

Dick Thompson arrived at Woodcrest in the first year when he was still an engineering student at the prestigious Cornell University. A Quaker by education and a nonconformist by choice, he, too, was won over by the special Woodcrest atmosphere. A year later, on completion of his studies, he returned and asked to be accepted as a candidate. "I was searching for meaning and an ideal in my life, which was then centered around my personal needs, and I found them at the commune," he would say in retrospect. "Those years in the United States saw a great deal of interest in communal life and I came to Woodcrest with that in mind. My Quaker education which tells us to seek the Word of The Lord possibly had some influence on guiding me towards the group."

Dick's wife, Collette, came from an entirely different background. She was born in New York and was active in pacifist circles. 1955 saw her working as an editor on a local newspaper when some material on the Bruderhof that had recently been established in New York State, crossed her desk. She and a friend found great interest in the Bruderhof story and as they were both tired of the city streets, they decided to visit the community on their bicycles. They reached Woodcrest in the early evening and were immediately enveloped in its special atmosphere; families with their children were sitting outdoors together, barefoot and simply dressed, spending their leisure time in song. It was something that was diametrically opposed to all that they were used to seeing in the big city and they were enchanted by all they saw during the two days they spent at Woodcrest. Collette recalls that on her return to the city she was restless and could find no further interest in her work, and so, a short time later she went back to Woodcrest and asked to be accepted as a candidate. "There was a unique spirit at Woodcrest that attracted young, idealistic people and those who were seeking a way," she says. She adds: "There were also young people in distress who were attracted to the community and who asked our help, but we were unable to help them all. Some of our efforts ended in failure. There were some requests that we rejected. We were not interested in conversion but rather in absorbing those people who had felt 'the call' to live as we did."[28]

The majority of the veteran members of Woodcrest have similar stories about the magic of those early days and the force that attracted them to the commune in its first years. It should be mentioned that of the thousands of visitors who passed through Woodcrest in the course of those years, a few remained and became members, thus increasing and strengthening the American sector of the population, which gradually became more significant in the wide and varied spectrum of the Bruderhof's ethnic makeup.

"Distant Brothers"—Relations with Kibbutz Members

It was at this time that contacts began to be made between the Bruderhof and the kibbutz movement. Shalom Wurm was the man who first opened the door to the world of the communes through his correspondence with Bruderhof members.[29] Evidence of Shalom Wurm's relations with the Bruderhof in the fifties may be found in several of his letters, which are in the Woodcrest archive. One of them, dated 30 September 1955, is entitled "An Invitation" and an excerpt reads as follows:

I have spread the news of your new community (in the United States) among some of the most active people in our movement. They felt encouraged. One of them came up with a splendid idea; he asked how your people would react to convening a joint conference of all the Hutterite Fraternal communes and the communal settlements in Israel to discuss the problems of community living, exchange opinions and establish close ties. Many of our friends seized on it and would welcome such a rare opportunity. Our veterans of the Jordan Valley suggested that should such a get-together materialize, it should take place in the Jordan Valley, where the Degania Kvutza has existed for forty-six years. They would like to be the hosts of such a symposium. Do you consider such a suggestion practicable?...We have to cope with many problems that would no doubt interest you.

The letter, written on behalf of *Ihud Hakvutzot Vehakibbutzim,* was signed by Shalom Wurm.[30]

The reply from Woodcrest was written by Hector Black:

Your friendly letter delighted us all. We read it to our members in the dining hall and sent copies to several of our communities in order to inform them of your proposal to organize a meeting or convention. The main obstacle is the fact that just now we are extremely busy in getting ready for a convention of communities that will convene in a couple of months in Paraguay.[31]

Two years after the first invitation, Shalom Wurm repeated it in a letter to Dick Whitty: "We would be happy to host several of your members here.... Both our communities would benefit much from such a visit." Going on to discuss the problems of young members, Wurm writes:

While some of your young people seem to be influenced by the cultural climate of your new country, ours aspire to achieve university education.... It is hard to fight these trends, but we are doing our best.[32]

In the years of Shalom Wurm's correspondence with Bruderhof members, other kibbutz members formed relationships with them that stemmed from visits to Woodcrest. Its proximity to New York City, the predominantly Jewish summer resorts, and in particular to the *Hehalutz* summer camp sites, made Woodcrest a frequently visited place for both incidental tourists and Jewish youth movement emissaries and camp counsellors. Roswith Arnold (Eberhard Arnold's granddaughter) recalls one such visit:

I remember one time that a whole group from a kibbutz came and they told us about themselves at supper. Then they began singing and one of them got up, took another by the hand, and before we knew it the whole room was dancing. It was just during supper and they were dancing the "hora" between the tables. It ended up as a very joyful dance evening and they taught us some Israeli dances, and that's how we slowly learned them.[33]

Woodcrest was also visited by some Israeli public figures who were interested in the communal settlement that looked like a kibbutz. One of them, Yosef Baratz, was one of the founder members of Degania. Despite its brevity, members of Woodcrest remembered his visit as a moving experience. Dick Domer recalls:

> Yosef Baratz visited us in the spring of 1956. It was a very special occasion. We had met with Jewish groups before; those who came from New York and the youth from the nearby summer camps. Baratz had evidently heard about us from them and was eager to visit. He arrived with his wife and three young people. It was a very cold day and I remember Baratz walking about in his winter coat. He met the community at lunchtime and told us about Degania and the Israeli kibbutzim. His story was fascinating because it was our first encounter with one of the kibbutz movement's founding fathers. The meeting led to warm feelings on both sides and we were very sorry that he could not stay overnight. His visit had a strong impact because he sent us his book on Degania, and for a long time we read chapters from it during our meals.[34]

Further testimony of the impact of Baratz's visit may be found in a letter he received from Hector Black, who wrote:

> We were very pleased to receive your book about the founding of Degania and the early pioneers' life. Thank you from the bottom of our hearts. The book interested our members very much.... From what we have read, it is evident that in the past as well as nowadays there is a keen aspiration for togetherness which leads to a large measure of unity and to profound relations between members.... Several days ago, a group of young Zionists from New York paid us a visit.... We are glad to have closer relations with kibbutzim and it is superfluous to emphasize that we expect such visits in the future.[35]

Some time after Yosef Baratz's visit, Israel Sheffer, a second-generation member of Kibbutz Ayelet Hashahar, visited Woodcrest and recorded his impressions in an article published in *Niv Hakvutza*.[36] The article is of special interest because it presented the first comprehensive impressions of an encounter between a kibbutz member and the Bruderhof in the United States. It also includes parts of a dialogue between the author and his hosts on their way of life and beliefs. Sheffer had heard about the Bruderhof from other kibbutz emissaries and was prepared for this encounter.

> Except for the different ideological concepts (regarding the place of nationalism in man's life on the one hand, and the place of religion on the other) which should not be disparaged, there is a great similarity between the way of life in these communities and life in the kibbutz.... We therefore prepared ourselves for a visit to a commune not unlike the *kvutza*, and assumed that the differences between us derived mainly from their religious and ideological origins.

But following his first impressions of the place and the people, when he conversed with Bruderhof members, Sheffer discovered that

> the way in which the kibbutz movement in general and its members in particular identify with the Jewish nation, society, and the State, is completely alien to them. They do not subscribe to the principle of the commune's active involvement with related outside society and the nation. According to them, the commune has rejected all that.

> In their encounter with us (the kibbutz), Bruderhof members continue to wonder how a commune can survive without religious foundations. The brethren are convinced that brotherhood ensures unity, which in itself is founded on religious values and experiences. Moreover, we learned that they are not motivated by the settlement factor or by a desire to return to nature.... Even though they live away from the cities, settling a tract of land is of no importance to them. They have no close attachment to their settlement because this might enhance economic considerations instead of ideological ones.

In this article, Sheffer gives a detailed account of long conversations he had with his hosts about their way of life, mode of education, means of consumption, ways of organizing work, culture, and the like. Summing up, he says:

> Even though in most cases we tried to avoid any recurring comparison between the Bruderhof and the kibbutz in Israel, our outlook is evidently influenced by the fact that we are kibbutz members.... One may approach the Bruderhof from three different aspects: first, as a human, spiritual, or social phenomenon, the values and very existence of which are of some interest; second, by perceiving the brotherhood as a chapter in the social Utopia of man's salvation; and finally by comparing the Bruderhof and the Israeli kibbutz, their differences and similarities. Despite the human, geographical and general remoteness, an observant kibbutz member employing a historical approach may learn quite a lot from this comparison.

Although Sheffer's article was not the only one to be published in the kibbutz press at that time, it was certainly the most comprehensive. From 1954, several letters and brief accounts about visits to the Bruderhof communities in the United States and England appeared in kibbutz movement publications.[37] From them one may learn about the character of mutual impressions and the kind of issues raised at such encounters.

In October, 1956, the *Kibbutz Hameuhad* weekly, *Bakibbutz,* published an article by Saul from Kibbutz Alonim in which he tells of his visit to Woodcrest.[38] His impressions were similar to those of Sheffer and he tells of a conversation with a Bruderhof member who had visited Israel and had stayed at several kibbutzim (in 1950, before he joined the Bruderhof). According to this member:

Their (the Bruderhof's) perception of equality is more far-reaching. Whenever a community acquires some property, for instance, if one of its members inherits, they share it with all the other communities. People are sent from one settlement to another in order to give a helping hand for unlimited periods of time.... They have no central organization and everything is arranged through correspondence between the various communities. Individual problems are solved without sets of rules, just by talking.... Their commune is based on their religious and emotional aspiration towards the renewal of man and more profound relations between one person and another.

Saul also received the impression that "there is a strong sense of adverseness towards society at large and the existing regime." When he inquired about their attitude toward socialism, he was told that "we don't trust people who preach socialism without actually living it in a commune."

One of the more interesting aspects of the published correspondence was the fact that they were willing to reveal acute problems in order to learn from mutual experience. For example, Hector Black wrote to Shalom Wurm in January, 1956:

For some time I have wondered how you deal with serious differences between members and whether you have adopted any regulations in case of anti-social behavior.

He goes on to relate certain instances of social tension he encountered on his visit to an Israeli kibbutz and asks about the means of dealing with them. Finally, he apologizes for "asking such serious questions... they ensue from my wish to understand how you cope with certain problems that we have in common and that are inherent in a communal way of life."[39]

It is evident from this correspondence that they were concerned about their younger generation, its behavior, education, and loyalty to the movement. These issues were raised in two letters that were written in October, 1957. In the first, from Primavera, Paraguay, Dick Whitty wrote about a convention on educational issues at which members complained that the young people were more interested in horse riding than in studies, that they were bored by rural life in Paraguay, and were seeking ways that were unacceptable to the community. He ended by saying, "I know that these problems are not unfamiliar to you."[40]

The second letter was written by Ruth David from a new commune near Farmington, Pennsylvania:

We are very eager to hear about the life of your younger generation. I am interested in education and especially in teenagers. It seems that our youth suffers from the same problems and difficulties as teenagers everywhere. It is not easy for them to decide on a communal way of life, even though eventually most of them reach that decision. We enable them to live outside for a while and experience a different way of life in order to make them think and reexamine their life more profoundly.[41]

Interest in the kibbutz was also found in the Bruderhof periodicals. Between 1954 and 1955, *The Plough* published two articles on the subject, one by a member of Kibbutz Giv'at Brenner[42] and the second by Harry Viteles, Professor of Economics at the Hebrew University of Jerusalem and Chair of Cooperations at the Eliezer Kaplan School of Economics.[43] It should be noted that the editor was inclined to add, "For some years our communities have felt a particular interest in the community life which is practiced in Israeli kibbutzim." In addition to the above-mentioned articles, *The Plough* also published short items on events in the kibbutz movements.

Renewal of Relations with the Hutterites and the Forest River Episode

The emigration of the Bruderhof to Paraguay caused a certain relaxation in their relations with the Hutterites and a diminishment of their influence on the Bruderhof. Relations were resumed at the end of the forties and Bruderhof delegations visited the Hutterites in order to strengthen the weakened ties.[44] Although during the war years and afterward the Bruderhof had maintained their loyalty to the values and beliefs that had previously guided them, there had been some movement away from the typical Hutterite way of life. The women did not adhere to the Hutterite dress code and the men were not obliged to grow beards in the Hutterite manner. Smoking, dancing, and the playing of musical instruments, all of which were anathema to the Hutterites, were prevalent in the Bruderhof. Yet in order to maintain good relations, the Bruderhof still made great efforts to preserve, even partially, the Hutterite customs they had adopted.

In 1949, two Bruderhof representatives, Bruce Sumner and Alan Stevenson, were sent to the Hutterites in North America who then numbered some 8,500 souls. Their mission was to allay the Hutterite's fears regarding the Bruderhof's conduct in Paraguay, to invite a Hutterite delegation to visit Paraguay, and to request material assistance. The mission was crowned with success and the Hutterites sent clothing,

implements, and agricultural machinery valued at $40,000 and also
$22,430 in cash.[45]

Some years later, in 1953, two Hutterite representatives visited Paraguay. The delegation (John Wipf and Samuel Kleinsasser) brought gifts
of boxes of clothing and although they were warmly received by the
members of the Bruderhof, they were shocked by what they found
there, especially by the widespread habit of smoking. They were also
surprised to find that the joining of new young members from the
United States had revived the tradition of the German youth movement. Work camps, folk dancing, theater, and even movies had become a matter of course in Bruderhof culture. Neither side was prepared
to compromise. The Bruderhof felt that modernization was vital for
attracting new members and the proof of this was manifest in their
success in attracting new members from the United States. The
Hutterites, on the other hand, felt that the desire to grow was distancing them from the Hutterite way. And so, when the delegation returned
to the United States and reported their findings, the Hutterite elders
served warning on the Bruderhof and demanded that they repent publicly and revert to loyalty to the Hutterite way. The Bruderhof were
not prepared to accede to these demands, and so twenty years of efforts at rapprochement ended in open crisis. This split with the
Hutterites saw the emergence of a period of liberalization in the
Bruderhof way of life and the expansion of their contacts with Europe
and the United States, which had begun immediately after the war.[46]

Despite the split with the Hutterite leadership, the first signs of bud-
ding personal relationships between the sister movements became apparent during these years and a number of Hutterites were among the
stream of visitors to Woodcrest in its first year. The first was Julius
Kubashek, the charismatic leader of a secessionist Hutterite group that
had settled near Toronto, who visited in January, 1955. Kubashek had
received prior notice of the Bruderhof's intention of moving to the United
States and he spread the news among the Hutterite communities. A short
time after Kubashek's visit, Woodcrest was visited by a number of
Hutterite men and women from the communities in North Dakota and
Canada. They were young people who were interested in becoming better acquainted with the world outside their communities and their visit
caused great excitement among the Bruderhof members. During their
stay they discussed their respective ways of life, the visitors pointed out

the differences between theirs and that of the Bruderhof, and the Bruderhof members replied that at a time like this, when there were so many prospective applicants for membership, dress as strange as that of the Hutterites was a barrier between them and the sincere people who were seeking a way. Dick Domer says of that visit:

> Despite the external differences between us, the four brothers felt an atmosphere of brotherhood and joy in the community. They were surprised to discover that young Americans had chosen to live the life of frugality and self-discipline that they had seen at Woodcrest. By the same token, the Americans were very moved and grateful for the opportunity of meeting Hutterite brothers for the very first time.

The differences in dress did not deter or keep the Hutterite visitors away; on the contrary, during these visits they suggested that they send some Hutterite carpenters to help with all the building work that faced the new community. And indeed, a series of contacts between Woodcrest and a number of Hutterite communities was established in the wake of their suggestion, and in the end, a team of five carpenters arrived in 1955 and made a very significant contribution in the construction of one of Woodcrest's new, big buildings.[47]

Those first Hutterite visits to Woodcrest, coupled with the assistance provided by the carpentry team, strengthened the ties with the Hutterite commune of Forest River in North Dakota. This community, which belonged to the *Schmiedleut* faction, had experienced some agitation for change and the need to establish contacts with the outside world, and now a large group of its members wanted closer ties with Woodcrest. The visits of "outsiders" like Clarence Jordan, leader of the Koinonia commune in Georgia who had visited them in 1954, had a fateful effect on the new community. It was Jordan, who had been warmly welcomed, who aroused the members' desire for the establishment of contact with the outside world together with Koinonia. This desire was expressed in the decision to send some people from Forest River to Koinonia and in turn to accept a couple who were teachers from there. This unilateral decision by the community was made without the approval of the Hutterite leadership and aroused their severe criticism, to which the Forest River people replied that they had a perfect right to decide independently on their way of life. At the same time, the Bruderhof delegation, which had come to seek their help in establishing their new community in the United States, came to see them. Their request was approved and the five carpenters left for Woodcrest to help in putting up the new buildings. It was these initial contacts that brought the Forest River community to seek permanent relations with the Bruderhof. The Hutterite elders tried to prevent this and the members of Forest River were divided: some 60 percent were for and approximately 40 percent against.[48]

However, the Woodcrest community was cautious; they had always held that Primavera was the mother community. To avoid anything that might appear to be inappropriately independent, Heini Arnold kept the Servants at Primavera and Wheathill informed about the Hutterites with regular reports. Gwyn Evans, a Servant at Primavera, responded to a letter from Heini on 25 May 1955:

> News about the visit of the Hutterites was joyfully received.... Here in Ibate we were all pleased with how things had gone.... It looks as if we are going to be concerned with a very important period in our dealings with the Hutterians and it may be determinative to our future as a community.

Unfortunately, there were tensions. Many at Forest River longed for freedom from restrictive legalism and hoped for deeper, more concrete relations with the Bruderhof. At the same time, some young members of Woodcrest who were perhaps too overzealous, were disrespectful toward the Hutterite elders who tried to maintain the stability of their colonies and shied away from too rapid a merger of the two groups. In the end, all this led to an even deeper breach.

The Woodcrest community decided to agree to the Forest River request and send a delegation that would establish relations with the Bruderhof. Among those who went to Forest River were Heini Arnold, Hans Meier, and Arnold Mason. In the light of the Bruderhof's strict observance of the custom of full agreement and consensus in their communities, this was an extraordinary decision. Later, when this episode was to become a crisis in Bruderhof-Hutterite relations, this readiness to establish relations with Forest River would be considered as the "original sin" that caused the decline.

In an interview with the author, Hans Meier said:

> I was in Forest River in 1955. I had been sent from Primavera and stayed there for six months. We all made a great many mistakes, both the Hutterites and us. We felt that we were better than them, and that was our problem. We felt superior and more modern than the Hutterites, and they, on the other hand, expected us to further their interests, but it should be remembered that it was they who initiated the contact with us.[49]

A short time after the Bruderhof families arrived at Forest River, the majority faction felt that they should consign the entire community to the movement. One of them describes it this way:

> We all had such a longing for something new in our lives, that when we heard of the Bruderhof...we decided that we really wanted to devote our lives and join the Bruderhof.... Heini challenged us quite often...that if we did not feel it completely in our hearts that this was the way we wanted to go, then it would be better that we turn around now. He told us again and again that he did not want to force anyone. It had to be a voluntary life.[50]

The decision caused a split in the Hutterite settlement, the minority left and went back to the mother community in Manitoba, and thus the break with the Hutterite communities was complete. Over half of the members of Forest River joined the Bruderhof and the community became one of the eastern communes of the Society of Brothers. An interesting and first-hand testimony of what went on in the community can be found an article by Ruth Baer-Lambach, who at the time was a young girl at Forest River. This is how she describes the coming of the Bruderhof families:

> This varied group burst into our 16th century farming village like a hurricane, upsetting our set way of life and changing it forever. The first ones arrived in the winter of 1955 and the last ones left in the spring of 1957. Their arrival and departure were full of unbelievable tension, anger, hate and bitterness and the results of that attempt at unification are evident to this day. The Hutterites live their lives without asking questions, but with the arrival of the Bruderhof, everything was put into question; the women stopped wearing the apron, shortened their skirts, gave up the traditional black and white spotted kerchief, and even cut their hair.... The Bruderhof put a stop to use of the children's dining room and we all ate together in the main dining room, in family groups. Twelve of us went to school at the local high school.
>
> The Bruderhof brought a number of exciting things into our set way of life. As far as I was concerned, the most beautiful of these was music, music without words...the Bruderhof were past masters at organizing shows that combined music, dance and art, and they knew how to get hundreds of people together in a common objective.... With the singing came folk-dancing.[51]

But despite the diligent efforts to advance unification, the amalgamation was unsuccessful. An admission of the difficulties they faced may be found in information published in *The Plough* in the summer of 1956:

> Woodcrest and Forest River have been working out the problems which inevitably arise when a newer and older movement come together.

The difficulties stemmed mainly from the vast differences between the two groups. The Hutterites found it difficult to get used to the Bruderhof's internationalism and to the ways of their people who had come from the outside world. Their lengthy long-distance telephone calls shocked the frugal and insular Hutterites, while the Bruderhof had difficulty in adapting to life on the midwest prairies and were depressed by the isolation of the small settlement, far from any centers of population. Another big difficulty was adapting to long days of farm work, especially at harvest time. The long work days prevented the community from spending time in the discussions that were an integral part of Bruderhof life.

Economic and practical problems became serious. It was difficult to run a large farm and at the same time gather the community for the meetings essential for maintaining its spiritual vitality, and this problem was particularly acute at seeding and harvest time. An added burden was the fact that Forest River consisted of two farms that were several miles apart.

Eventually, the brotherhoods of Woodcrest and Forest River decided to leave the North Dakota property; the families who wanted to farm it would stay there as a separate group, but the others could not move until a new location was found. By July, the brothers searching for a new location had found a property with enough living space to accommodate those waiting to move: Gorley Lake Hotel, a mountain resort near Uniontown in southwestern Pennsylvania, about 400 miles from Woodcrest, was up for sale. It was duly purchased and made ready for occupancy.

In 1957, there was a split at Forest River and the Bruderhof members decided to leave and move to the Oak Lake community, which was then being built in Pennsylvania, not far from Pittsburgh. The decision to leave the North Dakota settlement stemmed from Bruderhof movement considerations. At that time, there was a trend of growth and expansion in the eastern United States and Forest River was far from the center of events and could take no part in them. *The Plough* reported on this in no uncertain terms:

> Forest River was too remote from the main centers of activity in the United States.... The work proved to be too time-consuming during the summer months—the only time when guests would come.[52]

Merrill Mow sums up the leaving of Forest River:

Gathering in the East had certainly been a factor in our decision to return Forest River to the authority of the Western Brothers. It was far from our Woodcrest Bruderhof and more isolated from large population centers.

As an additional problem, the practical work there dominated life too much. It is just a fact that at seeding and harvest time, work simply has to take precedence over everything. During these times of intense pressure, brothers would be out on the tractors almost twenty-four hours to a shift.... And if the Servant of the Word saw the need to have a brotherhood or other important meeting in the evening, it was very difficult because the farm needed so many brothers.[53]

In 1974, at the time of the renewed efforts at rapprochement with the Hutterites, Hardy Arnold spoke of the Forest River episode in a self-critical vein:

The divisive, evil power at work in the communities brought about a break with the brothers known as Hutterians. This originated in Forest River, North Dakota, in 1955. At that time, several members of the Hutterian colony were seeking a closer relationship with the Society of Brothers in Woodcrest. Some of the members of Forest River even felt strongly drawn to "join" the Society of Brothers. In the ensuing conflict with our Hutterian Brothers of Manitoba and South Dakota, brothers and sisters acted sinfully. We [by] possession of the Forest River Colony for a time. This was legally in order but it violated the love of the Sermon on the Mount. We accepted some of its members into membership of our own group, and in this way forced those members who wanted to stay loyal to the Hutterian Brothers to leave their own colony. We deeply regret this arrogant act, which led to a complete break with the Hutterians.[54]

New Communities in the United States

On 15 July 15 1957, the new community in Pennsylvania was founded. Its establishment was designed to assist in the absorption of new Bruderhof members; those born in the United States (like the Macedonia pacifists), those who had decided to leave the Hutterite Forest River community, and also Bruderhof members from Primavera. The location, which had been known as Gorley Lake Hotel, consisted of woodland, meadows, a big house, and a large artificial lake that had been used for swimming, sailing, and fishing. The area had been in the past a farming and mining region, but had suffered economic decline in recent years and currently had numerous pockets of poverty and hardship. The establishment of the community aroused a great deal of external interest and even *Time* magazine, in its issue of 29 July 1957, devoted an article to the community and its inhabitants. The article mentioned, *inter alia,* that the purchase price of the hotel was $150,000.

From the beginning, the members of the Bruderhof had a definite interest in establishing relations with the local population and so, on 3 August 1957, a few weeks after the community's official opening, they held a "Bruderhof Open House" and according to the report that appeared in *The Plough,* it was attended by some 600 visitors. The schoolchildren put on sketches and there was an exhibition of the wooden toys they had begun to produce in the new factory. The number of people who wanted to come was so great that they decided to extend the open day by an additional day. In the exhilaration of the encounter, the Bruderhof members expressed their wish that the Bruderhof become a meeting point for those who were seeking ways to greater understanding between people. In general terms the open house was a great success that began a tradition of good relations with the local population.[55]

From the outset, the Bruderhof members began to provide assistance and welfare to the local needy, sometimes in cooperation with local welfare bodies such as the Food Bank, and sometimes independently by responding to direct approaches for help. The community also provided permanent jobs for a number of local people, especially skilled builders, plumbers, gardeners and so on.

Some time after the move to the new settlement, the Bruderhof members began to make changes on the ground. The first big operation they undertook was to change the somewhat luxurious décor of the dining room and adapt it to more modest Bruderhof tastes. The tapestries that covered the walls were taken down and the room was painted and enlarged. The living accommodation was good and everyone lived in a single, large building that contained the dining room, the school, and the office.

In the summer of 1965, they began an undertaking that would truly change the face of the settlement. It all began with Heini Arnold's visit when, in a discussion with him, the tensions, quarrels, and the troubled social atmosphere, all began to surface. Heini listened carefully and then asked, "What do you think about draining the lake?" (It will be remembered that there was an artificial lake on the property.) This suggestion was received with some astonishment and Heini was asked what that had to do with their social problems, but his intention quickly became clear: he had provided the community with a challenge that immediately raised their sagging morale. At the time, they were all living in the same house; "We had got used to living in comfort...you could walk around in bedroom slippers all day," some of the veteran members would later recall. Apart from the question of their morale, draining the lake was likely to provide a large play area for the children and allow access to the factory without having to cross a busy highway. And so they drained the lake, leaving a small two- to three-acre section of water at the southern end for its landscape features and sport, and once the drainage had been completed, the community's name was changed from Oak Lake to New Meadow Run.[56]

As work on the infrastructure continued, a new access road was laid in the autumn of 1965. The old route of the access road had joined the main highway at a dangerous intersection and needed to be changed. All these major undertakings had a great effect on the life of the community and significantly reduced the proclivity, even addiction, to excessive comfort that had tended to control their life in the past.

In its layout, way of life, and economic activity, New Meadow Run resembled the rest of the Bruderhof communities. The children attended both the community's school and the Uniontown high school. In the early years, they established their printing press and the offices of "The Plough Publishing House" and to this end, members from other communities who specialized in publishing were brought in.

One of the most notable characteristics of New Meadow Run was their good relations with the local population and a good example of this was something that occurred in the early days. Their next-door neighbors were a poor family who lived in a house that was unfit for habitation, which one day went up in flames. The Bruderhof came up with the idea of building them a new house, and so sixteen members of the community were mobilized and put up a new wooden house in one day. This, of course, had its effects and helped create very good relationships with the local population. In the turbulent seventies, when the wave of the flower childrens' communes swept the country, the Bruderhof was open to young people who were trying to find their way. A great many people visited the community on the main highway and some even found there the vision and the society they had been seeking and joined the Bruderhof as members.

The Bruderhof in Connecticut

In 1958, a short time after the land and buildings of Macedonia had been sold and the families had moved to Woodcrest, the Bruderhof began looking for a place for a new settlement that would be able to absorb the new people. They found it in northwestern Connecticut, not far from Norfolk, in the shape of an estate owned by Michael Pupin, a millionaire of Serbian extraction, on which he had built a home in the style of the Serbian palaces. The place was known to the Bruderhof from their search of 1954 when the estate had appeared to be far too grand and therefore unsuitable. This time, in the face of necessity, they decided to buy it. The estate had one very important advantage: its proximity to Woodcrest.

The ownership of the estate was transferred to the Bruderhof in the summer of 1958 and on 25 July the first families from Macedonia moved in and the rest of the members had arrived at their new home by the beginning of August. The estate had been neglected for many years and the buildings were in urgent need of renovation. Although the buildings were solid, stone-built, and spacious, they were unsuitable for living accommodation for the Bruderhof. The land was mainly swampy and a great deal of effort had to be invested in its drainage and preparation for the needs of the community. Among the first equipment that reached the new settlement was the machinery from the Macedonia toy factory, and only two months later the factory went into production.

The new settlement was first called Evergreen because of the striking firs that stood in the yard, and it was only fifteen years later that the name was changed to Deer Spring.[57] Here, too, a short time after the foundation of the community, the Bruderhof members invited the local population to an open day for getting to know one another and the establishment of good relations. The locality was a well-known resort area in the Berkshires and its population, which was thought to be relatively wealthy, displayed both curiosity and a sympathetic attitude toward this strange band of religious idealists. It may be said that their normal relations were maintained into the future.

Once the new settlement in Connecticut had been established, the number of Bruderhof communities in the United States in 1959 reached three, with a total population of some 400 souls. From that year onward, the Bruderhof communities in the United States began to play a leading role in the movement's development worldwide.

This situation was to gain significantly in intensity with the outbreak of the great crisis of 1960. Although the events of the crisis did not bypass the United States, their effect was not fatal as it was in other parts of the world.

The 1956 World Conference

Primavera, which in the past had been the connecting link between the communities, began to be shunted aside. In 1956, the total Bruderhof population worldwide numbered 1,100 souls, including approximately 450 members. The idea of a social-evangelistic movement became more established and from that time forward, internationalist elements, which stemmed from the Bruderhof's demographic makeup and its worldwide dispersion, were added. At this stage of their history, their sense of mission led them to view themselves as the bearers of a general message to mankind. Their publications proudly pointed at their multinational composition, which included Britons, Germans, Swiss, Americans, Dutch, Swedes, Austrians, Czechs, French, Italians, Letts, Indians, Spaniards, Argentineans, and Paraguayans. In much the same way they were very proud of the varied ideologies and cultures that characterized their members: Pacifists, anarchists, communists, agnostics, anticlericalists, clerics, and two native Paraguayan families, the mothers of which knew only Guarani.

It was under these circumstances and in this mind set that the second World Conference of the Bruderhof was opened at Primavera in 1956. The aims of the convention were to reinforce the ties between the various Bruderhof communities, which in recent years had become extremely ramified. All of the movement's communities sent delegates who represented approximately 1,400 souls in nine communities in South and North America and Europe. Numerous issues were discussed, among them the economic situation and the financial ties between the communities, educational policy, and youth training, and the policy of their publications in English, German, and Spanish. Hans Zumpe spoke enthusiastically of their activities in Germany, while admitting that although at present the achievements of the Sinntal commune were limited, he recommended that in the meantime the place should be used for seminars and conferences. He also suggested that additional effort should be invested in Germany. In contrast, Heini Arnold was in favor of expanding their activities in the United States. Regarding South America, the North American delegates were inclined to recommend a reduction of their activities there, and although Primavera was still considered to be the center of the World Bruderhof Movement, its status had been increasingly diminished due both to its remoteness from the centers of activity and its financial situation, which had turned it into a burden on the movement's communities in North America. A particular burden was the work in the Loma Jhoby hospital. Those in favor of cutbacks argued that as new hospitals had been established in the region, the hospital was not as indispensable as it had been in the past. They also claimed that the continuation of the hospital's work would be nothing more than a contribution to Paraguay's social welfare policy and that the Bruderhof, in the light of its current situation and its own needs, was unable to shoulder such a burden. The conference was concluded at the end of December with a feeling of disappointment.

Merrill Mow wrote of the conference and the disputes it aroused:

> The conference that took place during November and December at Primavera was not a happy event.... A very long letter by Hans Zumpe was read out before he arrived. Betty Robinson bravely stood up and said that it was an arrogant letter.... Nothing was straightened out...at best it was a conference that evaluated the Bruderhof and its tasks from a utilitarian viewpoint.[58]

In her autobiography, Elizabeth Zumpe also writes of the oppressive atmosphere that pervaded the conference:

> The brothers and sisters did not attend the conference in order to listen to one another but rather to promote their own views and obtain increased support for their communities' projects. There was no readiness to understand one another. Their only desire was to be understood. This will not bring unity. The blame for this lies with the office-holders involved in organizing the conference.[59]

The conference revealed a clear tendency to reduce the importance of the communities in Paraguay and move some of their central members from there to the European and North American communities. The Bruderhof leadership felt that the focus of their activities would henceforth be in those regions and not in remote Paraguay.

In a review of the conference, *The Plough* wrote:

> The twofold nature of community life came clearly before us as we worked out our plans. We again realized that we are called first to a life of brotherhood in the midst of a world of strife, so that a genuine testimony to the fact that people can dwell together in peace, holding all things in common, can be seen. To this end it was necessary that all communities be well-founded and strongly built, and at the same time maintain a real inter-Bruderhof unity. There should also be in each a good mixture of the different nationalities, age groups and skills. In the second place, we felt that we have to proclaim the life of brotherhood that springs out of a Christian faith, and challenge people to commit themselves wholeheartedly to such a cause. In this light we examined our nine communities; what were their inner weaknesses

and strengths, what possibilities have they to carry forward the outreach to people in their respective countries? Most opportunities lay in the United States, Europe, and the more populated parts of South America, whereas the greatest number of members is still in Paraguay. Therefore, a central concern of the conference became the question of how the work in other countries could be strengthened by moving members there from Paraguay.

> In South America we have been slow in finding the key to an effective outreach among Spanish-speaking people.... Primavera will seek to work much more closely with El Arado than it has in the past, carrying out joint journeys into Brazil and Argentina.[60]

Hardy Arnold, who visited South America during the conference, also received the impression that Primavera was overburdened and recommended shortening the front and concentrating on two communities:

> We had the impression that since so many people had left Primavera in the past few years to help at the other communities, it would be necessary either to replace them or concentrate our efforts in Primavera in two places, rather than try to keep three communities going with insufficient strength, both in an inner and practical sense.

At the same time, he had a positive view of the efforts being made in extending their mission in South America through groups of young people and he lauded the initiative to organize a work camp at Primavera in July, 1958.[61]

The work camp at Primavera that went ahead as planned in July, 1958, was an extraordinary event in the history of the Bruderhof in Paraguay. For the first time a group of thirty young people from five South American countries met at Primavera. The camp was aimed at putting up a new hospital building at Isla Margarita, to hold discussions on topical subjects and modern theological literature. The young people of the Bruderhof also participated in the camp and it proved to be an open encounter with young people from the outside world. Three weeks were devoted to the seminar and the discussions were lively and dealt with issues that touched the younger generation in South America at the time. One question was the stance that should be adopted by Christian circles in the face of communist ideology, something that was of great importance to the Brazilian students whose organizations were controlled by leftist groups. The camp ended with all the participants feeling very satisfied and filled with the desire to continue with this enterprise in the coming years. And indeed, relationships were formed both through correspondence and by sending young people for period of training, particularly to Brazil.[62]

Notes

1. Interview with Kathleen Hassenberg, October, 1992.
2. Zumpe, Bette Bohlken, in *The KIT Annual 1991* (The Collected Newsletters of the KIT Information Service, San Francisco, Calif.), 12.
3. See the memoirs of Bruderhof member Howard Johnson in *Sharing About the Beginning of Woodcrest* (June 1974); Also Zumpe, E. B., op. cit., 118; Wagoner, Bob and Shirley, *Community in Paraguay* (Rifton, N.Y.: Plough Publishing House, 1991), 249.
4. Ibid., 255.
5. *The Plough*, no. 2 (Quarterly of Bruderhof communities. Bromdon: The Plough Publishing House, 1954); Zablocki, Benjamin, *The Joyful Community* (Baltimore, Md.: Penguin, 1971), 220, views these missions to the United States as a manifestation of the liberalism which pervaded the Bruderhof in the 1950s.
6. Allain, Roger, *The Community That Failed* (San Francisco, Calif.: Carrier Pigeon Press, 1992), 183.
7. *The Plough*, no. 2 (1953).
8. Interview with Tom Potts, November, 1991.
9. *We Would Be Building*, 25th Anniversary of Woodcrest (1974), 8.
10. Mow, op. cit., 43.
11. *Sharing About the Beginning of Woodcrest*, chap. 1, 12.
12. Ibid., 9; On missions to the U.S., see also *The Plough*, no. 1 (1953); no. 2 (1953); no. 2 (1954).
13. See Wagoner, op. cit., 220-26.
14. Zumpe, E. B., op. cit., 130-31.
15. On the World Conference of 1953 see *The Plough*, no. 3 (1953); no. 1 (1954); Zumpe, E. B., op. cit., 129-31.
16. *The Plough*, no. 2 (1956), 26.
17. Interview with Art Wiser, October, 1992; and also *The Plough*, no. 2 (1954).
18. Ibid., no. 3 (1954).
19. *Sharing About the Beginning of Woodcrest*, chap. 1.
20. *The Plough*, no. 3 (1954).
21. Interview with Dick Domer, November, 1992.
22. Mow, op. cit., 36-42.
23. Interview with Tom Potts, November, 1992.
24. Interview with Art Wiser, October, 1992; and *We Would Be Building*.
25. Ibid., 19; Mow, op. cit., 72-79.
26. *We Would Be Building*, 17.
27. Interview with Dick Domer, November, 1991.
28. Interviews with Collette and Dick Thompson and Donna Ford, Woodcrest, December 1991.
29. Shalom Wurm was one of the veterans of the kibbutz movement in Israel and a polymathic scholar. In his youth he was a leader of the Hashomer Hatsa'ir movement, a member of Bitania Illit, and later Bet Alpha. When his kibbutz underwent a political split he moved to Ramat Yochanan. In 1941 he was sent to the United States as a movement emissary and remained there until the end of the war. During that time he was introduced to literature on communes in America and on his return to Israel he embarked on the writing of a series of articles on communes all over the world in *Niv Hakvutza*. The first of these appeared in issue no. 10 in

March, 1954, and the last in issue no. 32 in December, 1959. One of the last articles in the series dealt with the Bruderhof and was entitled "The Bruderhof's Open Door," and was based upon Bruderhof literature he had read and on his correspondence with one of the Bruderhof's members in South America. Letters from Dick Whitty are cited in the article and reveal a keen interest in the kibbutz movement, as well as an openness about events on the Bruderhof, without any attempt to cover up their hardships; See Wurm, S., *Communes and their Ways of Life* (Ayanot), 516 (Hebrew).

30. See document no. 35, *Postlist*, in the central Bruderhof archive.
31. This letter was published in *Igeret*, no. 227 (26 April 1956).
32. Shalom Wurm to Dick Whitty, 8 September 1957.
33. Arnold, Roswith, in *The Beginning of Woodcrest*, chap. 13, 9.
34. Author's interview with Dick Domer, Woodcrest, December, 1991.
35. *Igeret*, no. 246 (4 October 1956).
36. *Niv Hakvutza*, no. 24 (October/November 1957): 611-23.
37. See letter from Wheathill to S. Wurm about the visit of M. Mandel (Kibbutz Kiryat Anavim) and a group of Zionist youth; *Igeret*, no. 204 (10 November 1955).
38. *Bakibbutz*, no. 319 (17 October 1956).
39. *Igeret*, no. 247 (26 April 1956).
40. Ibid., no. 254 (October, 1957).
41. *Bakibbutz*, no. 366 (6 October 1957).
42. "From a Kibbutz Community in Israel," *The Plough*, vol. 2, no. 2 (Summer, 1954).
43. "Kibbutzim in Eretz-Yisrael," *The Plough*, vol. 3, no. 1, 11-17.
44. Zumpe, E. B., op. cit., 89.
45. Zablocki, op. cit., 92; Zumpe, E. B., op. cit., 89; On the Hutterite numbers, see Hostetler, John, *Hutterite Society* (Baltimore and London: The Johns Hopkins University Press, 1974), 292.
46. Zablocki, op. cit., 92; Zumpe, E. B., op. cit., 119-20.
47. Interview with Dick Domer, November, 1992.
48. The issue of *The Plough* (vol. 3, no. 4) that reported on the difference of opinion at Forest River describes the disagreement as one between those "who wanted a community based upon the spirit and love" and those "who wanted a community based upon law and tradition"; on the views of the local Hutterites, see *KIT*, vol. 5 (February, 1993): 8-10.
49. Interview with Hans Meier, October, 1992.
50. *Sharing About the Beginning of Woodcrest*, chap. 8.
51. Baer-Lambach, Ruth, *A Daughter of the Flock* (Yad Tabenkin, 1992) (Hebrew), 28-31. Ruth Baer-Lambach has left the Bruderhof some years later.
52. *The Plough*, vol. 5, no. 2 (1957), 59.
53. Mow, op. cit., 92.
54. Arnold, Eberhard and Emmy, *Seeking For the Kingdom of God* (Rifton, N.Y.: Plough Publishing House, 1974), 280-82.
55. *The Plough*, no. 3 (1957).
56. Mow, op. cit., 244-50.
57. *From Castle to Community: 25 Years of Community Life* (Conn.: Deer Spring); *The Plough*, no. 2 (1958).
58. Mow, op. cit., 62-63.

59. Zumpe. E. B., op. cit., 149–50.
60. On the Bruderhof World Conference, see *The Plough*, vol. 4, no. 2 (1956), and vol. 5, no. 1 (1957).
61. Ibid., no. 1 (1958).
62. Ibid., (1960).

8

The Great Crisis

The years 1959 through 1962 were years of great crisis, a dark period
in Bruderhof history. The divergences of opinion within the movement
that in the past had been swept under the carpet now burst out in all their
intensity, embracing all the Bruderhof communities and shaking the
foundations of the majority of them to the core. At that time, the end of
the fifties, the movement had ten communities: three in Paraguay, which
included Bruderhof House in Asunción, two in England, one each in
Germany and Uruguay, and three in the United States, with a total membership that was estimated at some 1,700 souls.[1]

It is worthy of note that the crisis erupted at a time when the
Bruderhof's economic situation was showing signs of improvement,
with the American communes' financial situation much healthier than
the others. They had also generated increased interest from the outside
world, they were the target of numerous visitors, and even the media
were showing interest in them.

The Americans who had joined the Bruderhof had brought with them
assets and a factory with a high production potential, and it was these
that had improved the economic situation. Prior to the acquisition of
"Community Playthings," the Bruderhof communities had been dependent, to a large extent, on donations for their physical existence. They
had always enjoyed a following of supporters who, because they themselves had been unable to join, had salved their consciences by donat-
ing generously and the Bruderhof felt that the use of this money was
morally justified by the mission they were fulfilling. But in the fifties,
opposition to this kind of fund-raising intensified together with the desire to place the communities on a sound economic footing. At the same
time, the development of the Paraguayan and Uruguayan communities

was making great strides forward; the farms had been expanded and new economic projects had been undertaken.

In contrast to the air of optimism that followed the improved financial situation, the communities were all deep in the slough of despond and there was talk of the Bruderhof's having moved away from its roots and the "spirit of Sannerz." The first signs of this distancing appeared in the settlements outside the United States.

Some of the communities, especially those in South America, were in a quandary. It seemed to be increasingly difficult to find a common direction for earning a living and there were those who wondered what the future would hold for the communities in South America and how they could be drawn together as a united brotherhood. One serious problem that faced the entire Bruderhof at that time was the lack of leaders—capable Servants of the Word—who were willing to fight for the spirit of unity among the different communities within the movement. After various confrontations that involved the leaders of several Bruderhofs in 1960, they realized that extreme steps had to be taken.

There was, at the time, no Elder capable of uniting the movement, no one who might be "called" to become the spiritual leader, and no one to oversee the movement's economic development. It is somewhat difficult to pinpoint the factors that were directly involved in this crisis that beset the movement in general and its communities in particular, but there were certainly a number of background elements that created the atmosphere of confusion and loss of direction that may be discussed. Those were years of dilemma for the Bruderhof: the dilemma between adopting Hutterite ideology and the spontaneity that so characterized the Bruderhof at its inception; between adherence to the Hutterite scriptures and the doctrine of Eberhard Arnold, and religious syncretism that combined a number of scriptures—socialist, Christian, and even Catholic. They were also faced with social and economic dilemmas: involvement in outside society or focusing solely on internal problems; democratic decision making or decisions made by an authoritarian leadership; making a living by the sweat of their own brows or depending on the donations of generous supporters. All of these split the Bruderhof and there was some evidence of regional variations, between Woodcrest and Primavera as the spiritual center of the movement, for example, and national variations between Germans, British, and Americans.[2]

Merrill Mow feels that the crisis had historical roots. In his view, its onset came following the death of Eberhard Arnold when the Bruderhof underwent what Mow defines as "the struggle between the atmospheres," or in other words, faith versus legalistic rationalism. A deciding factor in the revival of this struggle and the outbreak of the great crisis was the joining of new members at the end of World War II whose religious beliefs were not sufficiently deep. Mow claims that these new people came from movements, the perceptions of which were socialist and antiecclesiastical and although they identified with the Bruderhof way of life, they did not do so with regard to its inner beliefs. Not only did the new members change the movement's demographic make-up, they also undermined accepted beliefs, and hallowed concepts like "the spirit and will of The Lord," "Christian love," and "devotion to Jesus" all lost their meaning. This loss of faith signalled the opening of a new period of internal struggle.[3]

A similar assessment was offered by Hans Meier, who pointed at the debate held at Primavera on relations with the Hutterites, which were bound up with fealty to the legacy of Eberhard Arnold:

> It was against this background that opposing factions came into being and there were struggles and democratic decisions—government of the minority by the majority. Government by people and not by The Lord.... During that period of conflict, we lost our way; instead of seeking the Kingdom of God we were seeking the particular interests of the communes. The factions struggled over the power of rule and over resources. We lost our sense of obligation to our fellows. This led the way to the dictatorial rule of the minority and later to the rule of one man... because the people had lost their Divine leadership and preferred that of men. Under those circumstances, people were afraid of speaking openly. Those who opposed the dictator feared exclusion and held their peace and allowed perversion to strike roots.[4]

The first signs of the impending crisis became apparent in internal social relationships and this was particularly notable at Primavera. Minor incidents, which in the past had been speedily resolved by a reproof administered by one of the office holders, were now brought before the entire membership, and the discussion thereof became a veritable vale of tears for the accused in which they were publicly reprimanded and sometimes even sentenced to "exclusion." In 1959, the large number of these inquiries created a "purge" hysteria that spread like wildfire throughout all the Primavera communes. It was this atmosphere that caused numerous members to make public confessions and indulge in self-flagellation, which were designed to purify the community prior to a new beginning. But this fond hope was dashed in the continued decline and 1960 was an even more difficult year than its predecessor.[5]

The internal social tension at Primavera was exacerbated even further by the moral decline of the younger generation. Roger Allain, who was a teacher at the time, describes what occurred:

> It all began when we discovered that gangs had been formed among the schoolchildren which were engaged in petty theft and barter of the stolen property with the hired workers. The workers traded knives, slingshots and horse's reins. The cause of the greatest concern to the community was the relationships that had been formed between the boys and the Paraguayan workers, for in their view, these relationships put the childrens' puritanical sex education in jeopardy. The boys involved were brought before the entire community and those found guilty were punished by exclusion for varying periods of time. This episode heightened the tension among the children and their parents and served as a preface to other, more serious episodes which beset Primavera during that year.[6]

There then began a period of moral and educational stock taking and searching for ways of finding the correct basis for community life. The meetings at the various communes were stormy and ended in disagreement and for the Bruderhof, one of whose precepts is that of consensus, this inability to reach agreement signified a reality of deep crisis.

In October, 1959 there were sharp differences of opinion between the Primavera and European leaderships and that in the United States, in which the principal roles were played by Eberhard Arnold's three sons and his two sons-in-law, Hans Zumpe and Balz Trumpi. The struggles within the extended Arnold family, which had a long history, were bitter and tension laden. At the time of Eberhard Arnold's death in 1935, not only were his sons still too young too take over the reins of leadership, but they had also been smuggled into Switzerland because of the threat of compulsory military service that hung over them. It was these circumstances that led to the leadership passing into the hands of Hans Zumpe, who by dint of the fact that he was Eberhard Arnold's right-hand man, had carved out a niche for himself as the first among equals from the time of Arnold's visit to the Hutterites. Zumpe brought with him a turnabout in the style of leadership, albeit not in its centralistic character, and one of the first things with which he had to contend was a confrontation with the Arnold sons in Zurich (the *Zurich Handel*) in the wake of which the Arnolds were removed from the leadership.[7]

The Arnold family did not take kindly to this dismissal, which often included periods of exclusion, and in 1938, with the Hutterite interven-

tion in the crisis, they were reinstated for a while but the struggle intensified in Paraguay when the Bruderhof communities drifted away from
the Hutterite heritage. In the early forties, Eberhard Arnold's sons were
removed from the leadership for a period of several years. This had
been preceded by the establishment of internal factions, which nurtured
hostility toward the Arnold family and which left a residue of bitterness
in followers among the movement's older members, and this was to
nourish the divisions in the Bruderhof in years to come.[8]

A revealing testimony on the internal power struggles within the
Bruderhof and the factional organization against the Arnold family's
influence may be found in a letter from Gwyn Evans to Heini Arnold
that was written in 1961. This letter was written under the special circumstances of Heini being sent to hospital and the deep concern for his
life, and it begins with an expression of contrition:

> I am deeply grieved that what I have to write will be a great pain to you, for it will
> show you how very unfaithful and disloyal I have been to the great love and trust
> you have shown to me.

Evans goes on to review the periods of his activities as a central member of Primavera, as the leader of the young British faction that had no
confidence in the Arnolds, and then writes about his relationship with
Hans Zumpe: "I became suspicious and mistrustful...and it was while
I was in this state that Hans Zumpe and I 'found one another.'"

Following a review of various episodes of the internal struggles that
had led to the exclusion of Heini and his brothers in 1941 an 1944,
Evans reflects on the deep internal split in the leadership:

> There was no open, trusting relationship between us; we allowed suspicions to lurk
> and waited only for the strategic moment to strike.

He concludes with a confession of guilt:

> I have to stand before the fact that all my sorrow is powerless to put right what has
> been so deeply wronged: that I have quelled and destroyed life and that I have
> crushed or misled the spirits of many and that I have betrayed the vision that was
> once given to me, distorting it into a caricature of the truth, and that I have spurned
> and held in contempt the spirit of the Church.[9]

Two years later, when he was already outside the Bruderhof, Gwyn
Evans recanted in a letter to friends, claiming that he had written to
Heini when he was in a state of tension and temporary insanity, albeit he

did not deny the existence of the various intrigues he had revealed, including that of the secret plot between Hans Zumpe and himself.[10]

Some of the older members of the Bruderhof with whom I spoke verified the assessment that Hans Zumpe had indeed striven to establish his position as the sole leader. Hans Meier claimed that Zumpe had assumed the office of "acting Elder" without an election, and added that "the Bruderhof then supported Hans Zumpe...but they were not fully reconciled with either themselves or with what they knew in their hearts." Doug Moody had a similar assessment of Hans Zumpe's position in the fifties; he defined Zumpe as a Servant who saw himself as the *de facto* leader of all the communities albeit the terms of his office were not couched in those terms.[11]

After the war, Hans Zumpe, the man who stood at center stage in these power struggles, transferred his activities to Europe in general and Germany in particular. He was a controversial personality who during the long years of his leadership created a special set of relationships with his Bruderhof colleagues. On the one hand, there are many who remember him fondly and who remained true to him even after his removal from office, while on the other, there are many who remember him as an uncompromising and arrogant man. In the Bruderhof of today there are not many people who are willing to talk about him. Stan and Hella Ehrlich told me that they first met Hans Zumpe in 1956, at the World Conference at Primavera, and that he looked out of place in his business suit, surrounded by the Bruderhof members in their traditional Hutterite garb. They received the impression that he was a central figure at the conference, that he had influence and charisma.[12]

In 1958, two years after the Primavera conference, news reached the leadership in the United States that "there are problems regarding Hans Zumpe's functioning as Servant of the Word in Europe" and that he should be replaced as soon as possible, and as a result, Zumpe's standing began to decline. Benjamin Zablocki claims that Zumpe was the target of criticism as early as the Primavera Conference of 1956, which he rejected forcefully, but not a year went by and further criticism was levelled at him, this time by American activists and it was this that undermined his position.[13] In her autobiography, Elizabeth, Zumpe's daughter, defends her father while at the same time admitting that at the time, she felt that her father was undergoing a great deal of mental stress and that his behavior was strange and restless. Everyone agreed that he should be allowed to resign from the burden of his office and take a break, and so Zumpe was transferred from Sinntal to Bulstrode, where it was decided to release him from his positions of responsibility and recommend that he go to London for a vacation.[14] At a later stage it was decided to halt Hans Zumpe's activities in Europe and transfer him to the United States.[15]

Hans Zumpe's position became totally undermined in June, 1960 when it was revealed that at the time he had filled a central role in Europe, he had "lived in adulterous sin" with the woman who had been his secretary at Sinntal. His daughter Elizabeth, who was at Sinntal at the time, painfully recalls the difficult days she endured after she heard of her father's transgression. Initially and once the news had broken, it was heard that Hans Zumpe had disappeared, leaving behind a letter in which he wrote of his intention to commit suicide. Once this news reached the Bruderhof, its members began a search for Zumpe, found him after a short while, and prevented him from taking his own life. But the seriousness of the affair did not abate; adultery is one of the most serious transgressions against the Bruderhof code of ethics, and the transgressor faces ostracism and permanent expulsion from the Bruderhof unless he expresses repentance and pleads for forgiveness from the Church and the family. Hans Zumpe did not do so and so it was decided expel him and the woman from Sinntal with whom he had maintained the relationship, from the flock. As he did not have a resident's visa, Zumpe was unable to remain in the United States, and so he returned to Europe where he lived in seclusion until 1973, when on his return from a vacation in Palma de Majorca, he was killed in a plane crash.[16] In an interview with the author, Hans Meier spoke of Hans Zumpe's "sin of adultery" and criticized the conspiracy of silence between those who were aware of the affair in Germany and who did not act to prove it immediately, as dictated by the "First Law of Sannerz." Meier viewed this as further evidence of the atmosphere of insincerity that was prevalent in the Bruderhof at the time and symbolized the process of decline that led shortly afterward to the great crisis.[17]

After Hans Zumpe's expulsion, the Bruderhof publications stopped writing about the affair and Zumpe's personality, but some years ago, with the publication of Merrill Mow's book, they began to deal with these issues once more. Mow's book presents Zumpe in a negative light and as the one who was responsible for the authoritarian regime (which some people say was even dictatorial) that held sway in the Bruderhof during the Paraguayan period, and its publication aroused a sharp response from Zumpe's followers who had left the Bruderhof. His son and daughter, Killian and Elizabeth, who left the Bruderhof in the sixties, while not denying their father's breach of the code of ethics that ultimately led to his expulsion, have recently begun publishing articles, the objective of which is the rehabilitation of their father and his life's work.[18] But they claim that a sincere effort at conciliation with their father was not made, and the main thrust of their claims is directed against Heini Arnold. Their efforts are concentrated on highlighting Hans Zumpe's great contribution to the Bruderhof in the difficult years following the death of Eberhard Arnold.[19]

Following Elizabeth Zumpe's protestation that her father had sought a way back to his wife and the Bruderhof and had been rebuffed, Hans Meier was quick to refute this claim. He disclosed the correspondence he had maintained with Hans Zumpe when both of them were outside the Bruderhof in the sixties. Meier was in Buenos Aires at the time where he tried unsuccessfully to establish a community of Bruderhof ex-members and it was in the course of these efforts that he wrote to Zumpe. Zumpe replied to Meier's approach to try to establish a communal settlement and return to their past heritage thusly:

> To that, dear Hans, I have to give a different reply than that you will be expecting. I tell you frankly that I feel sorry to disappoint you in this because I feel myself closely bound to you through our standing and fighting together for many years. For me, as far as I can see, communal living with its special witness is a closed book. As far as I am concerned, I no longer cherish any further expectations or hopes in that respect.[20]

A second case of disagreement within the movement leadership occurred when a delegation from Woodcrest led by Heini Arnold visited the Oak Lake community. The delegation found that the community's way of life was not as "Christian" as it should be and that the man responsible was the chief office holder, Balz Trumpi, who had filled central roles in the school and leadership of the Paraguayan communities, and who was also Eberhard Arnold's son-in-law. It was decided to "release" him and his wife from their jobs forthwith. In his memoirs, Merrill Mow explains this step thusly:

> The feeling was that it was all too much for the Servant and his wife and that they should step down, rest, and allow the *Hof* to calm down and become internally rejuvenated.

Elizabeth Zumpe writes that Trumpi had not managed to find his way into the hearts of the Pennsylvania community's members and that they viewed him as standing for the Primavera tradition. The "release," which was supposed to be temporary, became exclusion and caused the removal of the family from the community, the pretext being that "the Oak Lake people feared that when the period of the Servant's and his wife's rest was over, they would return and they did not want to entertain such a possibility."[21]

The exclusion of the Trumpi family was further evidence of the crisis in the Bruderhof leadership and was the signal for additional conflicts in which leaders from the European communities were also involved. Trumpi himself was involved in additional confrontations with Heini Arnold and finally, in 1961, he decided to leave the Bruderhof of his own volition.[22]

The existence of this affair was concealed for thirty years and only came to light with the publication of Merrill Mow's book, which contains a condemnation of Balz Trumpi as the one responsible for the decline at Oak Lake and which fully justifies his removal. With the publication of Mow's version of the story, Trumpi finally broke his prolonged silence and in an open letter he described the chain of events in detail from his point of view, accusing Heini Arnold of undermining him with the intent of removing him from office because his loyalty to him was suspect. Trumpi also claimed that Heini schemed to attain a dominant position at Woodcrest, from which he would be able to control the movement. He further writes:

> With hindsight, I can see a clear line of Heini's intent to bring the Bruderhof under his control: first, his great concern to be the leader at Woodcrest without sufficient consultation with Oak Lake, attempts to intimidate other Servants of the Word...the attacking of other brothers, causing them deleterious self-examination while they were confident that they represented the real truth.[23]

It should be mentioned here that at the time, the Woodcrest community under Heini's leadership did indeed begin to carve out a hegemonic status for itself in the movement, and the elite of the newer American members was concentrated there. Some time later, the other communities accepted the fact that Woodcrest was indeed the leading community that held the key to the movement's future. Accepted opinion throughout the Bruderhof held that an atmosphere of unity and integration pervaded Woodcrest, which Merrill Mow describes thusly:

I believe there was a spirit that worked there and a will that came from God—a spirit of uniting, a spirit of fighting for a good atmosphere, a spirit that has been betrayed and has suffered greatly over the years.

Miriam Arnold also describes the special atmosphere at Woodcrest, but a trifle more sarcastically:

Woodcrest was always the place to be. That was where the true spirit was.... A lot of young groups used to go to Woodcrest for this and that. That was the thing to do. And while you were there, maybe you could catch a little bit of that wonderful spirit.[24]

Yet, that special spirit was unable to offer Woodcrest protection from the great crisis. Dick Domer, a Woodcrest veteran, recalls:

We all had to face the issue of combining communal life with a life of belief in the Gospel of Jesus. We had always faced the danger of putting our communal life before the experience of faith. The root of the problem in the crisis years was that some of our people thought that we could maintain our communal life without the inner content of belief and they placed the commune at the center of their existence instead of the reason which had brought us together as a commune—faith.[25]

In 1959, various groups in the Bruderhof communities expressed their concern regarding the large number of guests and candidates at Woodcrest. They said that although these people had expressed an interest in communal life, they did not meet its spiritual requirements. In general terms one may say that two separate camps had come into being: on the one hand, those who were defined as the "warmhearted" ones who had experienced redemption through belief in Jesus Christ and who wanted to build a closed and united community, and the "cold-hearted," in whose ranks were those who supported a secular, humanist ideology and who were interested in a community that maintained contact with the outside world. This division began to take on nationalistic connotations when some of the German members felt that the English were "cold-hearted" while the Germans and the Americans were "warm-hearted." The people from England who had joined the Bruderhof were viewed as being political and pacifist idealists rather than people who were seeking a spiritual and religious way, hence their tendency to respond to the challenges of communal life intellectually rather than emotionally. Truth to tell, this multiplicity, which during the previous decade had been one of the Bruderhof's greatest qualities, became an untenable and divisive force in 1960.[26]

The problem of "warmheartedness" also became linked to that of the policy that was to be adopted with regard to Bruderhof activities in outside society. In 1958, the "Woodcrest Service Committee" was founded in the United States with the objective of opening new avenues of activity outside the communities, but only two years later the very term *social work* became anathema at Woodcrest and in fact, the entire issue of work beyond the confines of the *hof* was pronounced proscribed for the brothers. Moreover, those who persisted in showing interest in work outside were defined as "cold-hearted" and as such constituted a threat to the integrity of the commune.

This *volte-face*, from the outside inward, was typical of the North American communities. In the past, when the Bruderhof had existed as an isolated sect in remote Paraguay, it had been capable of engaging in missionary activities without harm to itself. Its members were able to invest their best efforts in persuading their neighbors to adopt their way of life and it was their strangeness and their alienation from the Paraguayan population that endowed the Bruderhof with their sense of pride and exclusivity. The fact that the environment outside their communities was so impoverished obviated any danger of temptation and focusing on internal problems, so their outside activities posed no danger of shaking the faith of the veteran members.

The situation in the United States, however, was totally different. Woodcrest was only a two-hour drive from New York and numerous visitors and people seeking a way flocked to its gates without any intensive missionary activity. Unlike Paraguay, the society surrounding the Bruderhof in the United States was far more developed and sophisticated and, thus, posed more of a threat and demanded a greater effort in facing it, so protecting the borders of the community took on greater significance. The American communities accepted a greater number of prospective members, the majority of whom wavered between the Bruderhof and the other alternatives that were open to them. All this demanded efforts in finding a solution to the problems of community integration and the establishment of clearly delineated borders between the Bruderhof and the outside world.[27]

Woodcrest underwent a "housecleaning" in the course of which many of the "cold-hearted" were sent away, but the concern for the "unrepentant" hearts persisted. This soul searching created a great deal of bitterness among those who had been excluded. Those were years of tension and turmoil and many people sensed an impending total eclipse. In general terms, the Bruderhof members felt just how far away they were from the days of Sannerz, the time of togetherness and amity.[28]

While all this was going on in the United States, the general assembly of world Bruderhof representatives was convened at Primavera and on the agenda was the maintenance of the communities in the dispersion. The assembly's participants felt that there was something deficient in Primavera's economic structure that prevented it from maintaining an economy independent of outside donations. Proposals for the establishment of more profitable branches were tabled and steps were taken to reduce the economic burden of the Paraguayan communities. A 200 acre tract of land at Primavera was prepared for the cultivation of rice, and this project was to crown the efforts at turning Primavera into a viable economic and financial entity. There were many people who felt that rice had a great commercial potential in Paraguay and so the preparations got under way in 1958, with thousands of dollars being invested in the first year in land reclamation and the preparation of the road and water channel infrastructure. The sheer scope of the work involved obliged the Bruderhof to employ local hired labor in the hope that as time went by and with the introduction of mechanization, they would be able to manage without it. Although the rice fields were adjacent to Ibate, all the Primavera communities' people worked there. From numerous standpoints this was the largest economic project ever undertaken at Primavera, but it quickly became apparent that not all of the other Bruderhofs were unanimously in favor of the need for it, and when the first harvest was brought in, some harsh criticism was heard from the Woodcrest people. The project aroused a great deal of tension and as more serious internal problems had arisen, it was quickly shunted aside.[29]

Balz Trumpi, who was a member of the Pennsylvania community's leadership at the time, tells us something of the attitude of his fellow leaders:

> They were most concerned about the reports that had come in from Primavera on the rice project...they did a tremendous job there but at Woodcrest they felt that they had gone over the top.... Heini did not like the recurring requests for financial aid that came from Primavera.[30]

And so, just as the people of Primavera were celebrating their first rice harvest, a cable arrived from Woodcrest advising the Paraguayan communities to get out of agriculture and move into industry. The

Primavera communities' leadership were insulted by both the cable's wording and the lack of understanding that its authors had shown regarding the type of economy existing at Primavera (which was unsuitable for industrial expansion). The cable set off an acrimonious exchange between Paraguay and the United States, which deepened the schism between the two sections of the movement.[31] And indeed, it may be said that following the 1959 conference, Primavera's stock began to decline rapidly while that of Woodcrest was strengthened.[32]

A further cause of tension between the United States and Primavera was the question of Emmy Arnold's trip from England to the United States, the objective of which was to arrange an immigration visa for her to the States, where her children and grandchildren lived. There were those who viewed this as an act of favoritism toward the Arnold family and argued, in the name of equality, that the same hold true of all the grandparents whose grandchildren were dispersed throughout the movement's communities. This crisis, which further swelled the dregs of past insults suffered by the Arnold family, was settled a short time later, but it served to expose the weakness of the movement and showed that it was incapable of putting up a leadership capable of guiding all its communities with understanding and mutual agreement. In the opinion of those involved in those particular disputes, it seemed that one of the contributing factors in this situation was the dispersal of the communities in distant continents and so the idea of closing down the South American communities and transferring their members to Europe to reinforce the communities there, was raised once again.[33]

The Crisis of 1961 and the Dismantling of the South American Communities

The Paraguayan communities were dismantled in two stages. The two smaller settlements at El Arado and Loma Jhoby with its hospital were closed down first. The closure of the hospital involved a struggle with the members' consciences for it was the jewel in the crown of the community service offered by Primavera to the general public in Paraguay and in the past, emissaries had been sent abroad on fund-raising missions on its behalf and it held pride of place in their contacts with outside circles. But those in favor of closing it down had some very good reasons for doing so: the development of the regional and national health services had reduced the pioneering importance that the hospital had enjoyed in the forties and early fifties. New roads had been laid in the region that linked it with the medical centers in Asunción and a new hospital had been built at the Mennonite settlement, which had begun to provide the local population with efficient medical services. But in the final accounting, the main reason for closing the hospital down was that it had become a financial burden and the monetary sources for its maintenance were gradually drying up. An additional burden was the dearth of doctors and in fact, the hospital's professional staff had not increased in size since the early forties. It was under these circumstances that even those in favor of keeping the hospital open finally agreed that it should be closed down.[34]

The decision to close down these settlements and move their members to communities in England was made at the Bruderhof Council, which met at Oak Lake, Pennsylvania, in May, 1960. The proposal was also raised in the Bruderhof communities in Europe and won the support of the Paraguayan and Uruguayan communities' leaderships. The Council decided to charter an aircraft to fly the members of the South American communes to the North American and English Bruderhofs. In June, 1960, emissaries were despatched to organize the dismantling of the settlements and the transfer of their members to the United States and on the flight that took off on 24 August 1960, 176 people were airlifted from South America to Europe.[35]

It is worthy of note that the decision to dismantle the settlements did not stem from either the desire or needs of their members, but that it was a direct result of general Bruderhof policy to "shorten the front" and concentrate their members in Europe and the United States. At the time, there were 100 members at El Arado. They all felt that the settlement had achieved stability, the farm had been developed, their relations with the local population had been extended, and in 1959 they had even built a primary school for the settlement's children.[36]

Years later I had the opportunity of asking a number of the El Arado members how they had received the decision to dismantle their settlement, and they replied that they had done so "regretfully but with understanding." Furthermore, Charles Headland, one of El Arado's veteran members, told me that representatives of the settlement had gone to the United States with the idea of mooting the establishment of an additional Bruderhof in Uruguay, but their proposal had been rejected and they returned home bearing the decision to shorten the front and dismantle their settlement:

> We understood the rationale and felt the need to tell our friends in Uruguay about it. We wrote telling them of our decision to move to North America. The Comunidad del Sur anarchists came to make their farewells and were very discomfited. They could not understand our motives and felt that we were abandoning them.

Headland and Stan and Hella Ehrlich stayed behind to sell the farm and summed up their feelings this way:

> It was truly sad to leave the settlement in which so much effort had been invested, which had begun to develop, and just as the farm was beginning to produce results. But if our leaving was to help further the Bruderhof belief and mission, then our suffering was amply compensated.

They added that they had found some solace in the fact that the settlement's land and property (which were auctioned) fetched "a good price" and, thus, enabled a new beginning in another place.[37]

The shock waves that swept through the Bruderhof in 1960 did not die down with the decision to dismantle the two South American settlements. The United States was not immune to the events of the crisis, but in contrast to other regions their effects were not fatal, and among the North American settlements the one in Connecticut was hardest hit and was temporarily abandoned. The situation there deteriorated in the summer of 1960 with the emergence of a lack of confidence in both the local central office holders and the Bruderhof leadership. Veteran families began to leave and the congregate feeling was that Evergreen had ceased to function as a community. These circumstances led to the management of the settlement being transferred to Woodcrest, which was a two-hour drive away. In September, 1960, after several months of decline, Heini Arnold proposed that the settlement be closed down temporarily and that two families be left behind to take care of the property and buildings and adopt the small group of high school students who studied at the school in the nearby town. Once the community's members had recovered from the mortification of having to leave their home, Heini's proposal was accepted as the best way out of the no-win situation that the community was in. And so, in the autumn of that year it was decided to close down the new Connecticut settlement temporarily and leave behind a minimal presence until it became possible to repopulate it. Thus, the effects of the crisis were felt in all their force throughout all the Bruderhof communities. The atmosphere of gloom in the communities was so deep and so widespread that in 1960, for the first time in Bruderhof history, Christmas, the most significant festival in their lives, was celebrated as a family affair and not as a community event.[38]

By the beginning of 1961 it was clear that the leadership was no longer united and was not functioning as the world movement headquarters. Primavera, which was suffering a deep crisis, sent calls for help to Woodcrest and the leadership there decided to send a four-member delegation headed by Heini Arnold to reinforce the Paraguayan communities' leadership. The delegation reached Primavera in January, 1961 and not only did it not succeed in easing the crisis, it also caused a schism of vast dimensions, and for many people, this affair was a trauma from which they never fully recovered. In the wake of events such as these, there are differing versions of the chain of events and their ramifications, and I shall cite a number of them here.[39]

In his book, Benjamin Zablocki says that the despatch of the delegation from the United States to Primavera was arranged between the leaderships of Woodcrest and Primavera and that its objective was to set the Primavera house in order in the wake of the crisis undergone by the communities there.[40] In contrast, Roger Allain, who was at Primavera at the time, recalls in his autobiography that the news of the delegation's arrival was received with surprise and that the reason for its coming was unclear. For him, the events of January and February of 1961 were an earthquake that uprooted him and his wife from the soil of the Bruderhof, causing them to leave after twenty-five years of intense faith. Their decision to leave was formulated once it became clear that the discussions held in the general meetings had led the participants to the conclusion that the old Bruderhof had lost its way and should be dismantled, establishing in its place a "new" Bruderhof that would be begun by a small group of "faithful" to be selected by the brothers from the United States. Allain writes:

> What occurred during the next two months was like an avalanche that began its descent unnoticed and then suddenly gathered frightening speed, destroying everything in its path.

According to Allain, as soon as the brothers from the United States arrived, a number of the younger members of the commune asked them to help overcome the destructive spirit that was abroad in the two remaining Primavera settlements. Once this contact with the young people and some of the older families had been established a general meeting was convened, which was addressed by Heini Arnold, who said that the delegation had been sent out of concern for the decline of the Primavera communities, which was manifested by a lack of appreciation for the legacy of Eberhard Arnold and the dominance of a legalistic approach that neglected the foundations of their faith. At this meeting and the ones that followed, a number of members indeed confessed to harboring a disrespectful attitude toward the Arnold legacy, cold-heartedness and abandoning the faith. The assembly subsequently censured and excluded them.

Allain further writes that immediately following these events, the meeting went into recess for two hours and then the brothers from the United States presented a list of twenty names that were acceptable as faithful and worthy of becoming the nucleus of the new community. Additional names of people who were felt to be loyal were added to this list each day and, thus, the community was effectively divided, leaving many people feeling a great deal of tension and uncertainty. Dozens of members who were deemed to be "disloyal" were asked to leave without delay, taking with them their only possessions, a ticket to their country of origin and a small sum of money to help them in their first steps. It was under these circumstances that Roger Allain and his wife declared their intention of leaving before the committee asked them to do so, for they felt that they, too, would be deemed "disloyal." For reasons of their own they decided not to return to Europe, but to remain in South America.[41]

The Bruderhof members who were in South America at the time and with whom I spoke, all verified Zablocki's version of the story. According to them, a decision was made at Primavera at the beginning of January to ask the people from Woodcrest to come and help them settle the disputes that had arisen in the wake of their crisis of faith. Andreas Meier, one of the young Primavera activists, recalls the events of the great crisis of early 1961:

> We said, let us reconcile ourselves to the fact that the Bruderhof no longer exists and that we need to start over with everyone who is willing to do so, even though we are but few. We did not know how to form the first group. We were all in the same boat and we were all involved in internal debates. We suggested that brothers from Woodcrest, where a new spirit was abroad and whose members were not involved in our disputes, come to Primavera, speak to each of us, and see who wanted to renew our life and help us to do so by assisting in the formation of a new

group. This was proposed by the younger Primavera members of whom I was one. We did not know that at the time, and with no connection to our proposal, that four brothers from the United States were on their way to us with that same objective in mind. Later, a number of people who subsequently left alleged that the "Americans" had come and had taken over the commune. I vigorously deny that allegation. The actions of the American brothers were undertaken at our initiative and with our agreement.[42]

Regarding the events which took place during that visit, Andreas says:

I remember the first meeting we held with them. They were very emotional about meeting with the members of the mother commune at Primavera. Following a number of stormy meetings at which various members expressed various and contradictory opinions, we agreed that the "brotherhood" that had existed between us was no more and that we had to find a new way of renewing it. Following these meetings, there were some people who asked for some time to consider their options. My father, Hans Meiei, was among those who had lost his faith and he, too, requested some time to consider his way.[43]

According to all the versions of the story, the meetings were both stormy and fully attended. The disagreements were deep, there was no readiness to listen one to the other, and the inner unity that had characterized the settlements in the past was lost. All the versions are unanimous regarding the first issue to be raised at the meetings—the statement by one of the Paraguayan leaders that he had acted in the past to diminish the influence of the Arnold family. It all began when another leading member from Isla Margarita asked to confer privately with the delegation. He confessed painfully that the main inner conflict in his life was his opposition to Eberhard Arnold and the influence of the Hutterites. The brothers heard this admission in astonishment; the majority could not believe their ears and responded with skepticism, others responded angrily, while some made no response at all. As a result of the varied response, the idea was raised of clearing the air of internal division through the personal confessions of those who felt this way. It was against this background that the demand for "purification" talks that would bring about renewed unity sprang. A number of brothers raised the question at the general meeting and, thus, the internal split became unavoidable. The main subject raised at the meetings was the attitude toward Arnold's "witness" on the love of Jesus Christ.

Elizabeth Zumpe, who was at Woodcrest at the time that these events took place, writes that initially, worrying rumors about an "anti-Arnold" atmosphere at Primavera began to reach the United States and later came the bad news of the crisis that had overtaken the communities there, that brothers and sisters like the Allains and Bruce Sumner, who were counted among the bulwarks of the Primavera communities, were leaving. They also heard some shocking tales about the other members who had been excluded from the communities and of long queues of Bruderhof ex-members outside the British and German embassies in Asunción, waiting for visas and financial assistance for their journey back to their homelands across the ocean.[44]

Doug Moody and Art Wiser, who were both members of the Woodcrest delegation and who were directly involved in the crisis, provide me with their version of the events. Moody recalls:

At the beginning of January 1961, we received a letter from Bud Mercer who was Servant of the Word at Isla Margarita, in which he asked whether it would be possible to send a delegation from Woodcrest to Primavera. The request was discussed at Woodcrest and agreement was reached. As far as we were concerned, the journey was a wonderful experience because Primavera was then held to be the movement's mother-community.... Although we were received cordially by the settlements' members, we felt uncomfortable from the outset in the face of the furor that was part of the meetings. This was something that we were not used to at Woodcrest. People interrupted one another, interjected, and generally disrupted the speakers' efforts. But the most depressing thing was the request by one of the central members to make a public confession. In it he said that the two things he had always opposed in his life in the Bruderhof were the legacies of the Hutterites and Eberhard Arnold. He further felt that the good of the movement called for the evanescence of the leader once it had become established and that the death of Arnold in 1935 had been a good thing for the movement, for only then had it been able to stand on its own two feet. On hearing this, I recalled that he had said something similar to me many years previously when he had visited Woodcrest. I had attached no importance to it at the time, but his words gnawed at my brain. I asked myself how someone could live in a movement for so many years and yet have that kind of attitude towards its founder and spiritual mentor. The real question was why had he joined the movement?

It should be mentioned that the man in question was an Englishman who had joined on the eve of the departure from England to Paraguay. It is entirely possible that his joining was one of those hasty and ill-conceived actions undertaken by the English pacifists under the circumstances of that particular time. He adds:

After that particular meeting there were others in which people also stood up and revealed their innermost feelings. Much to my surprise, some of them expressed criticism of Arnold's legacy. It appeared that Primavera was suffering from an "Arnold problem" which was manifested in a discriminatory attitude towards those members of the family who were office-holders.... This made me think that there was something unpredictable here and that feelings of jealousy and enmity were polluting the atmosphere. That apart, I felt that there was no unity between the communities and between the members themselves, and that they were only interested in themselves and their work. It was these conditions that led to the communities being permeated by competition, ambition and power struggles. All of this surfaced at the meetings and were manifested in vocal disputes, unwillingness to listen and reach any kind of agreement. At a certain moment, people stood up and said that this could go on no longer. The Bruderhof must be started afresh! They then asked us whether we would help them to form a group that would start a new Bruderhof. Heini refused. He said that an act such as this must be undertaken by the brothers themselves. After much pleading, we finally agreed to prepare a list for the approval of the Bruderhof there.

That was how it happened! When we left for Primavera we had no idea that we would become embroiled in such a situation! And we certainly did not expect a wave of people leaving after the "new Bruderhof" was established. With the benefit of hindsight I admit that had we had more time for consideration we might possibly have prevented so many people leaving. It also never entered our minds that the temporary exclusions would lead to people leaving. One sad example was the departure of Hans Meier. Although we held him in high esteem, we knew that he was not reconciled with the new way. Under the circumstances, we told him, "Hans, stay away for a while and consider your way back." Fortunately, I still have the note containing the wording we presented to him, and it says categorically "that he will consider his way back." But under the prevailing tensions he did not fully comprehend our intentions and felt that we had told him that he had lost the calling...and that, of course, was something very serious that we had neither said nor intended. Years later, when Hans became reconciled, we showed him the wording, cleared up the misunderstanding and subsequently forgave each other.[45]

Art Wiser provides a similar description of the events as they occurred. He heard about the reservations regarding Eberhard Arnold's legacy from Francis Hall, one of the leaders of the Kingwood group that was about to join the Bruderhof, who had spent several years at Primavera. Francis told Art of the opinions he had heard voiced at Primavera to the effect that "Divine Providence had done the movement a favor by ridding it of Eberhard Arnold at the beginning, for then it had been able to free itself of its dependence upon him."

According to Art, the subject was raised among the members of the delegation during the flight to Paraguay. Heini's response was, "Ask the brother who said it—he is at Primavera." It transpired that the brother mentioned by Francis Hall asked to make a public confession of something that had occurred many years previously, and during the confession Doug Moody asked him if he still maintained his critical opinion on Eberhard Arnold's legacy. To the surprise of all present, not only did he not deny his criticism, but also verified the fact that he still held it:

"Yes", he said, "Eberhard Arnold and the Hutterites were the principal enemies in my life!"

"We were astounded," said Wiser. "It was beyond our comprehension. His words caused an uproar in the meeting and apart from the people who levelled criticism at him, there were also those who agreed with what he had said. The storm did not abate during the following meetings."

Art says that the hardest thing about this decline was the unwillingness to repent and seek forgiveness. Thus did they deviate from all accepted Bruderhof norms. He says that this was evidence of the new spirit that pervaded the Primavera community and that they were headed for crisis. But then voices were heard that called for a new beginning and Art, too, verifies that they were approached by some of the younger people with a request to compile a list of names for the first group of the new Bruderhof.[46]

Merrill Mow, who was a member of the second Woodcrest delegation to Primavera that went there a short time after the first, also tells of the confession of one of the active opponents of the Arnold family:

> Many asked for personal talks in the following days. After many meetings, and particularly after one disorderly discussion in which brothers and sisters refused to listen to each other, Heini Arnold asked the circle in Primavera: "Is this brotherhood?"...There were those who asked the visiting American members to form a new united brotherhood, even if only two or three were in it.

According to Mow's review of events, the meetings went into recess for a while and only reconvened at the end of February. It was at this meeting that Heini Arnold was asked that he and the four brothers from the United States compile a list of members loyal to the Bruderhof way who would form the nucleus of the new brotherhood in Paraguay. Heini refused and demanded that the group be formed from within the membership itself, without outside intervention. It was finally agreed that the guests from the United States and a number of central members would form the group and they would accept anyone who was prepared to join. The first group consisted of four brothers from Primavera, which grew to twenty-one and a few weeks later numbered sixty-seven (of a total of 150). The criterion for selection of the faithful was their attitude toward the "conflict between the atmospheres." "Each of us had to decide whether he was on the side of Jesus and the love and compassion that allowed a unhindered view of the way, or on the side of the power

of efficiency and talent that divert from the straight and narrow path
into crisis situations."[47]

"The faithful" were made up of veteran members who sought to bring
back the spirit that had been part of the Bruderhof in "the Sannerz days"
and a large group of second-generation young people who were looking
for a way of establishing a unified commune with a clearly defined objective and spiritual content, while the "other" camp included many
people who had joined the Bruderhof in recent years. In general terms,
the accepted division into two camps was the Germans and the Americans on the one hand and the English on the other. A more careful study
of the facts reveals that this division was incorrect and that members of
various national groups belonged to both camps, but the more commonly accepted version of the split is still heard today.

In his review of the events of the crisis, Zablocki claims that the delegation from the United States used two criteria by which those worthy
were selected for membership of the "new Bruderhof" group: belief in
the Eberhard Arnold legacy and the criterion of "warm-heartedness" or
"cold-heartedness." He also writes of the close relationship established
between the newer American members and the older Bruderhof members and the children of the founding fathers, in contrast to the unbridged
gaps between the Germans and the English members who had joined on
the eve of World War II, mainly out of pacifist motivation.[48]

Hardy Arnold's daughter, Miriam Arnold Holmes, who left the
Bruderhof in the wake of the great crisis, writes in her memoirs that
those who were forced to leave the Paraguayan settlements were those
who had joined in England while the faithful who remained were
Bruderhof veterans who had joined in Germany, and their children. In a
caustic criticism of the split and its causes, she writes:

> And so it happened that among those who were not forced to leave were the veteran
> members who had joined the movement at Sannerz and Rhön. The younger genera-
> tion, the sons of these veterans, were the "good boys" while the "bad boys" were
> those who had joined at Wheathill and the Cotswold Farm.... The overall charge
> was that the "bad boys" had opposed the Arnolds since the forties and that they
> plotted to "free" the Bruderhof from every last vestige of Eberhard Arnold's influ-
> ence. In their view, Eberhard Arnold had been an emotional romantic who should not
> be taken seriously. They were charged with being more "humanist" than Christian.[49]

A surprising verification of the existence of an ethnic division in the
ideological controversy can be seen in a letter from Heini Arnold that

contained his last testament, and which was written to his son Christoph in 1974 and opened after his death in 1982. Heini writes explicitly:

> Unfortunately, nearly all our English members shared the guilt of our terrible deviation from the way of Jesus Christ. This, of course, is only true of those who were in Paraguay or at Wheathill more or less from the beginning.... A most particular sign from God, I feel, was the coming of brothers and sisters from the intentional communities (the Americans).... These groups of brothers and sisters in no way detract from the significance of the youth movement in our feeling and attitude to life. On the contrary, they have enriched it and returned it to us.[50]

In this testament, Heini also reveals his displeasure at what he perceived to be an all-out attack on the Arnold family during the Primavera period:

> The cry "royal family" went around; there was talk of the common people and the brotherhood. From now on, the Servant of the Word was no longer to have the leadership but the people, the brotherhood.... All kinds of power cliques were formed consisting of "ordinary" brothers and sisters. Only one thing was broken up—the Arnold family.[51]

In an open letter, Roger Allain, who was one of the victims of the "purge," writes of Heini Arnold's motives in the exclusion affair:

> The chief reason was your obsession with the "Arnold Question"...that you were appalled by the hatred against the Arnolds and you wanted to find its cause. But you ascribed it superficially to the presumptive envy of a few individuals and you failed to see that through its history, the Bruderhof has been swayed by an ambivalent set of complex and confused feelings towards the Arnolds: love and gratefulness for their faith and courage in starting the community, but also vexation over the frequently and variously recurring expression of their patriarchalism. The term, "the royal family" offended your ears, but you failed to investigate the deeper reason for its use.[52]

It is therefore reasonable to assume that the question of attitude toward the leadership of the Arnold family was a predominant criterion in the selection of "the faithful" for the new Bruderhof. In the veteran members' field of consciousness, the Arnold family's leadership was inextricably linked to the Bruderhof's early days and this perception had been successfully handed down to the newer American members.

A short while after the stormy "purification" meetings on 8 March, the United States delegation met with ten leading members of the Primavera communities at the nearby port city of Rosario, and at what later came to be called "the Rosario Meeting," a proposal was raised to dismantle the Paraguayan settlements and move their members to the northern hemisphere—the United States and Europe. In the light of the vast difficulties involved in transferring such a large number of people, and particularly in the light of the difficulties that would be raised by the American immigration authorities at the time, this was a very bold-spirited suggestion.

Art Wiser, who participated in the meeting, recalls:

> As Heini left on his way back to the United States, he was accompanied by a group of leading members which included the American delegation and the witness brothers from Primavera. This group met with Heini in the port of Rosario for a discussion on the steps to be taken in the future. It seemed that the dispersion of the Bruderhof over three continents was causing great communication difficulties, the most pressing of which being the contact with Primavera which did not even have a telephone, in contrast to the American and European communities which did. The importance of close contact had become even greater under the new circumstances which had arisen in the wake of the crisis. It was then that the question arose of whether it would not be preferable to concentrate all our people in the north and close the Primavera settlements, but as the answer to that question would have to be given by all the Bruderhofs, Heini was empowered to raise it at the American Bruderhof. Although the question had not been raised officially at Primavera, it had been the subject of private conversations and it was an open secret that as the Primavera settlements were not part of the great developments that were under way in Europe and the United States, numerous people had shown interest in it. The number of people who troubled themselves to visit the Primavera settlements was very few, while their European and North American counterparts were flooded with visitors. Heini took the proposal to the United States where it was discussed together with the leadership of the European communities and later in general meetings. It was unanimously felt that the Bruderhof should be concentrated in Europe and the United States and that the South American settlements should be closed down.

This agreement was cabled to Primavera, and Art, who witnessed the cable's reception, recalls that it was received with an outburst of joy.[53]

Balz Trumpi, one of the people who left the Bruderhof after many years at Primavera, also provides verification of the desire to leave Paraguay by admitting that

> we at Primavera had a great longing to be a part of this new beginning, be it in Europe or North America, because we had been in the wilderness for fifteen long years. Life in Paraguay was very hard. There was no great response to community life in South America, at least not compared to the response we had experienced in the USA.[54]

There is some criticism in Roger Allain's retrospective assessment of the last years at Primavera:

Speaking of Primavera, where most of my community experience was, I think its collapse was due to many causes of which the Arnold question was only one. Other reasons were that we had become afraid of the voice of our own conscience, and often acquiesced in Bruderhof decisions without any personal conviction for or against; we had grown callous towards one another...we had become cold and puritanical with our children...contemptuous of social work, closing down the Primavera hospital...we had become artful and opportunistic with the outside world in our dealings with wage workers, businessmen and state officials; we had become proud and convinced of our superiority over other movements (while professing our own unworthiness)...above all we had been sinking deeper and deeper into a morass of frenzied clearances and collective introspection. These are not personal accusations against others—I fully include myself in the responsibility for it all.

A different tone may be heard in the words of an ex-member who lived there in his youth and left when the crisis erupted:

Our parents and us, their sons, spilt a great deal of blood, sweat and tears in the building and development of Primavera...no one asked us or sought our opinion when they decided to close the settlements down.[55]

Immediately following the decision made at the "Rosario Meeting," Heini left for the United States where he fell ill, and apart from a short visit to Primavera, he was absent from the commune's leadership for some two months and took no part in the process of separating the "faithful" from those who were excluded. The latter were asked to leave and take some time to consider their allegiance to the Bruderhof faith and this process stood at the center of the Paraguayan and European communities' experience; at its conclusion, there were some 600 people who were asked to "exclude" themselves or who chose to leave of their own volition.[56] This was the most difficult period in Bruderhof history.

How do the Bruderhof members who grew up at Primavera and who were still youngsters when the crisis erupted, view the abandoning of the Paraguayan settlements? I spoke with a number of them on my visit to Woodcrest in November, 1991. Christoph Boller said that personally, he was content with the decision to leave Paraguay and that moreover he had hoped that it would be made earlier:

We were refugees in Paraguay—shipwrecked. We did not succeed in establishing relations with the local population. We came from a different culture. The younger people among us felt isolated. They were unable to make contact with young people from the outside society.

And with regard to the crisis, he said, "We had become good commune members but our belief in God had waned."

In his view, this weakening of belief was a process that had gone on for many years in Paraguay and had reached its climax in 1961. Many people claimed that both they and their ideals had changed over the years:

> But we did not believe that the schism was that deep and that several hundred people would leave the commune for ever. Although many left of their own volition, there were others who were asked to leave by the first group of the new Bruderhof. Although the act of leaving was difficult, there was a feeling that the exclusion was temporary and for the purpose of moral stock-taking. The shortage of money dictated that those who were leaving were given only a small sum of money apart from their travel expenses to their country of origin.[57]

Andreas Meier held a similar view. He, too, felt that the crisis was unavoidable and claimed that it stemmed from a loss of belief:

> We made an idol of the community. Strangely enough, it was us youngsters who felt that all was not well in our life. The words had lost their meaning. We used religious terminology without its having any content of genuine belief. We felt that this was not the Bruderhof we had joined.

Andreas says of the decision to dismantle the Paraguayan settlements:

> After the crisis had passed and so many people had left, we were unable to maintain a large number of communes. We had to concentrate those who remained in a place that would allow a new beginning and we felt that the United States and England were the most suitable. Paraguay was unsuitable for this as it had no sound economic basis for development and we were isolated. Yet at the same time, I would like to emphasize that we do not perceive Primavera as a dark cloud in our lives. We loved the place. We even idealized it. I remember that in my youth I grew up with the belief that Primavera was a paradise chosen by The Almighty, a place in which trees must not be felled but left to grow.[58]

Peter Mathis describes the situation at Primavera thusly:

> We were like a lantern that shed no light, we were preserving an empty vessel. The decline had been going on for twenty years. We had lost our perspective of Eberhard Arnold's legacy. The foundation of love in our lives had been lost. We had lost the sincerity in our relationships. There was a whispering campaign. Everything was on the brink of collapse. Veteran families left because they had lost hope of a change for the better. Everyone felt that we needed to rediscover the center of gravity in our lives. And so, at the beginning of 1961, we decided that we must dismantle the old to make way for the new.[59]

Maureen Burn, who was also among those who left during the crisis, also speaks of the decline of belief at Primavera, and particularly about the move away from the beliefs of the founder, Eberhard Arnold:

At the time, there was a feeling that if the commune continued along this path, it would lose its way.... I was among those who had lost their way...I did not like the new direction and so I left and returned to Edinburgh to look after my sick mother.... Those first days outside were terribly difficult. We had no money and had to manage on our own.

Maureen concludes:

Heini was accused of being responsible for the situation. It was neither his fault nor that of the younger members from America. They were suddenly burdened with a grave responsibility without having sufficient experience to shoulder it. They were left alone with the responsibility because the majority of the office-holders avoided it and the way.... Later, I realized that I had erred and at the earliest opportunity returned happily to the commune.

And she adds, "One of the wonderful things about the Bruderhof is its ability to forgive."[60]

Hans Meier also recalls his decision to leave and the reasons for his return:

I was among those who decided to leave in 1961. I had in the past filled a responsible position in the commune and once I felt that we were no longer united I did my soul-searching and moved to Argentina, leaving my wife and children at the commune. I left not as a result of the disagreements, but because it was unclear to me how the commune could exist under the circumstances that existed at the time. I saw the internal split at Primavera and I wanted to know from what it had stemmed. I reached the conclusion that I represented an ideological commune while the brothers who remained represented one of the spirit and belief. That went on for twelve years. In 1972, I came for a visit and we were reunited. I felt that belief had returned and united us.[61]

Following the decision to dismantle the settlements, the Bruderhof had to make arrangements for the transfer of their members and the sale of the farm at Primavera. The farm was sold to "Friesland," the neighboring Mennonite settlement, and the money from the sale covered both the travel expenses of the members who were to be transferred and the cost of the tickets for those who were leaving, the majority of whom went to Europe. An additional source of financing was the reparations received from the German government in 1957.[62]

The obtaining of entry visas to the United States proved to be a tremendous problem. They were aided in this by a decision made a year earlier to empty the Connecticut settlement of its population but to hold on to the property. This empty property, which was capable of absorbing the entire population of the Paraguayan settlements, was a decisive factor in the decision of the immigration authorities to grant entry visas to the people from Paraguay. An additional contributing factor in swaying the immigration authorities was the growth in the activities of the toy factory. Thus, the way to immigration to the United States was opened, and the first group arrived there on 22 October 1961, and the last group on 29 January 1962. A number of members remained in Paraguay to deal with the transfer of the farm to its new Mennonite owners.[63]

The great crisis came to an end in 1962, with the membership of the Bruderhof having shrunk from 1,400 to 800. Many of those who left were completely unprepared for life outside the commune, which came as a shock that they found difficult to overcome. The mass exodus made life extremely difficult for hundreds of people—the elderly, infirm, and families with children—and they bore their burden stoically for many years. But the trauma was deeply etched on their memories, and some of their memoirs have been published recently. Among the writers are some of the Bruderhof's past leaders, like Roger Allain, whose criticism does not spare those responsible for their suffering:

> Those of us who were excluded or who left the Bruderhof, particularly during the crisis of the late fifties and early sixties, were deeply hurt by the wrench from dear friends and in many cases worse still from our own older children. We had very lean years working overtime to find a footing in the fiercely competitive world with next to no money.[64]

In his autobiography, Edmund Cocksedge, one of the Bruderhof members who had joined the movement in England and who left it at this time, writes of this watershed in his life:

> We had spent twenty years in Paraguay in the community, committed for our lifetime, and not anticipating any change in that relationship, yet now we stood before the possibility of leaving the community and trying to live life as a family on our own. This was a dreadful prospect but we just could not find our way to accepting the changes, which we felt were regressive rather than steps forward for the life in the communities.[65]

Bette Zumpe has also written extensively about the suffering of the 623 people forced to leave Primavera and alleges that the Bruderhof bore "moral guilt" as well as "financial guilt" concerning those who were excluded.[66]

This was a difficult time for a "purge" of this kind, not to mention the movement of the population that came in its wake. Twenty years in

Paraguay had not prepared the brothers for the reality that they were to face in their new locations. Moreover, the economic situation of the Bruderhof in Paraguay at that time was bad and this did not permit them to be generous with the people who were leaving. According to Bruderhof principles, each person joining contributes all his or her property and is not entitled to reclaim it, and as they had all made this undertaking upon joining, there were no grounds for appeal. With the outbreak of the crisis, there were some very hard cases from a human standpoint: families with many children found themselves in Asunción with the paltry sum of money they had been given by the Bruderhof and with no knowledge of Spanish, and in some cases they had to borrow money from the German or British consulates to pay for their tickets to their homeland.

Andreas Meier and John Winter were appointed to complete the sale of the property and the transfer of the people to the United States. In a letter to the author, Andreas reviews their activities in 1961 and at the same time rebuts the criticism regarding the Bruderhof's alleged ignoring of the needs and plight of those who left:

Heini Arnold asked us to ensure that no one remained in Paraguay unless he wanted to do so. Our first task was to ensure that all those who needed time to consider their actions received their travel expenses, that we would take care of their travel arrangements, and that each person received $100 in cash. In other words, a family of ten souls was given $1,000 in addition to boat tickets to their country of origin in Europe or to a country where they had relatives. It was made clear that the Bruderhof would not leave Paraguay until all these arrangements had been completed.

Our task was completed but it imposed a heavy financial burden on our communes in the United States. The travel arrangements were made through three different travel agents so we benefited from larger credit, and this was largely based on the knowledge that we would be able to repay our debts from the sale of Primavera and its inventory of equipment. At one stage we found ourselves overdrawn to such an extent that the court in Asunción ordered that the sale be stopped and ordered the police into Primavera for our protection until such time that we were able to prove that we had no intention of fleeing the country before our debts were cleared. During the litigation I was held by the police for a while but was released after we had proved our good faith. In the end, all those who had left the Bruderhof set off for the country of their choice with all their household goods and $100 in cash per person. Although this was not a large sum, those who left did not have to shoulder the burden of debt that was left for those who remained. Only three families elected to remain in Paraguay and all of them were provided with the means of beginning their new life: an apartment, furniture, land, and the same sum of money that had been given to the others.

It took five months to complete the sale of Primavera and repay all our debts and then the last of the Bruderhof members moved to the United States. We did not manage to sell everything and some expensive assets were left unsold. It took ten years for our communities to break the shackles of our debts and only then were we able to build our lives afresh...and that was how those who remained in the new Bruderhof shouldered the burden of debt and enabled those who left to begin their new life with a small sum of money, but free of debt.[67]

The baleful wave of crises was not only limited to the Primavera settlements, but also spread throughout the movement and reached Europe. Merrill Mow writes:

In England and Germany a pattern emerged similar to that in Paraguay, except that Heini was not able to participate at all.... The pattern was similar in that the brotherhood dissolved itself and a small group was formed from which a new brotherhood would grow. And the *hofs* moved together. Those who were in the brotherhood or close to it moved to Bulstrode from Wheathill and Sinntal. Sinntal was closed down and eventually sold... In a practical way this was the only workable solution, but inwardly it was not good. Words cannot express the upheaval and pain at that time.[68]

Merrill Mow writes of the crisis that broke out at Bulstrode in 1965:

An atmosphere of complacency and laxity threatened to destroy the life of the community and sapped its inner vitality. During the winter and spring, a number of brothers and sisters travelled from America to Bulstrode and called upon the members of the community to face challenges which would arouse them from their slumber.

He says that at the time, when almost all the Bruderhof were settled in the United States, and after all the *hofs* in Paraguay and Europe had been closed down, it appeared that there was no justification for the continued, separate, and isolated existence of the Bulstrode Bruderhof. In a joint decision made on 20 March 1966, by its members and members of the *hofs* in the United States, it was decided to close Bulstrode down and move its members to the United States. The decision was effected that same year and in December, 1966, the last of its members left Bulstrode Palace. The building and park were bought by a missionary association that invested large sums in renovation, and the proceeds of the sale of the property paid for the member's journey from England to America. Thus ended thirty years of Bruderhof communities in Britain.

Yet, with all the pain and suffering involved, Merrill Mow finds some good points in the crises as a means of purifying the movement:

The struggling process is truly tragic if it is directionless. But if there is clarity in the mind of even one person as to how the struggle should be rightly led...then the crises are a gift of God. They are the means by which a derailed train can be gotten back on the rails again and this happened in our community life again and again.

On looking back, one sees that the struggles were urgently needed and were tremendously important. And the most important thing about them was and is to know what they are about and what they are for. If that is not known, then the struggle can be extremely tragic and people can be hurt very seriously.[69]

Benjamin Zablocki, too, in his book on the Bruderhof, *Joyful Community*, claims that from the Bruderhof's point of view, the split was a drastic but necessary act:

Individuals were sacrificed for the church in the spirit of their own oath of allegiance. Had it not been for the exclusions of 1961, the Bruderhof would have become an eclectic community without the capability of survival. The harsh attitude was partly justified by the fact that none of the members were permanently excluded. The Bruderhof was always ready to accept the penitents with open arms.[70]

Over the years, the relations that had been maintained with those who had left brought about the return of many families to the bosom of the Bruderhof. Despite the fact that some of them lived outside the commune for many years, the communities' members had always perceived the people who had left as being in a temporary situation. Those who had left were viewed as still belonging to the church, and families who found themselves in financial difficulties were provided with assistance if the communities' economic situation so allowed.

Testimonies of Bruderhof members who left the movement in the year of the great crisis and who found their way back have been published recently with the objective of refuting the one-sided picture of suffering and of being ignored by the Bruderhof. One such testimony is that of the Keiderlings of Woodcrest:

In 1961, the whole community went through a hard time of terrible turmoil when everything collapsed.... Many went away into private life. We also did for twelve years.... Now all that Ellen and I had to do was to have a tiny longing for the life and to feel sorry where we had hurt love or were hypocritical. The rest came to us out of love. It was the most moving thing when after many years outside, Heini apologized for some lovelessness that was done to us.[71]

And the wounds of the crisis were slowly healed. The struggle for the preservation of the legacy of Eberhard Arnold ended in victory for his followers. In the two years that ensued from the outbreak of the crisis, a dozen or so Servants of the Word were excluded. Eberhard Arnold's three sons remained in the Bruderhof leadership. A number of the Americans, including those who had been members of the delegation to Paraguay, were advanced to senior positions in the leadership.[72] Some of the exiles returned but many continued to wander disappointedly in the world outside, and they, too, gradually found their places in it, but their efforts at maintaining contact with the Bruderhof were unsuccessful—a great deal of bitterness and deep emotional scars separated them.

Notes

1. Allain, Roger, *The Community That Failed* (San Francisco, Calif.: Carrier Pigeon Press, 1992), 229; Zablocki [Benjamin, *The Joyful Community* (Baltimore, Md.: Penguin, 1971), 240] claims that the membership was then comprised of twenty nationalities.
2. Mow, Merrill, *Torches Rekindled* (Ulster Park, N.Y.: Plough Publishing House, 1989), 299; Zumpe, Elizabeth Bolken, in *The KIT Annual 1991* (The Collected Newsletters of the KIT Information Service, San Francisco, Calif.), 169.
3. Mow, op. cit., 134-35.
4. Interview with Hans Meier, October, 1992.
5. Allain, op. cit., 291-99, and also Zumpe, op. cit., 169.
6. Allain, op. cit., 302-03.
7. Mow, op. cit., 110.
8. See chap. 5 on Paraguay, this volume; Also, J. Arnold in *KIT,* vol. 2, no. 2, 41, and Mow, op. cit., 121-24.
9. Mow, op. cit., 173-81.
10. Buddog Evans in *KIT,* vol. 2, no. 2, 41.
11. Interview with Doug Moody, October, 1992.
12. Interview with Stan and Hella Ehrlich, November, 1991.
13. Zablocki, op. cit., 213-14.
14. Zumpe, op. cit., 157-58.
15. Allain, op. cit., 305.
16. Zumpe, op. cit., 172-74; Mow, op. cit., 150.
17. Interview with Hans Meier, October, 1992.
18. In a revealing article that appeared in *KIT,* vol. 4, no. 9, 9, Bette Zumpe describes how she heard of her father's sin when she was at Sinntal in June, 1960. Heini Arnold was with her at the time and Bette admits that he did his best to ease her distress. See also her autobiography, *Torches Extinguished* (San Francisco, Calif.: Carrier Pigeon Press), 172-74.
19. On these articles, see Killian Zumpe in *KIT Annual 1991,* 4-6; Zumpe, Bette, in *KIT Annual 1991,* 41.
20. Hans Meier in *KIT Annual 1991,* 201.
21. Zumpe, Elizabeth, op. cit., 185-87; Mow, op. cit., 132-33.
22. Zumpe, op. cit., 185-87.
23. *KIT Annual 1991,* 248.
24. Miriam Arnold in *KIT Annual 1991,* 221-22.
25. Interview with Dick Domer, November, 1991.

26. Zablocki, op. cit., 99–102; Mow, op. cit., 14.
27. Zablocki, op. cit., 103.
28. Ibid., 107.
29. Allain, op. cit., 291–92.
30. Balz Trumpi in *KIT Annual 1991*, 241–42.
31. Zablocki, op. cit., 100.
32. Ibid., 100–01, 105.
33. On Emmy Arnold's trip, see: Zumpe, op. cit., 182; Mow, op. cit., 140–42; Allain, op. cit., 295.
34. Interview with Maureen Burn, October, 1992; Allain, op. cit., 296–300.
35. Mow, op. cit., 150–52; Allain, op. cit., 296–302.
36. *El Arado*, no. 9 (1959).
37. Interviews with Stan and Hella Ehrlich and Charles Headland, Woodcrest, November, 1991.
38. Allain, op. cit., 308.
39. Zumpe, op. cit., 196–98.
40. Zablocki, 106.
41. Allain, op. cit., 309–20.
42. Interview with Andreas Meier, Woodcrest, November, 1991.
43. Interview with Andreas Meier, Woodcrest, November, 1991; Also Mow, op. cit., 160, 42–44.
44. Zumpe, op. cit., 196–98.
45. Interview with Doug Moody, October, 1992.
46. Interview with Art Wiser, October, 1992.
47. Mow, op. cit., 169.
48. Zablocki, op. cit., 99, 107.
49. *KIT,* vol. 2, no. 10, 220; Zablocki, op. cit., 102, 107.
50. Mow, op. cit., 299–300.
51. Ibid., 305.
52. Roger Allain in *KIT Annual, 1989–1990*, 35–36.
53. Interview with Art Wiser, October, 1992.
54. *KIT,* vol. 3, no. 10 (October 1991), 4.
55. Hans Zimmermann in *KIT,* vol. 4, no. 7 (July 1992); Roger Allain in *KIT,* vol. 2, no. 1 (January 1990), 4.
56. Mow, op.cit., 172; Zablocki, op. cit., 108.
57. Interview with Christian Boller, November, 1991.
58. Interview with Andreas Meier, Woodcrest, November, 1991.
59. Interview with Peter Mathis, November, 1991.
60. Interview with Maureen Burn, October, 1992.
61. Interview with Hans Meier, 1978.
62. According to Zablocki, op. cit., 109, Primavera was sold to the Mennonites for $150,000; *The Plough,* no. 9 (Quarterly of Bruderhof communities. Bromdon: The Plough Publishing House, 1985): 16.
63. See Mow, op. cit., 183–86; In 1963, Roger Allain visited the abandoned Primavera settlements and the impressions of his tour, which include descriptions of the waste and desolation he found there, were published in *KIT,* vol. 3, no. 9.
64. Roger Allain in *KIT Annual 1989*, 235.
65. Cocksedge, Edmund, *Vagabond for Peace* (House of Freedom Christian Community Publication, 1991), 92.

66. Zumpe, Bette in *KIT Annual 1991*, 254.
67. Andreas Meier to Yaacov Oved, 3 November 1992.
68. Mow, op. cit., 186.
69. Ibid., op. cit., 48.
70. Zablocki, op. cit., 109, 236; See also Hans Meier's testimony on his leaving and return after the reconciliation in *KIT Annual 1991*, 200.
71. *KIT Annual 1990*, 242–43.
72. According to Zablocki, twelve Servants of the Word were excluded during the crisis. See Zablocki, op. cit., 237.

9

After the Crisis—Rehabilitation

The great crisis brought about some radical changes in the Bruderhof movement. Its numerical scope, the number of communes that were then concentrated in the United States, and the multinational composition of its membership, which had so characterized the movement over the past decade, were all diminished.[1] Prior to the outbreak of the crisis there were those who viewed the Bruderhof as a religious commune solely in the context of its past and the roots from which it had sprung, and they saw in religiousness the most appropriate way of maintaining a communal community. However, they also viewed the commune itself as a community that could avail itself of a number of varying options in order to maintain its continued existence, but as a result of the crisis, and the purges that came in its wake, these members were excluded.

The Bruderhof remained united in its concept of a church community in line with which the commune was organically linked to the existence of the church of the faithful. Moreover, once the crisis had abated, the movement's new regime began to relate to the period between the death of Eberhard Arnold and the beginning of the sixties as one in which an abundance of mistakes and deviations from dogma had been made, and they perceived the church community stage as a return to the Arnold tradition. This approach held that it was possible to combine the Bruderhof's existence as a social movement and a church that would be in keeping with the Arnold heritage.

In June, 1962, a short time after the end of the crisis, Heini Arnold was elected to the office of Elder of the entire Bruderhof flock and its communes and his election followed the hard lessons that had been learned from the harrowing experiences of the years of crisis. The four remaining Bruderhofs sensed an urgent need to maintain a stable church headed by a leader blessed with spiritual inspiration, and they were aided

241

in this by both the Hutterite tradition and charter, which obliged them to appoint an Elder who would serve as head of a group of *hofs*. In the past, when the Bruderhof had been accepted into the Hutterite church, the Hutterites had appointed Eberhard Arnold as Elder of the communes that were about to be established in Germany, despite the fact that there was only one such settlement. The office was abolished with Eberhard's death and although the number of *hofs* had increased, the matter was not brought up again. During the period in which there were nine Bruderhofs, the need to reinstate the office was discussed, but nothing came of it.[2] Under the circumstances that had ensued in the aftermath of the crisis, there was a consensus throughout the various brotherhoods that Heini Arnold should be asked to accept the office of Elder of all the Bruderhofs, and this consensus was an expression of the high esteem in which his leadership had been held during the period of the great crisis.[3]

Yet, despite Heini Arnold's election to the office of Elder, he did not succeed in attaining the status that had been enjoyed by Eberhard. On the one hand, he did not have his father's spiritual charisma, while on the other, the tasks that faced the leadership had increased in number and become extremely ramified. All of the things that the Bruderhof members had been able to accomplish in the framework of their small community could no longer be done in a movement that was comprised of four communities with a combined population of 800 souls. With great insight and skill, Heini built up a leadership that may defined as one of democratic centralism; the rank-and-file membership still had a great deal of power, while decisions that were reached by common agreement in accordance with Bruderhof tradition left a great deal of room for the involvement of the office holders. Heini did not take executive offices upon himself and the spheres of economic and everyday activities were left to his assistants. Yet despite this, and possibly even because of it, he managed to acquire the trust of the Bruderhof membership and in particular that of the newer American members who became, in the main, his supporters and disciples.

We can learn something of Heini's policies as Elder from a review of what occurred in the movement a short time after his election. The period of the movement's rehabilitation began in 1963 and the most significant event of that period was the return of some 200 members who had left the movement during the crisis. Many of these went to the new Oak Lake community in Pennsylvania, thus more than doubling its 1963 population from 120 to 245. The members of Oak Lake were eager to establish good relations with their neighbors and so, at an open house held in 1965, the audience was treated to a rendering of Haydn's oratorio, *The Creation*, by the Oak Lake choir. Although the Bruderhof membership felt that a new period of internal tranquility was dawning, it was not to be, for a short time later a new wave of crises, albeit limited and smaller in scope than those of 1960 through 1961, swept through the movement.

In 1965, a crisis erupted in the wake of a lack of consensus on the necessity for an air link between the New York and Pennsylvania communities. In November of that year the minister of New Meadow Run sought to bridge the long distance between his community and Woodcrest by means of an air link. As he was an ex-pilot, he obtained a civil pilot's license and flights between the two communities from the neighboring airfield got under way. It quickly became clear that unlike its predecessors, this innovation did nothing to improve the social climate; on the contrary, it caused increased tension, envy, and an ugly atmosphere between the two communities. Matters came to a head and it became necessary to convene a general meeting of all the members of the Bruderhof that was held at New Meadow Run at the end of that year. Prior to this assembly, an atmosphere of nonconfidence was prevalent, and the need for a general meeting was felt in order to bring down the barriers that had been erected between the camps. The experiences of the great crisis had taught them that disagreements should not be allowed to flourish and that every effort should be made to deal with them without delay. And so, once it became clear that crisis was in the air, work at all the *hofs* was suspended and the New York and Connecticut brothers travelled to the Pennsylvania community on chartered buses where they convened for discussions that lasted for five days. They then returned home and reconvened two weeks later, this time for a further four days. There were more general meetings of this kind that took place at the beginning of 1966 and at their conclusion the threat of crisis had passed and relations between the settlements were normalized.[4]

The success of the conference at New Meadow Run encouraged the Bruderhof leadership to organize additional meetings of this kind, with another one being planned for August, 1968. Packed buses from all three communities came to this conference, which was held over a weekend, bringing almost all the Bruderhof brothers and sisters. Tom Potts, one of the Woodcrest veterans, has this to say about these meetings:

> The brothers who came from all our communities suspended all their work and convened for discussions which lasted for two or three days. We discussed the future of the movement, its involvement in outside society, its publications, and the state of the communities and their stability.

Two years later, on 20 June 1970, some 300 members met at Woodcrest for a celebration of the fiftieth anniversary of the establishment of the Sannerz commune, and some of the Sannerz veterans who participated in the conference spoke of the atmosphere that had prevailed during those early days. These were meetings that brimmed with social and spiritual elation and Bruderhof members claim that it was at their inspiration that they experienced a kind of "rebirth" during the sixties. But there was another aspect to the new conditions that had been created: the Bruderhof began to concentrate on their internal problems and distance themselves from those of surrounding society and from what was happening in the outside world, and the evangelistic element of their life became seriously weakened.

In 1966 there were some signs of a trend to reorganize the Bruderhof communities that remained after the great crisis and it was under these circumstances that the Bulstrode community in England was dismantled and its members moved to the United States.[5] 1966 saw the beginning of a period of economic growth in the Bruderhof and new questions began to appear on the agenda. Should new members be accepted? Should the segregative Hutterite approach be adopted or should the Bruderhof open itself up to a new spirit? And then, after several years of seclusion, a new turning point became apparent and the Bruderhof opened itself to involvement in public struggles, first in the black civil rights struggle that was taking place in the southern states, when the movement come out openly on the side of Martin Luther King as an expression of partial involvement in the overall struggle for civil rights.[6]

In the sixties, the Bruderhof, increasingly concerned with the two national issues of the day—civil rights for the blacks and the Vietnam war—found themselves preoccupied with the outside world to an extent that they had not been for years. Brothers met with senators and congressmen in Washington, urging them to help stem the ever-increasing numbers of troops being sent to fight in Southeast Asia. Heini and others met with the members of the Senate Foreign Relations Committee chaired by senator William Fulbright, and had illuminating discussions with Wayne Morse of Oregon and Ernest Gruening of Washington, two senators who consistently spoke out against the war.

It was in the course of these efforts that the communities were reminded of the words of Eberhard Arnold in a letter to the brotherhood just before his death: "We must always respond to all current movements without becoming infected by them."

In February, 1965, Christoph Arnold and Art Weiser travelled to Marion, Alabama, to attend the funeral of a black teenager murdered by racists. The march to the cemetery was led by Martin Luther King, Jr. On 7 March, a second, larger march from Selma to Montgomery was called. The brotherhood responded by sending three brothers to Selma. The Bruderhofs, and the young people in particular, were challenged by this popular movement for social justice that swept America.

Miriam Potts, who at the time was one of the Bruderhof's younger members, recalls:

> One of the most important things we decided then was not to close ourselves off but to take part in struggles we felt were just, like civil rights, identifying with the blacks and the fight against the war in Vietnam. These struggles linked us to groups of friends and broadened our relations with the outside world.

Klaus Barth, a Bruderhof member from Paraguay, tells us something of the significance that these activities held for him:

> We had a great longing to get to know people from the outside world and learn about their problems. Our involvement in the civil rights struggle opened a new and uncharted world for us, one we had not known in Paraguay. We identified with that struggle because we viewed it not only as a political one, but also as a struggle for social justice.[7]

The turnabout in the approach to external social involvement fell into line with Eberhard Arnold's heritage (see quotation above). It is worthy of note that in their external activities, the Bruderhof members were also involved in a kind of religious revival, which brought Arnold's theology into sharp focus and their publishing house, which had renewed its activities in the sixties, devoted itself to the publication of all his writings.

1964–1974—Reconciliation with the Hutterites

It was at this stage of Bruderhof history that there was a renewed call for reconciliation with the Hutterites, relations with whom had been broken off in the wake of the Forest River episode and in this matter, too, a special effort was devoted to the revival of the Arnold heritage. The Hutterites were viewed as a communal movement *par excellence* that had succeeded in maintaining its beliefs and way of life and had avoided crises of the kind that had beset the Bruderhof in recent years.

Heini Arnold played an active role in this reconciliation and he was aided by Jacob Kleinsasser, who at the time was acting Elder (a kind of deputy to the incumbent Elder, who was very old) of the *Schmiedleut*. At the time, Heini felt a profound need to seek ways and means of reconciliation with the Hutterites, of joining the schism and abrogating the Hutterite ban on contacts with the Bruderhof, which had been declared in the wake of the Forest River affair. Heini felt remorse about the mistakes made by the Bruderhof in this affair and sought a way of correcting them by means of a public apology. He raised the issue at various Bruderhof meetings and indeed, he found agreement throughout the movement on the need for reconciliation. It may be assumed that among the factors that came into play in this matter was the desire to renew relations with the sister movement, the stability and numerical growth of which aroused much admiration (in the year in question, the Hutterite population numbered some 20,000 souls).[8]

The first signs of the possibility of renewed relations became apparent in the fall of 1963 when two Hutterite "ministers" from Canada visited the three Bruderhof communities in the United States. The visit took place in a congenial atmosphere and there was a feeling among the Bruderhof membership that this was a Hutterite signal of their desire for reconciliation and that the time was ripe for talks. Heini Arnold yearned for a renewal of relations with the Hutterites and so he contacted one of their Elders in Canada, seeking approval of a visit to them at the head of Bruderhof delegation. The request was duly approved and in January, 1964, two central Bruderhof members who had not been involved in the Forest River affair, left for Manitoba. They were received warmly and affectionately, albeit a certain alienation was felt on the church and movement levels. Their Hutterite hosts hinted that they were still officially "ostracized" and therefore they were not allowed to eat at the same table with their hosts [*sic*]. Comments were made about their dress and appearance, "which was not Hutterian." They did not wear beards and, heaven forfend, they wore watches on their wrists. It was patently clear that the memories of Forest River still clouded their relationship.

It was during this visit that the delegation met with the Hutterite elders and Heini begged forgiveness for the sins of Forest River. Initially it seemed that the elders were prepared to forgive him personally, but on the eve of the delegation's departure they were handed a letter in which the Elders' demands were set out which included, *inter alia,* that all the Hutterites who had joined the Bruderhof must return to their church in order to undergo a formal exclusion ceremony and that Heini himself would have to be symbolically excluded for a certain period. Heini was prepared to accept the exclusion but his fellow Bruderhof leaders would not accept these conditions.[9] And so the first attempt at reconciliation was shot down almost before it had got off the ground.

But the Bruderhof leadership did not capitulate and looked forward to a further opportunity of renewing the relationship with the Hutterites, and indeed, it was not long in coming. This time, too, the signal came in the form of a visit to Woodcrest by Hutterite elders who came to meet with Heini Arnold on 6 June 1973, accompanied by the eminent sociologist John Hostetler, author of some important books on the Hutterites and the Amish. The meeting took place in Heini's home and although brief, it was extremely warm and emotional. Bruderhof member Joseph Ben-Eliezer, who participated in the meeting, described it in detail in an interview with the author and said that it resulted from an initiative taken by Jacob Kleinsasser during a tour of eastern Canada that he had made with Jacob Hoffer in the winter of 1973. During the tour, Kleinsasser suddenly decided to visit the Bruderhof and, thus, fulfil a long-standing wish. Their surprise visit occurred during a festive meal (love meal) in honor of Heini's safe return from a visit to the English commune. The surprise and excitement knew no bounds and both sides left the meeting with the feeling that the road to reconciliation had been opened.

Kleinsasser sensed the strong desire on the part of the Bruderhof members to return to their mother church, but at the same time he was aware of the great obstacles that the opposition of his colleagues from the other *leute* had placed in their path. On his departure he promised nothing, but he immediately began to act among the Hutterite leadership with the objective of bringing about a meeting of reconciliation between his own leadership and that of the Bruderhof. It will be remembered that numerous differences separated the Bruderhof and the Hutterites; the Hutterite form of dress had long been abandoned by the Bruderhof and the external appearance of the settlements was not in the

Hutterite style. But these external effects did not deter Kleinsasser from moving the parties toward reconciliation.[10]

And indeed, a short time later, on 21 June 1973, Heini received an invitation to visit the Hutterite settlement at Crystal Spring, Manitoba, with a delegation of Servants of the Word. The delegation was to be comprised solely of members who had not been involved in the Forest River affair. The group's departure was delayed as a result of some fears that they would again be faced with demands that they would be unable to accept, but after deliberation it was decided to send the delegation, which included Heini Arnold and active members from among the newer American membership who had not, of course, been involved in the Forest River affair: Don Alexander, Glenn Swinger, Merrill Mow, and Dwight Blough. The delegation left on 4 January 1974 and the following day reached Crystal Spring where the Council of Elders of all the Hutterite settlements from all three *leute* had convened. There were some fierce discussions and the Bruderhof delegation was asked to provide clarifications on their position on matters of education, baptism, the family and marriage.

The next day, the extended council of all the elders convened at the neighboring Hutterite settlement, Sturgeon Creek. There were some seventy people present, representing all the settlements and *leute* and it was there that Heini Arnold rose to his feet and on behalf of the Bruderhof, pleaded for forgiveness. After he had finished speaking, the Bruderhof delegation was asked to wait for the decision of the Council of Elders outside the hall. The Council's deliberations continued well into the night until the delegation was finally informed that it had been decided to accept Heini's plea for forgiveness. In order for the act of forgiveness to take effect, Heini had only to take part in an additional symbolic ceremony in which he would declare his contrition and further undertake that henceforth he would prevent the Bruderhof from reverting to its errant ways. After Heini had done as he had been asked, the members of the delegation thought that the matter was closed and the road to reunification had been opened.[11]

However, to their great surprise, the Hutterite delegates rose at the conclusion of the ceremony and announced that in order to completely erase the bad feelings of the past, the Hutterite members of Forest River who had joined the Bruderhof would have to submit to exclusion for a short period and to this end, five Hutterite ministers would go to

Woodcrest to perform the exclusion ritual. This unexpected addition surprised and discomfited the Bruderhof delegation, for it constituted a reiteration of one of the rigid conditions with which they had been faced in the past, but as the ceremony of forgiveness had already taken place, the Bruderhof members were chary of breaching it by giving their assent without the approval of the Bruderhof general meeting. Heini was torn, and in a letter summarizing this episode he wrote:

> Had we said that we were unable to do this prior to discussing it at home, we would have been liable to find ourselves in the middle of a new Forest River affair.[12]

In any event, in order to alleviate their fears, the delegation called Woodcrest next day and were given unequivocal approval and in addition, on 8 January, a cable arrived from Woodcrest that formally approved the agreement reached with the Hutterites. Yet, despite the congenial atmosphere that had prevailed at the meetings, the delegation returned home with heavy hearts at the thought of what might happen when the Hutterites visited Woodcrest. But their fears were rapidly dissipated when the Hutterite delegation arrived and conducted the ceremony in good spirits and an understanding of the Bruderhof's exclusiveness. The issue of unequivocal adoption of the Hutterite mode of dress did not arise and the Bruderhof were simply requested to adopt a uniform form of dress. In the atmosphere of goodwill that prevailed between the two sides, the Bruderhof membership decided unilaterally to adopt the Hutterite dress: dark clothes for the menfolk and long dresses and head kerchiefs for the women.[13]

Thus were the relations between the Bruderhof and the Hutterites renewed and a new and rich chapter in the relations and cooperation between the two sister movements was opened. During the first year of the renewed relations delegations travelled back and forth between Manitoba in Canada and the eastern United States. Although those first days were filled with enthusiasm and mutual understanding, the great differences in the culture and way of life of the two movements did not simply disappear. Samuel Kleinsasser of Sturgeon Creek, who attended the funerals of two Bruderhof members who died in an air crash in January, 1975, expressed these differences well. In a long letter in which he set down his impressions of his visit to the Bruderhof communes, he wrote:

> Many things among them are still different from the way we have it, but this is not to be despised or rejected.... Just think: a thousand people of the world—they

enter the church—they give up everything. We do not have a single soul visiting our communities while they have visitors daily.... There is no over-abundance of clothing in the families and selfishness is not encouraged.

Church discipline and the ban are used just as they are with us. Total discipline is maintained, not superficially as it is with us.

He concludes his letter with these words: "One cannot describe everything, but these people have much that is good."[14]

The Seventies

With the opening up of some very wide markets for its products, "Community Playthings," the Bruderhof toy factory, began to show signs of impressive economic success at the end of the sixties and the enterprise's reputation spread rapidly. Tom Potts, who managed the factory for many years, tells us something of its success:

The possibility of expanding our production coincided with the beginnings of the Bruderhof movement's expansion in the United States and this provided us with solid economic foundations for our activities.

Tom repeatedly emphasized that "we view our success as a gift from God and believe that He guided, and will continue to guide us along the right road." Regarding the factory itself, he says:

We feel that the work in factory is particularly suitable for our way of life...there is work for all sectors of the population and it can be adjusted to meet a particular need. Work is not seasonal and there is no need to work on festivals and holidays. Our products are not patented but we are not afraid of competition for the products enjoy a fine reputation, thanks to our high work ethic. Some stages in the factory's development evolved from bottom-up initiatives and experience. The majority of our special products were invented by our members, often springing from a home-made toy that had been made as a gift for a child...and indeed, the Bruderhof has a long-standing tradition of woodwork which can be traced back throughout the movement's history and this, without doubt, is extremely helpful. There is no hired labor in our factory and there never has been. Expansion of production has usually come together with population growth and we manage to maintain the production of large orders by mobilizing our work force. All our sales are done through catalogs and in order to avoid large numbers of orders which we are unable to fill, the number of catalogs released to the market is limited. This was something we learned from a book salesman who taught us the secrets of distribution in the United States and since then we have marketed our products by using this method, and today the factory has some 250,000 customers on file. In 1977, a new department for the manufacture of aids for the disabled was opened and is currently highly developed as we are the only company specializing in the manufacture of these products. This enterprise, too, was started up by chance. The family of one of our neighbors at Deer Spring had a disabled son and they asked us to make a special aid for him. Our people accepted the task, invested a great deal of effort and initiative in it, and came up with an aid that filled the bill completely. Word of the quality of this piece of work spread rapidly and we soon received further orders.[15]

Tom Potts and all the other Bruderhof members with whom I spoke about "Community Playthings" stressed that the Bruderhof takes great care not to be carried away by the dynamics of economic success and wealth. They said that in 1978, with an improvement in the Bruderhof's financial state, Heini Arnold cautioned them against being caught up by materialism:

It has to be in the whole household that a clear stand is taken against all greed and all mammonism.

I want to challenge us all to go the whole way. If we have more than we need as it seems at the moment, then we have to ask God to show us the way to share. We want to share with everyone who wants to follow Jesus, even if they are not yet united with us.... We must have open hearts for seeking people and also open hands.

We must find ways of outreach and mission at a time when standards have gone downhill.[16]

Further evidence of this trend may be found in the 1983 decision to lower the standard of living, concentrate on expanding the Bruderhof and engage in social work in outside society:

Many members were troubled about the standard of living in the communities: was there not a danger that they would forget the years of poverty, that they would fail to remember that their income from "Community Playthings" was a God-given gift?...And if worldly goods become too important, or if they accumulate, complacency and materialism would follow.

The trend toward curbing materialism did not slow the rate of the factory's development and new channels for excess income were quickly found. The economic success of the seventies enabled the Bruderhof to invest in the rehabilitation of the movement by financing the establishment of new communities, and the first and most prominent of these was Darvell in England. The new community was established in order to absorb the people who had left the movement and later returned after wandering through Europe seeking renewed ties with the Bruderhof. Merrill Mow describes the circumstances that surrounded the new beginning in England thusly:

Early in 1971, the Servants of three communities met: they wanted to do more for the unreconciled members who lived in England and elsewhere in Europe—America was too far away for them to visit. Heini suggested building a new Bruderhof in England to make it easier for brothers and sisters to find their way back to the community.

Heini's own words in 1971 about Darvell were: "The main reason for starting a Bruderhof in England was to find a way to those who once belonged to us, to find a new relationship. We felt that our door should be open to everyone who is truly called by God. So we felt that we should go to a country where there was more of an open door for all foreigners, and England seemed to be that country. We long very much to come into real contact with more people and also with former members.

Darvell has the special task for, if I may use the term, lost sheep. Every Bruderhof has this task.... There are some in America but they are mostly in England and Germany.... There will be much joy at Darvell, but there will also be much pain. Contacts with former Bruderhof members will be partly very painful, but sometimes a great joy."[17]

The brotherhood's response was enthusiastic. In early February, a party of three was sent to England to look for a suitable location, and by July a former tuberculosis sanitarium had been purchased.

Darvell Hall Hospital, which had earlier been an estate, was built on rolling hills near the Channel, fifty miles south of London. The property was small but it had considerable housing available immediately. Darvell, an old Saxon word meaning "Deer Spring," was kept as the name of the new Bruderhof.

Throughout the first months at Darvell, several members living outside the communities in England and Germany reunited with the brotherhood at the new Bruderhof, and more visited. This gathering was the result of frequent visits by brothers and sisters to Germany, Switzerland and England over the previous ten years.

The new community at Darvell was not immune to the social crises that had beset the older settlements and a short time after its establishment, it underwent a social crisis that was brought upon it by the local leadership.

The Servant of the Word, abusing the trust placed in him by the brotherhood, ruled the brothers and sisters with a strong hand. This came as a great blow to the small, newly founded brotherhood, which had supported him in his responsibilities. The wounded brotherhood and household at Darvell needed support and so another Servant was sent. Thus began a spiritual battle for the continued existence of the English community. Members from Woodcrest visited Darvell several times in 1973 and 1974 to help the community through its difficulties, and in particular to overcome the ambition and hardheartedness that appeared to be the root of the community's problems.

Some years after the crisis at Darvell, a similar one broke out at the Connecticut Bruderhof. It seemed that at Evergreen, under the guise of piety, a small power group under the Servant of the Word was oppressing 400 people. The Evergreen brotherhood suffered greatly over the subsequent period; several people left or were asked to leave and it was a struggle to restore unity and trust and to help bring succor to those who had been hurt in the process. Evergreen was not alone in its problems and eventually the internal struggle there encompassed all the Bruderhofs and led to a purification process, which was important for the future. During the crisis, the brotherhood changed the community's name to "Deer Spring" as a symbol of a fresh start in a new spirit.[18]

The seventies were marked by a return to the Bruderhof of some central members who had left the movement during the great crisis. The most prominent of these were the Swiss veteran members, Hannes and Else Boller, who decided to leave their home in Zurich and return to the fold, but unfortunately, Hans was killed in a road accident on the eve of their departure. This tragedy, however, did not affect Else's decision and she rejoined her big family, who had remained in the Bruderhof.

In October, 1972, Hans Meier, in response to talks he had held with three brothers who had visited him in June, flew from Argentina to visit his wife and family at Evergreen. His visit was significant not only for him; everyone wanted to become reconciled with him after eleven years of separation.

About a month later there was an important household meeting at Woodcrest; Hans Meier and others who wished to become reunited with the brotherhood were also present. Heini Arnold put the problems of the past into the perspective of repentance and forgiveness and at that meeting everything that had separated Hans Meier from the brotherhood disappeared and a few days later he became a fully united member. In order to speak of what had been wrong in the community since 1935, he and several others wrote open letters to each brother and sister who were living away from the community.

Renewal of Ties with the Kibbutz Movement

At the beginning of 1970 relations between the kibbutz movement and the Bruderhof were reestablished. This was mainly due to the efforts of two people: Hans Meier, an old friend of the kibbutz movement who had recently rejoined the Bruderhof and his family, and Amitai Niv, who was then a member of Kibbutz Misgav Am and who visited Deer Spring while preparing his doctoral dissertation at the Harvard School of Business Administration. The two met for the first time at Deer Spring. Niv had heard about the Bruderhof at seminars organized by the *Kibbutz Hameuhad* movement and while he had some vague ideas about them, he was anxious to learn more.

Amitai Niv's curiosity about contemporary communes and his interests as a researcher encouraged him to seek a subject that would combine his professional sphere with the subject of values and, thus, the idea of a comparative study of the kibbutz and the Bruderhof for his doctoral thesis was born. The idea was accepted by the university and he embarked on his fieldwork, which included visiting the Bruderhof over a period of two years (1974–76), during which he spent a day or two each week with them. Longer visits were possible only during vacation time. He was the first kibbutz member to meet the Bruderhof for such a long and intensive period and moreover, his systematic observations raised their encounter to a higher theoretical and research level than had ever been previously attempted. The result was his thesis that was submitted to and accepted by Harvard University: "A Search for a Theory about the Survival of Communes."[19]

This lengthy encounter between a kibbutz member and scholar and the Bruderhof marked an important stage in the development of relations between the two movements, so I therefore felt it important to interview Amitai Niv today, quite a few years after the completion of his research project. Niv explained that there were a number of contributory factors that assisted him in the good relations that existed between him, as a scholar, and the Bruderhof: (a) the trust in which they held kibbutz members; (b) his good relations with Hans Meier and later with Heini Arnold, who at the time was Elder; and (c) the high esteem in which he himself held the Bruderhof and their way of life. He added that "that esteem was preserved long after I had completed my study and I continue to maintain it towards them and the communal system they have built to this day." He believes that the Bruderhof's positive attitude toward kibbutz members springs from a number of sources. First, kibbutz members are Jews. The persecution suffered by the Jews at the hands of the Church and those suffered by the Bruderhof and the Hutterites because of their Anabaptist beliefs have created a sense of a profound common destiny with the Jewish people. Although the Bruderhof members repeatedly stress that they have no part in the actions of the established Church, they feel, as Christians, a certain sense of guilt toward the Jews. A further common fate came into being in the thirties when they, too, were oppressed by the Nazi regime and forced into exile by it.

Second, the kibbutz came into being in the Holy Land, which holds a deep spiritual significance for them, and third, the kibbutz is part of a communal movement that has existed successfully for more than eighty years. Apart from the Hutterite sister movement, there are not many communes of this kind anywhere in the world, and compared to modern communes that were established from the sixties onward, the kibbutz is closer to them and their lifestyle. So therefore, a kibbutz member who had made the effort to come to visit them from afar was viewed as a brother from an enchanted and distant world, which aroused deep emotion.[20]

In reply to my question of whether such sympathy for the kibbutz was evident in his conversations with ordinary Bruderhof members, Amitai replied in the affirmative:

> There were many questions asked about the kibbutz by the Bruderhof members with whom I spoke. The majority stemmed from simple curiosity while some were aimed at comparison. In my talks with the elders, the object of which was comparison, the kibbutz was perceived as inferior in matters of family and community life. I neither entered into a debate with them nor did I make any attempt to persuade them to accept my viewpoint.[21]

Two years after Amitai Niv completed his study, I visited Deer Spring on his recommendation during a tour of historical communes and their archives. Before I left for America, Niv suggested that I visit the Bruderhof and went so far as to initiate correspondence between us. The visit itself turned out to be both an unforgettable experience and a milestone on my road to the study of communes. I therefore found it fitting to accord it a place of honor in the opening chapter of my book on American communes.[22] Since that encounter, our ties have become stronger and for the first time in the history of our relations, a delegation of Bruderhof members visited Israel and the kibbutz movement. I returned for several further visits during a sabbatical at Harvard University in 1982 and it was during these visits that I formed closer ties with Hans Meier with who I spent many happy hours in conversation.

The Eighties—Renewal of the Mission and Social Involvement

On 23 July 1982, Heini Arnold passed away. Five years later, his brother Hardy, eldest son of Eberhard Arnold, who had filled central offices in the Bruderhof, followed him. Heini's son, Johann Christoph, who had been his father's assistant since 1974, was elected to the office of Elder. His election was finally ratified on 17 April 1983, after internal struggles that were only terminated by the intervention of *Schmiedleut* leader Jacob Kleinsasser, who recommended the election of an Elder for all the communities. Merrill Mow, who reports on this in his book, admits that there some internal struggles had indeed occurred:

> We eastern brothers and sisters did not listen and brought much harm to the church before and after Christoph Arnold was confirmed in the Elder's service on April 17, 1983. There was envy and ambition on the part of some eastern brothers. This sin, carrying with it critical thoughts, grumbling, and slanderous gossip about our Elder Christoph, was deliberately committed even by brothers entrusted with the Service of the Word.[23]

Evidence of the problems that were bound up in the transfer of leadership to another member of the Arnold family may be found in the letter written by Heini to his son Christoph in 1974, which contained his last will and testament and which was opened after his death in August, 1982.

In his will, which is a document more revealing than any other in Bruderhof history, Heini Arnold writes of episodes in the movement's history in which, he alleges, "factional organizations were formed, the objective of which was the undermining of the spiritual status of Eberhard, head of the Arnold family, and the removal of his sons from office." He remonstrates against the deviations from the spiritual and theological source of the Bruderhof that had taken place at Primavera and that had been manifested by the addiction to reading "external" Catholic or socioreligious literature. The full force of his criticism, however, is reserved for the English contingent, which had hastily joined the movement on the eve of the Bruderhof's departure for Paraguay. On the other hand, he is full of praise for the new American members who had joined them in the fifties and who he compared to the movement's founders of the Sannerz generation.

A large part of this letter is devoted to counsel, cautions, and advice for a young leader, and its main points are: "the need to examine religious belief," "to be aware of the Word of The Lord which finds expression in agreement within the community," and "be true to the consensus of brotherhood by accepting it as the source of the spirit of Divine unity." He calls upon his son to preserve and protect the Hutterite heritage which he describes as a "Gift of God." Heini, who in his lifetime was continually troubled by the complacency that had infected the Bruderhof in the United States, cautions against it, saying that there must be no submission to the false spell of tranquility and the absence of persecution. All could suddenly be changed and they must be ready to repel the dangers with which, in the era of radio and television, they might suddenly be faced.

In his letter, Heini tries to inculcate in Christoph the sense of vocation and mission that was part of the leadership that he was about to assume. He extols the importance of the leader of a Christian community and writes:

> It is impossible to maintain a Christian life in a community which has no clear foundations of leadership.... Misapprehension of the meaning of leadership and the ambitions for rule held by others were the root of the evil.... A true Christian communal life cannot be a living organism unless it has a clear leadership.

He tells his son that being a leader means being involved with one's fellow men and being attentive to them. "The leader should not shut himself off. Only through close cooperation with the brotherhood and humble service can complete guidance in all matters be given."

In this letter, Heini openly expresses his derision for what he defines as "democracy." In his view, majority rule is an open invitation to power struggles and factional organizations and he perceived this as one of the main reasons for the split that had taken place in the sixties. The letter denounces those who called themselves "simple brothers" and, thus, camouflaged their canvassing for the votes that would have aided them in gaining power in the Bruderhof.

The letter closes with a concise review of the Bruderhof way. It was the formative years in the youth movement that Heini viewed as the primary source of the struggle for sincerity and honesty, the search for the truth, and the repugnance of the fraud they had discovered in religion and the way of life. It was the desire to find the root cause of things that brought the Bruderhof's founders, the youth movement youngsters, to find what they sought in togetherness and a communal settlement. The second source was Christianity and the Gospel of Jesus and it was here that the commune cried out for incessant renewal. But he cautions against any tendency toward "new Christianity" and goes on to elucidate:

> We of the Bruderhof experience the living Christ within ourselves. We express it in our daily prayers. But at the same time we see Him as the Sovereign of the Kingdom of Heaven who guides our way.[24]

With the election of Christoph to the office of Elder, a new period began, one which in some respects continued the line laid down by Heini during his last years in office. A number of Bruderhof members attest to this:

> In the early 1980's, the brotherhood became increasingly concerned with mission.... Heini voiced his longing that the brotherhood become more active in its outreach. The Bruderhof's witness to Jesus needed to become more visible; not in order to gain members or draw attention to the communities themselves, but in response to individuals and groups who felt called to a life of brotherhood.

> On December 23, 1981, Heini spoke to the brotherhood of his hope for mission: "I long that we can become more active in the new year...the time is urgent.... We live in this big country where there is lots of room for outreach."

In 1983, Christoph Arnold's first year in office, the Bruderhof numbered 1,200 souls living in four communities; three in the eastern United States and one in Great Britain. In November of that year, after an interval that had lasted for twenty years, publication of *The Plough* was resumed and this was the signal that the period of seclusion had ended and that a new era of renewed relationships with, and involvement in, outside society had begun. This was expressed in the first issue's format and by addressing potential outside subscribers with the appending of an application form. The first editorial said:

> Today many are calling for a spiritual revolution: the inner life must come into harmony with the outer. Under the tension of politics and the preparations for nuclear warfare, humanity hungers for an order of peace and justice—now! There is the greatest urgency for a public outcry against atomic weapons.

And on the magazine's editorial policy:

> We want to include individual testimonies and the witness of historical and current movements. There will be a discussion of issues; book reviews; and articles on education, family life, prison ministry and the life of a Christian community.[25]

The content of the first issue fulfilled this editorial promise: the opening article spoke out against the threat of nuclear warfare and the magazine also contained reports on Bruderhof involvement in the black civil rights struggle. We learn from these articles that on 27 August 1983, nine brothers and sisters travelled to Washington, D.C. to take part in a demonstration marking the twentieth anniversary of the historic march headed by Martin Luther King. The issue also contained an article by Vincent Harding, a professor of theology from Colorado, who had visited Woodcrest and lectured on Dr. King, and one by John Perkins of Pasadena, California, the leader of The Voice of Calvary community, on social work in disadvantaged neighborhoods. He, too, had visited Woodcrest, called for Bruderhof cooperation with his own community, and took his leave of them with these words:

> I pray that the Hand of God will bring about a true exchange between us and that people from your community will be able to visit us, live with us for six months, and thus become partners in our life and struggle.[26]

A special column in this issue, which later became a permanent fixture in the magazine, was entitled "From Behind Bars," and it described the activities of the Bruderhof members with the inmates of local prisons. These activities, which involved young, old, and even the elderly, became one of the Bruderhof's most humane contributions toward its involvement in outside society and they found expression in writing letters, mutual visits, and efforts at prisoner rehabilitation in Bruderhof communities. This work had begun almost by chance and in the first edition of "From Behind Bars" its writer, Daniel Moody, wrote that some time previously, while reading the 16 February edition of the local paper, *The Kingston Daily Freeman,* he had come across a letter to the editor from an inmate of the county jail in which the writer complained of the inhuman conditions at the facility. Daniel was shocked by what he read and immediately contacted the local sheriff, who was so impressed by the interest shown by a member of the Bruderhof, that he invited him to tour the jail and see the conditions there for himself.

> A relationship developed between the county sheriff and those in his prison on the one hand, and our Bruderhof on the other. We started visiting regularly, small groups going from cell block to cell block. This expanded into Tuesday and Saturday night meetings.... Our first big meeting developed very slowly. Twenty-three men came. We met in the jail library and sang two songs. There was not much response, but as time went by the atmosphere warmed and our relationship was cemented.[27]

The determination and devotion to the humane task that the Bruderhof members had taken upon themselves rapidly brought about wide-ranging relations between the members of all three Bruderhof communities and the inmates of nearby prisons. These relations included regular, twice-weekly visits, talks on faith and life, and correspondence between the prison inmates and the Bruderhof children, young people, adults, and even the older veteran members. One of the highlights of these relations was a visit to New Meadow Run by a group of prison inmates that took place in November, 1983. It was a very emotional encounter, which was reported in issue number 3 of *The Plough* under the headline, "They Warmed Our Hearts." The writer of the report amplified his description of the emotional experiences undergone by both sides during the encounter, which lasted for several hours and included a communal meal, singing, and meetings in small groups.[28] A similar meeting was held several months later between a group of Bruderhof members and prison inmates at the Ulster prison—this time inside the prison walls—to mark the first anniversary of the establishment of the joint relations, and it was devoted to a talk on the problem of marriage and the family as a basis for the establishment of a moral life which forms a barrier against a decline to drug use and crime.[29] Apart from these meetings and weekly visits, there was also some very emotional correspondence with prison inmates who were awaiting execution, and in its wake the magazine's editorial board decided to make its contribution to the public struggle against capital punishment by devoting space to a debate, the four contributors to which were well known for their fight against the death penalty.[30]

Participation in the struggle against the death penalty was not the only public sphere in which the Bruderhof were involved in the United States. On several occasions and on matters that were close to Bruderhof hearts, Johann Christoph Arnold wrote to Presidents of the United States. In the first, written on 15 July 1983, he called upon the President not to use force of arms in the struggle against communism:

> We are not able to fight communism by killing communists.... All the bombs thrown at the Prince of these powers, the Devil, do not harm him and his cause but rather fulfill his intention of bringing death to millions of innocent people.... Seeing the danger coming nearer, we pray and implore you with all our hearts...to seek by all peaceful means the prevention of such a disaster which may bring the end of God's Creation on this earth.[31]

Some years later, on the eve of Desert Storm (the Gulf War), Bruderhof members demonstrated against United States involvement in the war and Hans Meier wrote a personal letter to the President:

In the present situation in which we are thankful to God who gave you and the political leaders of Russia the courage for ending the Cold War...we feel an urge and task to warn you not to shed blood. Recognizing the injustice which the President of Iraq has committed by occupying the small country of Kuwait by force, we feel, and history has shown again and again, that real justice is not achieved by the shedding of blood of thousands of soldiers and civilians.[32]

It is worthy of note that the Bruderhof members' pacifist posture did not cause them or their young people to experience alienation from the soldiers serving in the armed forces. The Bruderhof youngsters, for example, in the framework of their citizenship education, were given the opportunity of meeting Pentagon staffers for talks. *The Plough* reports on one such visit of ten Bruderhof youngsters to the Pentagon:

Our arrival at the Pentagon was memorable for the warm way in which the officers welcomed us.... They expressed appreciation of our direct approach and for the effort we had made in making the trip. A course of action consisting of protest marches, they said, would have done far less in establishing mutual respect and understanding.

The opportunity to witness for peace and hold our positions in the face of diametrically opposing opinions was invaluable. We found warm respect for honest conscientious objectors who are willing to make sacrifices for what they believe. We were able to meet "the military" on a personal level and could clearly see that they were not faceless machines or sinister dragons, but human beings, blessed like the rest of us with hearts and consciences.[33]

Outreach for Faith

From 1983 onward, numerous Bruderhof delegations were sent to distant American states and abroad, states and countries that the delegations' members had never before visited. A large part of the membership of these delegations was comprised of young people for whom this was to be their first experience beyond the confines of the commune and it proved to be a thrilling encounter with the fascination and problems of the outside world. This trend, which began after many years of Bruderhof seclusion, was the brainchild of the new Elder and it won overall approval. In one of the first issues of *The Plough* there appeared an open letter to the young people of the Bruderhof written by Maureen Burn, one of the movement's veteran members, which opened with the words:

Beloved Christoph and Verena,

How I thank God for the movement of the Spirit. I am so glad that you encourage our young people to seek for themselves. Nothing is so convincing as what we have become convinced of for ourselves.... Opening ourselves to what God says to others is actually partaking in the movement of God's Spirit today.

The writer goes on to demonstrate the many ways that were open before the young people for placing their talents at the disposal of all outside society, and she concludes her letter with these words: "Perhaps our young people who have found something inspiring could share it with others."[34]

Leafing through the issues of *The Plough*, in almost every copy one can find information about a planned trip or a report on a trip that had taken place. Some of these trips brought responses from the Bruderhof members and about one such journey to Southern California, the group's members write:

> We were a three-member team sent out by the Bruderhof to travel through Southern California simply to listen, learn, and encourage wherever God led us. We were paying our way through *Plough* book sales and staying wherever friends would put us up. The brotherhood had chosen Southern California because our friend John Perkins had recently started an outreach center for his Voice of Calvary ministries there in Pasadena. That was our first stop. Later, a Christian magazine editor directed us to Los Ninos (a non-profit organization working on the US-Mexican border).

Their encounter with the Los Ninos farm for abandoned children was a shocking experience for the Bruderhof group, one that underlined the sheer magnitude of the Mexican immigrants' distress in their abandoning tens of thousands of their children along the U.S.-mexican border. At the same time, the group was very impressed by the devoted team of workers there:

> We had met brothers and sisters in spirit who believe that "it is possible to create a world in which fewer innocent children suffer."[35]

The journey through California brought about close relations with Cesar Chavez, veteran activist in the nonviolence movement, labor leader, and organizer of migrant farm workers. Chavez visited Woodcrest in October, 1986 and told the Bruderhof members about the hardships endured by the migrant farm workers and of his efforts and those of his small group of assistants, to organize the workers in their struggle for improved living and working conditions. These relations with a farm workers' leader caused a number of young people to go to his aid in his fight on behalf of the Mexican migrants in southern California, and this in turn served to contribute to a deepening of social awareness among the Bruderhof youngsters and caused them to initiate a struggle for improved living and working conditions for farm workers. One such initiative took the form of a letter to Congress, which directed attention to the plight of the farm workers in California. The writers warned, *inter alia,* of the dangers of exposure to toxic pesticides and insecticides, which the workers sprayed with no cautionary explanations from their employers and without being provided with protective clothing.[36]

Another trip to a totally different region took place in 1985. This was to Sweden and was organized by Nils Wingard, a veteran Bruderhof member of Swedish origin, who had maintained close contact with groups and individuals in that country that had been strengthened in recent years. Some Swedish journalists had visited the Bruderhof and it appeared that there was increasing interest in communal life in Sweden. *The Plough* reported:

> The Bruderhof decided that it was time to learn more about it firsthand. In May 1985, three of us were sent to visit anyone who would take us in—simply to try to find out how God was working there and to encourage anyone who was trying to live more in keeping with Kingdom values. So we went.... Many wanted to hear about life at the Bruderhof. We had slides to show and questions to answer. Eight different newspapers and magazines wanted interviews. We talked to dozens of different people from every conceivable background.[37]

During those years many Bruderhof members visited Germany and central Europe for a variety of reasons. For some it was a pilgrimage to the historical locations at which the Bruderhof had started on its road and in which Hutterite communities had lived in the sixteenth century, but the main reason for those journeys was linked to the renewal of the Bruderhof's mission in Germany. One such journey took place in May, 1983, and was made by Johann Christoph Arnold, his wife Verena, and Christopher and Else Winter. The tour lasted for four weeks and included visits to all the Bruderhof communities in Germany, Liechtenstein and England.[38]

In May, 1985, a delegation was sent to the Whitsun Youth Conference, which took place in Frankfurt and a second one left for the *Evangelische Kirchentag,* which took place in Dusseldorf in June. At the conclusion of the conferences, the delegations toured the country, meeting with various groups and media journalists.[39]

Between 1986 and 1989, Bruderhof delegations attended conferences of historical churches from the reformation period. The first two conferences took place in Prague and were attended by thirty delegates from the Waldensians, Hussites, Mennonites, Hutterites (and the Bruderhof), Quakers, and the Church of Brethren. The subjects discussed at the conferences were eschatology and social change. The position presented by the Bruderhof delegation asserted that social change has its beginnings in everyday life, and the conference was a platform for the presentation of some of the tenets of their faith; and so it was at the third conference, which took place in 1989. This journey, which took place after the collapse of communism, enabled the delegation to tour countries that had previously been behind the Iron Curtain—East Germany, Slovakia, and Hungary—and in all of which the Bruderhof members met people from church circles, radical sects, people who were seeking a way, and those who sought to establish communes.[40]

The changes that had occurred in what had been the Soviet bloc and the establishment of new relations between the United States and the new Russian federation of states had their effect on the Bruderhof's activities. In December, 1991, the members of Pleasant View participated in the despatch of medical supplies to hospitals in Belorussia.[41]

The Bruderhof had contacts and friends in India, too, the most notable of whom was K. K. Chandy, a well-known public figure and a student and disciple of Mahatma Gandhi. Chandy had heard about the Bruderhof as early as the thirties and was profoundly influenced by their vision and way of life. Inspired by the Bruderhof, he established a Christian community in India that devoted itself to the care and education of orphans and this community, Christavashram, exists to this day. In 1960, during the great crisis, a rumor reached India to the effect that the Bruderhof had fallen apart and during the years that followed, the Bruderhof's seclusion was so complete that no one bothered to inform their friends in India of the true state of affairs.[42]

In 1963, during a tour of the United States, Chandy visited Woodcrest in order to learn about what had become of the Bruderhof. His surprise on seeing that the movement was still in existence despite the crisis that had beset it was great indeed. Following that visit, relations between them were renewed and in 1983, Chandy and his wife visited the three Bruderhof communities in the United States and it was on that occasion that Chandy invited the Bruderhof members to visit his community in India. The visit took place in 1984 and coincided with the fiftieth anniversary of the founding of Christavashram, and the Bruderhof delegation took the opportunity of visiting other groups that were close to them in spirit.[43]

Another country that has recently been added to the map of the Bruderhof's foreign relations is Japan. For some twenty years there has been a Christian commune in Japan that began its communal life according to the traditions of the early Christians. Later, its members learned of Anabaptism and the Hutterites in the United States, united with them, and became known as The New Hutterian Church of Owa. There are currently twenty-four brothers and sisters in the church and their commune is located in a mountainous region north of Tokyo.

The opportunity of visiting the Japanese commune came about under special circumstances, when a Woodcrest high school student, Laura Johnson, won first prize in an essay competition. Her prize was a trip to Japan to take part in the remembrance day ceremonies of the bombing of Hiroshima and Nagasaki in World War II. The Bruderhof allowed her parents to go with her on her three-week trip and, thus, the family got to visit The New Hutterian Church of Owa.[44]

The new Bruderhof openness toward the outside world was also demonstrated by the number of visitors from outside to their communes, and although they had always maintained an open-door policy, the eighties saw an increase in the number of visitors. Some visits were the direct result of Bruderhof involvement and influence in outside society, particularly among groups who sought inspiration for an alternative way of life. One such encounter took place in October, 1983, when a group from Harlem, New York, came for a visit, and this proved to be a very emotional event; blacks and whites meeting to seek ways of maintaining an alternative society. Joseph Holland, founder of the group, Harlem's Ark of Freedom, told his hosts:

> We want to set up an alternative economic system in Harlem and we want to start with each other. We are living in one household now.

And their hosts reported:

> During their hours among us we experienced a lively heart-to-heart exchange. We were privileged to share their love for each other and for all people.[45]

By far the biggest event took place in June, 1988, when all the Bruderhof communities in the eastern United States organized and hosted an international conference sponsored by other organizations, the subject of which was "A New Testament Church in the Twenty-First Century. Is It Possible?" There were hundreds of participants from the United States and all over the world, from Great Britain to Japan. The conference sessions took place at the three Bruderhof communes on three separate June weekends and during its course some sixty workshops were organized on such diverse subjects as social justice, the peace policy, education, teenage problems, the Third World, nonviolence, capital punishment, the American family, ethics and modern medicine, women in the church, sex education, AIDS, and church and state.

The conference demanded a tremendous organizational and ideological effort on the part of all the Bruderhof communities and it threw them into a period of frenzied activity that lasted from Easter right up to the opening. A special edition of *The Plough* was dedicated to the conference, its discussions, and a number of the keynote lectures. It is worthy of note that the conference participants were an extremely varied group, from representatives of churches in disadvantaged neighborhoods to the Senate chaplain, who in one of the sessions, said:

> We are told to be in the world, but not of it. Now, that is a tension. How can you be in the world but not of it? How can you be a "Kingdom of God" person living in the kingdoms of men? Through these years, the Church of Jesus Christ has tried to escape this tension one way or another, either by totally withdrawing from the world, or becoming so much a part of the world that it was indistinguishable from the world.... If you are going to take Christ seriously you must live in tension. You can't avoid it...tension is not bad. You would never get music out of a guitar if you didn't have tension in the strings.[46]

An additional way of opening the Bruderhof to surrounding outside society has been found in recent years; Bruderhof members provide emergency medical aid. Each community has a team and an ambulance ready for immediate action. *The Plough* had the following to say about this:

> Over the years, we have looked for ways in which the caring we experience in our own life together could spill into the wider community. Since the communal life of our Bruderhofs offer a unique concentration of people living and working at the same location, and we need a core of medically trained people on-site, emergency medical assistance seemed a natural avenue of support. With this in mind, thirty brothers and sisters have been trained as emergency medical technicians, volunteering their services with local ambulance corps. The commitment to assist in daytime staffing means a financial burden in terms of factory hours lost and our involvement fluctuates...but even at times of minimal involvement, we have been thrust into the lives of our neighbors, together sharing moments of pain and triumph.[47]

Notes

1. According to Benjamin Zablocki, at the beginning of the 1950s there were members of twenty different nationalities in the Bruderhof, while at the beginning of the 1960s this number had dwindled to only seven. See Zablocki, Benjamin, *The Joyful Community* (Baltimore, Md.: Penguin, 1971), 202.
2. Ibid.
3. Merrill Mow, in his review of the stages of Heini Arnold's rise to a central position, mentions the process of the consolidation of that position after he had been relieved of office in the 1940s. When Heini moved to Ibate, he was a teacher in the school there and was later elected to a central office. These positions were of such prime importance that in 1951, ten years after his exclusion, he was re-elected Servant of the Word. Two years later he was again re-elected to this office. During the years that had elapsed since Eberhard Arnold's death, no one had been elected Elder. For a short period between 1940 and 1941, Heini was Servant of the Word for all of the Bruderhofs in Paraguay and could have elevated his status to that of Elder, but with regard to the two decades during which Hans Zumpe had controlled the leadership, an Elder had not been elected. Mow, Merrill, *Torches Rekindled* (Ulster Park, N.Y.: Plough Publishing House, 1989), 124.
4. Ibid., 252-55.
5. Interview with Tom Potts, November, 1992.
6. Mow, op. cit., 231-33; *The Plough*, no. 1 (Quarterly of Bruderhof communities. Bromdon: The Plough Publishing House, 1983).
7. Interview with Miriam Potts and Klaus Barth, October, 1992.
8. Interview with Joseph Ben-Eliezer, October, 1992; For the Hutterite population figures see Hostetler, J., *Hutterite Society* (Baltimore, Md.: The Johns Hopkins University Press, 1974).
9. Mow, op. cit., 188-99.
10. Interview with Joseph Ben-Eliezer, October, 1992.
11. Interview with Glenn Swinger, November, 1991; also Mow, op. cit., 202-20.
12. Mow, op. cit., 217.
13. Interview with Glenn Swinger, November, 1991.
14. Mow, op. cit., 287-91.
15. Interview with Tom Potts, November, 1992.
16. *Memories of Our Early Years*, vol. 1 K (Collection of pamphlets published by the Plough Publishing House, Rifton, N.Y.: 1973-79), 18-20.
17. Mow, op. cit., 265-56.
18. From an interview with Chris Zimmermann.
19. The contents of the study and its contribution are beyond the scope of the present work. A summary of the thesis may be found in an article written by Amitai Niv for the Israeli periodical, *Kibbutz*.
20. I was able to sense Hans Meier's deep admiration of the kibbutz movement in all the interviews I had with him. During one such interview he quoted Professor Salo Baron, who lived close by and who sometimes came to visit. Hans claimed that Baron viewed the kibbutz as the last remnant of the true heritage of the Jews as "the chosen people."
21. Interview with Amitai Niv, March, 1992.
22. Oved, Yaacov, *Two Hundred Years of American Communes* (New Brunswick, N.J.: Transaction Publishers, 1987).

23. Mow, op. cit., 289; Zumpe, Elizabeth Bolken, in *Torches Extinguished* (San Francisco, Calif.: Carrier Pigeon Press), 238.
24. Mow, op. cit., 304–18.
25. *The Plough,* no. 1 (November, 1983): 1.
26. Ibid., 13.
27. Ibid., 15–16.
28. Ibid., no. 3 (March, 1984): 12–14.
29. Ibid., no. 5 (July, 1984).
30. Ibid., no. 18 (January, 1984). Bruderhof involvement in the public struggle against the death penalty in the United States gained momentum when, on 5 May 1990, a large and varied group of Bruderhof members and young people took part in a march for the abolition of the death penalty. The march began in Starke, Florida, and ended in Atlanta, Georgia. Twenty-two high school students who paid for the trip by working overtime, and four couples, including Elder Christoph Arnold and his wife, took part in the march. The Elder himself wrote the article describing the march, the personalities who had taken part, and the Bruderhof's total identification with its objectives from both a humane standpoint and also that of their religious and pacifist beliefs [*The Plough,* no. 25 (1990): "Hutterites March Against Death Penalty"].
31. Ibid., no. 2 (1983).
32. Ibid., no. 28 (February, 1991).
33. Ibid., no. 18 (January/February 1988).
34. Ibid., no. 3 (March, 1984).
35. Ibid., no. 7 (November, 1984).
36. "Fruits of Labor for Farm Workers," ibid., no. 18 (January/February 1988).
37. Ibid., no. 15 (1986).
38. "A Visit to our Early Bruderhofs in Europe," *Ranger's News,* vol. 3, no. 5 (1983).
39. *The Plough,* no. 14 (February/March 1986).
40. Ibid., no. 19 (May/June 1988) and no. 24 (April/May 1990).
41. Ibid., no. 30 (1992).
42. On relations with India in the fifties, see Ibid., vol. 5, no. 2 (1957): 54–56.
43. "India Collage," Ibid., no. 2 (1983) and also no. 9 (March, 1985).
44. Ibid., no. 30 (1992).
45. Ibid., no. 2 (1983).
46. Ibid., no. 20 (November/December 1988).
47. Ibid., no. 28 (February/March 1991).

10

A Window to the Outside World

The Delegations to Israel

In 1983, the board of directors of the Yad Tabenkin Research Institute in Israel initiated an international conference of commune scholars, researchers of the kibbutz, and kibbutz members, that was to be held in May, 1985. Invitations were also sent to the Bruderhof, who immediately replied that while they welcomed the invitation in principle, they preferred not to commit themselves at present. As the opening of the conference approached, the organizing committee received a letter from Hans Meier, dated 5 December 1984, in which he confirmed the participation of a six-person delegation, five from the Bruderhof and one from the Hutterite commune in Minnesota. Meier also mentioned that the delegation intended to arrive in Israel three weeks before the conference opened in order to tour the country and visit the kibbutzim in which they had friends. In reply to the organizers' question about their preferences regarding visits to the Christian holy sites, they wrote:

> We are not interested in church buildings and the religious "*klim blim*" around them at the different historical sites, but rather to get to know and receive impressions of the region in which God made history through the people of Israel, their prophets, Jesus, and also at present. We are far more interested in getting to know something of what God's creative spirit is doing among the kibbutz-communes than visiting spots where the crusaders put the cross on others rather than on themselves.[1]

The Bruderhof delegation landed at Ben Gurion Airport on 30 April 1985. Even in the short history of relations between the two movements it was an historical and exciting event for the people involved.

During their three weeks in Israel, the guests visited many kibbutzim. They toured the country, saw its sights, visited Jerusalem and Nazareth, and met scores of kibbutz members for talks; it turned out to be a most moving and interesting encounter for all concerned.

At the "Old-Timer's Exchange of Ideas," which took place on the final evening of the conference, Hans Meier had the following to say about their encounter with the kibbutz:

> In every kibbutz, we were received as though we were part of the family and I very much hope that when you come to visit us, you too will feel the same way. The fruit is proof of the tree from which it comes, and since we feel that the fruit is the same in many ways, it follows that the tree must be the same, too.

He laid stress on the Bruderhof belief in God's spirit, which guides their actions and supports them in their failures. This also applied to the future, he said, and in an appeal to kibbutz members added:

> In this sense we feel that you *kibbutzniks* can only live together too because there is something which unites you...it does not matter what we call it, but it is something beyond man which brings us all together here...shaping the truth which frees the world. We cannot force anyone to think as we do, but we feel that if we are open and seek together, God will give us what we are longing for.[2]

A short while after the delegation's return to the United States, their initial impressions were published in booklet form and entitled, "Two Letters to the Kibbutz Movement in Israel," written by Hans Meier and Georg Barth. Hans Meier wrote:

> In order to learn something of our lives in community from each other, many of you ask us to share openly something of our experience as 450 year-old "old" Hutterians and 65 year-old "new" Hutterians, which has relevance to the present situation.... We are aware that we can only open a dialogue for mutually seeking the best way to fulfill our task in the present hour of history.

Meier opened the dialogue by presenting his creed as it relates to the history of mankind, a history that is controlled by God's will and, thus, he immediately focused on the points of view that separated the two movements. He did not believe, however, that such a great gap existed between them and claimed:

> If you seek for the spiritual roots of the kibbutz movement, you will probably look first at the beginnings and teachings of the history of the Jewish people which are reported in the *Tanach*.... From it we should all learn the purpose and tasks of our lives and the consequences if we do not fulfill them. In the Bible, we are warned again and again that it is not us men, but God, the Creator, who has history in His hands.... In His love He does not force us to do His will, but to a certain extent He allows us human beings to "make our own history" which is still limited by Him.

Meier concluded his letter with an expression of hope:

When this letter is read, many questions may arise which we await with open minds and hearts. We feel that both our movements are called by God in this present situation and time, to give realistic witness that it is possible to live in Shalom here and now. In this we must help one another for the benefit of all mankind.

Georg Barth, who was unable to attend the conference because of his advanced years, joined Hans Meier in his expression of esteem of the kibbutz movement. He recalled his experiences in Germany during the thirties, when he first met with members of the religious kibbutz movement, and wrote:

> In the life of the rapidly spreading kibbutzim, especially in the sacrifice and complete dedication of their first years, we saw and responded to the struggle for the ideal of the future brotherly society of justice, peace, and freedom. You and we look upon our community life as a forerunner of a future new order of society. In this we both feel the great responsibility we have. . .

> Dear friends at the kibbutzim! We feel near to you because you and we in the Hutterian Bruderhofs have lived in community of goods, life and work for so many years. We should not become soft or give way in these things.... In the struggle for the common life which we all go through, we think of you very much and wish to stand by you. We have read about despairing people in your movement who no longer had the inner strength to continue the struggle. This shakes us very much. It is part of the reason that I felt the urge to share openly with you and stand by you.

The Contribution of the International Conference

The Bruderhof delegation's visit to Israel strengthened relations between the two movements, chiefly because it had given them public expression. Previous contacts between them had been on a purely personal level, but after the conference there was a significant increase in both official correspondence and visits.

The September, 1986 edition of *The Plough* (no. 16) was devoted entirely to Israel, under the heading, "When Brothers Dwell in Unity. Reflections on a Visit to the Holy Land." In the opening article, Hans Meier evaluated the visit and emphasized that:

> Surely this trip signifies more than friend visiting friend; Jew and Christian had turned to each other for help—help to live in "Shalom." We immediately felt at home with the kibbutzniks.... We were thankful to discover many similarities between both our movements. It is not far-fetched to conclude that they grow from similar spiritual roots...but obviously there are differences. The time spent with our "distant brothers" (as they call us) left us awed and deeply respectful. At the same time, in answer to their request, we will spell out concerns we have felt for the kibbutz movement, "the experiment that has not failed," as Martin Buber called it.

Hans Meier was careful not to generalize and explained that "we can only exchange experiences and grope together for the way in which we must each proceed." He criticized the kibbutz members' political approach and their attempt "to improve society at large by cooperating with the state." He recalled how a particular kibbutznik had said:

> One difference between you and us is that you withdraw from American society. You isolate yourselves on beautiful islands. Your reaching out is actually reaching out without ever becoming a part. American society has no meaning for you.

Meier admitted that this was a frequently voiced criticism, but insisted that

> the Bruderhof, like the kibbutz, is different from society "outside." Both of us are islands, whether we like it or not. In the society outside, people do not live in community helping one another. Ultimately, both the kibbutz and the Bruderhof will survive as a group only if they unite in will and purpose for the Truth.

He summed up by expressing his belief in both movements:

> Every sincere Christian and every sincere kibbutznik is called by God to witness that it is possible to live in "Shalom" here and now. To this we challenge and awaken one another for the benefit of all people.[3]

That issue of *The Plough* contained diverse subjects and questions that the editors hoped would foster a dialogue between the Bruderhof and the kibbutz movement. All in all, the editors tried to piece together a mosaic of ideas and present a balanced picture, albeit not with complete success, but the special edition of the magazine served as a milestone and enhanced mutual relations, which expanded significantly following the conference. It is worthy of note that although the Bruderhof maintained relations with other communes throughout the world at the time, none had enjoyed the distinction of having an entire issue of *The Plough* devoted to it. Moreover, relations between the two movements were given an official imprimatur after a committee was set up under Hans and Klaus Meier, with Klaus maintaining official correspondence with the International Relations Department at Yad Tabenkin, while other members corresponded privately.

In one of the first letters he wrote after the conference, Klaus Meier mentioned the visit of Mussa Bar-Semech and Danny Gal, two members of Hakibbutz Ha'artzi (one of the kibbutz federations). He concluded his letter by expressing a wish:

We would like to have interested kibbutz visitors for longer periods in order to continue the dialogue that was begun during our visit to Israel.

Mussa Bar-Semech of Kibbutz Yad Mordechai, who was studying in the United States at the time, recalls that he first encountered the Bruderhof while serving as a counsellor at a Hashomer Hatza'ir summer camp near Woodcrest. His meeting with the Bruderhof came after an extended stay in the United States, just as disturbing rumors about the decline of communalism in the kibbutz movement began to reach him. He was therefore profoundly impressed by the flourishing community, the members of which maintained their communal life out of internal convictions. Back in New York, he expressed his impressions in an appreciative letter and added that the Bruderhof's very existence was an asset to the kibbutz movement. He explained that while he was aware of the great points of dissimilarity in their doctrines, he felt that the similarities between them were even more pronounced.

His letter was distributed throughout the Bruderhof communities, and some time later he was invited to visit Deer Spring, Connecticut, where he met Hans and Klaus Meier who had just returned from Israel and were still affected by their encounter with the kibbutz movement. During their conversation they decided that the time had come to move from theoretical talks to practical action in order to strengthen the ties between the two movements. At the time, the Bruderhof was just beginning to establish their new community at Pleasant View and Bar-Semech's hosts suggested that young people from kibbutzim in Israel and youth movements in the United States might be interested in participating, while at the same time, Bruderhof youngsters would assist in similar projects in Israel. Bar-Semech, who feared that such a project would not be practical at that stage, proposed an exchange program for older, more experienced kibbutzniks.[4]

The plan took shape in 1987, after first being presented to the Elder, Johann Christoph Arnold by Klaus Meier, and then endorsed by Hans Meier. The first couple, Martin and Burgel Johnson, left for a four-month stay in Israel, from October, 1987 to February, 1988, and they were followed by a second couple, Jim and Jeanette Warren.

The Johnson's visit to Israel marked an additional step forward in the relations between the two movements as they were the first family to spend an extended stay at one community: Mussa Bar-Semech's kibbutz, Yad Mordechai. Using Yad Mordechai as their base, they travelled widely throughout the country and the kibbutz movement and had the opportunity of studying varying perspectives. Some of their first impressions were conveyed in letters home:

> October 15:
>
> To us it is still amazing that so many people give their lives without pay to help in these large communities. I am still trying to find reasons for this dedication. There are certain facts that are different from our life in the Bruderhofs. They send their young men to the army after high school for two or three years. They do not agree with many of their government's policies.... Despite that, they have great interest in finding out what holds us together.[5]

During their visit, Martin suggested that the kibbutz movement invite the Hutterite and Bruderhof elders to visit Israel. The invitation was sent jointly by Yad Tabenkin and the Kibbutz Federation and resulted in nine people, seven of whom were Bruderhof members and two Hutterites, arriving in Israel on 17 October 1988. They stayed until 10 November and managed to visit seventeen kibbutzim and also the research institutes at Yad Tabenkin and Giv'at Haviva. Toward the end of their visit, they visited the Kibbutz Federation offices where they met with the movements' general secretaries and during their talk, they expressed their desire to strengthen relations between the two movements and special committees were set up for that purpose.

Shortly after returning home, Johann Christoph Arnold wrote a letter in which he summed up their visit and expressed deep appreciation for the welcome and consideration they had been given by every representative of the kibbutz movement. Like others before him, he also wrote:

> We felt like we were in one of our communities.... But one obvious trend made us very sad. The kibbutzim seem to be very well off materially. This has bad fruits for the young people. The trend now seems to be: "What can I get out of the kibbutz?" when it should be, "What can I and my children give the kibbutz?" Only if this trend is changed to giving instead of taking will there be hope for the future of the kibbutz and the Hutterian communities.[6]

The significance of the visit was also expressed in *The Plough* (no. 22), which published a letter by Elder Johann Christoph Arnold in which he expressed his attitude:

> Our hearts go out to the kibbutz movement in their struggle for economic survival and to win their people.... These struggles we have in common. We of the Hutterian

communities long that the contact with the kibbutzim continue. This contact has been a great enrichment to our communities and there is real hope for the future. This hope is best realized by a close working together of both movements for the brotherhood of all men.[7]

In January 1989, Hans Meier, too, summed up the visit to Israel in a long letter addressed to friends of the Bruderhof in Israel:

> When our people visit your communities and when kibbutzniks visit our Bruderhofs, we always feel many similarities...which led to your calling us "distant brothers." The deepest reason for this is probably the fact that we know ourselves called to the same historical task: to prove realistically that it is possible, here and now, for ordinary people as we are to live "Shalom." We understand that the word "shalom" has the combined meaning of peace, justice, and organic unity. We feel that the best help we can render one another is to share our positive and negative experiences; the positive ones as mutual encouragement, the negative ones as mutual warning.

After this introduction, Meier reviewed his *Weltanschauung* of the evolvement of early Christian communalism, its corruption by the Church, and its preservation by the Hutterites. He also elaborated on the fate of the Jewish people as "God's chosen people," whose ability to live righteously on earth was to serve as a model for other nations. He concluded his letter with these words:

> The foregoing is meant only as a beginning of our open-hearted seeking together for "Shalom" for all mankind. We do not wish to tell you what to do, but to find together with you the true reasons of why we live together in full communalism.

This letter, which was full of good intentions for the opening of an ideological dialogue, did not achieve its purpose and this may have been due to the strong and exclusive emphasis it placed on the Bruderhof's religious doctrine. It was never answered to Meier's satisfaction and he has continued to seek the reasons for this ever since. One may assume that his kibbutz correspondents were somewhat reticent about dealing with unbridgeable religious issues and preferred instead to maintain open, less sensitive channels of dialogue.

In an oblique attempt to relate to the difficulties involved in a dialogue that concerned the creeds of both movements, I wrote:

> If I may use a metaphor, I would say that our worlds are like the two banks of a river in which communal life flows. Both banks are very different and distinct; they are close but run parallel to one another and therefore are unable to meet. Only bridges can join them and I perceive these bridges in the similar patterns of our ways of life. The links could be strengthened by our visits, encounters, and mutual

assistance. It is very important that each of us assert his identity and try to describe it as thoroughly as possible. In this way we can get to know one another more appropriately. Mutual understanding will buttress the bridges.[8]

Hans Meier's reply was not long in coming:

Your comparison of the kibbutzim and the Bruderhof as the two shores of the same stream, which run parallel but never come together, intrigued us very much. We thought a lot about it and came to the following conclusion: you are right; when we follow the river downstream, the two shores separate more and more. But when we return to the sources of the stream, the two shores come together and unite. It is a question of swimming upstream and arriving at the source which takes more effort than swimming with the current.... Should not the kibbutzim and the Bruderhof and all the communities in the world give a clear witness of the Source of life for the whole of humanity by their life in common, like a living, organic body?[9]

In 1991, a breakthrough in the relations between the two movements occurred, thanks to the private initiative of the Regev family from Kibbutz Kfar Hahoresh, who spent over six months sharing the life and work of the Deer Spring and Spring Valley communities. They returned home in June, 1992, after having spent a longer period with the Bruderhof than any other kibbutz member, and as I was extremely interested in their fresh impressions, I met Shlomo (Shulti) Regev only a few days after their return from America.

I was curious about the nature of their relations once the excitement of the initial encounter had abated, for after all, their extended stay should have presented them with an opportunity of getting to know the Bruderhof not only at moments of elation, but also during the monotony of their daily life. I wondered whether their amiability had been maintained throughout the Regev's stay, to which Shulti replied:

That question had bothered us, too. As people who had been educated in the manner of Western society with all its facade, we wondered when "the genie would emerge from the bottle." It didn't! We soon realized that their friendliness was real and it was maintained throughout all our relationships. It was obviously most evident during our reception and I believe that it is simply their way of overcoming embarrassment when meeting strangers, and later, although they do not smile continuously, they always maintain their friendly manner.

I believe that their amiability stems from the very nature of their direct relations with one another. They are expected not to bear a grudge, and whenever problems concerning another person arise, they are expected to talk with him that same day. This was something we experienced personally; it helps to maintain good relations, prevents the forming of an atmosphere of hostility, and promotes mutual understanding as a natural expression of their interpersonal relationships.

Another thing which may explain their cordiality is the extraordinary attention they pay to one another. No event escapes their attention, they congratulate you on your birthday, celebrate the birth of a baby, and even sing under a sick person's window.

Every personal experience becomes a community experience in the fullest sense of the word. One of the things that attracted me to them was their evident pleasure in giving to, and sharing with, others.

Without generalizing, I think I can say that we felt as though we were living with people who enjoyed their togetherness. Let me give you an example. Towards the end of our stay, we wanted to visit other parts of the United States and enquired about their vacation arrangements. We were told that they had no specific arrangements because they did not need regular vacations; they were content to stay at home where there were plenty of holidays and days of rest which they could use for hiking with their families or rest. They did not imply that they would be loath to enjoy travelling to other communities in distant states; there were simply no regular vacations to relieve stress.

We told them about our life and the current crisis [in the kibbutz movement] and felt that they were troubled by what they had heard. They follow the kibbutz from a distance, but with deep concern.

According to Shulti, the Regev's stay with the Bruderhof also revealed some divergences of opinion:

During our conversations, there were ideological confrontations on a number of subjects: their Christian doctrine, pacifism and the right to defend oneself, the lessons of the Holocaust, the place of women in society, their puritanical sex education which tends to suppress vital issues, and their education of teenagers. Even though they send their youngsters to outside schools, they are not given enough scope to experience any real conflict and deliberation concerning their future. They guide their youngsters closely and steer them towards community life. We had talks and discussions on these issues and just as they appreciated my candor, I was impressed by their ability to listen and to respect another person's view, even though they disagreed with it.

Some time later, the Bruderhof furthered relations between the two movements by initiating an essay competition that encompassed all their communities, on the theme, "Israel: Past and Present" and under the slogan, "Easter in the Holy Land." The competition's questions were based mainly on religious and historical issues: the first concerned Judeo-Christian tradition and its significance for the Bruderhof and the present-day Christian Church, while the second focused on problems of modern Jewish nationalism and the Israeli-Palestinian conflict. The nine best essays won their writers a prize of three weeks in the Holy Land during Passover, 1992. Two weeks were spent in kibbutzim, where they were hosted by old and new friends, and they also visited the Yad Tabenkin Research Institute for an exchange of ideas on problems common to both movements.

Milton and Sandy Zimmerman summed up their visit thusly:

> To experience the currents of life in Israel today was very stimulating and challenging. We need to keep in contact with our friends.... We need to work and pray for peace not only for Israel, but also for our Bruderhof movement which likewise experiences the stresses of growing pains and recurring shakiness in holding firmly to its inner foundations.[10]

At the conclusion of their visit to Yad Tabenkin, they were asked to follow the tradition of signing the visitor's book. On browsing through the book, I noticed that since the first Bruderhof visit in 1985, fifty members of the movement, young and old, had visited the Institute. It is worthy of note that the number of kibbutz members who had visited the Bruderhof was much greater.

New Communities and New Relations

The intensive Bruderhof activity devoted to relations with the outside world was not the cause of any reduction in their internal activity, but rather the opposite. Through their encounters with "seeking people," links were forged that brought many new members to the Bruderhof's ranks, but the greatest source of this numerical expansion was their own young people, an extremely high percentage of whom decided to become members—including those who had spent a number of years experiencing life outside the commune. This expansion was reflected in membership numbers, which increased from 1,400 in 1983 to 2,400 in 1994, and it was this, together with their estimate that the growth trend would continue over the coming years, that brought the Bruderhof to decide on the allocation of manpower to the establishment of new communities.

In the summer of 1985, the first new community to be established as a result of this decision was founded at Ulster Park, which stood on 100 acres of land several miles from Woodcrest, and the first Bruderhof members moved there in October of that year. All the Bruderhof communities sent young people to help with the work of setting up the community; the Hutterite communities in the West sent help too and, thus, all the housing and farm buildings were built in the first year. The new community was named Pleasant View and by the summer of 1986 there were seventy souls, adults and children, living there.[11]

Two years later, work was begun on a new community in Pennsylvania, which stood on 145 acres of land adjacent to the established community at New Meadow Run. The land was purchased in 1987, but unlike other communities that had been established in the past, there was not a single building on the site and so the construction of the new settlement had to be done from the ground up, and it was only in July, 1990 that the first settlers were able to move into their new home, which was named Spring Valley. Within a single year there were 160 souls, half of them children, living there. In line with the new functional division that had been instituted in the Bruderhof, the new community became the home of the movement's central archives and the publishing offices, and a branch of the toy factory was set up there in accordance with accepted practice in all the communities.[12]

In 1990, the Bruderhof acquired a vacation hotel situated in the heart of the breathtaking mountain scenery of the northern Catskills. The hotel's previous owner had been the New York Police Department, but a serious drop in demand by police vacationers had led to bankruptcy and the subsequent sale of the property. The purchase had placed a severe financial strain on the Bruderhof and it was only effected thanks to a generous loan at easy terms, which they received from three Hutterite communities in the West.[13] In this case too, all the Bruderhof communities harnessed themselves in a joint effort: the largest building was renovated and the hotel rooms were converted into family apartments according to Bruderhof practice in all their communities. In April, 1990, the first families began to move in and within a year there were 100 souls, adults and children, living there. As the new community was relatively isolated, great efforts were invested in building all the necessary educational services on site, including the construction of a school.[14]

While the establishment of new communities in the United States continued apace, it was decided at the same time to reestablish the Bruderhof in Germany. The first stage was the purchase of a house with joint financing provided by the Bruderhof and the Hutterite communities in the West and, thus, Haus Waldfrieden, located not far from Bonn in northwest Germany, became the Bruderhof contact address for seeking people in Europe. In March, 1988, the first family moved in and the foundation stone of the revivified Bruderhof in Europe was laid. Within a short time they were joined by other Bruderhof families and new people from Europe, and the second stage, the purchase of sixty acres of land and a number of buildings which would house a small community, was completed. And so Michaelshof, the new Bruderhof community in Germany, was founded and by 1989 its population numbered eighty souls. Its location in a densely populated area soon turned it into an attraction for visitors and some 2,000 people visited the new community in the first year.[15]

One of the greatest difficulties the new community had to face was its proximity to the village of Birnbach, some of the inhabitants of which were closely identified with the Republican (neo-Nazi) party. These people were not entirely happy with their new Anabaptist, pacifist neighbors, and did everything in their power to place obstacles in their path, particularly by preventing the granting of permits for the construction of new buildings. They managed to prevent, *inter alia,* the construction of new buildings that were to house the factory and the dining hall, but in general terms it can be said that positive public opinion slowly began to be generated in the immediate area and the entire state. The media report on Bruderhof activities quite frequently and in a supportive vein, especially by responding positively to the harassment perpetrated by some of their neighbors.[16] (In the meantime, this Bruderhof was closed; see Post Script.)

In the wide network of relations fostered by the Bruderhof with the outside world, those with other Christian communes held pride of place. The great awakening in this sphere was particularly apparent in Germany and one of the expressions of this phenomenon was the appearance of the Basisgemeinde communities, the communal way of life of which was very similar to that of the Bruderhof. From 1983 onward, economic relations were also established between the two movements when the Basisgemeinde took over the distribution of "Community Playthings" products in Germany. Visits to the Basisgemeinde communities are included in Bruderhof tours of Germany and relations between the movements have been strengthened, despite the differences of opinion between them regarding Christian, Catholic, or Protestant dogma.[17]

The widest and strongest area of Bruderhof relations with outside society was, of course, in the United States, where they could find expression in mutual visits and strong ties of cooperation. Relations of this kind were established with the Christian commune, Jubilee Partners, which had been established in 1979 in Georgia, and which had been influenced by the Koinonia commune with which the Bruderhof had maintained relations since the fifties (see above). The members of this commune perceived social work and the provision of assistance to the Third World refugees who had found a haven in the United States as their principal vocation. Their work in this field provided help for refugees from Cuba, Vietnam, Laos, and Cambodia, initially with their absorption in the United States and later with their subsequent emigration to Canada or any other country prepared to accept them. They were helped in their work by sister churches, including the Bruderhof, with whom they maintained special ties which included mutual visits and the provision of information on their activities through their respective magazines.[18]

Relations that had been formed with the small Christian commune of Ransom House, which is located in Utica in northern New York State, culminated in unification and economic integration with the Bruderhof. This group, which had its beginnings as a Christian commune in 1977, underwent numerous changes and moved from place to place over the Northeastern United States until it reached Utica, but there too, it did not find fertile soil for its activities. Their encounter with the Bruderhof was through literature that reached them and in which they found the way they had been seeking. Relations were rapidly established, and following visits and correspondence, they asked to join the Bruderhof. In April, 1991, they received a positive response and in its wake they decided to move their members and assets to Woodcrest and begin the accepted process of joining the Bruderhof.[19]

The Bruderhof and *KIT*

At the beginning of 1990, a number of factors that inhibited the growth of the widening network of Bruderhof relations with outside society became apparent. These were concentrated around a bulletin called *KIT*, which was published by a group of people who had left the communes and which became, as time went by, a sounding board for the dissemination of writings that showed open hostility to the Bruderhof way, its values, personalities, and spiritual beliefs. The bulletin, which first appeared in August, 1989, began its career as a kind of round robin letter launched by Ramón Sender, one of the people who had left the Bruderhof nursing numerous personal grievances against the movement.[20] The letter revealed that many of the people who had left the Bruderhof, or had been excluded from it during the great crisis, were interested in maintaining social contact, an exchange of information, and having a platform through which to voice their claims. The bulletin's aims were succinctly embodied in its name, "KIT," or "Keep In Touch," and within the first few months of its distribution it boasted a readership of some 200 people.

By January, 1990, the original round robin letter had become a regular monthly bulletin, the editorial board of which displayed both initiative and persistence and which, by the end of its second year of publication, had widened the bulletin's distribution to some 700 readers from various circles, a small number of whom were from outside the communal sphere. The bulletin's primary function was to serve as a platform for people who had left the community, who were spread all over the world, and who expressed their satisfaction about the renewal of old ties through *KIT*. As the majority of the articles expressed critical, if not downright hostile views about the Bruderhof, a number of the correspondents expressed their concern that the Bruderhof leadership might impose constraints on the possibility of their visiting relatives in the Bruderhof communities. These concerns brought a clear response from Elder Johann Christoph Arnold, which was aimed at alleviating their fears.[21]

After some time, letters from Bruderhof members began to appear in *KIT,* and it seemed that a long-awaited dialogue might ensue. The Bruderhof's readiness to embark on such a dialogue motivated the *KIT* people to draft an open letter to the Bruderhof membership in which they set out a number of their claims, including one for a grant to those who had left and who were in financial difficulties. The letter's authors requested that it be read in public at all the Bruderhof communities.[22] Although the Bruderhof had some reservations about the letter, it was not rejected out of hand, but the trend that had become apparent during the bulletin's second year of publication, one of increasing hostility, did not allow a practical dialogue to come about. The editorial board neither filtered nor edited the material in an appropriate manner, and the bulletin's issues became a platform for personal attacks, defamation, and slander, which had no place in a bulletin whose wide readership had no interest in personal and family feuds.

The bulletin's editors were not satisfied with an expression of views in print, and during the course of the first year they initiated a social gathering that took place at the Friendly Crossways Hostel guest house in Massachusetts. Some fifty people took part in the event which, apart from its social aspect, included discussions on the future of their relations. Following the success of this first meeting, another was organized a year later at the same venue and there, too, the event comprised a combination of a social encounter and discussions. A number of Bruderhof members took part in this second meeting to answer the charges that had been levelled against them, but the organizers imposed a time limit on their participation in the talks and asked them not to attend the plenary session, which included a discussion on the subject of "What would you like to say to or ask from the members of the Bruderhof?" The participants in this discussion spoke freely and the organizers decided that the subjects that had been raised should be summarized in writing and presented to the Bruderhof members, so that they could be raised before the entire membership as a basis for a dialogue with those who had left the movement. The subjects raised comprised thirty different points, the majority of which were no more than gross intervention in the Bruderhof way of life and beliefs, intervention by a heterogeneous group of former members who were living their lives outside the Bruderhof and who had usurped the right to dictate to the Bruderhof membership how they should live *their* lives. Among the claims listed were such things as:

1. "Make it easier for children to leave";
2. "Every baptized member should read *KIT*. And *KIT* should be read in baptism preparation groups and discussed. Unless you know your own history you will be condemned to repeat it";
3. "People in the Bruderhof cannot give up their inalienable rights. Suggested list of rights:
   a. If children are physically disciplined (by a parent), another adult should be present.
   b. All laws of the land should be respected."
4. "Half of Bruderhof assets towards survivors of [the] Bruderhof for therapy, school, medical or whatever anyone needs."[23]

The decision to demand that the Bruderhof respond to the thirty points was both strange and unfortunate as it completely destroyed the already shaky basis for dialogue between the parties. The thirty points were communicated to the Bruderhof and their reply came on 19 August 1991, and stated that the points had been read out at a general meeting of all the Bruderhof communities. The reply read as follows:

Dear Participants of the KIT Conference,

We received your 30 points to our brotherhood from your KIT Conference and yesterday afternoon we met jointly, including also Darvell and Michaelshof. As points were read, the feelings of shock and disbelief were felt and expressed. Then upon discussing quite extensively the points brought forward, we concluded that the spirit behind this letter was divisive, destructive, and totally against Christ and His will and command for those who seek to follow Him. And therefore we reject the spirit behind your letter and will not communicate further regarding it. However, if there are those among you who wish to sincerely sit down with us and in the spirit of the teachings of Jesus find peace and love together, we will welcome that with all our hearts.

Yours sincerely,
The brotherhoods of the Hutterian Brethren in the East[24]

One may say in retrospect that the "Thirty Points" successfully buried the dialogue that had begun to take shape and an atmosphere of mistrust was created, and although some faltering efforts at seeking new channels of dialogue are periodically made by the parties, they usually end up in stalemate with each side accusing the other of insincerity. Not only has no progress been made in the dialogue, but there are also signs of decline in the minimal goodwill that initially existed between the parties, and so it would appear that at the present stage, the gaps remain unbridgeable. *KIT* occasionally publishes letters or articles by Bruderhof members, and while the bulletin's subscribers sometimes have thoughts of a moral stock taking on the need to cease probing the wounds of the past, neither brings about a renewal of the dialogue. The impression received is that each of the parties is fully entrenched in its position.

During my meetings with Bruderhof members in the fall of 1991, I tried to encourage them to provide me with some kind of assessment of the likelihood of a renewed dialogue with the *KIT* people. I talked to Dick Domer and Christoph Arnold, who had both participated in direct talks with them, and their prognosis was not optimistic. Dick told me:

The bulletin has become a platform for besmirching the Bruderhof image.... They have tried to distance friends like John Hostetler (the sociologist who has studied the Hutterites) by planting distorted ideas about the Bruderhof in his head. But what is even worse is that the bulletin reaches young people who know nothing about us and who learn about us from what the bulletin publishes, and thus a barrier is erected between our message and them. This, and not their effect on our life, is our greatest concern in this affair. We know the writers and their motives and they have no effect upon us from within. I personally have travelled to San Francisco in an effort to meet with the editors, but nothing came of it.

Christoph Arnold also acceded to my request to relate to this affair, and in an interview he granted me in November, 1991 he was pessimistic about the future of the dialogue and expressed his concern about the negative effects inherent in the deteriorating relations between the two parties. He said that the Bruderhof had shown its goodwill by supporting the dialogue from the beginning and that they had even promised to cooperate in finding a suitable place and providing food for the annual meetings, but the *KIT* people had refused and later had limited and even prevented the participation of Bruderhof members in the meetings. With regard to the charges of hardheartedness toward those who had left the movement and those who had been excluded, Christoph replied with great frankness:

I do not deny that there were some harsh deeds committed in the past, but to lay all the blame upon my late father, Heini, and upon the present Bruderhof leadership is totally unacceptable. Those who are at present outside the commune and who filled central offices during that period acted no less harshly.... In general terms, it is irresponsible to judge events which took place thirty years ago in articles published in a bulletin like *KIT* and which rely solely on personal memory, which by its very nature is selective, and without allowing an examination of the claims by hearing both sides of the argument. A large part of what *KIT* publishes is at best half-truths, which in themselves are worse than lies.... There are also deliberate lies and distortion of the facts.

In various issues of the bulletin, Christoph stoutly defended his defamed father and claimed that contrary to what the bulletin had published, it had been Heini, more than any other individual, who had striven to bring those who had left closer to the movement and even return them to the fold, and in so doing he had travelled the length and breadth of the country to renew contact with them. He had this to say on this sensitive subject:

One of the recurring claims against us in *KIT* was with regard to our rigid and puritanical sex education policy. I want to make it clear that a great part of this severity of ours is not the fruit of Bruderhof ideology but rather a result of the rigid education that our parents brought with them from Germany. And in this matter, too, it was Heini who sought a more liberal approach to sex education.[25]

The main thrust of Christoph's criticism was directed at the thirty points and at the proposal contained in them to the effect that the Bruderhof be made to sign a "Bill of Rights."

> I think that it is a ridiculous proposal, but if one examines it seriously it is both degrading and inflammatory. What right do people who no longer live with us have to impose a set of rules upon us? Does it not hint that the commune infringes the laws of the land? We live in a country in which the citizens enjoy the basic right of choosing their way of life according to the dictates of their conscience, and this is what we do. We act openly and anyone who comes to us is fully aware of our way of life, and if he or she is not aware of it, we make sure to make it clear in talks preparatory to baptism. We ask for nothing but to be left alone to live our lives according to our beliefs.

In reply to my question on the chances of a renewed dialogue, Christoph was pessimistic, and referring to the most recent publications he said that he felt that the *KIT* group was heading toward a serious confrontation with the Bruderhof. They continue to dig into the past and come up with new stories with which to fan the flames of defamation. "Confrontation is unavoidable...we must be patient. Even though damage has been caused it will pass." And he concluded with the words of Jesus, who said:

> "Blessed are ye, when men shall revile you, and persecute you, and shall say all manner of evil against you falsely, for my sake." So in the long term there is nothing to worry about—the truth will eventually come out.[26]

In the meantime, the *KIT* editorial board has managed to establish a sound economic base and has founded a publishing house for books on the Bruderhof.[27] They have also succeeded in publishing a monthly that is largely devoted to correspondence and memorabilia on various episodes in Bruderhof history. The bulletin's hostile tone has not diminished and even reached new heights with the publication of a "scholarly" article comparing the Bruderhof to the Nazis [*sic*].[28] The editorial board's "non-intervention" policy, which allows the occasional publication of wildly defamatory pieces, defeats every effort at reaching a *modus vivendi* for contact with the Bruderhof. It is my view that there might have been some chance of this happening were it not for the aggressive tone of the criticism, which causes the Bruderhof to bristle as it does. Recently, articles dealing with the debate between the Bruderhof and conservative Hutterite circles, and which have been reprinted from external sources, have appeared. This might seem surprising if one failed to understand that the publication of these articles simply served the objectives of the editorial board in giving free rein to anyone and anything that might attack and revile the Bruderhof.

Bruderhof-Hutterite Relations in the Eighties and Nineties

For a decade after the 1974 reconciliation between them, Bruderhof relations with the Hutterites developed satisfactorily, particularly with the *Schmiedleut* communities in the United States and Canada. Economic, social, and family ties were formed, together with religious-church relations between the communities. The Bruderhof adopted many forms of Hutterite dress and did everything in their power to attain complete unity with the Hutterites and this found its greatest expression in their publication policy. The publishing house published a number of books on the Hutterite heritage, the most notable of which was an English translation of the ancient Hutterite history, *The Chronicle of the Hutterian Brethren; Volume 1,* with the translation being accomplished in the most scholarly and praiseworthy manner. Apart from the *Chronicle, The Plough* published a series of articles on Hutterite history and martyrology.[29]

Over the years, dozens of mutual visits took place between the Bruderhof and the Hutterites, and after a while the Bruderhof bought a bus for ferrying visitors between the Eastern communities and the Midwest and Canada, where the *Schmiedleut* communities, with which they had particularly strong ties, were located. Although the majority of these trips were for business purposes, some carried people who had been sent to help at work, and this was particularly notable during the period in which new settlements were being established. Work missions from "our brothers in the West," as the Bruderhof called the Hutterites, played a particularly important role in various work projects, like the construction of the roof of the Pleasant View dining room.

In January, 1984, a twenty-five strong Bruderhof delegation travelled to Sturgeon Creek in Manitoba to attend a celebratory assembly marking the tenth anniversary of the reconciliation and reunification. It was there that the subject of sending joint missions abroad was discussed and it was decided that, henceforth, a special effort would be made to have Western Hutterite members take part in every important mission (one result of this decision was Hutterite participation in the official delegations that visited Israel; see above).

It is worthy of note that during that time, when it seemed that relations with the *Schmiedleut* were becoming stronger, a parallel process was not apparent with the *Dariusleut* and *Lehrerleut* communities of the more orthodox Hutterite stream that maintained their reservations about relations with the Bruderhof. These reservations intensified, gradually becoming open opposition that finally came to a head in December, 1990, somewhat surprisingly and in quite an embarrassing manner as far as the Bruderhof was concerned, when they received a long and detailed letter from the leaderships of the two *leute* informing them that as far as the orthodox streams were concerned, the union with the Bruderhof was null and void. Here follow the main points of that document:

> The Hutterian Brethren Church of the Darius and Lehrerleut Conference to the Society of Brothers who call themselves Hutterian Brethren
>
> 11.12.90
>
> The reuniting of the Hutterian Brethren, January 1974...with the Society of Brethren or Arnoldleut, Woodcrest, was the topic of the meeting. We were all in unison that you were accepted on a probational basis, so that you would get acquainted and accept the teaching and tenets, rules and principles of the Hutterische Church as they were practiced by us at that time and by our forefathers, so that you may adopt and adhere to them, which up to that time you shunned and trod with your feet, and in fact disgraced and abused the messengers that were sent to you from time to time, all out of love for your salvation.

First: Regarding Millennium. You still cling to the false doctrine of the Millennium...which is against the Apostolic Creed...our forefathers made no mention of the Kingdom of God here on earth.

Second: The Rearing of Children. We cannot agree with you on the issue of sending your people to school outside of your communities at the age when they need the most protection from the wiles of the devil which are rampant in this world as never before...

Third: March to protest the Death Penalty (*The Plough*, no. 25, August 1990).... Surely Christians are against any kind of killing...but have you ever heard of Hutterites marching with other denominations or taking part in such activities? No! Never in Hutterite history . . .

Fourth: Torches, Idols. Your use of fire and candles in your gatherings and services is also foreign to us...We believe that this is on the road that leads to idolatry.

Five: Presentation of babies to the Church.... It seems to us as being only half a step away from infant baptism.

Seven: Hutterite Sermons, Music, and Acting.... Where in the 500-year history of the Hutterites have we ever heard of play-acting, putting on a live show.... How did you dare to wilfully violate the ordinances and humble practices of the church by introducing musical instruments on any occasion? Has this not infiltrated in some of our dear Schmiedleut Colonies and caused a drifting in your direction?

This is why we are so concerned and therefore try by all means not to let this happen to our Lehrerleut and Dariusleut colonies.

Although it is true that in 1974 the Schmiedleut, Lehrerleut, and two of the Dariusleut ministers agreed to the uniting with the Arnoldleut after they heard the pleas of the then present Arnoldleut, we earnestly thought you would adopt the Hutterian Brethren customs and traditions and ordinances as much as possible (and all elders acted in good faith), however, we are well aware that you did not keep your promises and instead of coming closer to us, you are, so to speak, deliberately drifting in the opposite direction. Especially like in the case of the musical instruments and radios, you seem to have no concern whatsoever whether we agree with you or not. Therefore, even if it is hard for us to do, we are forced to revoke the 1974 unification.

Although it is said, that you say, you don't live on customs but on love, may we point out to you that a church without customs and traditions is not a true church.

Therefore we, The Dariusleut and Lehrerleut Congregations, declare and reveal to you, The Arnold Congregation, that hereafter you are not recognized as Brothers in Faith, and ask you to refrain, yes, stop using and tarnishing the Hutterite name with your anti-Hutterian deeds. We ask that in the future you not send any of your literature and *The Plough* for fear of being led astray.

Signed,
For the Dariusleut: John.K. Wurz, M.S. Stahal
For the Lehrerleut: John.S Wipf, John Kleinsasser[30]

Approximately one year after the publication of the *Dariusleut* and *Lehrerleut* letter, I visited Woodcrest and asked to hear the Bruderhof response to the crisis that had broken out between them and the two Hutterite orthodox streams. Glenn Swinger, a Woodcrest Servant of the Word and one of the participants in the 1974 reconciliation assembly, related the situation that had arisen in the wake of the letter.

He told me that the Bruderhof delegation had left the 1974 assembly with the feeling that, as representatives from all three Hutterite streams had been present and all the issues had been fully agreed upon, complete unification had been achieved. There had been a spirit of understanding and reconciliation throughout the meeting and all present had been unanimous on the main points discussed: the Anabaptist faith and fulfillment of the principle of community of goods. Although the existing differences had not gone unnoticed, there had been no call to do away with them, and while the adoption of the Hutterite form of dress had not been tabled as a demand, it had been decided upon unilaterally by the Bruderhof in order to reinforce their reconciliation with the

Hutterites. According to Glenn Swinger, the arguments presented by the *Dariusleut* and *Lehrerleut* elders as divisive factors that prevented unification were not new, and had been public knowledge at the time of the reunification.

The Bruderhof maintains a clear-cut position on matters of war and peace, and participation in demonstrations is not part of their permanent policy, but rather an issue that is occasionally raised as a result of members', and sometimes young peoples' and children's, personal initiatives. The decision to approve or reject such activities depends upon the type of demonstration in question and the message it is trying to convey. It should also be noted that a historical divergence of opinion on their mission in the world exists between the Bruderhof and the Hutterites, one that has been preserved since the first contacts between the two movements were established during Eberhard Arnold's mission of 1930. The Bruderhof view the mission as their vocation in the world and their way of life as a "witness," and therefore the movement's members are prepared to go anywhere, meet any group that is ready to listen to them, and open their doors to thousands of visitors from close and distant circles, while the Hutterites, on the other hand, have not done this since their "Golden Era" in the sixteenth century. The Bruderhof also fulfill this mission in their various publications and through their relations with surrounding society.

A divergence of opinion between the two movements also exists in the sphere of education, particularly with regard to sending teenagers to local high schools, and more recently, to college. The Hutterites do not do this, while the Bruderhof maintain this educational policy for two main reasons: first, because of the need they feel to give their young people a knowledge of all the facets of the outside world in preparation for the day when they will make their decision to become members, and then do so of their own free will and in complete awareness of the differences that exist between them and the outside world; and second, because of the need to prepare their youngsters to fulfill their role in their own society and economy so that they will be able to communicate with the society that exists beyond their communes, comprehend it, and later face up to it from an ideological and cultural standpoint.

Glenn Swinger added that with regard to the use of musical instruments, nothing new had emerged as the difference of opinion between the two movements had also existed since 1930. He felt that this subject was a matter of little consequence, and certainly not one of principle, as it stemmed from the different cultural backgrounds of the two movements. "We make every effort not to flaunt our playing musical instruments at religious assemblies and do not play when we meet them out of respect for their feelings," said Glenn, and added with a touch of humor, "we don't blow our trumpets in their ears!"

According to Swinger, their approach to the question of a standard form of dress is similar. Despite the fact that the Bruderhof membership accepted the modest Hutterite style in principle, they do not observe it pedantically and moreover, variations in dress style exist between the three Hutterite streams. The orthodox Hutterite approach, which adheres rigidly to every point, is unacceptable to the Bruderhof.

> We believe that what is truly important is faith, love of God and Jesus, and our day-to-day way of life, which is the fruit of our belief, and not items of clothing. Although we made this clear to them, we know that their more orthodox members feel that if one is not dressed exactly as they are, then one does not believe with the same degree of faith, and this is unacceptable to us.

With regard to the possibility of bridging these gaps in the future, Glenn avoided giving me a direct reply and said that he found it difficult to forecast relations with the more orthodox streams. In the meantime, the Bruderhof would continue with the line it adopted in 1974 and strengthen its ties with the *Schmiedleut,* which was both close to the Bruderhof geographically and more tolerant of the differences that exist between them. In his estimation, these differences will continue to exist in the future; the Bruderhof will not become identical to the Hutterites simply because the Hutterites have a centuries-old history of closed agricultural communities that have not absorbed new members from outside, while more than half of the current Bruderhof population is composed of people who joined the movement from the outside worlds of America or Western Europe. Nevertheless, Glenn Swinger repeatedly stressed that all of the above-mentioned differences pale into insignificance in the face of the two movements' common Anabaptist faith and communal way of life, and this is the foundation upon which a narrowing of the gap leading to unification will be achieved.[31]

Swinger's hopes have not come to fruition. Since 1991, relations between the Hutterites and the Bruderhof have become seriously weakened and there has also been a marked decline in Bruderhof relations with large sections of the *Schmiedleut.* The campaign is currently centered around the leadership of *Schmiedleut* Elder Jacob Kleinsasser who, since his election as chairman of the board of managers of all the Hutterite communities in 1978, has played a vital role in the reconciliation moves between the Bruderhof and the Hutterites.

During my stay at Woodcrest and my talks with Glenn Swinger, litigation was taking place in Manitoba by a group of people who had left the Oak Bluff community after being "excluded and excommunicated" as a result, among other things, of their opposition to the strengthening of ties with the Bruderhof. After their exclusion, their children were forbidden to attend the community's school and it was only after the intervention of the county court that a compromise was reached: a temporary building was erected so that the children could continue their schooling until their parent's legal battle was concluded. Apart from this particular episode, since 1987 there have been some other struggles with "dissidents" who fought against Jacob Kleinsasser's leadership. Kleinsasser's economic policy was centralist and as a result he imposed taxation on the communities to finance a central fund for joint activities and the provision of assistance for the weaker communities.[32]

Kleinsasser's supporters claim that his economic policy was motivated by his desire to deepen cooperation and mutual assistance between the Hutterite communities and narrow the gap between the richer and poorer ones, and in this he was influenced by the example shown by the Bruderhof, whose communities maintain joint finances. In contrast, Hutterite tradition permitted autonomy for its communities and this provided an opening for what Eberhard Arnold had critically described as "collective egoism." Kleinsasser had tried to curb this independence and create financial tools which, apart from mutual assistance, would streamline and reduce the costs of the economic activities of each community through the joint purchasing of fuel, agricultural implements, and vehicles. It was this rationale that led him to establish an independent agricultural insurance fund that would reduce dependence on outsiders and the exploitation of the Hutterites by external financial institutions.[33]

Kleinsasser is also striving to deepen relations between the Hutterites and the Bruderhof. He views these relations as a source of positive and fruitful influence on the more conservative Hutterites, who tend to isolate themselves in their farming communities, avoid modern influences, and abstain from high school education, and it is this approach that sets him apart from the other Hutterite leaders. He understands the developing trends of the modern world which, he feels, the Hutterites can no longer ignore; he knows that they must change in order to survive in this developing world: economically, through the introduction of industry and dispensing with the exclusivity of their farming, and also by providing their children with an education. It was as a result of his firm stand that certain of the *Schmiedleut* communities have recently begun sending their boys and girls to institutions of higher learning, while at the same time the number of classrooms at their schools has been increased and previously unheard of subjects, like electronics, for example, have been introduced into the school syllabus. There is also evidence of a trend to extend their compulsory education to the twelfth grade, which so far has been unacceptable to them. On these issues, too, Kleinsasser found support and inspiration in the Bruderhof. A special relationship has developed between Kleinsasser and Bruderhof Elder Christoph Arnold, and for some years now they have been working together in mutual understanding and respect, and sometimes even travel together on their different missions.[34]

The more conservative elements of the *Dariusleut* and *Lehrerleut* factions were not happy about these trends and it was they, together with conservative elements in the *Schmiedleut,* who formed the opposition to Jacob Kleinsasser's leadership. The struggle began at the board of managers of the Hutterite settlements, of which Kleinsasser had been Senior Elder since 1980. The Bruderhof were represented at the board's 1987 meeting, and this was not favorably received by the more conservative elements, who questioned the Bruderhof way of life and its incompatibility with Hutterite tradition in matters pertaining to dress and other issues. But despite the opposition of the *Dariusleut* and *Lehrerleut* delegates, Kleinsasser decided to co-opt the Bruderhof representatives as permanent board members and this decision exacerbated the already severe internal tension, and according to the conservative factions it constituted the last straw, which caused them to decide unilaterally on the severing of relations with the Bruderhof in December, 1990.

The *Dariusleut* and *Lehrerleut* elders have a whole string of claims against Kleinsasser that state that influenced by the Arnolds, he has abandoned the traditional Hutterite way of life and committed misdeeds: the subpoenaing of Hutterites to state courts, extended travel—which is unacceptable to the Hutterites—and worst of all, the embezzlement of public funds, which had been brought to their attention by attorney

Donald Gibbs. Therefore, in the light of all Jacob Kleinsasser's "transgressions" and the great damage he had caused the Hutterites, they no longer recognized him as Elder of the *Schmiedleut*.[35]

With the severing of relations and the denial of Kleinsasser's leadership by the two conservative factions, opposition to his leadership also began to take shape within the *Schmiedleut* and manifested itself in opposition to the strengthening of relations with the Bruderhof and the trends toward openness and modernization. Kleinsasser's opponents had no qualms about obtaining help from external lawyers and accountants and embarking upon a smear campaign against him, which was in itself a unique occurrence in Hutterite history and one that rocked their way of life.

I heard some echoes of this crisis with the Hutterites when I visited the Bruderhof communities in October, 1992. My hosts painfully told me about the deterioration of relations with part of the *Schmiedleut* and the spreading of accusations to the effect that Kleinsasser had embezzled millions of dollars. According to them, the rumormongers were a small minority of avaricious people who rejected intercommune cooperation, who only wanted to isolate themselves in their own communities, to fight the spirit of modernization, and avoid the mission in the outside world—which was the reason behind their attacks on Kleinsasser's trips to England, New Zealand, and Nigeria. My Bruderhof hosts defended these trips, saying that they were movement missions and not for pleasure or vacation, and gave as an example Kleinsasser's trip to Nigeria, during which he had been taken ill and feared for his life. They took comfort in their assessment that Kleinsasser's opponents within the *Schmiedleut* were a small minority and that the majority supported him.[36]

A short time after this conversation took place it became clear that the assessment that the opposition represented only a minority group did not, in fact, reflect the true state of affairs. On 27 November 1992, the Bruderhof Council was convened by the accepted means of intercommunity telephone calls between all the Bruderhof members in the United States, England, and Germany. The Council discussed the movement's response to the charges that had been levelled against the Bruderhof and Jacob Kleinsasser by the *Schmiedleut* oppositionary faction. The Council decided this deed should be punished by the excommunication and ostracism of the opposition faction members until such time as they retracted their charges. This decision was communicated to

the leaderships of all the *Schmiedleut* communities together with a re-
minder of Kleinsasser's invitation to the leaders of all the 160
Schmiedleut communities to the General Council meeting that was to
discuss the crisis and was scheduled for December, 1992.[37]

The council of *Schmiedleut* leaders took place on schedule, but there
was a nasty surprise in store for Jacob Kleinsasser: it rapidly became clear
that he did not have the support of the majority of the council and moreover, at his opponents' instigation it was decided by majority vote to re-
move him from the office of Elder of the *Schmiedleut*. Kleinsasser viewed
his removal from office by majority vote as an oppositionary conspiracy
in the "democratic spirit" that was so alien to the Hutterites. He refused to
accept the decision and called for a meeting of his followers that would
take place in January, 1993 in order to decide who was entitled to represent the *Schmiedleut*. The meeting took place as planned and was attended
by representatives of approximately half of the communities. The assembly decided that those present were the *Schmiedleut*'s authentic representatives.[38] On 8-9 February 1993, the opposition convened at Delta Colony,
ready to take the battle to the "enemy's" gates. This meeting was attended
by attorneys who counselled the participants on their course of action
against Kleinsasser, and this resulted in each community being requested
to contribute $5,000 toward the legal fees incurred.[39]

After the meeting, which took place at the beginning of 1993, it appeared that each side was digging in and the split in the *Schmiedleut*
became a incontrovertible fact. Further evidence of this may be found
in a letter circulated by the leaders of the oppositionary faction in which
they called upon all the colonies to elect new officers, thus openly undermining Kleinsasser's status by which, according to state law, he was
the only one authorized to appoint officers, and fill official religious
positions. In an address he gave to Bruderhof members at Darvell in
March, 1993, Kleinsasser took the opposition leaders to task and settled
accounts with them in public:

> You all know that there is a big struggle going on in our communities in Man-
> itoba.... it is more of a rebellion than anything else.... It is turning out to be
> quite tragic, as it involves breaking up colonies where there are some families
> who want to stay in the church and others who say they want to go with the
> opposition.... The leader of the opposition is getting all his reasons and argu-
> ments from a Connecticut banker.... They are accusing me of lies and deception
> and even of stealing millions of dollars.... The southern and dissident colonies
> have hired two people to investigate the whole church's financial affairs and are

trying to come up with the millions of dollars which they say have been stashed away or given away or stolen.

These two men made quite an investigation. It was terrible to have them digging around in all the church affairs...and they are charging our unfaithful brothers a tremendous sum of money...

They fool the poor brothers, who are so blinded that they believe anything.

As far as I am concerned, records have been kept as straight as possible. I'm not afraid of that. I never have been. I am only afraid of the great harm and damage this attack will do to the church and to the many brothers and sisters who want to remain faithful.

I also heard some sad comments on what was happening to relations between the Bruderhof and the Hutterites from Andreas Meier when he visited Israel with his wife and Sybil Sender, a Woodcrest member, in August, 1993. In a talk we had he admitted that there was a serious deterioration in relations with the Hutterites and that the worsening situation had also penetrated the *Schmiedleut*. In Andreas's estimation, there is an increasing tendency among the more conservative Hutterites toward isolating themselves from the world and they are trying to protect themselves by building walls of alienation and estrangement between themselves and the modern world. They were again debating with the Bruderhof on items of clothing—aprons over the skirts, loops instead of buttons, kerchiefs of a certain type—instead of devoting themselves to belief and mission in the world. "It is a tragedy that a movement so important to our generation has descended to debating such trivia...and is prepared to divide communities and families for them." According to Meier, there are scores of young people in the conservative communities who are not reconciled with the idea of isolation and who are seeking a way to the Bruderhof, despite the decision of their Elders to ostracize the Bruderhof and prohibit any contact with them.

They view us as being responsible for the new spirit which caused the split. If the truth be told, the reason for the deterioration in our relations should be sought in the cooling of the Hutterian Brethren's love which was replaced by their avarice and greed. Many of their communities became very wealthy and did not want others to share their wealth.[40]

Jacob Kleinsasser, too, views wealth as the cause of the change in values and the subsequent schism, and in his address to the Bruderhof at Darvell, he said:

Brothers, maybe this is happening because we live too well. We're living in prosperity, and our whole aim is to prosper more. And it disengages us from the responsibility upon us as followers of Christ. We have become so cold; our only desire is for more money. Jesus said that before the "unrighteousness will increase, love will grow cold, and faith will die." So maybe God is showing us that to many of us are living in our communities because we were born there, without sufficient inner conviction. I think we all need to examine ourselves and see why it is that way.

He saw the way out of this morass in the renewal of the Hutterite awareness of their mission.

We are here in brotherhood not for our own individual benefits—and they are plenty, we must admit—but to shed love and warmth to others...

When my grandfather was the Elder, he often said, "A church that has no mission is dying."

He concluded his address with some remarks about what was happening in Nigeria:

Yet something encouraging is also happening. At the same time that the devil is working to break down in one corner, God is building up in another corner, in Nigeria.

And he did not miss the opportunity of sending a few barbs in the direction of the more conservative elements:

Many brothers in the West are totally opposed to it, let me tell you. The statement was made me, "We don't need black people among us," and some said, "What do you want there with those heathen?"[41]

Palmgrove—The Hutterian Brethren Community in Nigeria

The first steps toward the formation of a Hutterite community in Nigeria were taken in 1989 when a young pastor, Reverend Inno Idiong, was seeking his way through the veritable maze of Christian churches. He said that he experienced a revelation in 1987 when he was shown a vision of the communal society as the realization of a pure Christian way of life. He then began his search for a church that would fulfill his expectations in this regard in both its faith and way of life, and it was in the course of this search that he was given the address of Paul Gross of the conservative branch of the Hutterite church in the Western United States. Gross had no real interest in these African Christians and directed Reverend Idiong to Christoph Arnold of the Bruderhof.

Christoph replied to Idiong's letter and the two embarked upon a regular correspondence in the wake of which Idiong was invited to visit the United States, but his request for an entry visa was denied. He then approached Jacob Kleinsasser with a request that he obtain a Canadian visa for him and once this was forthcoming, he decided on a six-week visit to Kleinsasser's community, Crystal Spring in Manitoba, together with one of his assistants. In the course of their stay there, the two visitors experienced community life first hand and were so affected by it that they decided to turn their flock into a Hutterite community and join the movement.

Fired by their decision to establish a Hutterite community in Nigeria, Idiong and his assistant returned home, their correspondence with Kleinsasser and the Bruderhof at Woodcrest flourished, and the Bruderhof agreed to their request to strengthen their ties with the Nigerian group. A short time later, pilot missions were sent out to obtain a first-hand impression of this Christian flock, which lived in a remote corner of southeastern Nigeria. The first visitors reached Africa in May and June of 1991 and found there a small group of some sixty adults who wanted to become part of the Hutterite church with all that such a move entailed. The large majority of the flock were pitifully poor and scraped a living from farming and the production of palm oil. From the time of Inno Idiong's return from Canada and with financial aid from the Hutterites and the Bruderhof, they had managed to purchase two hectares of land close to their town where they intended to establish their community.[42]

In September, 1991, Inno Idiong's wife arrived at the New Meadow Run community for a four-month stay. She was followed by her husband, who paid a shorter visit to Woodcrest during which he asked to be baptized and be accepted as a full member of the Hutterite church. This request caused some perplexity among the spiritual leadership, and so Jacob Kleinsasser and Christoph Arnold met with Idiong for several days of discussion, at the conclusion of which it was decided against baptism, but in favor of his acceptance as a novice. It was at this time that Idiong requested that a delegation of Elders visit Nigeria and help them lay the foundations of a Hutterite community according to the communal principles of Apostolic Christianity and it was this request that brought about the decision to send a delegation headed by Jacob Kleinsasser and Christoph Arnold to Nigeria for a three-week visit.[43]

The Elders' historic visit got under way as planned at the end of May, 1992, but unfortunately, as a result of a combination of the long and arduous journey and the heat and humidity, Jacob Kleinsasser fell ill and so they were forced to curtail their visit to eight days. The delegation was very warmly received and good relations were quickly established. They were, however, besieged with numerous requests for baptism, and so the Elders decided that the remaining days of their visit should be devoted to a series of talks on the significance of baptism, the church, and the communal way of life. During these meetings they talked about matters of principle and day-to-day problems, replying to all the questions put by their hosts. Although most people present understood English, everything they said was simultaneously interpreted into Annang, the local dialect. The delegation comprised ten members of the Bruderhof and the Hutterite *Schmiedleut* faction and their meetings took place under the most primitive conditions; sometimes under a thatched lean-to and usually by the dim light of a kerosene lamp. One delegation member, David Johnson, related his emotional impression of the strange scene thusly:

> There were the two Hutterite Elders, members of a religious group which had sprung from German-speaking countries in the Europe of the Reformation...sitting in a lean-to in the dim light of a kerosene lamp, singing old hymns together with African brothers and sisters who were possessed of the same drive to serve God in a community of brotherhood.[44]

At the conclusion of the preparatory talks it was decided to baptize Inno Idiong and accept his wife and another eight members of the flock as novices. The delegation was very impressed by the enthusiasm they had seen and by the efforts invested in the building of the new community. The members of the flock devoted all their free time, including Saturdays, to preparing the land and putting up the first new buildings. At the conclusion of the visit it was agreed that the brothers would conduct an appeal in the United States in order to finance the building of the new community; in the first stage they would raise money for the drilling of a well and the purchase of a pickup truck for hauling goods and easing the transport problem between the community and centers of population.

On the eve of their return home, "the distinguished visitors from America" were invited to an official reception hosted by the local chiefs of the Abak district. It was at the reception that Jacob Kleinsasser and

Christoph Arnold were invested with the honorary title of "Chief," and in their addresses, the local chiefs praised the readiness of their guests to visit that remote part of Africa and live together with the local population—unlike the white missionaries, who usually closed themselves off in their houses and set themselves apart from the natives.[45]

There can be no doubt that the establishment of a Hutterite community in Nigeria was a special event and its distinctiveness became clear after the delegation's visit and the strengthening of ties with the American communities. The Eastern Bruderhof communities in particular revealed a sense of responsibility and identification, and the number of American brothers who visited the new community for extended periods increased. The emissaries sent in 1993 included Servants of the Word and Stewards who helped manage the new community's developing financial affairs.

On 15 February 1993, a small mission headed by Christoph Arnold left for a two-week visit during which they held pre-baptismal talks and later, the actual baptism of additional novices. There were seven novices to be baptized and a further six people who had asked to be accepted into the novitiate. In accordance with accepted Bruderhof practice, a wide range of subjects was discussed in these preparatory talks, from the Principles of the Hutterian Doctrine according to Jacob Hutter, church discipline, to questions of married life: courting, marriage itself, and even adultery and divorce. The minutes of the talks, which were later published, indicate a serious effort on the part of Christoph Arnold and his assistants to endow the new African community with solid ideological foundations and fully elucidate the Hutterite principles. At the conclusion of the preparatory talks, the baptism was performed before an audience of some 200 people from the local population. Later, on 24 February, a closed ceremony, "the Lord's Supper," which is of particular historical significance, was held. This was the first time in the 450 years of Hutterite history that black and white brothers had sat down to the Lord's Supper, for at this ceremony there were eleven black brothers who had been duly baptized. The supper took place on the site of the new community, in a hut specially erected for the purpose. The lack of a dining room, the center of Hutterite communal life, was sorely felt, and so it was decided on the spot that a special effort should be made to accelerate the construction of living quarters, and in particular of a dining room and kitchen and so enable the taking of communal meals, that central Bruderhof custom in which, in the words of Christoph Arnold, "each meal is one of thanksgiving for communal life."

This led to a proposal made by Christoph Arnold at a Bruderhof meeting held at Woodcrest, that brothers capable of directing the construction project be sent to Nigeria. At the beginning of May, 1993, Martin and Burgel Johnson were called upon to go to Nigeria for a year and help lay sound economic foundations in the new commune. In early June, 1993, Burgel Johnson wrote a letter to some friends in Israel in which she told them about the spurt of construction: the completion of three buildings for living quarters and the construction of a temporary dining room that would serve until the completion of the permanent building. Everything pointed to an early move to the new settlement and the beginning of a new, Bruderhof-type communal life, which would be adapted to local Nigerian conditions. An estimated 130 souls would move into the commune in the first stage and these would include members' families and novices. The letter also indicated that many people were interested in joining the new commune and were seeking ways of doing so, and it also related to its readers that the settlement had electricity supplied by a generator, water from a well, and the beginnings of western-type toilet facilities; but the difficulties were still great: there were no laundry facilities and the sisters did their washing in the river; they had made a start on a small farm, which supplied them with eggs and vegetables; and they had begun the construction of a palm oil plant, which was to be the community's main source of income. One receives the impression from Burgel's letter that in that year of the laying of the foundations of the new community, the spirits of the Bruderhof members in Nigeria were high and that in their life there, they were experiencing the spirit of mission and pioneering. She concluded her letter with the following emotionally charged words:

> We are amazed at how the Holy Spirit is at work here, calling together people from all races and nationalities to live a life of full cooperation as a witness of communal life and brotherhood.[46]

But only a few months had elapsed before Burgel and her husband Martin drafted an open letter to all the readers of *The Plough*, the content and spirit of which were totally different and told of a dramatic turnabout that had occurred in the Nigerian community:

Recently, to our great shock, the very leaders who originally pleaded to join with us, secretly assumed control of all assets, properties and bank accounts belonging to the Hutterian Church in Nigeria. They declared their wish to be independent and made it clear that we are no longer wanted.

In a talk I had with Martin and Burgel in the fall of 1994, they said that in their estimation, the Nigerian community's leaders were not fully prepared to accept the Bruderhof movement's principle of community of goods. After a period of two years, during which they had enjoyed unstinting Bruderhof support, both financially and with manpower, they had decided to sever their economic and financial ties with the Bruderhof in America and become an independent Nigerian community. Under circumstances such as those an internal struggle, in which the American Bruderhof people had no wish to become involved, was likely to erupt, and as Martin and Burgel explained in their letter,

> because of the general control they have over Palmgrove, we felt that we should not become involved in a power struggle that might seem to be seen as a question of "black versus white" leadership. So we have decided to withdraw from the property with all those wishing to remain faithful to their promises to the church.... We have made all efforts to leave everything in order for those remaining in Palmgrove...
>
> This was a very hard decision for us to make, but it seemed the only way to keep things peaceful up to the last departure of our American and European members.

The most difficult problem was, of course, what was to become of the five mixed couples who had married during that period and who had expressed their desire to move to Bruderhof communities in America and England. With the help of the British and American legations in Nigeria who interceded on their behalf, their emigration was approved. We learn from Martin and Burgel's letter that apart from the five couples, there were some other Nigerians who wanted to move to Bruderhof communities:

> We currently have nine Nigerian brothers and sisters living with us already in our other communities. The door remains open to all those unfaithful ones to be reunited through repentance. We have hope and longing for each one. The struggle is not over, but it must be fought with the weapons of the spirit, not with the weapons of the world.

It appeared that as far as the Bruderhof members were concerned, this chapter was closed, but despite the disappointment and sense of failure that stemmed from the establishment of the Palmgrove community in Nigeria, Bruderhof spirits remained high. The failure did not bring in its wake a desire to isolate themselves within their communities and reduce the scope of their outside activities; on the contrary, their efforts to present their community to the general public have continued unabated. In the fall of 1994, in accordance with their tradition, they held open houses for their neighbors in all their communities, and as in the past, their hundreds of guests included people from all walks of life in the neighboring areas.

In addition, from 21 through 23 October 1994, they held conferences in three of their communities to discuss current issues and they wrote of the motives behind the meetings:

> This conference grew out of a deep longing of the Bruderhof for dialogue and to seek, with like-minded folk who are struggling for justice, peace, and community in the world.

In the circular that contained the invitation to the conference, they elucidated the background to the dialogue:

> As a society, as churches, as families, as individuals, all of us feel the effect of our culture's increasing fragmentation and steady moral decline. Its evidence is all around us: violence, substance abuse, divorce, family breakdown, abortion, suicide, sexual promiscuity and its attendant diseases, and homelessness.

> Today's moral crisis affects us all. We long to search with you in the hope that something new and genuine can be given in the world, even if it turns our world upside down!

> We invite you to join us as we seek a way of hope and new life. Together, we want to address problems and questions that affect us all today.

A few days after the conferences, on 4 November, Martin Johnson and Charles Moore summarized the proceedings in a letter to me:

> The conferences were held on three communities simultaneously: Spring Valley and New Meadow Run (Pennsylvania) jointly, Deer Spring (Connecticut) and Pleasant View (New York). In Pennsylvania there were over 170 guests, while Deer Spring and Pleasant View each had around ninety. Newcomers as well as old friends came. There were Jews, Protestants, Evangelicans, Anabaptists, Catholics and Eastern Orthodox. Quite a number of small community groups joined as well: Shepherds Field from Missouri, the Church of the Servant King from Southern California, Reba Place Fellowship from Illinois, and others.... Peace and justice groups also attended.

> On Saturday afternoon, small groups gathered together around subjects of concern: living a consistent life of reverence; educating and nurturing children; establishing a growing, pure and faithful relationship with one another; living free of materialism; pursuing justice for the poor and the oppressed; creating community, and so forth.

They wrote the following about the atmosphere at the conferences:

People came to discuss important matters. There was very little conjecture, specu-
lation or analysis. Even when there were disagreements (and there were some)
there was the realization that all of us need to change and that all of us get into the
way of God's spirit of justice, love, and "shalom." The atmosphere at all three
places was one of openness and mutual listening. Guests as well as community
members were able to get beyond differences to address core issues. There were
very few answers but plenty of self-searching instead.

The letter was concluded with a question:

What would it be like if this humble way of being together could extend beyond a
weekend conference to the daily practical living of brotherhood?

This rhetorical question, which contains so many hopes and dreams,
remains unanswered. Only time will tell what the contribution of the
Witness of the Brothers to the fulfillment of those hopes and dreams
will be.

Notes

1. The letters are in the file "Communes; preparations for the international conference, 1985," Yad Tabenkin archives.
2. Gorni, Yosef, Yaacov Oved, and Idit Paz, eds., *Communal Life, An International
   Perspective* (New Brunswick, N.J.: Transaction Publishers, 1987), 744–48.
3. *The Plough*, no. 16 (Quarterly of Bruderhof communities. Bromdon: The Plough
   Publishing House, September 1986): 2–8.
4. Interview with Mussa Bar-Semech, June, 1992.
5. "Common Ground," *The Plough*, no. 19 (May/June 1988).
6. Johann Christoph Arnold to Yaacov Oved, 2 January 1986.
7. *The Plough*, no. 22 (1989): 10–12.
8. Yaacov Oved to Hans Meier, 7 May 1989.
9. Hans Meier to Yaacov Oved, 26 August 1989.
10. *The Plough*, no. 31 (May/June 1992).
11. Ibid., no. 14 (1986), and no. 15 (1986).
12. Ibid., no. 19 (1988); no. 26 (1990); no. 29 (1991).
13. See *KIT Annual*, vol. 4, no. 2 (San Francisco, Calif.: 1992).
14. *The Plough*, no. 26 (1990).
15. Ibid., no. 19 (1988); no. 21 (1989); no. 29 (1991).
16. *Mennonite Weekly Review* (U.S.: 3 October 1991).
17. *The Plough*, no. 5 (July 1984): 6–7; no. 8 (January 1985): 9.
18. Ibid., no. 26 (September/October 1990): 6–9.
19. Ibid., no. 29 (November/December 1991).
20. Ramón and Sybil Sender joined the Bruderhof in the United States at a time when
    they were going through a difficult period in their marriage. At the conclusion of
    their novitiate, Ramón was found unsuitable for baptism (acceptance as a mem-

ber), while Sybil was accepted and remained in the Bruderhof with their daughter. As a result, their relationship was severed and contact between father and daughter was limited in the extreme. The daughter later married and raised her family in the Bruderhof, but unfortunately she contracted cancer some years later and subsequently died. The news of his daughter's death reached Sender after some delay, and in an effort to learn something of her life during the years she had lived in the Bruderhof, he sent out a round robin letter to the members and also to those who had left the movement, and it was this correspondence that laid the foundations of what was to later become *KIT*.

21. *KIT*, vol. 2, no. 8 (September 1990); vol. 2, no. 11 (1990): 3.
22. Ibid., vol. 1, no. 3 (1989).
23. Readers interested in seeing the complete list will find it in Ibid., vol. 3, no. 9 (1991).
24. Ibid.
25. On the attitude of the Bruderhof veterans towards sex education and German educational tradition, see Zumpe, Elizabeth Bolken, in *KIT Annual 1991*, 32.
26. Interview with Dick Domer and Christoph Arnold, Fall, 1991.
27. Allain, Roger, *The Community That Failed* (San Francisco, Calif.: Carrier Pigeon Press, 1992). Bohlken, Zumpe, E., Torches Extinguished.
28. See article by R. Sender in *KIT*, vol. 5, no. 1 (1993): 8.
29. *The Plough*, nos. 5, 6, 8, 11, 12, 17, 19, and 20.
30. *KIT*, vol. 3, no. 2 (February, 1991): 1-2.
31. From an interview with Glenn Swinger at Woodcrest, November, 1991. The transcript is the author's.
32. *Reasons for Judgement Delivered* (Winnipeg, 31 October 1989; *Saturday Night* (Toronto, April 1992).
33. Interview with Andreas Meier, Joseph Ben-Eliezer, and Derek Wardle, October, 1992.
34. *Saturday Night* (April 1992).
35. See the Elders's letter that was published in *KIT*, vol. 5, no. 2 (February, 1993); *The Mennonite Reporter* interviewed a number of Kleinsasser's supporters who replied to the charges, see *KIT*, vol. 5, no. 7.
36. Interview with Andreas Meier, Joseph Ben-Eliezer, and Derek Wardle, Fall 1992.
37. *KIT*, vol. 4, no. 10.
38. Ibid., vol. 5, no. 1.
39. *Mennonite Reporter* (19 April 1993).
40. Interview with Andreas Meier, Kibbutz Palmachim, 1993.
41. "The Present Struggle of The Church," *The Plough* (1993): 91-95.
42. "The Genesis of The Hutterian Brethren in Nigeria," *The Plough*, no. 29 (December, 1991).
43. Kleinsasser, Jacob, "A Visit to Palmgrove Community," *The Plough*, no. 3 (May, 1992).
44. Ibid., 10.
45. Ibid., 72; *The Plough*, no. 32 (September, 1992) and no. 33 (November/December 1992).
46. Burgel and Martin Johnson, letter from Nigeria, 7 June 1993.

Epilogue

In retrospect, one may conclude that the Bruderhof has withstood the test of time while overcoming the crises that beset the movement, and that their "witness" has been maintained from its inception to the present day. A study of the movement's history confirms that the Bruderhof has shown a rare ability to wander the world as a united community that did not disintegrate as a result of the emigration that was forced upon it four times in the course of its seventy-four-year history. During that history, the movement established twenty-three settlements in seven countries under varying conditions, absorbed new members of various nationalities, and despite these adverse conditions, the Bruderhof has succeeded in maintaining stability in its way of life and communal tradition from its beginnings to the present day. Descriptions provided by foreign visitors reveal the unchanging way of life during the various periods of the Bruderhof's history and highlight a most characteristic and impressive phenomenon: the ability to maintain stable communal relations in the community.

Moreover, the Bruderhof's present vitality has not become diminished, but rather the opposite. The movement's communes have grown in recent years and currently number eight, and they are spread over four countries and three continents, while membership is also larger than it has ever been, reaching 2,200 souls at the beginning of 1994. The membership continues to preserve its international characteristics, and consists of members of fifteen different nationalities; 49 percent of the total population is comprised of children, teenagers, and young people, and 51 percent are adults of all ages up to ninety years of age, and at the time of writing the fourth generation of commune children is growing up in the settlements. The children, who start their education at local schools, are later sent to outside high schools and institutions of higher education and this openness is the touchstone of an educational policy directed at enabling the children to become acquainted with outside society before they decide on their future. It appears that this approach does not discourage the young people from deciding on a future in the Bruderhof; on the contrary, the experience of recent years has shown that the majority of Bruderhof children join the commune and play central roles in the community's activities. Over the past ten years 464 candidates of both sexes were "baptized" (in other words, they joined the church and community as full members) and of these, 70 percent were children of the commune. The remaining 30 percent were people who had joined the communities from outside and who come to the Bruderhof in a small but steady flow. Of the people who joined from "outside," ninety-one were Americans, twenty Germans, sixteen Nigerians, eight Britons, and various people from Canada, Morocco, and Holland.

The Bruderhof's economic situation has become firmly established over recent years. "Community Playthings," the industrial enterprise that had its beginnings producing toys, has extended the variety of its products and established a factory at Rifton for the manufacture of aids for the disabled. Both factories enjoy a wide market and an unblemished reputation. As in the past, surplus revenues are not plowed back into the community for raising the standard of living, but are used for reinforcing the "witness" the world over. It was under these circumstances that the Bruderhof was able to take upon itself the task of establishing a settlement in Nigeria, which placed an extremely heavy financial, organizational, and social burden on the movement. This taking up of a fresh challenge in Africa is not only something quite rare in the world of communes, but also of the inner strength of the membership in facing new challenges. Although the experiment ended in failure as a result of deceit perpetrated by the leadership of their Nigerian allies, according to the tone of letters received from Bruderhof members they have not capitulated, are certainly not shying away from fresh challenges, and their readiness to accept new tasks is not limited to the African continent. At the beginning of 1995, the Bruderhof decided to send a couple from each settlement to establish contact with people seeking an "alternative way" to the materialism prevalent in outside society. The emissaries remained outside their communities for several weeks, making contact with various circles, and the motivation behind this mission is their increasing awareness that it is incumbent upon them to do their utmost to change the reality of our world and expose people outside to their witness of the possibility of an alternative way of life.

At present, with the processes of privatization invading the majority of the world's communes (there are even some accounts of the erosion of communal relations in the Hutterite communities caused by the penetration of a market economy), the Bruderhof is a shining example of communal stability. Not only are there no signs of privatization, but there is also a ramified system of an intercommunity cooperative economy that has achieved great success, a kind of "general commune" of all the Bruderhof settlements. But even more impressive is the Bruderhof's ability to maintain its members' inner morals, which act as a buffer against consumerism *per se* and the pursuit of luxury. A visitor to the Bruderhof communities cannot but be amazed by the balance that has been created between the filling of all the members' needs at a good standard in which nothing is lacking, and the absence of luxury items and everyday things like radios and television sets, which are part of the standard furnishing in every home in the surrounding environment.

There is, however, one unavoidable question: How has the Bruderhof movement managed to maintain its stability over three generations and overcome the crises that beset it? What is the secret of the inner strength that enabled it to survive the many years of wanderings, suffering, and crises?

A review of the history of the movement raises a number of hypotheses regarding the factors which sustained the Bruderhof's ability for survival and these are worthy of note in general terms in this chapter.[1]

The first and foremost factor in the Bruderhof movement's long history of stability is the exceptional combination of deep religious belief and the centrality of harmonious community life. This religious belief is rooted in a system of values that endows the communal way of life with meaning and is nurtured by the belief that the Hand of God directs the universe, guides history, and pilots the Bruderhof along their route. According to Bruderhof belief, the maintaining of communal and community life is a manifestation of God's will and it forms a bridgehead for the Kingdom of Heaven that will come with the millennium, *ergo*, living a communal life means the fulfillment of God's will. They view joining the community as an expression of an "inner calling," a response to a Divine commandment, and they feel that the act of joining has a double significance: on the one hand, it provides a framework for people who are striving toward a life of belief, while on the other, it provides them with the sublime meaning of the fulfillment of the Kingdom of

Heaven on earth. In both instances, commitment to the community is equivalent to total devotion to a lofty, transcendental ideal.

It should be emphasized that members of the Bruderhof take a pessimistic view of the nature of man. They recognize the fact that a constant struggle between good and evil exists in the world, that man alone is too weak to combat his selfish instincts, and that greater forces are required to keep him on the straight and narrow path. The role of the commune is to assist man in improving himself and to aid him in his inner struggle between good and evil. Moreover, according to Bruderhof perspective, only in community life is man able to conquer the selfish instincts that lie within him.

Interpersonal relationships within the community are maintained as in a big family; are based upon harmony, caring, and a sense of brotherhood toward one's fellow-man; and require the total integration of the individual within the community and the relinquishing of all personal aspirations. The Bruderhof's social ethos dictates that the development of an individual's personality occurs while devoting oneself to the community and its aims. There is strict observance of close interpersonal relationships and, hence, efforts are made to maintain the community's optimal size. The Bruderhof membership does not aspire to grow beyond these optimal limits and does not view growth in itself as either an aim or a measure of success. From their standpoint, the success of the "witness" is not evaluated by the number of people who have joined them on their way, but by the inner truth that radiates from it. They accept the fact that they are a small minority in the world and that they will continue to be so.

They ascribe great importance to social life within the commune and it ranks even higher than work obligations on their list of priorities. Work and its concomitant arrangements are adapted to fulfil the needs of the community and in accordance with this approach; they endeavor to integrate work obligations with social and community needs. It should be mentioned here that the accumulation of wealth is not the chief objective of their economic activities, for sufficing with little is a basic principle of their communal life. Their ascetic approach enables them to effectively combat materialism and consumerism, which they view as an expression of man's baser instincts, and this struggle is maintained while strictly avoiding any spiritual enslavement to assets. According to Bruderhof belief, they do not perceive themselves as owning the assets they hold, but believe that the assets belong to The Almighty and have been placed in their custodianship, so that through them they may maintain their witness.

Their social ethos is sustained through a system of socialization that is active in every sphere of their life and begins with intensive education from childhood. Through this system, the Bruderhof members internalize the movement's accepted moral norms and it should be emphasized that community life itself is an active ingredient in the socialization processes throughout all the age groups. Worthy of special mention is their success in bridging the generation gap; people of different ages live and work together and cooperate in community life. The education of the younger generation constitutes a preparation for life in small communities, the objective of which is to become exemplary.

From an administrative and organizational standpoint, the Bruderhof is a hierarchical community that is managed according to an authoritative doctrine and by a charismatic leadership. The authoritative source of their doctrine is in the belief that they are doing God's work and this finds expression through the general agreement of the community, so decisions are not made by a majority vote, which is standard practice in democratic societies. If, at the conclusion of the discussion, full agreement has not been attained, it is continued until consensus is reached. Sovereignty and authority are vested in the general meeting, from where they are passed on to the committees and individuals. Community matters are put into the hands of the "Elder," who is deemed to know the will of his flock and has been elected to be the instrument for the fulfillment of this will, but yet is attuned to the will of God. Acceptance of the leader's authority is therefore perceived as the acceptance of Divine authority. From this standpoint, the Elder may be discerned as a charismatic leader according to the characteristics put forward by Max Weber.[2] The guidance and supervision of the conduct of the society and the individuals in it are vested in the Elder and in the application of his authority. He is assisted by the communities' central office holders, the Servants of the Word, and public opinion. Any deviation from accepted norms meets with a swift response, and the direct response, the "admonition," may be delivered by a member, an office holder, or the Elder. In more severe cases sanctions may be imposed, and it should be borne in mind that the Bruderhof maintains a system of sanctions by which punishments may be imposed for deviations from accepted norms and other irregularities. The majority of these find expression in varying degrees of exclusion for varying periods of time. This use of sanctions reflects the pessimistic view held by the Bruderhof members on the nature of man and the perpetual struggle between good and evil. The lessons of history have taught them that a significant increase in the number sanctions imposed usually indicates the development of a crisis situation.

Crisis in itself is not perceived as a situation of destruction and disintegration, but as an expression of the struggle between good and evil in the world and as the Almighty's response to occurrences in their community. They believe that in this way the Hand of God helps them to discern processes that endanger the community's existence and so, according to this approach, crises are a process of purification for they impel them to reexamine their ways. Despite the fact that a crisis is accompanied by a collective sense of guilt, the brothers do not relate to it in either positive or negative terms, but rather as an unavoidable necessity. Furthermore, Bruderhof members view the crises that have beset them as corrections of deviations and as a witness of the struggle against the weaknesses of man that have been caused by external influences.[3]

All the Bruderhof communities are exposed to external influences. This is particularly prominent in the United States, where the tolerant and pluralistic climate creates an open and comfortable relationship with the outside world. Yet, the Bruderhof and its leadership foster a consciousness of the past that cautions them against laxity and warns of the dangers that may bring persecution and expulsion in their wake, and so they maintain an even balance between openness and seclusion. On a personal level, the effect of the community's seclusion is somewhat alleviated by belonging to a movement that permits mobility and the broadening of community life. Movement between the communes and the numerous missions help take the brothers out of their isolation and reinforce the awareness of belonging to a large movement. Thus, despite the consciousness of exclusivity and seclusion, the Bruderhof members are not isolated or detached from what is going on in the world around them.

I have discussed a number of factors which, in my view, have sustained the survival of the commune in both the past and present. It should be emphasized that in my estimation, the ability to survive and the vitality that are apparent in the Bruderhof do not provide a true and complete picture of the "witness," and the fact that a high price has been paid for that special witness must be taken into account. The exclusive combination of a community with a rich social life and a church imposes an unremitting authority on the community together with all of the advantages it holds for the stability of the community. This authority finds expression in the binding belief that is imposed upon the individual members of the Bruderhof and on the movement's member communities. Obligations to the church invade social life and while they are a source of strength and stability, they are also a source of tensions simply because permanent tension is created between the needs of the community and its members and the needs of the church, particularly in the triad of the community, the church, and the leadership. The historical review contained in this book presents only a few of these tensions, particularly those that found outward expression in the life of the community. But there are also hidden internal struggles that a person carries within him and which remain concealed until the storm blows over, albeit on occasion he is unable to keep them concealed and they burst out and become part of the public domain. Once central members were involved in cases such as this, conditions became ripe for a decline into crisis and situations of this kind recurred on a number of occasions throughout the movement's history and there can be no guarantee that they will not occur again in the future.

Numerous obstacles in the path toward realization of the historical ideal set out by Eberhard Arnold have recently become apparent. So far, the Bruderhof have not succeeded in realizing the vision of their founder by uniting with the Hutterites and becoming a single movement. The sixty-year-old history of efforts at unification is currently at a low ebb, with the majority of the Hutterite settlements against amalgamation and a small minority in favor of continuing cooperation with the Bruderhof (in this context, see Post Script).

Despite the steady population growth of the Bruderhof in recent years, the movement's witness has not succeeded in its efforts at persuasion that it might be a universal gospel. Not everyone is able to shoulder the burden required by the exemplary life of the "witness"; many have tried and failed. Some left with a sense of personal failure, while others felt that it was the community that had failed, and there are many people who are still living under the effects of the trauma of leaving the Bruderhof. The groups of people who left the Bruderhof and who recently united around the *KIT* magazine, are diligently opening the wounds of the past and fully intend to become a platform for critical views of the

Bruderhof. Most of their criticism is centered on episodes from the distant past, is one-sided, selective, and ignores the historical context. A cautious appraisal of their criticism is called for because of the fact that the critics themselves were active participants in some of the Bruderhof's "injustices" that they are currently revealing. But despite these drawbacks, the objective scholar cannot ignore this criticism because it is of some assistance in becoming acquainted with the phenomenon from a critical point of view.

For many years, the Bruderhof publications tried to conceal the existence of the crises. In those most trying times during which shock waves shattered the Paraguayan settlements, not a word was published about the events taking place and the outside reader could only apprise himself of them through Benjamin Zablocki's book. But as the Bruderhof harbored deep reservations about the book, it was difficult to obtain disinterested information. This situation was rectified with the publication of Bruderhof member Merrill Mow's book, which revealed some unpleasant episodes and described power struggles that had taken place within the Bruderhof.

While the book aroused angry responses from those who had left, the discord allowed the collection and verification of information from varied and opposed sources and the cross-referencing of various testimonies. This situation enabled both the reader and the objective scholar to move much closer to the historical truth than they had been able in the past.

True to the guidelines he set for himself, the author has endeavored to review the development of the Bruderhof movement through all its struggles, as objectively as possible. Each scrap of information, even though it might have come from hostile sources, was studied until its factual basis was established. The author harbors no pretensions of sitting in judgement or proffering advice; he has simply filled the role of an objective, albeit sympathetic observer who has tried to review the history of the Bruderhof according to the criteria of historical writing that strives to understand and explain how events took place.

Yet, even employing this approach of maintaining an objective distance, the witness of the Bruderhof still leaves a number of conjectures and questions unanswered. For example, can a pacifist movement that professes to be a "witness" to a communal life of brotherhood avoid facing up to the monumental problems that face the society in which it lives? Can it be satisfied solely with protest demonstrations and signing petitions? Or could it have returned to Germany without conducting a political and moral stock-taking concerning the rise of Nazism which had destroyed the very soul of its own generation and brought about the movement's exile?

And with regard to internal matters: Is the movement's hierarchical structure that was formulated in the course of its history as vital today as it was then? Can the concerns regarding the concentration of authority in the hands of one man be ignored? Does the need to reach consensus not prevent free expression in that it suppresses criticism and dissenting opinions? Do the recurrent crises not indicate that communal life and faith have failed in uprooting struggles for power and authority?

These are but a few of the conjectures and questions to which the author has found no plausible answers. But in the final accounting and beyond the conjectures and the hidden and ostensible flaws, there is no doubt in my mind that the brothers bear a special and particularly significant witness for our generation. The Bruderhof experience, even though it be inimitable, constitutes a challenge for every communal movement, including the Israeli kibbutz movement. And not only for them, because those who believe in a rejuvenation of faith in the pluralism and mini-Utopia of communal life in the wake of the collapse of the communist and authoritarian regimes, can find a source of inspiration in the Bruderhof experience. Indeed, those who in their naivete thought that an ideal and perfect social structure that was free of flaws existed, will be disappointed at not finding it in the Bruderhof. But anyone who does not labor under the delusion that there is a straight and simple path to a just society, will find in the Bruderhof one of the most enthralling experiments of our time at maintaining a lasting communal way of life.

Notes

1. See the description of communes' ability to survive that is based upon a comparison between Bruderhof communes and the kibbutz in Niv, Amitai ["A Search For a Theory About the Survival of Communes" (unpublished doctoral dissertation), Cambridge, Mass.: Harvard University, 1975].
2. Weber, Max, "The General Character of Charisma," in H. H. Gerth and Wright Mills, eds., *From Max Weber* (London: Kegan Paul, 1947), 245-50.
3. Amitai Niv views the internal crises as making a positive contribution to the existence of a high level of awareness and as guarding against internal processes that have ramifications on the existence of the commune in the future, which in turn assists in the prevention of stagnation.

Postscript

After the manuscript had been delivered to the publisher, news reached me of some important developments in the Bruderhof movement that had occurred during the course of 1995, which I felt should be brought to the attention of my readers, even in the form of informative excerpts from the correspondence, articles, and other documents in my possession.

The first significant event was the Bruderhof's decision to close down the Michaelshof commune in Germany and move its members to England. This decision was first aired publicly in an interview given by Servant of the Word Jorg Barth to the *Rheinische Zeitung* on 25 January 1995, in which he spoke of the background and motivation that led to the decision:

> We never were able to start a real Bruderhof here...Since 1988 we have done our utmost to build a real community. We had to struggle with great opposition to all our plans, and I would like to mention the "Citizens Union" here. This union has been active since 1990 and has done everything in its power to frustrate our building plans.... For four years we have taken all our meals in a big tent on the lawn and have held all festivities and prayer meetings in this tent.... In our search for a place where we can truly concentrate all our abilities and strength, Hastings in England seemed a much better choice.

In January, 1995, once it had become clear that the Schmiedleut stream, headed by Jacob Kleinsasser, had broken off its relations with the Bruderhof, a deep and total schism was revealed between the two movements. The cause of the schism was the differing approaches to the affair of the Palmgrove community in Nigeria. As mentioned above, the Bruderhof broke off its relations with this community, while the Hutterite stream ignored this fact and continued its activities in Nigeria, claiming that they must maintain the mission and take care of the assets there. The Bruderhof viewed this act as one of betrayal. The signal for the break was given in an open letter from Elder Christoph Arnold, in which he denounced the internal deterioration of the Hutterite settlements[1]:

In many Hutterite colonies in Canada and the Dakotas, members withhold money and other good for themselves in spite of their membership vows to relinquish all private property and share everything. Some work outside the community to earn money for their personal use. Communal work departments have become independent "kingdoms," and a sense of common work and a common purpose has been lost. There is little or no spiritual leadership, and ministers are no longer true servants of their flocks, but lord it over them, seeking to increase their personal authority. Young people no longer receive clear guidance and direction from their ministers, teachers and parents.... Alcoholism is rampant, even among some community leaders. Premarital sex is widespread, and there are illegitimate children. In other words, the church has lost its salt and become lukewarm, shallow and superficial...

We in the Bruderhof long to embrace the call of the Apostles of 2,000 years ago: "Repent and be baptized; save yourselves from this crooked generation." ...Together with those Hutterites who seek for change we ask for a reawakening by the Holy Spirit. The God of present-day Hutterianism has become too small. The understanding of the true Church has been lost. We want to seek anew the living God of Judaism and Christianity, who alone is unchangeable.

This open letter, which publicly and caustically voiced criticism that had been expressed only implicitly in the past, opened the schism and made it irrevocable. Although both parties to the dispute are keeping the option of "forgiveness and reconciliation" open, there are no signs that it will be taken up in the near future.

While these events were occurring, the activities of the Bruderhof's "mission" in the world were being reinforced. On 17 January 1995, it was decided to send "brothers and sisters" to various American cities—Philadelphia, Boston, Washington, Pittsburgh, and Rochester—and even to London. The objective of these emissaries, who left with only a little money and no contacts, was to see the reality at close quarters, experience its exigencies, and listen to "seeking people." These activities have been continued over the past year with missions to countries as distant as Japan, Korea, Russia, Ukraine, Latvia, Central and South America, and only recently a group of forty young people visited Israel. This "missionary" trend of the Bruderhof has been given further expression in the movement's active involvement in the fight against the death penalty in the United States. The 1995 summer edition of *The Plough* was devoted almost entirely to the struggle against the execution of Mumia Abu-Jamal that was due to take place in August, 1995 (at the time of writing it became known that the court had granted a stay of execution). *The Plough* editorial (no. 44), deals with this matter; herewith a number of excerpts:

Why should the Bruderhof get worked up over the case of this one man, Mumia Abu-Jamal? On one level, it is simply because he has become much more than a death row statistic to us. Through his writing, and through the visits of several of our brothers to the nearby federal prison where he awaits his execution, Mumia has become a friend. More than this, his witness for justice and his championship of the oppressed have moved us. On another level, the case of Mumia Abu-Jamal is an example of this country's justice system at its worst.

Some of our readers have expressed concern about the Bruderhof's "new" social activism. First, we'd like to point out that this is not new; since the founding of Sannerz, the Bruderhof has attempted to be a voice for social justice. We do not consider this to be a contradiction of our primary calling to be witness for Christ and for a life of discipleship. At the same time, we are not social Utopians who believe that human perfection can be legislated into existence. Nor are we blind to the human imperfection, the sinfulness, the power-seeking and even violence that can infect movements that stand for peace and justice. But we cannot stand by in holy isolation when suffering presents itself at our very doorstep!

Against the backdrop of the changes that have taken place in the relations between the Bruderhof and the Hutterites and the widening of Bruderhof openness to the world, an interesting and extremely significant development began to emerge in the relationship between the Bruderhof and the *Integrierte Gemeinde,* a Catholic movement whose center is in Munich and whose members maintain partial cooperation. For some years this movement has maintained good relations with the Bruderhof and the Israeli Kibbutz Movement.

In *The Plough,* no. 45 (Winter, 1995), John Christoph Arnold and Eckhard Muller published an article entitled "Steps toward Reconciliation," which reviews the relations between the Bruderhof and *Integrierte Gemeinde* and describes the contacts between both movements and the leaders of the Catholic church.

Because of the importance of the article, we have chosen a number of verbatim excerpts that have some bearing on the new spirit abroad in the Bruderhof. The article opens with a clarification of the relationship between the Bruderhof and *Integrierte Gemeinde:*

What does a decidedly Roman Catholic group have in common with an Anabaptist Bruderhof? For the *Integrierte Gemeinde* as for us it was clear from the beginning that we cannot be satisfied with the growth and prosperity of our own groups. We must be on the lookout for other related movements in which Christianity demands the whole life. And so we discovered—in spite of obvious differences between us—a common task, that is to show the world that harmony among people is indeed possible: through faith.

At the beginning of February, a Bruderhof delegation handed over a letter from Christoph Arnold to the *Integrierte Gemeinde* leadership, in which Arnold asked them to mediate between him and the heads of the Catholic church in order to bring about a meeting with Pope John Paul II (*sic*). The letter itself is a most interesting document, as the following excerpts show:

> I have eagerly followed and deeply respect the firm stand Pope John Paul II takes on many unpopular issues—divorce, abortion, homosexuality, women in the priesthood (and lately the death penalty). His recent book, *Crossing the Threshold of Hope,* is a much-needed and prophetic word in our corrupt and violent times.

> It would be a great gift from God if Pope John Paul II and I could offer each other the hand and embrace each other as a sign of reconciliation and forgiveness for the terrible persecutions our Hutterian church has suffered in the past.

> I long for a new, mutual understanding between the Roman Catholic Church and the Hutterite movement, so that we can again look into one another's eyes and know that the past is forgiven, then together we will be able to seek more deeply what true and living discipleship of Jesus means as we enter the 21st century. Most of all, Roman Catholics and Hutterites will be able to encourage and support each other in becoming more dedicated and convinced Christians.

As a first step toward the hoped-for papal audience, the friends of the *Integrierte Gemeinde* planned a meeting between Christian Arnold and a group of Bruderhof members with Joseph Cardinal Ratzinger. Thus, on 28 February the heads of the *Integrierte Gemeinde* met with Cardinal Ratzinger in Rome and agreed to convene a meeting with him, J. Christoph Arnold, and an *Integrierte Gemeinde* delegation as a preparation for this visit to the Pope. It was accepted that the meeting should take place on 24 June in Rome.

In the meantime, J. Christoph Arnold met with Cardinal John O'Connor, the Archbishop of New York.

> On March 4...I drove to New York City to attend the "Respect for Life" seminar. The main speaker was Cardinal O'Connor...

> When there was a break for lunch, the Reverend Monsignor James F. McCarthy, secretary to the Cardinal, introduced us to the Cardinal. I think this was the first time that any of our people had talked to a cardinal of the Roman Catholic Church. It was a great joy. I shared with him the persecution of the Hutterites by the Roman Catholics 450 years ago.... I pointed out that as far as I know, this was the first time that an elder of the Hutterian church was talking to someone in the Roman Catholic hierarchy. I shared with him the necessity and urgency I feel, that as leaders in the Christian church from both sides, we must seek reconciliation and forgiveness, and that it is much better to set something right in this world than in the next.

I gave the Cardinal brochures about our "Gulfstream II" charter service (the Bruderhof aircraft) and suggested that the next time he goes to Rome, we would like to fly him there. He was surprised and said, "Four hundred and fifty years ago you wanted to get out of Rome, and now you are offering to take us there!" We invited him to Woodcrest to speak to our community. He was very open to this and told his secretary to make the necessary arrangements.[2]

On 24 June 1955, the planned meeting with Cardinal Ratzinger took place in Rome. Johann Christoph Arnold and Eckhard Muller reported on it in the article mentioned above thusly:

On Saturday, June 24, we gathered at the place of the *Integrierte Gemeinde* in Rome with Cardinal Ratzinger. Some thirty persons were gathered.... The Cardinal arrived at about 4 P.M. After coffee and mutual introductions, the meeting began in earnest. It lasted for three hours.

We expressed our longing to have a personal audience with the Pope.... As the meeting progressed, it was clear that we were not merely partners in a discussion, but participants in an encounter of deep inner content. The desire for reconciliation prompted us all to ask ourselves where the common task of the *Integrierte Gemeinde* and the Bruderhof lies. One hope expressed by the *Integrierte Gemeinde* was that we might become joint witnesses to our faith.... Cardinal Ratzinger remarked that in the conjunction of the Bruderhof-*Integrierte Gemeinde*-Kibbutz Movement, it is significant on the one hand, how the kibbutzim, with their questions about community, are acting as a catalyst between Christians who have been historical adversaries, while on the other hand, how we Christians might help them to rediscover the Scriptures, not as a kind of political blueprint, but as a Divine promise that gives meaning to all of life. Referring to the hoped-for encounter with the Pope, the Cardinal said that he would like to see something that transcends the usual protocol that attends papal audiences: "We want to stay out of the headlines." On leaving the meeting, each of us felt that it had been an encounter of deep significance.[3]

At the time of writing, there has been no news of the expected meeting with the Pope, but even without it, these events can be seen as extremely significant with regard to future trends of The Witness of the Brothers.[4]

Notes

1. J. Christoph Arnold, "An Open Letter from the Bruderhof," *The Plough*, no. 41 (January 1995).
2. From J. Christoph Arnold, *Report of Our Visit to Cardinal John O'Connor: March 5, 1991*; "An Historic Meeting," *The Plough*, no. 43 (May/June 1995)
3. *The Plough*, no. 45 (Summer 1995).
4. We received a note of a planned meeting between Cardinal O'Connor, Pope John Paul II, and the Elder of the Bruderhof for 7 October 1995. The meeting was to take place at Cardinal O'Connor's residence.

Appendix

A Chronological Table of Important Dates in Bruderhof History

July, 1920	The Sannerz commune is founded by Eberhard Arnold.
October, 1922	The split at Sannerz. Seven "loyal" members remain in the commune.
1925	"The First Law of Sannerz" is adopted.
January, 1927	The move to the farm at Rhön (the Rhönbruderhof)
1928	Establishment of the *Gemeinschaftsverlag Eberhard Arnold* publishing house.
1930–31	Eberhard Arnold visits the Hutterite communities and is "ordained" as Elder.
1931	Adoption of the Hutterite way of life and dress.
1932	The first meeting with the Jewish "Religious Pioneers Federation" group.
16 November 1933	The first Gestapo raid on the Rhönbruderhof.
1934	The establishment of an additional *hof* in the Principality of Liechtenstein.
22 November 1935	Death of Eberhard Arnold. Hans Zumpe is appointed as his successor (until 1937).
September, 1936	Purchase of the Cotswolds farm in England.
14 April 1937	A further Gestapo raid on the Rhönbruderhof and their expulsion from Germany.
May, 1937	The entire Bruderhof moves to Britain and settles on the Cotswolds farm.
1938	Establishment of the publishing house and the English-language magazine, *The Plough*.
July, 1939	Absorption of the twenty-five German refugee members of the *Hashomer Hatsa'ir* training group.
August, 1940	The British government indicates its intention of interning the Germans, and the decision to emigrate.

December, 1940	The first group leaves Britain for Paraguay, which was prepared to offer asylum.
January, 1941	Purchase of the Primavera farm and the establishment of the Isla Margarita communities.
April, 1941	The last Bruderhof group leaves Britain for Paraguay.
December, 1941	The three members who remained in Britain form the nucleus of a new *Bruderhof*.
January, 1942	The second Paraguayan Bruderhof, Loma Jhoby, is established.
March, 1942	The Wheathill Bruderhof is established in the west of England, near the Welsh border.
1942	Opening of Bruderhof House in Asunción.
1942	A leadership crisis in which Heini Arnold is removed from office and replaced by Hans Zumpe.
1944	A second crisis incited by seventeen members who were "excluded" for one to two years.
1946	The establishment of the Ibate settlement for the absorption of war orphans.
August, 1948	The Wheathill community is officially accepted into the Bruderhof.
1949	Bruderhof emissaries are sent on missions to the United States. One delegation is sent to visit the Hutterites.
1952	The El Arado settlement is established in Uruguay.
1953	A Hutterite delegation visits the Primavera communities in Paraguay.
1953	The General Council of Bruderhof communities meets at Primavera to discuss the continuation of the Bruderhof mission in the world.
June, 1954	The first community in the United States, Woodcrest, in New York State, is established.
April, 1955	The Bruderhof House at Hoenstein Castle in Germany is established.
May, 1955	Launching of the Spanish language magazine, *El Arado*.
1956	The German Bruderhof moves to its place of permanent settlement at Sinnthal.
December, 1956	An assembly of representatives of the Paraguayan, North American, and European *hofs* is held at Primavera.
1956	The Forest River community joins the Bruderhof.

February, 1957	Fire destroys the central building at Woodcrest.
June, 1957	The decision to leave Forest River and transfer its members to the community in Pennsylvania.
July, 1958	Establishment of the Bruderhof in Connecticut, at Deer Spring.
July, 1958	The International Youth Camp at Primavera.
August, 1958	Bulstrode, the second Bruderhof community in Britain, is established.
1959	A general assembly of Bruderhof delegates held at Primavera decides to reduce the number of communities.
May, 1960	The Bruderhof General Council held in Pennsylvania decides to close two communities.
June, 1960	Hans Zumpe is excluded from the Bruderhof and moves to Germany.
August, 1960	176 members from the communities that were closed down are flown to reinforce the European communities.
January, 1961	A delegation from Woodcrest is sent to Primavera to deal with the crisis there.
February, 1961	The decision is made to close down Primavera and transfer its "loyal" members to the communities in the United States.
1961	"The Great Crisis": some 600 members leave the Bruderhof and return to their countries of origin.
1961	Wheathill and Sinnthal are closed down and their members transferred to Bulstrode.
22 October 1961– 29 January 1962	Emigration from Paraguay to the United States.
July, 1962	Heini Arnold is elected Elder of the Bruderhof.
1964	An attempt at reconciliation with the Hutterites ends in failure.
1965	Small social crises in the United States communities are settled quickly.
1966	The Bulstrode Bruderhof is closed down and its members transferred to the United States.
1966	The Bruderhof toy factory begins to flourish.
July, 1971	Darvell, the new Bruderhof in Britain, is established.
1972	A wave of members excluded during the Great Crisis begin to return to the Bruderhof, among them, Hans Meier.

1974	A delegation of repentance and forgiveness meets the Hutterites.
23 July 1982	Death of Bruderhof Elder Heini Arnold.
17 April 1983	Johann Christoph Arnold is elected Elder.
November, 1983	Publication of *The Plough* is renewed.
May, 1985	The first Bruderhof delegation to visit Israel participates in an international congress.
August, 1985	The Pleasant View community is established near Woodcrest.
October, 1987	A number of Bruderhof families visit kibbutzim for a few months.
June, 1988	The Bruderhof communities in the eastern United States host a Christian theological and ecumenical conference.
March, 1988	Purchase of a house in Germany that will serve as a Bruderhof bridgehead in that country.
1989	The Michaelshof Bruderhof is established in Germany.
April, 1990	A *hof* is established in the Catskill Mountains.
July, 1990	The Spring Valley Bruderhof is established in Pennsylvania.
December, 1990	The Hutterite *Dariusleut* and *Lehrerleut* leadership sever ties with the Bruderhof.
July, 1991	A Bruderhof delegation visits Nigeria and the nucleus of a Bruderhof community there is established.
May, 1992	The Palmgrove community is established in Nigeria.
June, 1994	The Bruderhof members leave Nigeria and ties with Palmgrove are severed.

Bibliography

Allain, Roger. 1992. *The Community That Failed.* San Francisco, Calif.: Carrier Pigeon Press.

Arnold, Annemarie. 1974. *Youth Movement to Bruderhof.* Rifton, N.Y.: Plough Publishing House.

Arnold, Eberhard. 1988. *Brothers Unite.* Ulster Park, N.Y.: Plough Publishing House.

———. 1984. *God's Revolution: The Witness of Eberhard Arnold.* New York: Paulist Press.

———. 1976. *Children's Education in Community.* Rifton, N.Y.: Plough Publishing House.

———. 1973. *A Testimony of Church Community.* Rifton, N.Y.: Plough Publishing House.

———. 1967. *Salt and Light.* Rifton, N.Y.: Plough Publishing House.

Arnold, Eberhard, and Emmy Arnold. 1974. *Seeking For the Kingdom of God.* Rifton, N.Y.: Plough Publishing House.

Arnold, Emmy. 1964. *Torches Together,* 1st ed. Rifton, N.Y.: Plough Publishing House.

Arnold, Heini, and Annemarie Arnold. 1974. *Living in Community.* Rifton, N.Y.: Plough Publishing House.

Arnold, Johann Christoph. 1993. *Palm Grove Diary.* Farmington, Pa.: Plough Publishing House.

Bouvard, Marguerite. 1975. *The Intentional Community Movement.* Port Washington, N.Y.: Kennikat Press.

Burn, Maureen. 1986. *Outcast But Not Forsaken.* Rifton, N.Y.: Plough Publishing House.

Cocksedge, Edmund. 1991. *Vagabond For Peace.* Queensland: House of Freedom Christian Community.

Community In Britain. 1938. Cotswold Bruderhof Press.

Durnbaugh, Donald. 1991. "Relocation of the Bruderhof to England, South America." In *Communal Societies,* vol. 11. Evansville, Ind.: Communal Studies Association.

Eggers, Ulrich. 1988. *Community For Life.* Scotsdale, Pa.: Herald Press.

El Arado, Montevideo. 1955–59.

From Castle To Community: 25 Years of Community. Deer Spring, Conn.

Hindley, Marjorie. 1993. "Unerwunscht: One of the Lesser Known Confrontations." *German History,* vol. 11, no. 2. German History Society.

Idiong, Inno. 1992. *The Genesis of the Hutterian Brethren in Nigeria.* Rifton, N.Y.: Plough Publishing House.

Keep In Touch (KIT), vols. 1-4. 1989-92. (The Collected Newsletters of the KIT Information Service.) San Francisco, Calif.: Carrier Pigeon Press.

Kleinsasser, Jacob. 1992. *A Visit to Palm Grove Community.* Rifton, N.Y.: Plough Publishing House.

Lambach, Ruth Baer. 1993. "A Colony Girl." In Chmielewski, Wendi, ed., *Women In Spiritual and Communitarian Societies.* Syracuse, N.Y.: Syracuse University Press.

Meier, Hans. 1979. *The Dissolution of the Rhön Bruderhof.* Rifton, N.Y.: Plough Publishing House.

———. *Hans Meier Tells His Story To A Friend.* Rifton, N.Y.: Plough Publishing House.

Memories Of Our Early Years, vols. 1-3. 1977. Rifton, N.Y.: Plough Publishing House.

Mow, Merrill. 1990. *Torches Rekindled.* Rifton, N.Y.: Plough Publishing House.

Sharing About The Beginning Of Woodcrest. June 1974. Mimeographed collection.

Sonnherzbuch. 1920-26. Mimeographed collection.

The Plough. 1937-39; 1953-61; 1983-95. Quarterly of Bruderhof communities. Bromden: The Plough Publishing House.

Volmer, Antje. 1973. "The Neuwerk Movement (1919-1935)." Berlin: Unpublished doctoral dissertation.

Wagoner, Bob, and Shirley Wagoner. 1991. *Community In Paraguay.* Rifton, N.Y.: Plough Publishing House.

The Wheathill Bruderhof. 1952. *Ten Years Of Community Living.* Bromdon, UK: Plough Publishing House.

Whitworth, John Mackelvie. 1975. *God's Blueprints.* London and Boston: Routledge & Kegan Paul.

Yoder, John Howard, ed. June, 1979. *We Would Be Building: 25th Anniversary of Woodcrest.* New York.

Zablocki, Benjamin. 1971. *The Joyful Community.* Baltimore, Md.: Penguin Books.

Zumpe, Elizabeth Bohlken. 1993. *Torches Extinguished.* San Francisco, Calif.: Carrier Pigeon Press.

Primary Sources

Papers, documents, correspondence, press cuttings, articles, and archival material from the Yad Tabenkin archives, Israel, the Bruderhof Central Archive at Spring Valley, Pennsylvania, and the Woodcrest archive, New York; personal interviews with Bruderhof members (see chapter notes).

Index